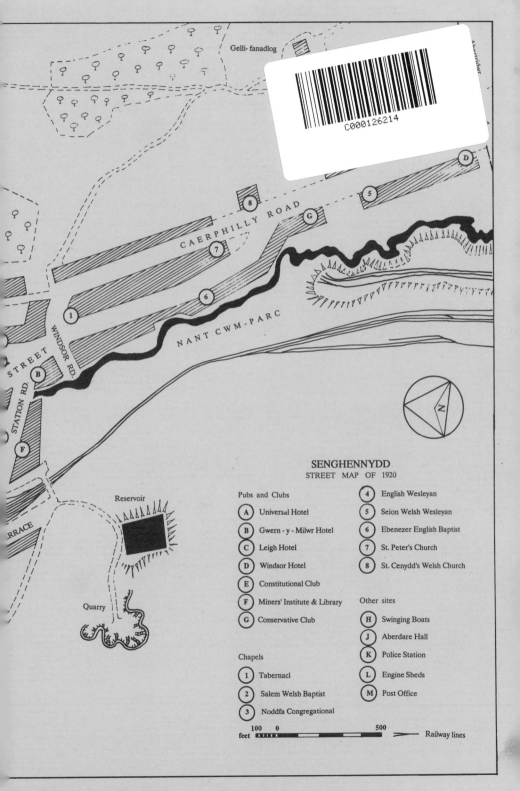

SENGHENNYDD
STREET MAP OF 1920

Gelli- fanadlog

CAERPHILLY ROAD

NANT CWM-PARC

STREET
STATION RD.
WINDSOR RD.
TERRACE

Reservoir

Quarry

Pubs and Clubs

(A) Universal Hotel
(B) Gwern - y - Milwr Hotel
(C) Leigh Hotel
(D) Windsor Hotel
(E) Constitutional Club
(F) Miners' Institute & Library
(G) Conservative Club

Chapels

(1) Tabernacl
(2) Salem Welsh Baptist
(3) Noddfa Congregational

(4) English Wesleyan
(5) Seion Welsh Wesleyan
(6) Ebenezer English Baptist
(7) St. Peter's Church
(8) St. Cenydd's Welsh Church

Other sites

(H) Swinging Boats
(J) Aberdare Hall
(K) Police Station
(L) Engine Sheds
(M) Post Office

100   0   500
feet   Railway lines

SENGHENNYDD, THE UNIVERSAL PIT VILLAGE
1890-1930

Senghennydd,
The Universal Pit Village
1890-1930

Michael Lieven

First Impression—1994

ISBN 1 85902 043 7

For the people of Senghennydd and the south Wales mining valleys.

This volume is published with the support of the Welsh Arts Council.

Printed in Wales
at the Gomer Press, Llandysul, Dyfed

Contents

List of Illustrations

List of Maps

Maps drawn by Jane Monahan.

Abbreviations

The following abbreviations are used in the footnotes:

Birmingham Daily Post:	BDP
Caerphilly Journal:	CJ
Daily Mail:	DM
Glamorgan Free Press:	GFP
Glamorgan Record Office	GRO
National Library of Wales	NLW
New Tredegar, Bargoed and Caerphilly Journal:	NTBCJ
Pontypridd Chronicle:	PC
Public Record Office	PRO
The Times:	Times
Western Mail:	WM

Introduction

In the nineteenth century what is now called Senghennydd was a small hamlet surrounded by sheep farms and isolated by hills from the communities in the neighbouring valleys. Even the area indicated by the name was uncertain since it referred not to the farms around what was sometimes called Parc Hamlet but to the broader area which had once formed the Welsh feudal Lordship of Senghennydd.

The modern search for coal in the area began in 1890 and Senghennydd became the site of a chaotically expanding pit village drawing in a labour force from throughout Wales and from other parts of Britain. The village became a melting pot, typical of the new Wales that was created in the nineteenth century. By 1900 the community supported nine chapels, seemingly numberless social, political, sporting and religious clubs and a school designed for over 900 children.

On one level its history for the next thirty years was that of any other mining community: a catalogue of strikes, brief periods of boom, and economic depressions and a pattern of domestic life, social events, self-important civic functions and petty crimes common to other isolated communities during the processes of industrialisation.

On another level Senghennydd became a symbol of the destructive capacity of industrialisation. In 1901 there was a catastrophic explosion which almost destroyed the mine and killed all but one of the 81 night shift workers who were underground at the time. In the following years the village was notorious for violence and drunkenness. In 1913 there was a second explosion which killed 439 miners and affected every family and institution in the small community. 90 men were killed in the next four years at Gallipoli and on the Western Front.

The community shared in the short lived post-war boom and in the depression of the 1920s. In 1928 the Universal Colliery was bought by the Powell Duffryn Mining conglomerate which closed the mine as part of a strategy of cutting production in order to reduce the glut of steam coal from the south Wales Coalfield.

In a period of 40 years, Senghennydd had experienced the full industrial cycle of growth, economic depression and withering away. It stands as a symbol both of the destructive power of industrialisation uncontrolled by communally agreed social purposes and of the capacity of communities to create meaning and order from intolerable circumstances.

Many of the events in Senghennydd presented two faces. One was immediate and real, the life to which the participants were inescapably bound: the other was a piece of theatre, sometimes tragic, at other times pure farce, carefully observed by the inhabitants and reported by the specialist critics of the local press. At times of disaster for the community Senghennydd was an 'amphitheatre' into which people poured to observe the 'tragedy': on other occasions it provided the material for long running comedies for which the magistrates court and the streets provided the stage and which drew large and appreciative audiences. The reports, in turn, affected the way in which the inhabitants saw themselves.

In the prosperous years, sandwiched between the sometimes unbearable pain of Senghennydd, one can often share in what the locals themselves saw as a comedy: 'there is a great quantity of eating and drinking, making love and jilting, laughing and the contrary, smoking, cheating, fighting, dancing, and fiddling: there are bullies pushing about, bucks ogling the women, knaves picking pockets, policemen on the look-out, quacks. . . bawling in front of their booths, and yokels looking up at the tinselled dancers and poor old rouged tumblers, while the light-fingered folk are operating upon their pockets behind'.

Other writers have reconstructed the history of the mining valleys from the record of trade union activities or by reflecting on their own experience. The story as it is told here is closer to the rhythm of apparent inconsequentiality to be found in the pages of the local newspapers. From the seemingly random juxtaposition of farce and tragedy, of social commitment and personal irresponsibility, of enjoyment and brutality, thieving and altruism, lovemaking and violence, despair and faith in the future, there emerge patterns in the development of the community and meanings in the lives of its members.

PART I
THE BIRTH OF THE VILLAGE

Chapter One
Senghennydd and the Coalowner

'Senghennydd' was a place set apart. Senghennydd Dyke runs for
seven miles along the tops of hills and through high moorland until it
drops into the narrow valley to complete a rough circle. This small
ditch and mound separates the outside world from an area of moorland
and bog, hill pasture and rough valley. The physical barrier is so
slight as to seem largely symbolic. Nevertheless medieval inhabitants
who ignored this boundary were punished with the same ruthlessness
that was to be the fate of their descendants in the valley.

Close to the circumference of the imperfect circle the inhabitants
built monuments which gave meaning to their lives. Vast rocks stood
majestic in the fields and circular cairns of small stones and mounds mark
meanings lost in prehistoric times. In the middle ages Senghennydd
denoted a large territory belonging to the Welsh princes, one of the
last Welsh lordships to be unconquered by the English invaders. The
castle at Caerphilly, four miles from the modern Senghennydd at the
southern entrance to the Aber Valley, is the unchallangeable symbol
of the English domination which followed: a castle so overpowering in
its strength and also in its visual message of power, that its destruction
seemed almost inconceivable. Senghennydd Dyke was an extension
of that visual symbol, etching on the landscape the boundaries of the
hunting park belonging to the castle; inside the dyke it was illegal for
the native Welsh to hunt for food. At about the same time the
inhabitants of the surrounding area built a Christian church at
Eglwysilan: the small gothic chapel is almost domestic and comforting,
standing isolated at the top of the bleak moorland near the dyke.

Within the dyke later generations divided the land into fields, which
they separated by tall dry-stone walls. The walls criss-cross the hillsides, ascetic, upright and finely dressed; as bleak and uncompromising
in their own way as the walls of Caerphilly Castle. Each of the walled
fields belonged to a local farm: Caer Moel, the Fort on the Bare Hill;
Graig-yr-Hyvan, the Rock of the White Stag (*Craig yr Hydd Wen*);
Gwern-y-Milwr, the Warrior's Meadow; Gelli Ddu, the Black
Grove. The origins of these names are lost in time.

Even in the middle ages there were hints of the wealth hidden beneath the mountains. In 1376 a document relating to Edward le Despenser referred to a coal 'mine' in the Lordship of Senghennydd worth thirteen shillings and fourpence. In the sixteenth century this apparently barren land was granted by Edward VI, a minor, to the Earl of Pembroke. It is unlikely that the Earl ever visited this remote and unproductive glen. Nevertheless leases for the digging of coal were granted by the Earls in 1611, 1625 and 1677 for between ten shillings and one guinea per annum.[1]

Over the centuries this dark and forgotten place, and more importantly its mineral rights, passed by inheritance to the Crichton-Stuarts, the Marquises of Bute. The family owned tens of thousands of acres of land and mineral rights in south Wales, vast and apparently barren areas whose value was transformed by the industrial revolution and the growth of the British Empire during the eighteenth and nineteenth centuries. The production of iron and steel, the demand for manufacturing tools, the need for ships and railways to export these goods and defend this trade to the burgeoning late nineteenth century empire all required an apparently endless increase in the supply of steam coal to power these developments; and the Bute lands and mineral rights lay across one of the richest coalfields in the world.

At Castell Coch, five miles from Senghennydd, John Crichton-Stuart (1847-1900), the third Marquis, built an eerie; a French medieval castle with turreted and canopied towers and high, massive, walls. From the valley below, the architecture is so convincing that it has the power of illusion and mirage. Within the castle, John, Marquis of Bute, Earl of Dumfries and of Windsor, Viscount Ayr, Viscount Mountjoy, Viscount Kingarth, Lord Crichton of Sanquhar and Cumnock, Lord Mountstuart, Cumrae and Inchmarnock lived out a medieval fantasy, paid for in large part by the labour of many thousands of south Wales miners.

From this fantastical hill castle he looked out on his very real wealth which, nevertheless, also had some fantastical qualities. The castle overlooked the railway lines which brought coal from the mines of Aberfan, Merthyr Tydfil, Pentrebach, the Aberdare Valley and the Rhondda Valleys. Several of the mines in these valleys were owned by the Marquis or by his agent: others paid a royalty to the Marquis for every ton of coal they produced, since he was also the owner of vast mineral rights. The coal was taken South past the Castle to the Bute

Docks in Cardiff which his agents had developed and which he owned.

The Marquis received all this wealth, but he had not summoned it up. To the extent that, in his lifetime, it was done by any one human being, it was done by William Thomas Lewis. Lewis was born in 1837, the son of the chief engineer to the Plymouth Ironworks and Collieries, and the descendant of generations of coalowners. William Lewis was not, however, born into wealth: his father left only £3,263 when he died in 1900. In 1864 William Lewis married into a family of coal owners. His wife was Anne Rees, the grand-daughter of Lucy Thomas, a legendary figure in the south Wales coal industry. As William Lewis developed his empire, the Rees clan became directors of his various concerns. Also in 1864, when he was only twenty seven, Lewis became mineral agent to the Bute Estate, directing their mining operations during a period of rapid expansion. Using his great entrepreneurial and technical skills and the resources of his wife's family he simultaneously started developing his own mines. In the 1870s he opened mines in the lower Rhondda at Coedcae and Hafod. Other mines followed in the Merthyr, Aberdare and Rhymney Valleys.

In 1880 Lewis became the Agent and Trustee of the Bute Estate, responsible for the entire network of railways, ironworks, mines, docks, housing schemes and other enterprises. He was credited with founding the coalowners' association for the Aberdare Valley in 1864 and thereafter he became the main figure in creating employers' associations in south Wales to resist the trade unions. In the 1870s he initiated the Monmouthshire and South Wales Coalowners' Association. In 1875 he was the prime mover behind the Sliding Scale Agreement which for twenty five years linked the wages of south Wales miners to the selling price of coal—always, according to the miners, to the owners' advantage. Beatrice and Sidney Webb described him as 'the best hated man in the principality'. His services to the coalowners were marked by cheques for 1,000 and 3,000 guineas, a sign of the value of his services to a group not noted for their personal generosity. He was also involved in various associations for supporting sickness and injuries benefits to miners: his dislike of the undermining effects of charity and his belief in self-help ensured that, in the main, the organisations would be funded from the wages of miners. He made major contributions to hospitals in Cardiff and Merthyr and founded

Sir William Lewis, Lord Merthyr of Senghennydd.

the Chair in Mining at University College, Cardiff. As a result of these activities, he had a reputation for philanthropy in some circles.[2]

His courage and determination as an entrepreneur and organiser brought him great wealth and even greater industrial power. He was a major shareholder in, and often the chairman of, the Lewis Merthyr Consolidated Collieries, the International Coal Company, the Melingriffith Tin Plate company, the Forest Iron and Steel Company, the Cardiff Railway Company, the Rhymney Railway Company and the Newport Tinplate Company. In his collieries he employed up to 10,000 men. Most of these companies were, in effect, extended private partnerships with small groups of wealthy people owning the company and being responsible for finding capital and meeting debts. It was not until 1900 that he decided to realise the capital of his, by then, eminently safe and reliable coal companies. In that year his main company, Lewis Merthyr Consolidated Collieries, was publicly floated and further share issues of £125,000 were made in 1906 and 1912.[3]

His success brought him a knighthood in 1885, the first of many titles and honorary positions. He was president of the South Wales Institute of Engineers, president of the Mining Association of Great Britain, president of the Iron and Steel Institute, vice-president of the Institute of Mechanical Engineers and a fellow of the Royal Geological Society.

He was also active in local politics and encouraged his senior employees to take a similar leading role in their local communities. In his political activities he suffered some of the rare setbacks of his life. He was defeated as the nominally Independent (although in effect Conservative) parliamentary candidate for the iron and coal town of Merthyr Tydfil in 1880, and his eldest son was defeated in East Glamorgan in 1892 and Merthyr in 1895: from these attempts one historian concluded that hereditary insanity was not confined to the old aristocracy.[4]

His unbending Toryism and his authoritarianism in industrial matters were coloured by a romantic attachment to Welsh history and culture. His complex loyalties are indicated in a letter to Thomas Ellis, the Liberal and Nationalist M.P., whose early death left the movement for Welsh political autonomy bereft. Lewis wrote a warm personal letter to Ellis, sometimes breaking into Welsh, and assuring him that 'if sympathy would assist your recovery you would have been quite robust long ago'. He then went on to discuss trade union difficulties in the Cardiff Docks caused by 'the extraordinary demands of Tillett & Co- I am afraid from present appearances we are on the eve of a very serious crisis between Capital and Labour in pretty well every trade in the kingdom'.[5]

Lewis was a member of the Aberdare Board of Health, a member of the Merthyr Board of Guardians and a member of the Glamorgan County Council. He served as a member of Royal Commissions on Mining Royalties, Shipping, Coal Supply, Industrial Disputes and Railways. He was a man immovable in his belief in the deference owed to his authority. Even his hagiographer conceded that his appearance was daunting despite his fine qualities: 'imperious and haughty he may have been in personal demeanour, but in spite of his somewhat terrifying presence there was no kinder heart'.[6]

Sir William was a passionate defender of a rigorous competitive market, fighting a hard battle against any assertion of union power, and an equally tough battle against fellow coalowners, led by his cousin D. A. Thomas, (later Lord Rhondda), in their attempts to form a cartel to limit production and thus raise prices and wages. Lewis bore an uncanny resemblance to Keir Hardie, both with their long white hair and patriarchal beards: Lewis's relentless emphasis on the virtues of the industrial entrepreneur in the age of imperialism forms a reverse image of the passionate and idealistic socialism of Keir Hardie.

In the 1890s this archetypal industrialist and entrepreneur turned his attention to the area at the end of the Aber Valley to which he was to give the medieval name of Senghennydd. In 1890 this was still a small hamlet of a dozen scattered farms. The end of the valley where the modern Senghennydd was to grow had no name on the map: the 1891 census referred to it as the hamlet of Park, echoing its medieval origins. Less than 100 people lived in what was to become Senghennydd and of these only one was recorded as a coal miner; lower down the valley in Penyrheol and Aber-tridwr, however, miners already represented a significant section of the population. In upper Park the householders were all farmers or farm labourers. Most of them had been born in the area and almost all were Welsh speakers although a significant minority could also speak English. Many of the families were to play an important part in the development of the valley: the Bussells of Caermoel, the Johns of Parc Newydd and the Phillips clan of Graig-yr-Hyvan and Garth farms. Some, like Daniel Lewis, his wife Mary Lewis and their young son at Gwern-y-Milwr, were farm labourers, but others lived in relatively substantial farms which were the homes for an extended family. At Caerllwyn, John and Maria Richards lived with their three sons, one daughter, an uncle, brother Henry and his wife Jemima, a niece, and an agricultural and a domestic servant. The other Richards family at Cefynllwyd farm also had two servants in a household of ten people. This was a small enclosed community without a shop, pub or chapel although all these could be found two miles down the valley in Aber-tridwr.[7]

By 1900 Sir William Lewis was to transform this quiet hamlet into an explosive pit village. Elsewhere he had developed mines which extended existing communities. Here he summoned a new community into existence: his pride in that achievement is indicated by the fact that, when he finally received a peerage in 1911, he was to take the title of Lord Merthyr of Senghennydd.

CHAPTER 1
    [1] C. Wilkins, *The History of the Iron, Steel, Tinplate and other Trades of Wales,* (Merthyr Tydfil; 1888), 24-29
    [2] B. Evans, *A History of Trade Disputes and the Formation and Operation of the several Sliding Scale Agreements. . .,* (University of Wales Thesis; 1944), 1-9: W. D. Rubinstein, *Men of Property,* (London; 1981), 78: E. Phillips, *Pioneers of the Welsh Coalfield,* (Cardiff; 1925), 200
    [3] R. Walters, 'Capital Formation in the South Wales Coal Industry 1840-1914', *The Welsh History Review,* 1980 Vol 10, 79: PRO BT 31/16355/65300 [hereafter cited as PRO]
    [4] W. D. Rubinstein, op cit, 77
    [5] T. Ellis Archive, NLW 1421
    [6] E. Phillips, op. cit., 202

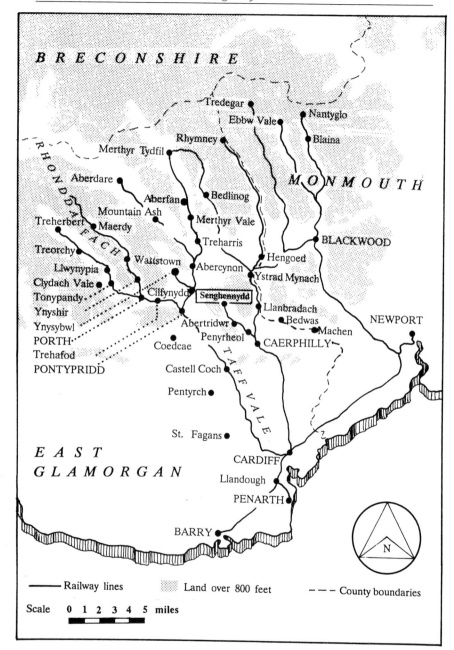

B R E C O N S H I R E

Tredegar
Ebbw Vale
Nantyglo
Rhymney
Blaina
Merthyr Tydfil

M O N M O U T H

Aberdare
Bedlinog
Aberfan
Mountain Ash
Merthyr Vale
Treherbert
Maerdy
Treharris
BLACKWOOD
Treorchy
Watttstown
Hengoed
Llwynypia
Abercynon
Ystrad Mynach
Clydach Vale
Cilfynydd
Senghennydd
Tonypandy
Llanbradach
Ynyshir
NEWPORT
Ynysybwl
Abertridwr
Bedwas
PORTH
Penyrheol
Machen
Coedcae
CAERPHILLY
Trehafod
PONTYPRIDD
Castell Coch
Pentyrch

E A S T
G L A M O R G A N

St. Fagans

CARDIFF
Llandough
PENARTH

BARRY

N

———— Railway lines   Land over 800 feet   – – – County boundaries

Scale   0   1   2   3   4   5   miles

Chapter Two
Developing the Pit Village

Sir William was fortunate that the Aber Valley was still available for mining in 1890 since it had come close, in 1881, to being flooded as a reservoir for the burgeoning town of Cardiff. The surveyor had reported at the time that 'there are no underground workings in the positions I have chosen and the coal measures in the valley have again and again proved to be worthless. The lower measures lie at great depths and I believe very irregularly, and I am given to understand on the best authority that if they are ever worked, the proper way to get at them is from the Taff and Rhymney Valleys, not by sinking in the Aber Valley'.[1]

The outlay and risks at Senghennydd were very great compared to the sinking of a mine in an already established mining valley. After the area was surveyed by Sir William Lewis and (Sir) William Galloway in 1889, a new railway had to be built from Caerphilly and the development work continued for several years before there was any hope of a return on capital. Lewis was well aware of the risks. In 1885 he had been the prime mover in the formation of the Cardiff Steam Collieries Company, created to develop pits in Llanbradach. The method of raising the necessary capital costs, an estimated £100,000, was the traditional one in south Wales of involving a relatively small number of wealthy shareholders. In this case the 26 unfortunate shareholders were called on to put up a further £95,300 towards costs which escalated yet further to £248,071 in 1894, by which time the construction stage was still not completed: the shareholders were probably aware of the epitaph, 'He sunk the Ystrad Pits, and the Pits returned the compliment'. Lewis was also unfortunate in his timing at Senghennydd. After a brief boom in 1890, the price of Welsh steam coal fell throughout most of the 1890s, only reviving after the strike of 1898: the process of recovering the company's development costs was thus greatly slowed. In order to protect his other companies from the consequences of failure, Lewis formed a new company to exploit Senghennydd. The Universal Steam Coal Company Limited leased mineral rights over two thousand acres, the larger part of it belonging to the Marquis of Bute.[2]

For the first stirrings of this community one relies on stray bits of information ranging from christenings to the business dealings of Sir William Lewis, information as apparently inconsequential and unrelated as broken pieces of pottery on a disused rubbish heap. From these, however, one can trace the arrival of individual labourers and the struggle of small entrepreneurs, greedy for opportunity, in the unhealthy building site as they slowly developed the expansive pomp of self-conscious civic dignitaries.

The sinking of a shaft was started in 1893 under the direction of David Thomas, but the project ran into difficulties almost immediately. The workers discovered an underground stream which poured over two thousand gallons of water an hour into the workings: five thousand bricks per yard were needed to hold back and divert the flow. In the early stages serious thought was given to cutting the losses and abandoning the project.[3]

At the start of 1894, when the place was still referred to variously as the Aber Valley or Park Hamlet, an explosion ripped through the shaft in which sixteen men were working. A frozen charge of nitro glycerine, used for blasting, exploded under slight pressure, immediately killing one man and critically injuring another. After a protracted discussion the inquest jury returned a verdict of accidental death 'but held that there was a great deal of negligence and irregularity in connection with the management. They also recommended that a competent man should examine all cartridges before being used'; which might be considered a fairly obvious precaution.[4]

In these early days the place was little more than a work site with a small colony of engineers and workmen involved in sinking the new mine. The sinkers who built new pits worked in appalling conditions as they dug down through the rock formations, deposits and streams left behind by millions of years of geological development. Their work involved extreme physical hardship and stress: it was assumed that they rarely put down local roots and by definition they lived on sites removed from the security of an established community. The sinkers gained notoriety as a group of wildly drunken and dangerous men. This, at least, was the way in which they were stereotyped in the mythology which surrounds mining communities. Since there was no pub until the end of 1894, the men brewed their own beer and sold it

Some of the men who built the mine.

The sinkers wearing clothing to protect them from the underground streams. Behind them is the temporary wooden winding machinery.

in the huts where they lived. Although the settlement was isolated at the end of the valley, with only farm roads connecting it to Caerphilly, there was an attempt from the start to limit the sale and use of alcohol. In March 1894 John Mapps was charged with drunkenness and in April he was charged with selling beer without a licence. Twenty six men were counted by the police going into Mapps's hut and several were counted 'coming out for a purpose' and then returning. Some of the men were so drunk that they had been put into the same bed to sleep off the effects. Mapps was fined the enormous sum of £10 while his customers were fined ten shillings each. One of them, John Lewis, complained to the magistrates, 'it is too bad; it is bad enough for a fellow to have to pay for his beer without having to go to Caerphilly to pay for it over again'.[5]

To house these and other workers the company built rows of corrugated iron huts, near the pit head: low, one storey buildings with a single window and a door at the front and tall chimney stacks rising above their squat frames. In later years the huts formed a poignant and impoverished setting in which widowed mothers, nursing babies, leant in their doorways waiting for news of the latest tragedy. Other workers lived in accommodation of tarred canvas stretched over wooden frames, which was provided by the company, or in varied temporary accommodation on the surrounding farms. Evan Evans lived for three years in a disused roadmender's van on a picturesque site by the brook on Gelli Farm.[6]

Not all were peripatetic workers. William (Windsor) Williams was a local man who lived at Windsor Cottage, Abertridwr, before moving to Graig-yr-Hyvan Farm in Senghennydd. He had a reputation as a bricklayer and was employed on the new pit as well as on the railway bridges from Caerphilly. Legend, possibly boosted by his own stories since he outlived his contemporaries, credits him with having built the first of the new houses in the village, and he had a considerable reputation as a dry stone waller for the surrounding farms.[7]

Other sinkers lived in the first small terraces built beside the railway line. Athough it was still predominantly a town of single males, some sinkers did raise families in Senghennydd and stayed on to work in the mine. Mary and Richard Surridge lived in Parc Terrace, overlooking the station on the far side of the railway line from further housing developments. Their first child, Ivor Octavius, was born there in December 1895, to be followed in November 1896 by William John and in August 1898 by Mark Thomas, by which time they had moved to a larger house in Caerphilly Road. Their neighbours in Parc Terrace, Charles and Fanny Waddon, had a daughter in December 1895: Blanche Esther Waddon was christened with Ivor Octavius Surridge in the medieval church at Eglwysilan on December 8th. Charles Waddon was an electrician in the pit and he too stayed in Senghennydd where his presence is marked by various appearances in the magistrates' court; a son, David Henry, was baptised in February 1898. Both families were still in Senghennydd and the Aber Valley in the 1930s and were to be the victims of tragedies in the later years. In all, the families of at least twelve sinkers were still in Senghennydd in 1912.[8]

Even before coal was won building had started on permanent houses in the village. In 1894 it was estimated that 130 men were working on the site and by the end of the year about 90 houses had been occupied while another forty were nearing completion.[9] By then the inhabitants were beginning to learn the name of the place where they lived. When the railway station was opened, the Pontypridd local newspaper reported:

> the new place has a rather peculiar name. It is, by what we can see at the railway station, to be called 'Sengenith'. We have many inquiring as to the meaning of the word, and, also, as to the coiner of it. Perhaps some of the readers of the Free Press will explain matters.

As an afterthought the paper added: 'We believe it was Sir W. T. Lewis, Aberdare'. It was to be some time before the spelling was commonly established as 'Senghenydd', part of a wider campaign to preserve the spelling of Welsh place names: and even then the spelling should, correctly, have been Senghennydd.[10]

Parc Terrace and Kingsley Place, on opposite sides of the railway line, were followed by developments in Windsor Road, Eleanor Road and Stuart Road. Much of the early evidence comes from reports to the Caerphilly Local Board, which was responsible for enforcing planning laws in Senghennydd. Complaints that building and health regulations were not being respected set a pattern for the next thirty five years.

In May 1895, the Caerphilly Medical Officer of Health, Dr Thomas, reported that the supply of water to some houses resembled an open sewer which arrived in the village via a duck pond and in which floated dead cats as well as less obviously visible health hazards. The drains and sewers emptied out into the rough lane, stagnating in foetid pools by the roadside. Many houses did not even have outlet pipes.[11]

The local government officers tried to ensure that standards were maintained in the construction of the new development but from the start they fought a losing battle against two local builders and developers, Henry Williams and Josiah Morgan. In August 1895 Dr Thomas together with the borough clerk, the building inspector and the surveyor visited Senghennydd and reported that 'bye-laws on building and sanitation were a dead letter'.[12] Despite warnings several months earlier, it was found that cellar dwellings had been built below the houses in what was to be Stanley Street: these cellars were to figure largely in the epidemics which swept through the village in the future.

In the first of a series of battles, Henry Williams, the Senghennydd builder, entrepreneur and ratepayers' representative on the council, had been prosecuted in 1895 for letting a house which had not received a certificate of fitness from the Council. As always he claimed that the house was in fine condition and that the matter before the court was a mere technicality. The magistrates' court decided against Williams but fined him a derisory ten shillings which, in future, he seems to have regarded as a minor license fee. When he was summonsed for the same offence in April 1897 the fine was reduced to five shillings for each of eight houses.[13]

Similarly, when a certificate was refused for nineteen houses belonging to a building club in Senghennydd, it was Josiah Morgan, the 'developer', who led a delegation to the council.[14] The Senghennydd Building Club showed an expenditure of £10,529 10s 3d in 1898: of this £9,407 went to their building contractor, so Morgan's support for the delegation was not entirely disinterested.[15]

The Caerphilly Urban District Council had major difficulties in coping with the speed of the new developments in its area. The councillors were hampered by the fact that Caerphilly Council was responsible for only some aspects of public services in Senghennydd: the village was in the jurisdiction of the Pontypridd Board of Guardians as far as poor law relief and medical services were concerned, in the area of the Eglwysilan School Board for the provision of education, and in the area of the East Glamorgan Constituency for parliamentary elections. The problems were exacerbated for the next few years since this was a period in which local government was, understandably, being reorganised; the next decade was therefore one of continual change in local administration. Old established officials, such as the town clerk, were ill prepared for the demands made on them by the rapid industrialisation and urbanisation of the area.

In October 1897 a crisis was reached in the affairs of the Council and a group of councillors carried out a coup against their clerk. The unusual presence at the meeting of eleven out of the twelve councillors was a warning that something was afoot. The council's officers were asked to leave and it was then proposed that Mr Lewis, the clerk, who had refused to leave the room, should resign. The formal reason given was that a clerk with sound parliamentary and legal knowledge was needed in order to deal with all the new legislation but it was apparent that this justification shrouded older more personal animosities. The record of the clerk was defended by Councillor William Thomas, but his supporters were outnumbered by an alliance between the military, Major Lindsay and Captain Dowdeswell, and members of the local bench. At the last moment the clerk pre-empted his opponents by resigning. Just as the time came to vote on whether to accept his resignation, Major Lindsay, with more tactical sense than courage, unexpectedly left the room and failed to return. Mr Lewis appeared to accept his dismissal with some dignity, but he had a spectacular and immediate revenge when he asked the members to leave instantly as they were on his property: 'The offices were in his possession and they were to go out at once'. The councillors were thrown into disarray by this move and the chairman asked nervously about the position regarding the furniture. Mr Lewis, the Clerk, replied that they would have to pay for it: he 'then put his pen on the table and walked out, saying, "Good afternoon, gentlemen"'.[16]

'This evidently caused some consternation, as none of the members thought that he would finish so soon'. They blustered for some time about whether they could demand a month's notice, but whatever the legal niceties of the situation, in practice they accepted defeat. They went on to discuss whether the next meeting should be at the Clive Arms or at the Police Court, leaving with rather less civic dignity than at the start of the proceedings.

Williams and Morgan, the developers, were not content with simply defending themselves in the courts against the council, but took the war into the enemy camp: the debacle over the sacking of Mr Lewis, the council clerk, offered the ideal material to Henry Williams. In December 1897 he launched a ferocious attack on the competence and integrity of the councillors and the council officers. Behind his personal onslaught was the conflict between, on the one hand, business interests anxious to limit council expenditure, and thus rates, to the provision of basic services and, on the other hand, 'progressives' who sought to harness the potential power of the council to the improvement of the local environment. Williams's conviction for building insanitary houses, (as far as he was concerned a symptom of council interference), was of a piece with his attack on council expenditure on a new sewage works. The recent battle between the council and the clerk provided him with a cartload of muck, which he proceeded to throw at his colleagues with immense gusto. It also produced a significant minority of councillors who had defended the clerk and who were obvious potential allies for Williams.

Williams's attack reached a climax at a Council meeting in December 1897 and started well.[17] Pointing to the expenditure of 10 shillings per inhabitant in a six month period, he declared that 'this monstrous extravagance is known to keep many good financiers from speculating within the area of this council'. His populist attack drew roars of approval from his audience of ratepayers and a voice shouted out 'quite right; give it to them, Harry'. Henry Williams did not underestimate the broad principles which were involved, as the weighty historical references in the peroration of his speech made clear:

> ... the schemes of the council are nothing but a comedy of errors, leaving for each councillor no alternative but to confess that he has done wrong in the past and promise to do better in the future. If they would not make that admission, I will conclude by repeating the words of Cromwell, 'Be gone, ye knaves, and make room for honest men'.

The chairman, J. E. Evans of Brynawel, countered the attack with restrained sarcasm, stating that 'Mr Williams has taken 35 minutes to make himself understood, and I purpose limiting every speaker (excepting Councillor Thomas) to 7 minutes'.

The inexperienced council and its small administrative staff undoubtedly had a difficult task on its hands in trying to cope with the extraordinary rate of expansion in the district. In the circumstances William Thomas gave a fairly lucid explanation of the Council's actions and the audience's reaction suggested that Henry Williams had shot his bolt. They began to cheer Thomas and by the time Henry Williams began his summing up they were getting out of control. When Williams started to lay into the exhorbitant salary of the surveyor, the audience had had enough and a Mr Rossiter shouted out, to the cheers and laughter of his fellow spectators, 'Hurry on man, it is getting late and we have had quite enough of this'.

Williams, sensing the mood, attempted to save the day by having the meeting adjourned, but by this stage he could not even find a seconder. A splendid evening had been enjoyed by everyone, and a vote of thanks to the wretched chairman 'who had presided so ably and impartially' was generously proposed by the defeated Henry Williams and seconded by Councillor William Thomas. The speed with which the proceedings were finally brought to an end may have been connected to the closing times of the Caerphilly pubs.

If, however, his fellow councillors or the council officials thought that the Senghenydd entrepreneur was finished, they had mistaken their man. He now turned to the newspapers, writing a high blown article in which he glorified the Onward March of Progress and Freedom: 'after centuries of struggle and persecution, our forefathers have succeeded in handing us the privileges and rights we now enjoy'. The result, he argued, had been a vast range of benefits at local level. Unfortunately one area of Britain was almost uniquely excluded from the general evolution of progress: 'In drawing this picture of progress and advancement resulting from wise and careful administration of the laws passed for the people's well being and comfort, I regret to admit it is not one which can be said to reflect the results of local government in the area of Caerphilly District Council'.[13] He concluded with the threat that he would return, in future articles, to the case of the Council's large sewage scheme and the connected purchase of a farm.

The more righteous members of the council may well have thought that divine retribution had been exacted on the troublesome developer when, a few weeks later, he fell and broke his skull in his quarry above Senghennydd.

In August 1895 the winning of a seven foot seam of coal in the Universal had dramatically accelerated the pace of development which was obviously outstripping the capacity of most local institutions to plan the new community. The company purchased further mineral rights, now extending to 3,000 acres, and it was already estimating a future workforce of about 2,000 men. The Aber Valley was spoken of as the 'Rhondda of the future', an opinion much aired by Morgan and Williams. The road to Senghennydd was still little more than a country lane, the railway line was incomplete, the number of houses was wholly inadequate for the workers beginning to pour into the new community and the institutional structure was almost non-existent, despite the rapid growth of some nonconformist congregations. By August 1897, when the population was already 1,775, 314 houses had been completed; over ten people were crammed into some of them and many families lived in just two rooms of the divided houses.[19] The country lane clearly needed to be tarmaced and with some reluctance Caerphilly Council agreed to the extravagance though they drew the line at hiring a steamroller from Newport at 28 shillings in order to produce a flat surface. The Council Clerk objected that the road was very uneven for cyclists to which Captain Dowdeswell, who had a reputation to preserve for curmudgeonly behaviour, retorted, 'Hang the cyclist'.[20]

The developments were hurried along by pressure from small entrepreneurs in Senghennydd anxious to speed up the process. In February 1896 Towyn Jones, the Secretary of the Senghennydd Chamber of Commerce, and Robert Lougher, proprietor of the Universal Hotel and Treasurer of the Chamber, were urging Caerphilly Council to demand improvements in the postal facilities, the opening of a telegraphic office, improvements in lighting and general cleanliness, an expanded police force and a polling booth in Senghennydd during elections. A sub-committee was formed and letters were sent to the relevant bodies.[21] These demands were made against a widespread perception that the mining valleys balanced above a precipice of social disintegration.

The threat of violence associated with drink in the unstable atmosphere of a new town largely peopled by young single males was a recurring theme in the history of Senghennydd. Even the established coal districts in the neighbouring valleys were extremely volatile and at times reverted to the bestial. In Treorchy, a few miles away in the

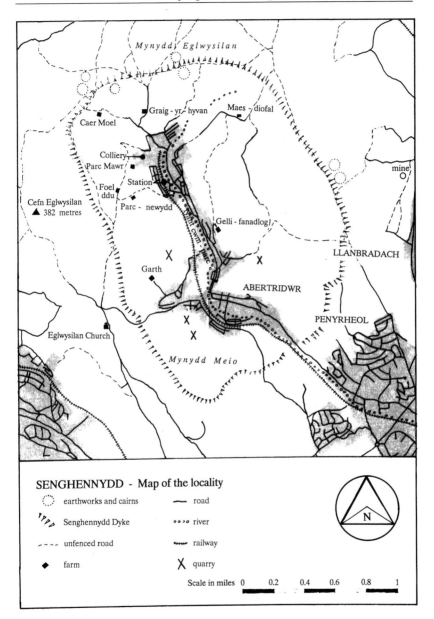

SENGHENNYDD - Map of the locality

Mynydd Eglwysilan

Graig - yr hyvan   Maes - diofal

Caer Moel

Colliery
Parc Mawr

Foel
ddu   Station

Cefn Eglwysilan
▲ 382 metres   Parc - newydd

Gelli - fanadlog

LLANBRADACH

Garth

ABERTRIDWR

PENYRHEOL

Eglwysilan Church

Mynydd Meio

mine
O

SENGHENNYDD - Map of the locality

◌ earthworks and cairns	— road		
🗲 Senghennydd Dyke	∘∘∘ river		
- - - unfenced road	⧉⧉⧉ railway		
◆ farm	X quarry		

Scale in miles 0   0.2   0.4   0.6   0.8   1

N

Rhondda, a gang stripped and assaulted a woman, while a crowd held back her husband and a policeman. In Ynysybwl a crowd of about twenty young men raped a woman in the street, leaving her unconscious after beating up her husband.[22] In Pontypridd, four miles away across Cefn Eglwysilan, a husband was harried by a gang of nine youths as he tried to carry his sick wife home, and when he was unable to carry her further and went for a policeman, four of the gang viciously raped her. Another gang, this time consisting of fifteen youths, was accused of raping a fifteen year old girl at a fairground in Treherbert. She was assaulted against walls, on the river bank, on coal tips and elsewhere: in the main their defence was that they had paid her a penny and that she was willing.[23]

Alcohol often corroded the life of the village and its inhabitants; at other times it could produce a leaven of humour in the otherwise grim routine of extracting coal. The Universal Hotel won a license in August 1894 and the battles to get licences for the other hotels became an annual event which combined high moral principle with a splendid, and free, public spectacle.[24]

The first major battle in the saga of the pub licenses, a saga which ran for a decade, occurred in the same month that the seven foot seam was discovered. In August 1895, the *Pontypridd Chronicle* headlined its report, 'Temperance Victory at Senghennydd' and 'Flying Colours'. In the words of the Secretary of the temperance lobby, 'the magistrates courageously refused every application that came from Senghennydd'. The following August two renewed applications from Senghennydd were heard before thirteen magistrates sitting together. The matter was becoming urgent for the applicants since they had already built hotels and were unable to open as public houses. As early as 1893 there had been sufficient confidence that coal would be found for the owners to begin to spend £4,647 in building the Leigh Hotel, which was completed in 1895. In a meeting of high drama Dr Franklin Evans, the chairman, first cast his vote in favour of the Leigh Hotel and then withdrew it under pressure. The remaining twelve justices divided equally, with the result that there was no decision. A five hour meeting was then held in September: again the temperance lobby were victorious, with licences for the Gwern-y-Milwr, Parc and Leigh Hotels all being refused.[25]

The war reached one of many climaxes at the licensing session in 1897. On the one side there was an unholy alliance between Robert

Lougher, the landlord of the Universal Hotel which did have a licence, and the temperance members of the rapidly growing chapels whose development is described below: the Welsh Wesleyan Chapel, the Calvinistic Methodist Chapel, the English Congregational Chapel and the Welsh Independents. Members of the established church were noticeable by their absence. On the other side were the owners of three hotels which had no licence: they were hampered by the need on the one hand to maintain a common front but, on the other hand, to attack their allies to ensure that if only one or two new licenses were granted then the licenses should go to their own establishment. The local newspaper headlined its report, 'Another Battle Royal', and the spirit of the occasion was caught in the opening sentence: 'It was a great day in Caerphilly on Tuesday for on that occasion the battle of the licenses was fought'.[26] The large audience for the event, despite the bad weather, meant that the court was overcrowded, but the audience was recompensed for its discomfort by a memorable performance.

The barristers and solicitors for the competing hotels accused each other's clients of complex dirty tricks campaigns. The owner of the land behind the Leigh, for example, was accused of building a slaughter house there with the deliberate aim of preventing the Leigh from getting a license: meanwhile he was, all unbeknown, actually an interested party in the development of the Gwern-y-Milwr Hotel down the road. This was Josiah Morgan, the ubiquitous property developer. Smears were thrown at each other's urinals, staircases and religious connections. The lawyers probably had the most fun, having a special indulgence to exchange repartee and flippant broadsides: Bowen Rowlands, opposing the applications on behalf of a group of local residents, said of the applicants that Senghennydd 'was a veritable Klondyke, towards which the rush of benevolence was almost unexampled and which would probably end in the annihilation of one or more of the combatants'. The bench finally awarded licences to the Leigh and the Gwern-y-Milwr Hotels and the temperance party left vowing to oppose the licenses at the Confirming Court in October.

Fortunately for the afficianados, the magistrates' decision was indeed overturned and the battle was renewed in 1898. Again Bowen Rowlands Q.C. and George David appeared for the cynical alliance of temperance chapels and Robert Lougher, and again Rowlands effectively attacked the new applications with a combination of innuendo and public petitions. Much of the argument hinged on the extent to which the long coal strike of 1898 had reduced trade and thus the need for another public house. As a result of this hearing the Gwern-y-Milwr got its licence, but the other two were turned down.[27]

Robert Lougher was to pay a price for his machinations with the temperance lobby. When Senghennydd finally gained an additional place on the council, he was defeated in the election for the council by David Thomas, an under-manager in the colliery. Lougher lost some of the beer drinkers' vote by his actions in preventing more pubs from opening and, as a publican, he could count on little support from his temperance allies.[28]

In these battles we can trace the emergence of the institutions which were to dominate the village socially and physically. The solid stone mansions of the pubs and chapels were to outlast the industrialists, the trade union, the mine and most of the inhabitants although few even of the grandiose chapels and pubs would survive for three score years and ten.

Among the first institutions to have put down roots in the new

Tabernacl Chapel.

village had been the churches. In the early days they had to make use of any rooms that were available. The manager of the Leigh Hotel was proud of the fact that the club room had been used as a church, with its own pulpit, while the dissenters were accommodated in the coffee-room. This willingness to help the religious life of the village was not purely altruistic, since the evidence of respectability and civic concern was also very useful in the annual battle for pub licenses.

Salem Welsh Baptist Church was founded while exploration work was still going on and before coal had been raised. In an event whose symbolism they made much of, the four founder members of the congregation first met in the carpenter's shop belonging to one of them, John Thomas. The first preacher travelled from Mardy in the Rhondda to preach in the shop and the congregation received financial assistance from the Baptist Home Mission Society. When the Reverend Dan Davies of Porth visited the congregation, they had to borrow the vestry of the Welsh Congregational Church in order to hold a meeting. At that meeting Lewis Walters was converted, and sixteen people remained behind after the meeting. These sixteen consisted of eight men and eight women, and from this group a committee of men was formed to start the formal process of building a church. The first step was to build a vestry. The foundations were dug by volunteers and the vestry building was completed for £600, a vast sum for such a small congregation. In 1896 preachers from Cardiff, Brynmawr and Treorchy took part in the opening ceremony of the vestry, which was only a prelude to even greater efforts to build the chapel itself. The land for the Chapel was leased from Josiah Morgan. The fact that Morgan, who was also a part owner of the Gwern-y-Milwr public house, paid for the fittings of the chapel seems to confirm the view that the gap in social intercourse between chapel and pub has sometimes been exaggerated.[29]

Their first pastor was the Reverend David Roberts. In the small world of Welsh nonconformity, ancestries of learning, as well as those of birth, are important and there was pride in the fact that Senghennydd had attracted the descendant of the Reverend Daniel Davies, pastor of Felinfoel Chapel for 54 years. Before coming to Senghennydd he had been the minister at Talog, Foelewan and Cwmchydrin in Carmarthenshire, bringing to this raw new community the values and hopes of rural Wales. As one of his colleagues was to say of him, he 'was wonderful in prayer, and at home when before the throne of

Grace, he was familiar with his father. There was no twist in his character, his conversations were always interesting and elevating and always centred around preachers and his native Pembrey and Carmarthenshire'.[30] His simplicity would have been an asset anywhere, though it is less certain that the attitudes and concerns developed in the Welsh countryside were the most appropriate for developing an adequate response to the experience of rapid industrialisation in the Aber Valley. Some of the younger members of his congregation would try to test him by learning peculiarly obscure bible passages before meetings. They would then falter in their delivery, only to have the quotations completed by David Roberts on each occasion. Even his expert knowledge of the Bible was, however, outclassed by his piety. T. W. Chance, a fellow Minister, 'felt that a halo of sanctity surrounded him and that piety seemed to ooze through every part of his being': although this tribute by his colleague was less than felicitous, (it sounded better in Welsh), David Roberts is indeed remembered as a saintly but wise and sympathetic human being. His wife also seems to have been a perfect person in the eyes of others, since 'in Mrs Roberts he had an ideal Minister's consort and worthy of the great calling of her husband'. Her own strengths are not recorded. Like many of the early inhabitants David Roberts and his family were to stay in Senghennydd and to play a major part in the life of the community over the next thirty five years: he is still remembered with great respect and affection.

Even the Anglican Church had opened a 'mission' in 1895, holding services in the assembly room of the Leigh Hotel. The rector, the Reverend Henry Morgan, hurried developments along: the foundation stone of a mission church was laid in August 1896, the church was completed in March 1897 and the first curate, the Reverend David Jones, took up his post in the same month. There was from the start an active congregation which included both long time residents such as Gwenllian Phillips of Graig-yr-Hyvan farm and newcomers like Richard Surridge who had come with the sinkers and who became one of the organists of the new church.[31]

From the early days a variety of social events were instituted by the clergy, mine officials, tradespeople and respectable miners. Already by 1897 traditions had formed and gatherings could be described as annual events. In August 1897 the numerous Sunday schools held their second 'annual demonstration' with a procession, teas and a sports day at Gelli Farm, and an address by Edward Shaw, the manager of the mine. The owners of the various hotels which were waiting for licenses were anxious to prove their respectability and fell over themselves to help the non-conformist chapels. So on New Year's Eve 1897 a 'grand soiree and supper' was held at the Gwern-y-Milwr, kindly lent to the English Congregational Church by Josiah Morgan. So great was the festive goodwill that Robert Lougher of the Universal Hotel loaned the piano and the building was so overcrowded that the assembly rooms had to be opened. Just before midnight the gathering moved to the church.[32]

Another typical event was a grand concert held to raise funds for the ambulance (first aid) class in 1897. There were songs, violin duets, piano solos and recitations delivered by a number of performers. On this occasion the evening belonged to Miss Phillips: with Miss Howells, she 'beautifully rendered' the duet, 'Over the Hawthorn Hedge'; gave a 'delightful rendering' of 'What's a little Maid to do', which was loudly encored; gave a 'sweet rendering' of 'Bid me to love'; and ended the evening with 'In the dusk of twilight'. The reporter was probably not the only listener to be slightly smitten by Miss Phillips.[33]

The development of the school was a further indication of the rapid growth in population and the extent to which the community was beginning to include stable family structures. In 1894 there were already complaints about the lethargy of the local board in setting up a school in Senghennydd but by 1895 there was still no record of any capitation fee being paid although the Eglwysilan School Board, whose district included Senghennydd, agreed to look for a temporary room in which to start a school. The meeting was enlivened by John Morgan, the previous chairman, who stormed out in protest at the election of a clergyman of the established church, the Reverend Daniel Lewis, to replace him as the chairman of the Board.[34]

In August 1895 the School Board appointed a school attendance officer at a salary of £75. There were 37 applicants for the post, from whom a Mr Millward was chosen: he had the advantage of a testimonial from Mr David Thomas, the under-manager of the Universal Colliery. At the same time Miss England was appointed as head teacher. She was the only applicant and her salary was £45 a year. The salary was considerably less than that of the male attendance officer or the clerk of works, who was soon to be appointed, since women teachers were not expected to support a family, it being the practice for them to resign when they married. The policy was supposedly designed to support the breadwinners of families who were defined as men. By the time of her appointment there were 78 children on the books and the Board agreed to employ an assistant and a monitor. They also set aside £500 to build a school.[35]

Miss England recorded the historic first day of the school with a mixture of formality and simple pride:

> This (Senghennydd) Infant School was opened today (12th day of September 1895). I (E. A. England) commenced duties on the day of opening. Mr Sherrah (member of the Board) and Mr [Thomas] Thomas (clerk) present. Admitted 55 children.[36]

From the start Miss England won praise for achievements at the School, though all the praise was given on the basis that anything would be an achievement in the light of the problems faced. The report for 1896 commented that 'the school has been conducted with care and diligence. The children shew very satisfactory proficiency, considering the difficulties connected with the premises etc'.[37] The log book of the school demonstrates that for the next few years these difficulties were at times very great, though it needs to be borne in mind that the log book was a head teacher's method of communicating to the managers her extraordinary abilities in overcoming almost insurmountable problems.

The school, like those at Llanbradach and others in the area, was often closed as the result of epidemics in which many children died: in 1898 Miss England recorded the death of two of her 'little scholars' from the diptheria epidemic of that year. Again as at the Llanbradach School, she had a continual struggle with the unqualified assistants on whom she was forced to rely, recording their absences without permission and their weaknesses in basic skills. In 1899 she noted the 'gross insubordination of Margaret Gould (3rd Year Pupil Teacher). She refused to draw lines on the floor and went home'. In that year both her third year pupil teachers (Miriam Rowland and Margaret Gould) failed their exam and her third pupil teacher achieved a result of 'below fair'. Eliza England's report on one of her monitors illustrates the material with which she had to work: 'Harriet Roberts commenced duties as a monitor today. She is very backward in her studies not having attended any school for a period of two years. She is 17 years of age'.[38]

The buildings themselves seriously limited the scope of the school, an inspector reporting that '..the rooms are barely warm enough on a cold day. The smoke blows down in the main room'. Finally, inspectors noted that despite the achievements of the school the level of many of the pupils was disappointingly low. Of the slower children it was suggested that '. . .their backwardness may reasonably be accounted for by the circumstances of the district', and it was later argued that 'this backwardness will doubtless disappear when the district becomes more settled'. Eliza England resigned in April 1900, along with her deputy, after a difficult four years.[39]

While she struggled in the infant school, the plans for building a senior school, with greater resources, were developing. The matter of a house for the headteacher nicely illustrated the workings of the Eglwysilan School Board. The Board agreed in early 1898 to spend up to £450 on the house and then received tenders all of which were for over £500. Attempts to ignore or rescind the previous decision were talked out. The architect helpfully remarked that if the board had acted sooner then the house would have been cheaper. It was suggested that new tenders could be invited, at which the chairman irritably pointed out that the number of bidders had dropped to four

The Senghennydd Council Schools.

and that there would soon be no-one left to tender. The architect then commented that if the plans were further reduced they would end up with a cottage rather than a house, at which Mr Evans insisted that they must have 'a building worthy of Senghennydd'. The other Mr Evans seconded the motion, but Mr Jones insisted that as he had previously voted for £450 he could not now vote for the higher sum. In desperation the chairman asked 'whether his mind was not open to enlightenment', but Mr Jones replied 'I have not received it yet'. The local paper reported that 'this short passage of arms was wound up when Mr Jones said he was open to conviction'. At this point, however, the second Mr Evans said that he now wished to withdraw as seconder of the motion to increase the sum available. The chairman said 'Well gentlemen, this is not business', and was faced with a motion by the two Evanses to accept yet another tender, at which 'the business now became rather confused and the chairman laconically remarked "Where are we now?"'. The meeting ended where it had begun, by agreeing to a tender above the original limit.[40]

The beneficiary of all this discussion, Dan Lloyd, took up his position as headmaster in 1898: he was to play a major part in the life of the village for the next 25 years. The new school was opened in late 1897. With an eye to future growth it had places for 260 boys, 260 girls and 280 infants and by 1900, when the population of the village was over 2,000 people, the average school attendance was just under 350.

The 1901 edition of *Kelly's Directory* listed about 80 businesses and individuals in its commercial section, another indication of the rapid growth of the village. This included some self employed tradespeople, but also a large number of shops. Grocers, outfitters, fish and chip shop proprietors, hoteliers, two doctors, two part-time bank managers, stationers, tailors, insurance agents, butchers, drapers, bakers and cafe owners had all set up shop in the bustling Commercial Street. These respectable ratepayers were immensely serious about the civic dignity of the new community.

In 1898 they were given the opportunity of naming, and in some cases renaming, the existing streets. The changes allowed the ratepayers simultaneously to mark their disapproval of the catholic and tory Marquis of Bute, John Crichton-Stuart, Earl of Windsor, and to express the utilitarian and commercial image of the

Senghennydd which they wished to establish. The titles and family names of the Crichton-Stuarts were replaced by names which reflected the world view of the shopocracy. Windsor Road became Commercial Street, Stuart Road became Cross Street (it linked two other terrace streets), and Eleanor Street became High Street.[41]

With the sun shining on the small terraces, and the hills forming a glowing backdrop, the small town could take on a festive appearance. Already it was as large as some of the market towns of mid-Wales and to the inhabitants who had come from country areas it probably had the excitement of those towns which they had visited as children for special occasions. Senghennydd *en fete,* in the years of growth and relative plenty, was a place of hope and excitement for its inhabitants.

A sign of the growing importance of the village was the attention paid to it by Alfred Thomas, the Liberal member of parliament for East Glamorgan although, in expansive mood, his largesse tended to be spread widely rather than focussed on particular communities. In June 1897 he gave tea parties for all the children of East Glamorgan, (21,000 in all), to celebrate the Queen's Jubilee. In Senghennydd the children paraded the streets before the tea, supervised by Miss England. The parade was led by the Universal Colliery Band. Various dignitaries were present including members of the School Board and officials from the mine such as Edward Shaw. Among the banners was one which read 'Thanks to our generous M.P.'. The inhabitants lined the streets, cheering the parade and glowing with pride at the columns of well scrubbed children in their best clothes. After tea the National Anthem was sung in Welsh and William Brace, the miners' leader, proposed a vote of thanks to their Member. The *Glamorgan Free Press* commented that 'Mr Thomas's large hearted generosity is proverbial, but in this he excelled himself, and his name will be handed down to posterity as that of the greatest benefactor to young East Glamorgan on the occasion of the great Diamond Jubilee'.[42]

Historians such as Ieuan Gwynedd Jones have contrasted early colliery settlements, (mere aggregations of people; 'condensations of labouring people'), with the structured and ordered societies or 'civic' communities of later periods. Though facets of life in Senghennydd certainly echoed the experiences of the early settlements, it slowly developed the institutions and patterns of behaviour which helped to counterbalance the raw and sometimes dangerous forces within the community.[43]

The second annual banquet of the Senghennydd Chamber of Commerce, held in 1898, was a splendid affair, reported in suitably high blown prose, which celebrated the growth in size and confidence of the burgeoning new pit village. The guests included many people whose names recur in the history of the Senghennydd: Councillor Thomas; Major Lindsay the landowner, coalowner and soldier; Henry Morgan the vicar; Edward Shaw from the Universal Company; Thomas Jones, the assistant overseer of the workhouse; Charles Goodfellow, the leading local freemason and a solicitor whose cases enlivened local discussion; Charles Isaacs the gentleman's outfitter; Dan Lloyd the head master; Robert Lougher, proprietor of the Universal Hotel and Treasurer of the Chamber of Commerce and Josiah Morgan, the developer. The food was lavish, the musical entertainment was 'capital': endless mutually congratulatory toasts were drunk, drawing attention to the various developments which had occurred during the year.[44] It is doubtful that victorious generals, industrial barons, ministers and great administrators had ever sat down to a government banquet with a stronger sense of their status and importance than did these leading citizens of Senghennydd and the local gentry.

Yet their importance, real, pretended or self proclaimed was based, materially and socially, on a world which most of these participants at the banquet had never visited. It was a world which existed a thousand feet below them, inhabited in blackness and fear by human beings who suffered injury and debilitation to support an existence which, if they were lucky, might temporarily raise them above the level of mere survival.

CHAPTER 2

[1] *Cardiff Times* 12/3/1881. My attention was drawn to this story by Neil Thomas of Coleg Harlech

[2] R. Walters, op. cit., 75: B.Thomas, 'The Migration of Labour into the Welsh Coalfield 1861-1911', in W. E. Minchinton, *Industrial South Wales*, (London; 1969), 43: GRO D/D B1/3/1: see also D. G. Sellwood, Llanbradach: 1887-1914, (Caerphilly; 1988),17-25

[3] J. B. Phillips, *A History of Senghenydd up to 1918*, (typescript; nd; Abertridwr Public Library), 11: GFP 25/8/1894

[4] GFP 13/1/1894
[5] GFP 14/4/1894
[6] PC 2/10/1896
[7] CJ 23/3/1931
[8] Eglwysilan Parish register; GRO
[9] GFP 25/8/1894: GFP 19/5/1894
[10] GFP 27/1/1894: *Welsh Leader* 4/8/1904. There continue to be different spellings of the place name. Though 'Senghenydd' is in common use 'Senghennydd' is identified as the correct spelling in E. Davies (ed.) *A Gazetteer of Welsh Place Names*, (Cardiff; 1967). I have used the latter spelling except when citing titles or quoting sources which use alternatives.
[11] PC 24/5/1895; PC 21/6/1895
[12] PC 30/8/1895
[13] PC 30/4/1897
[14] GFP 14/8/1897
[15] GRO D/D X 299/1
[16] GFP 13/10/1897
[17] GFP 11/12/1897
[18] GFP 15/1/1898
[19] GFP 25/8/1894: GFP 28/8/1897
[20] PC 28/2/1896: PC 31/1/1896
[21] PC 14/2/1896
[22] PC 14/6/1895: GFP 20/6/1891
[23] PC 30/10/1896: GFP 30/10/1896: GFP 13/8/1898
[24] GFP 25/8/1894
[25] PC 18/8/1896: PC 25/9/1896
[26] GFP 28/8/1897
[27] GFP 27/8/1898
[28] J. B. Phillips, (n.d.), *op cit*, 14
[29] T. M. Bassett, *The Welsh Baptists*, (Swansea; 1977), 351
[30] CJ 10/12/1932; CJ 13/2/1937
[31] M. J. Mainwaring, *History of St Peter's Church Senghenydd: 1895-1945*, (Abertridwr; 1946), 4-7
[32] GFP 8/1/1898
[33] GFP 10/7/1897
[34] PC 31/5/1895: GFP 25/8/1894
[35] PC 20/9/1895
[36] Infants' School Log 12/9/1895
[37] *ibid* 8/6/1896
[38] *ibid* 4/12/1898: *ibid* 14/4/1899: *ibid* 25/1/1900: *ibid* 4/10/1897
[39] *ibid* 30/4/1899: *ibid* 30/4/1897: *ibid* 30/4/1898: *ibid* 30/4/1900
[40] GFP 30/7/1898
[41] J. B. Phillips, (n.d.), *op cit*, 13
[42] GFP 26/6/1897
[43] I. G. Jones, *Communities*, (Llandysul; 1987), 335-336
[44] GFP 19/2/1898

Chapter Three
The Miners and the Strike of 1898

The coalmine is death: it is the tomb. Both in metaphor and in reality the two are inseparable for the miner. The blackness of the mine is that of the grave and the experience of the mine is wrapped in that blackness. The experience of the miner is timeless: a bond between all miners living and dead. 'The darkness of the mine is indescribable. You push out your hand to feel it, and your hand goes through solid blackness. There is no gleam of light or even relief of shadow. The darkness weighs on a man'.[1] Will Paynter wrote that the darkness of the pit 'is absolute blackness, impenetrable and eerie. Sounds appear to be magnified, the creaks of the roof sounding like cracks of doom. . .'.[2] The blackness became a shroud for Robert Morgan as he waited alone while his father went to tend an old miner dying after being crushed by a fall:

> alone with the silence and a glowing lamp I began to picture all kinds of odd things. I felt the darkness was slowly wrapping itself around me and that at any moment something tremendous was going to happen. I tried to dismiss such thoughts and feelings, but they persisted and even grew stronger. I felt cold and began to shiver.[3]

The adjectives used to describe the mine echo from the grave: 'sinister', 'oozing', 'wet', 'damp', 'eerie', 'black'. The memories of miners contain ghostly encounters, experienced in the heightened awareness engendered by the mine; experiences often laughed at afterwards.

Each time the miner goes down the pit he drops hundreds of feet in a matter of seconds, descending in his fright through the sediment of millions of years of death and putrefaction.

> I heard the gate click as it was locked by the banksman. I seemed unable to breathe properly as the cage plunged down the shaft. Bodies were pressed tightly against each other and my arms were pressed against my sides. As the cage moved I had a curious feeling in my stomach and I must confess the feeling was one of fear and, although I was to make hundreds of descents down the shaft, I was never once at ease going down.[4]

Even on the surface, the winding machinery is a symbol of the grave, throwing its shadow of death across the small communities whose existence depended on the thing which destroyed them. The young Arthur Horner 'felt the shadows of the pit . . . the fear of sudden death or mutilation still hangs over the miners and is felt in every mining village'. For miners the touch of death is tangible in the mine; it is not merely a private sensation, but also part of the observable reality.

> Then one Sunday, somebody left a ventilation door open in the Glynmeal Level and my grandfather, going in at evening to examine the pit, was blown to pieces by an explosion. . . My uncle worked in the mines until his back was broken by a fall. Another uncle went nearly blind with nystagmus. I learned very early that there was blood on the coal.[5]

The dramatic explosions which killed large numbers of miners, particularly in south Wales, were responsible for only a small proportion of the hundreds of accidents which killed miners in ones and twos every day of the year, and these hundreds of accidents affected only a small proportion of the men who died from the direct and indirect results of silicosis, 'black spit', (sometimes known as 'miners' phthisis'), and the other lung diseases from which most south Wales miners suffered to some degree. And the deaths from the diseases and accidents taken together represent a very small fraction of the number of men suffering accidents and disease who struggled on in the mine because they could think of no other way to earn a living and keep their family. Possibly the most dreadful of all was nystagmus, a form of blindness caused by the darkness, which produced strange visions in the brain and could be associated with a kind of madness. It was not uncommon for miners to break down and to be unable to enter the pit until economic necessity drove them back, sedated by alcohol.[6]

It is not possible to understand the miners' impact on society without some sense of this background. The religious involvement of some, as much as the alcoholism and aggression of others, is related to their experience in the mine. Their dry verbal humour, boisterous practical jokes, apparent indifference to death, absenteeism, ferocious political beliefs, commitment to profound egalitarian change, deep social conservatism, all are related to the experience of the mine.

The interaction between that shared individual experience of the miner and the changes wrought in the coalfield by social and economic factors outside their control was, to a large extent, what determined the future of Senghennydd as a community.

The expansion of the Glamorgan coalfield slowed down in the 1890s. In 1893 the mining inspectorate reported that 'the only new winnings of any importance commenced during the year were that in the Aber Valley in the parish of Eglwysilan, by the Universal Colliery Company Limited'.[7]

By the start of the new century the Universal Colliery was employing over 800 men. Many of the workers came from neighbouring parts of Glamorgan or Monmouthshire. Others came from rural Wales; from Breconshire, Cardiganshire, Carmarthenshire and Pembrokeshire. Once one person had come from a village others would follow. From Trawsfynydd, for example, came a group of families who were to play an important part in the life of Senghennydd for the next thirty years: Evan Parry, John Griffith Owen, David Hughes and Robert Simon Hughes.[8] Several came from Somerset, and some from the tin mines of Cornwall. A significant minority were Irish and there were individuals who had been born in almost every part of Britain. Edward Shaw, the manager of the mine, brought with him some fellow members of his Baptist congregation from Aberdare, notably Thomas James and his daughters Catherine and Maggie May and his son Thomas, who were to make a major contribution to the Aber Valley in the years to come.

They entered a mine heavy with the burden of development costs and one in which the mine officials were under pressure to increase production in order to overcome the slump in prices. Throughout the south Wales coalfield wages for face workers were paid according to the amount of coal actually cut by the colliers: they were not paid for the small coal. In those collieries which belonged to the Monmouthshire and South Wales Coalowners' Association the wage paid for the output achieved was on a sliding scale based on the selling price of coal. The Sliding Scale Committee was chaired by Sir William Lewis who, according to D. A. Thomas, carried 'the coal owners' association in his waistcoat pocket'.[9] The base line of 100% was taken as the selling price in 1879. In 1890, prices, and therefore wages, were 50% above the baseline of 1879. By 1895 they were barely 10% above the baseline, representing a great drop in the weekly income of a family since 1890. J. T. Robson, the district inspector of mines who lived (philosophically) in the best of all possible worlds, was able to give a positive gloss to these developments in 1895:

> ... probably the workmen generally and their families are not much worse off now than when their wages are considerably higher, for the men work more regularly, and they have less time to spend money uselessly, as too many of them do in periods of high wages.[10]

The Inspector, whose main task was the overseeing of safety arrangements, was so taken with the advantages of the lower wages which automatically followed lower prices, that he failed to note their obvious effect on working patterns. It was now not only in the interest of miners to increase personal productivity working for longer periods, with greater physical exertion, often for less wages: for most it would be a necessity in order to maintain a standard of living to which mining families had become accustomed, even if that standard of living was regarded as profligate by the Mines Inspector. This in turn created pressures and risks to safety which would have been great in any mine, but which were to have particular significance at Senghennydd. In fairness to Robson it should be added that he was responsible for legislative improvements on mine safety and for attempts to remove from the south Wales colliers the responsibility for safety work which, as far as they were concerned, was in effect unpaid.[11]

The system of piece rates put pressure on individual miners to minimise attention to safety. Thus the Inspector's report in 1892 noted that the miners had not, in general, availed themselves of their power to inspect the mine monthly: 'so far as I am aware the owners and managers have not encouraged inspection by the miners, and are probably indifferent in the matter'.[12] There was a constant price to be paid for these pressures in the injuries and death suffered by miners.

In the early years the deaths mounted only slowly at Senghennydd. In 1896, the first full year of production, though still on a small scale, Daniel Evans, who was thirty two, was killed by a truck, which ran over his thighs. In 1898 Charles Oliver died when the coal face at which he was working collapsed on him. On December 28th in the same year the twenty two year old John Sullivan was killed: he fell from a truck on an incline.[13]

One of the effects of the sliding scale system for determining wages was greatly to reduce the strength of the union, since the union's role in setting wage levels was largely limited to applying a fixed procedure. To the extent that negotiation was needed, it was mainly at a local level, and therefore exaggerated the tendency of colliers to think of trade unions simply in terms of their autonomous organisation in each individual colliery or district. None of this was accidental: it was the direct result of the sliding scale system of which Sir William Lewis was the prime mover and of whose committee he had been the chairman since 1880.

Sir William was a committed and principled opponent of trade unionism in any but the most benign form. In 1898 David Morgan (Dai o'r Nant), a local trade union leader in Aberdare, declared that 'he regarded Sir William Thomas Lewis as the greatest enemy to the working classes whom he had known for the last thirty years'. One historian, L. J. Williams, has written that '. . . Sir William had spent a lifetime dealing with industrial disputes, but had never been able to reconcile himself to the need for trade unions': another, Brinley Evans, wrote that Lewis's aim was first to 'supplant, and later eliminate trade unionism among the men in the south Wales coalfield'.[14] For Lewis, one of the attractions of opening a new mine in an undeveloped valley was its freedom from the taint and tradition of unionism. A definitive history of British trade unions has argued that Lewis 'had a fair claim to be considered the leading industrial opponent of trade unionism'.[15] In 1893 he had been associated with William Collison's National Free Labour Organisation, which was used as a weapon to break strikes by providing non-union labour, and in 1897 he was present at a small meeting of major employers to found the Free Labour Protection Association aimed, in part, at protecting non-unionists in strike breaking activities.[16] In a hostile portrait by a kinswoman, Sir William was described as the 'the last of the industrial barons', the representative of 'the old feudal spirit'.

> The only relationship which he really admitted between himself and the workmen was that of master and man . . . he either did not grasp or refused to admit the fundamental equalities and interdependence of capital and labour in the production of wealth: and he lacked the imagination which would have enabled him to envisage the future development of industrial action and adopt statesmanlike measures to

meet them with a minimum of disturbance to the common interests of employers and workmen.[17]

From the point of view of the workforce it was not all that important whether he was evil or simply a hard headed realist. The practical reality for them was that they were working in a pit where they must expect few concessions and where they would have to look to their own protection. Lewis's attitude to wage bargaining may be summed up in his comment that 'I am satisfied that the men are much easier [to manage] once they find the owners determined to resist their claim for increased prices. . . '.[18]

The system of piecework gave power to managers and mine officials to reward individuals and to punish trade union activists so long as most of the men were not in the union. The amount of coal that a miner could cut in a week depended not only on the collier's skill and energy but also on the particular place in the mine where he was working, for each part of a mine has distinct geological features which alter as the coal faces are pushed forward. Thus apparently trivial decisions about where men were to work formed a major part of relations between men and the management. Only if the men negotiated collectively could they ensure a fair system, but the nature of their trade and some aspects of their traditions emphasised individual skills and earnings.[19]

Although some of the colliers in Senghennydd were individual members of the Cambrian Miners' Association, (in any case something less than an independent trade union), the management were successful in discouraging unionism until 1897. In August of that year William Abraham, M.P., the miners' agent of the Rhondda District Miners' Association and leader of the Cambrian Miners' Association, addressed a meeting in the Gwern-y-Milwr Hotel. Abraham, generally known by his bardic title of 'Mabon', was a legendary figure. He had dedicated his life to building up the miners' organisation on the principle of the common interest between owners and workers. For nearly twenty years he had worked as vice-chairman of the Sliding Scale Committee under the chairmanship of Sir William Lewis, and he had a profound respect for the qualities of his chairman. The mutual respect between them was such that Lewis was kind enough to employ Mabon's eldest son as a clerk in his office. Mabon practised his beliefs, so far as the identity of interests between capital and labour was concerned, and he was to die with more directorships and much more capital than his former trade union colleagues found acceptable.[20]

Mabon was given a warm welcome when he spoke at the Gwern-y-Milwr, which in those days did not have a licence, and with his famous oratory, which he sometimes interspersed with hymn singing, he encouraged the men to organise within the Cambrian Miners' Association. The Association had certain interesting features: in particular it was notable for its insignificant contribution of 2d a month, too small to create a strike fund, which was deducted in the colliery offices and forwarded to the 'association'. It was also significant that the organisation had no workplace structure in the form of lodges or branches, but was organised directly through Mabon's office in the Rhondda.[21]

The speed and enthusiasm with which the Senghennydd miners now organised must have produced mixed feelings in William Abraham, since the weapon of the strike, except in extreme circumstances, was one which offended his religious and moral beliefs. As a result of the economic pressures on the work place and the miners' growing enthusiasm, the effect of their new organisation was soon felt. Less than a month after Mabon's visit the pressures came to a head and the colliers at the Universal struck. The strike started when it was rumoured that a few miners had negotiated a price for the coal and were to sub-contract men to work the coal in their headings. Such a system would undermine the men's unity and any collective action in the future. Numerous meetings failed to resolve the issue and by the first Saturday of the strike the company took the initiative. The night shift of 150 was paid off, making it clear to the men that, whatever the outcome of the particular issue, the cost to the workers would be the loss of 150 jobs.

The following Tuesday Mabon again attended a meeting in the assembly room of the Gwern-y-Milwr. This time he had the measure of the situation and he was able to negotiate a return to work between his members and the Company of his chairman on the Sliding Scale Committee. A delegation of the men 'waited' on the manager, who was now happy to 'confirm' that there would be no sub-contracting of production. Other agreements were made which ensured that the managers could not use their power to give better workplaces to particular men: in future 'the oldest men in each heading and stall should have the priority in these places; and an arrangement was made that the whole of the workmen would have priority over any newcomers'. Nevertheless the management tried to ensure that punishment was exacted by imposing single shift working and stopping 'the double and treble shifts' at a threatened loss of between 100 and 150 jobs. Granted the growth of the mine, the threat of lost jobs sounded hollow.[22]

In fact Mabon's influence in the coalfield was reduced in this period as a result of his commitment to the sliding scale mechanism for fixing wages. It was felt by many miners that the sliding scale kept wages down and moreover, since it was a condition for joining the Miner's Federation of Great Britain that local unions should not be party to sliding scale agreements, it also had the effect of separating the Welsh district unions from the greater industrial strength of the British union. The battle between Mabon and his followers on the one hand, and William Brace and his colleagues who wished to join the British union, on the other hand, had continued for several years. When the latest sliding scale agreement ran out at the end of March 1898, after years of wages depressed by low prices, the miners of south Wales voted for a determined effort to dispose of the agreement and demand a minimum wage, combined with a 10% wage rise. Moreover, suspicious as they were of Mabon and the leadership, the men refused to give their negotiators full powers to settle, insisting instead that any new contract should be put to the men before it was formally agreed. Sir William, on behalf of the owners, in turn refused to negotiate with any representatives of the workers who did not have full powers to settle the dispute.

As a last attempt to avert a major strike, the miners' conference for the coalfield 'agreed to make a direct personal appeal to Sir William, reminding him of his previous [conciliatory] utterances'.[23] This judgement of Lewis's attitude, if it was more than tactical and rhetorical, was soon shown to be wildly inaccurate.

By then, in any event, the preparations had been made and the leaders on each side, who were for the moment in the ascendant, were determined not to give way. As April 1st 1898 approached, both sides organised for the coming struggle. One result of the lack of any centralised union structure was that there was no proper strike fund; all that the leaders could do was to agree a procedure to relieve cases of extreme hardship. The owners, thanks to Sir William Lewis, were better prepared. At their April meeting they paid out £32,522 in compensation to those owners who had already been withstanding strikes by their workers: this was estimated at one shilling a ton for lost production for members of the owners' association, a figure related to the average profit on a ton of coal. The total funds available to indemnify members in the coming strike stood at over £300,000.[24]

The strike started in the first week of April when the men began 'unofficial action', despite last minute attempts to find a solution. In Senghennydd the situation was confused by the fact the the Universal Colliery Company, unlike Lewis's mines in the Rhondda and the Bute mines, was not a member of the owners' association and therefore not a party to the sliding scale agreement. Some of the workers struck immediately, but there were hard words about the many more who continued to work. R. Humphreys, one of the Senghennydd men on strike, wrote that

> in most cases the hauliers have the name of being the ringleaders in the present strike. Such is not the case at the Universal Colliery however, for at that colliery the hauliers have worked up to now without even asking for an advance, and not only have they done their own work but have taken the places of repairers and labourers, and I am sorry to say that they are not by themselves, for many of the colliers have also gone in to repair the workings on the same terms. The men who have remained out have found it necessary to post a notice up to the effect that these men are blacklegs and therefore cannot be tolerated.[25]

Later in April Tom Richards, one of the miners' leaders, accused Sir William of blacklegging on his fellow owners by continuing to work the colliery while the members of the organisation which he led were engaged in a major strike. Windfall profits were being made as the shortage of coal forced up prices. By the end of April, however, the Universal Colliery Company had joined the owners' association and the entire workforce came out on strike.[26]

The lack of any centralised strike fund meant that hardship was immediate for many families. Proposals were put forward to the Pontypridd Board of Guardians, of which Eglwysilan Parish and therefore Senghennydd formed a part, to set up projects for relief work. Other proposals were put to Caerphilly Urban District Council, of which Senghennydd also formed a part. A further attempt was made, for example, to construct a lane from Pontypridd to Senghennydd, potentially drawing trade to Pontypridd and away from Caerphilly.

Tempers flared in various meetings, bringing out the antagonism and overlapping roles between the unelected magistrates and the elected local boards and forcing into the open the view that, by providing relief work, councillors and poor law guardians were supporting and prolonging the strike. The surveyor of the Great Western Colliery, Mr Valliant, argued that 'the council could find fitter work to do by endeavouring to use their influence to bring the present lamentable strike to an end, and not endeavouring to prolong it'. Valliant also accused Watkin Williams, a landowner and a proponent of the scheme of public works, of hiding his personal financial stake in the proposal. Williams robustly replied 'that is a lie' and, after scenes of wild disorder, Williams announced that 'if Mr Valliant wanted to attack him . . . he would take him to the back and see if he could do so'. The Chairman struggled heroically to produce an ordered conclusion from the chaos by putting a motion for public works to the vote. He 'declared the motion carried, but this was ridiculed by the opposition and the meeting broke up in disorder'.[27]

Though this was by no means the only example of farce enjoyed by the locals during the strike the grim reality of widespread distress was almost immediate. Soup kitchens were set up in sympathetic chapels and free soup was provided in the schools, under the Poor Law, for destitute children.

At other meetings the poor law guardians made large scale arrangements for stone breaking at their yards. This work was not available for single men unless they could prove that they had dependant brothers, sisters or parents. At Pontypridd, the rate for a man with a wife was a shilling a day with 2d a day for each child. Thus the weekly rate for a family of five would be ten shillings and sixpence at a time when it was agreed that £1 a week would barely provide subsistence. Destitution became widespread with reports in the local papers of babies having only water, and of children going for two days without food.

In this situation the churches were an essential part of the relief effort; and they were therefore important, indirectly, in supporting the strike. The English Wesleyans in Senghennydd decided that, before they could appeal to an impoverished public for money for their food kitchen, they should first exhaust the money in the fund for building a chapel. They distributed food to the destitute each day in the vestry. It was reported that the food kitchen behind the Gwern-y-

Milwr Hotel fed 350 children daily on bread, butter, cheese, rice pudding, pea soup, potatoes, beef, broth, cocoa and tea: 'in fact, the children in this town are excellently provided for, although funds are greatly needed'. As well as providing food the kitchens offered opportunities for popular enlightenment. On the day of Gladstone's funeral all shops were closed between eleven and one o'clock and the blinds were drawn. In the food kitchen there was a meeting before the food was served, addressed by the Reverend David Jones: the other speakers were David Edmunds, the grocer; M. E. Price, the chemist; David Towyn Jones and Thomas Thomas. A vote of condolence to Mrs Gladstone was carried before the hungry mass could tuck into its food.[28]

By the middle of June people were becoming desperate. A long article in the *Western Mail* summarised conditions throughout the coalfield, illustrating the report with 'typical cases'. The article argued that 'the destitution among the miners' families of which we have heard so much in the general way is far more serious than anyone can imagine'. From every quarter the reporter heard stories which 'have been extremely harrowing, telling tales of want and suffering to a numerical extent that is appalling'. The reporter claimed that people were actually starving in south Wales. In the place of the normal frantic industrial bustle there was a 'a horrid stillness as of the tomb'.

The tone of the piece is sentimental in a way which would become familiar to the inhabitants of Senghennydd over the years; but some of the imagery retains its power to shock. The reporter wrote of 'the pale and pinched faced children' who had 'to weep away their hunger until sleep comes to let them dream of food. Their very clothing is a dirge, for everything but the merest rags are gone and naked feet and bare heads do but finish the tale of poverty that they tell'.

This and other reports emphasised the extent to which family possessions had been pawned. 'The homes are broken up; everything that the pawnbroker will take has gone—sold for a few pence with which to buy food—and amid the barren walls and empty cupboards the mothers have the additional hardship of having to refuse when their starving offspring clamour for food'. Chests of drawers were sold for fifteen shillings, sheets for ninepence and children's clothes for a few pennies.

The report focused in particular on the position of women in the

An anti-trade union cartoon published in the *Western Mail* during the strike
of 1898.

strike. 'Upon the mothers falls the greatest burden. Pale, weak, and
shrunken, they try to do their housework, but there is no money in the
purse, no food in the cupboard to give their children, still less for
themselves. . .'. The writer cited cases of children going to school
without breakfast and of empty cupboards throughout the weekend.

A member of the Pontypridd School Board, John Johns, argued
that the people 'are being terrorised by starvation'. By June, relief
funds were beginning to dry up leaving the heads of families to rely on
pay from public works. Interestingly, at least one workhouse master
claimed that he did not personally 'know of a case of extreme poverty.
There are less women and children coming here now than before the
strike'. Pressed by an incredulous journalist, the master of the
workhouse said that people preferred to 'stay at home and receive one
meal per day, rather than visit the workhouse and receive three meals

a day . . . [they] do not like to break up their homes and go into the workhouse'.[29]

The universal hardship created even greater solidarity in Senghennydd together with a stubborn pride. At the end of May the Senghennydd miners created a stir when they apparently refused to work in the stoneyard, despite the fact that the distress 'was very acute in Senghennydd'. E. Morris, the miner's delegate insisted that they had been misunderstood. 'The men were offered road mending at 2s 6d a day with a shovel, and 2s 3d without a shovel. As this was less than the ordinary men employed on this work are paid, they refused, thinking that an advantage was being taken of their hopeless position. 'They would,' Morris claimed, 'be only too glad to work if they were paid at the usual rate'.[30] This suggests a high degree of solidarity and morale even if, as the distress intensified, they were forced to alter their position.

The entire community at Senghennydd shared the hardship since it was the miners' wages which fuelled all the activities of the town. The small commercial class was immediately affected, producing a Senghennydd rates crisis for Caerphilly Council. The auditor helped by postponing the audit until June 13, but Captain Dowdeswell tried to make the meeting face the worst by asking what would happen if the strike continued for another month: events were to show that his gloomy realism was much too optimistic. The auditor clearly regretted that he could not surcharge the councillors for the overdue revenue, feeling that the threat of this would stiffen their resolve towards their electors: the auditor 'was of the opinion that the council was too lenient with the ratepayers'.[31]

Given the suffering of the Valleys communities it is unsurprising that Sir William was the target of much personal abuse. David Morgan (Dai o'r Nant) declared that 'Sir William had a splendid brain, but he had the heart and conscience that were governed by the Devil' and that he 'could tell falsehoods like a dog could trot'. Keir Hardie claimed that many miners were losing their Christian faith and that it was not surprising 'that this should be so when they saw how Christians of the type of Sir William Lewis and Mr Cory were acting towards the men'.[32] Against this view it is worth noticing that Lewis could be sympathetic to those who, in his opinion, had not brought suffering on themselves and their own families: at the end of April he offered money to relieve cases of hardship among the families of railwaymen thrown out of work by the strike.[33] His critics might cynically argue that such displays of sympathy had more to do with engaging public support than with empathy for the suffering although, in fairness, it should be said that sensitive public relations were not Sir William's favoured tactic.

While the strike raged on Sir William Lewis maintained an appearance of unbothered detachment. When the men, anxious for continued negotiations, asked for a further meeting, Sir William announced that he would be unavailable for a week. When asked whether, in that case, the owners' committee could meet the men's representatives without him being present, he crisply replied from the chair, 'No'. D. A. Thomas's claim that 'it is well known that the Monmouthshire and South Wales Coalowners' Association is a one man affair' may have had some truth.[34]

In the third week of May it was announced that 'Sir W. Thomas Lewis Bart, left Aberdare on Monday for London, and will proceed thence upon private business to Scotland. He is not expected to return to Wales until the end of the week'.[35] In fact he was visiting the Marquis of Bute who, as the greatest 'industrialist' in south Wales, was an important element in the situation.

As far as the strike was concerned Sir William's air of autocratic distance, almost of indifference, was not a mere pose; and he weathered other equally explosive issues of public concern with a similar air of disdain. In Llandaff, on the outskirts of Cardiff, two young children were drowned on a weir over the River Taff, land owned by the Bute Estate of which Sir William was the agent. The Vicar of Llandaff claimed that children were drowned in the same spot each year, and suggested that Lewis refused to spend the necessary few pounds to fence the area of the weir because the estate wished to use the situation to stop rights of way over all the neighbouring land.

At the inquest the surveyor for Llandaff and Dinas Powis District Council said,

> I shall report the fatalities to my council, my council will instruct me to send a petition to the Bute Authorities, the same old answer will be received, and the matter will be allowed to drop once more until some more children meet with their deaths.[36]

The Vicar personalised the attack on the head of the Bute Estates, a tactic that was to produce results. He claimed that 'probably now that two more young lives have been lost Sir William will give the matter his attention'.

Even Sir William, despite his enormous presence and his nerves of steel in the face of pressure, must have felt under some stress in this period. The marriage of one of his daughters produced a happy interlude in the midst of the worsening crisis. He was a patriarchal figure with real affection for his daughters and grand-children, and the wedding of his children brought considerable pleasure. His daughter Mary married William Forest of St Fagans near Cardiff. Together they made a beautiful and charming couple. The reception was a grand affair attended by the Marquis and Marchioness of Bute, Lady Margaret Crichton-Stuart, Sir John and Lady Gunn and other fairly prominent people, though it was noticeably not a society or aristocratic wedding. Nevertheless the newspapers published two columns on the wedding including lists of the presents: gold, jewellery, Meissen porcelain, silver services and cutlery and antique furniture. It was a fine summer, the couple were young, attractive and gifted, and the villagers of St Fagans danced and fired salvos of artillery to celebrate the wedding taking place 200 miles away at St Peter's, Eaton Square, Belgravia, before the enchanted pair left to honeymoon in Paris.[37]

Back in Senghennydd the festivities were distinctly more muted throughout the period of the strike and some magistrates were happy to note the vast drop in drunkenness as a result of the widespread poverty. A fairly typical example of celebration in the context of the strike was illustrated under the headline, 'Sheebeening at Senghennydd'. Annie James of Stanley Street was found selling beer without a license and was prosecuted in keeping with the determined attempts to limit drink in the village. When the police entered her house they found two men there. Her explanation that 'Dick came here for the loan of 3d but that she gave him a pint of beer instead', was barely adequate though it has an authentic ring to it. The police claimed that she then said, 'you have not got such a case as you had last time'.

Unfortunately one of her customers was less than determined in his denials. Asked by the court if he had paid for the beer he replied, 'No, not that day': which was adequate. But when further asked if 'he paid for it at all', he replied, 'I think I did'. Annie James, who had previously been fined the fabulous sums of £5, £10 and £50, was gaoled for a month. The 'defendant who was the worse for drink, gave a curt "thank you", and added that 'she did not know what she was sent to prison for'.[38] The law and the cause of temperance had been strengthened to some infinitesimal degree.

Slowly the strike was having its effect, for in late June the Government announced that the Navy's Summer manoeuvres would be abandoned as a result of the stoppage. The announcememt predictably claimed that this was merely a precautionary measure and that the Navy was weighed down with coal stocks, but the news gave encouragement to the miners.[39]

In July the Government, in the person of Charles Ritchie, the President of the Board of Trade, made an attempt to settle the strike by appointing Sir Edward Fry as a conciliator. There were signs that a compromise with the coalowners might be found but the optimists underestimated the personal force of the chairman of the Coalowners' Association. Whatever the feelings of the other coalowners, including several with larger concerns than that of Sir William, their chairman firmly held his position and the members of the association followed his lead. On the Ist of July it was announced that 'Sir William T. Lewis maintains his decision not to accept the intervention of a third party, and declares that Mr Ritchie's conciliator will not be recognized by the employers'.[40] Just in case the President of the Board of Trade mistook this for a mere public smokescreen, a tactic to alarm the miners' leaders, the next day the *Western Mail,* which echoed Sir William on most issues, stated that 'Sir William has informed Mr Ritchie. . . that the Welsh Coal Owners will tolerate no interference from the outside in the settlement of the dispute'.[41]

During the following week Sir Edward Fry persevered regardless, while his mission degenerated into farce. He was installed in the Park Hotel almost opposite the headquarters of the owners' association in the South Wales Engineers' Institute. At the end of a meeting of the owners 'Sir Edward Fry's private secretary crossed to the Institute from the Park Hotel and soon afterwards returned. Dalziel [secretary to Sir William's Committee] then crossed to the Park Hotel and later returned to talk to Sir William. Sir William then crossed to the Park Hotel and remained there for some time.' At the end of all this to-ing and fro-ing, which aroused great expectations, Sir Edward Fry was finally forced to face the facts: he announced that Sir William Lewis

Sir William Lewis and Mabon defy Sir Edward Fry's attempt to settle the
strike of 1898.

'declined to recognise my position as conciliator in any way, and
stated that he called merely out of courtesy'.[42]

In the growing crisis Senghennydd and other villages and towns
resorted to every possible method of survival. Crowds could be seen
on the coal tip, trying to find coal to sell or to use for their own
cooking. The village also responded to the crisis by deploying one of
its established strengths: concerts were given in Senghennydd and
elsewhere to raise money for its central relief fund. On August 9th, by
which time the situation was becoming desperate for some families, a
'Grand Sacred Concert' was held on a Sunday night at the Gwern-y-
Milwr. Solo performances were given of 'Lead Kindly Light', 'O rest
in the Lord' and 'Arm, Arm ye brave'. Welsh hymns and songs
included 'Pa le mae'r Amen' and 'Cartref yr Amddifad'. 'A very
substantial amount was realised by silver collection from the crowded
audience' and there were hopes that this would prove a rich source for
future funds. Ithel Thomas and Tom Wigley organised other concerts

in Llanbradach and Caerphilly in which further 'substantial' amounts were raised. However in the impoverished coalfield in which singing was a universal activity this initiative had obvious limits, and other groups went further afield beyond the south Wales coalfield in their attempts to raise money.[43]

The long report in the *Western Mail* in June had suggested that 'it is feared that starvation will make the workmen reckless in anything they might undertake so as to provide their foodless families with proper nourishment'.[44] Certainly as the weeks dragged on, with families and relief organisations exhausting their savings and funds, a desperate and dangerous undertow became increasingly apparent.

Throughout the coalfield there were mass demonstrations against colliery officials and miners who continued to work. In Dowlais police were injured during demonstrations. In Abercynon there was allegedly a riot outside the house of an official: the demonstrators numbered 5000. In Merthyr Vale 10,000 marched to the door of a miner who worked for Nixon's Collieries, one of the largest companies in south Wales. The marchers carried sticks and the leaders held long poles. The demonstration had a large police escort headed by Captain Lindsay, the Chief Constable of Glamorgan, (and brother of Major Lindsay), who was prepared to read the riot act. It is a sign of the union's discipline that in the circumstances, and with what the newspaper described as a 'mob' of 10,000, the demonstration passed off with no disorder, no damage and no arrests.[45]

By this stage the coalfield was filling up with troops. These were called in by the magistrates, an unelected body, largely representative of older, often landed, interests in the county; confronting them were the elected councillors who, along with the Boards of Guardians and School Boards, were more responsive to the demands of their constituencies. 100 dragoons were stationed in Pontypridd at the request of the magistrates, an act which drew an 'emphatic protest from Pontypridd District Council'. Over the mountain from Senghennydd, in Cilfynydd, troops were billeted in the Albion Colliery to protect working miners, a situation which did not arise in Senghennydd where no coal was being produced.[46]

At the end of June the miners were amused and encouraged by the news that Sir William was temporarily leaving south Wales. The *Pontypridd Chronicle* announced that 'Sir William Thomas Lewis and family have taken up their residence in London for the season, or at any rate, until the labour troubles in South Wales are over'.[47] The *Western Mail* was apparently worried that this might be seen as a craven retreat, and therefore emphasised that it was not his personal safety that worried the owners' leader. Rather he had been 'greatly worried by the fear that some attack might be made by the strikers on his family'.[48] To forestall any suggestion that Sir William might be jumping at shadows, there was a remarkable account, in the following day's edition, of an abortive attempt on Sir William's house.

> A night attack on the Mardy, Sir William Thomas Lewis's home at Aberdare, was organised last week and relinquished merely because it was discovered that the house was defended. Riots, where they are perfectly safe for the rioters, are the regular order of the day.

Since the account was taken from *The Times* rather than directly from the *Western Mail*'s own local sources, it is possible that Sir William had been able to help the national newspaper with information during his stay in London, though the evidence for the existence of a plot was not provided. Later the *Western Mail* referred to the family as being in exile, reiterating the point that Lewis had left because he was 'directly informed that his safety could not be guaranteed'.[49] The miners' leader, Mabon, was also subjected to threats on his life and was accused of selling out the cause of the workers to his old colleague, Sir William: he remained in his house in the Rhondda.

Though Sir William Lewis may have been driven temporarily from the Valleys, his memory was kept alive in a popular song, 'Sir William Rules us All' which was sung to the tune of 'Rule Brittania'. The song demonstrated the affectionate hatred in which the man was held; it was an accolade not given to other wealthier coalowners. The last three verses give the tone of the whole song:

> Sir William Rules the Sliding Scale
>   Sir William Rules on land and sea
> On acres Broad, on dock and dale
>   Sir William rules both you and me.

> *Chorus:*
>   Rule Sir William , Rule Sir William,
>   Sir William—Rule the Waves
>   Colliers ever, ever, ever
>   Shall be Slaves

In Heaven above, on earth below,
   Down in the pit, where'er you go
Upon the tip, or neath the fall
   Sir William rules as Lord of all.

Chorus:

Oh may deliverance not be long
   From one man rule throughout the world
And may oppression by the strong
   From man's domain be swiftly hurled.

Chorus.[50]

But it was not to be. In the end the miners were forced to accept the continuation of the sliding scale together with the loss of their monthly holiday (Mabon's Day): in return they won a 5% rise and an agreement that if the price of coal forced wages below 12½% on the standard, then the workers would be able to withdraw from the agreement after September 1899. The miners were defeated, but they were not humiliated: indeed they had inflicted considerable financial losses on the owners who were to be more wary of confrontation in the immediate future.

CHAPTER 3

[1] B. L. Coombes, *These Poor Hands*, (London; 1939), 80

[2] W. Paynter, *My Generation*, (London; 1972), 20

[3] R. Morgan, *My Lamp Still Burns*, (Llandysul; 1981), 95

[4] *Ibid.*, 66

[5] A. Horner, *Incorrigible Rebel*, (London; 1960), 11

[6] T. Boyns, 'Work and Death in the South Wales Coalfield, 1874-1914', *Welsh History Review*, (vol 12, 1984-5), 515: J. Benson (1980), *op cit*, 38-42

[7] Inspectors' Reports, PP 1894 C.7339 (p3), xxiv

[8] CJ 2/7/1932: CJ 14/1/1933: CJ 12/3/1932: CJ 18/7/1931: *Merthyr Express*, 7/6/1924

[9] B. Evans, *A History of Trades Disputes and the Formation of the Several Sliding Scale Agreements. . .*, (University of Wales Thesis; 1944), 85

[10] Inspectors' Reports, PP 1895 C.7667 (p3) xxii

[11] T. Boyns, (1984-5), 521-3

[12] Inspectors' Reports, PP 1892 C. 6625 xxiii

[13] Inspectors' Reports, PP 1899 C.9264 xv

[14] L. J. Williams, *The Monmouthshire and South Wales Coal Owners' Association, 1873-1914,* (University of Wales thesis; 1957), 255: Brinley Evans, *op cit,* 87

[15] H. Clegg et al, *A History of British Trade Unions since 1889,* Vol I, (Oxford; 1964), 324

[16] *Ibid,* 171 & 173

[17] Viscountess Rhondda (Ed.), *D. A. Thomas, Viscount Rhondda,* (London; 1921), 118

[18] L. J. Williams, (1957), *op cit,* 229

[19] M. J. Daunton, 'Down the Pit: Work in the Great Northern and South Wales Coalfields, 1870-1914', *Economic History Review,* 2nd Series, XXXIV (N0 4), (November, 1981)

[20] E. W. Evans, *Mabon,* (Cardiff; 1959): E. W. Evans and John Saville, DLB, Vol I, 3

[21] E. W.Evans, *op cit.,* 20-22: GFP 21/8/1897

[22] GFP 25/9/1897

[23] WM 30/5/1898

[24] NLW, Records of the Monmouthshire and South Wales Coal Owners' Association

[25] WM 18/4/1898

[26] B. Evans, *op cit,* 92

[27] PC 20/5/1898

[28] GFP 7/5/1898: GFP 18/6/1898

[29] WM 17/6/1898

[30] WM 27/5/1898

[31] WM 12/5/1898

[32] WM 31/3/1898: WM 23/6/1898: quoted in B. Evans, *op cit,* 101

[33] WM 25/4/1898, quoted in B. Evans, *op cit,* 93

[34] B. Evans, *op cit,* 96 & 91

[35] WM 24/5/1898

[36] WM 11/5/1898

[37] WM 13/6/1898

[38] PC 22/7/1898

[39] WM 20/6/1898

[40] WM 1/7/1898: NLW, Records of the Monmouthshire and South Wales Coal Owners' Association

[41] WM 2/7/1898

[42] B. Evans, *op cit,* 102-3

[43] GFP 27/8/1898

[44] WM 17/6/1898

[45] PC 10/6/1898

[46] PC 24/6/1898; PC 17/6/1898

[47] PC 17/6/1898

[48] WM 13/6/1898

[49] WM 14/6/1898: WM 16/6/1898

[50] PC 15/7/1898

Chapter Four
The Disaster of 1901

In this period the village entirely depended on the mine for its existence. When the colliery stopped working the village immediately started to shrink. As a result of the strike the population fell from 2,583 in 1898 to 2,221 in 1899. Nevertheless the setback was only short lived and the town continued to grow as further seams were opened up in the mine.[1]

An indication of the continued growth was the number of shops and commercial concerns opening in the village. Towyn Jones, the secretary of the Chamber of Commerce, was established as a bootmaker in Commercial Street; Albert Fine, the furniture dealer, was creating his 'emporium' and Joseph Williams combined the jobs of carpenter, builder and undertaker, a lucrative combination in the brief history of Senghennydd. Although, like many others, it was unsure of how to spell the name of the village, the 'Senghenith Industrial Co-operative Society' was also quickly established.

Many of the shopkeepers were involved in the efforts to improve the amenities of the village: they continued to harry Caerphilly Council and ensured that Senghennydd received more than its fair share of attention, demanding better lighting, sewage and water supplies and a polling booth.[2] The Sloggetts, Bussells, Marshalls and Snailhams all played significant roles in the town. Mrs Snailham kept a shop in Station Road, while the men of her family worked in the pit, giving their name to Snailham's Dip. The Bussells now farmed Maes Diafol, provided the village with a watchmaker, worked in the mine, and above all ran the post office. Miss Elizabeth Bussell, the postmistress, was to be one of the most enduring citizens of the village, playing a significant role in the major events of the future. There was a china warehouse, refreshment rooms, shoe makers and endless hardware shops selling the tools of their trade to the miners.[3]

An important symbol to the inhabitants was the presence of no fewer than two banks, Lloyds and the London and Provincial, both open from 9.30 to 11.30 on Tuesdays; an indication of the village's importance. The police were also now firmly established with a sergeant, John Davies, and one constable, a force which was to double in the next decade.

By 1901 the school was well established and its pupil numbers almost trebled between 1901 and 1910 as the mine reached full production, sucking in more workers and their families. At the beginning of the century average attendance at the school was 110 boys, 110 girls and 115 infants. Miss Mary Davies was the school mistress, Miss Margaret Austin was the head of the infant school and Dan Lloyd was still the headmaster.

In the saga of the pubs the Universal and the Gwern-y-Milwr were still the only hotels to have licences, with the Leigh and the Parc still making their annual attempts. They were again refused licences in 1899. The epic battle was given new colour when it emerged, in 1901, that an attempt had been made to bribe the chairman of the Licensing Committee, for a pub lower down the valley.[4]

The number of chapels was also growing although, compared to other mining areas, there was already a remarkable number of them measured against the number of pubs. There were English and Welsh Congregational Chapels, a Welsh Baptist Chapel and a Welsh Calvinistic Methodist Chapel, an English Wesleyan Chapel, a Welsh Independent Chapel and a Roman Catholic presence. Senghennydd was a part of the the Anglican parish of Eglwysilan which also had a 'mission hall' in the village in the charge of a curate, Henry Evans.

The development of the railway station from a mere object of utility was also an indication that the village was passing from its first stage of growth. The *Pontypridd Chronicle* claimed that Senghennydd Railway Station was now 'the prettiest in Glamorgan at the height of the flower season. It is a midget flower shower in perspective panorama, and speaks volumes of the sense of taste and beauty of the stationmaster'. Even Penyrheol, at the entrance to the Aber Valley, which twelve months previously had been compared 'to a lunatic asylum in the midst of an African Karoo', was complimented on its improvement and the Aber Valley line was sharply distinguished from the appearance of the stations on the main line.[5]

In the midst of this burgeoning growth the Senghennydd miners were far from demoralised by the result 1898 strike. On the contrary the strike had been the catalyst for the creation of a single unified union in south Wales and this had a direct impact on events in Senghennydd. In the Universal there were several confrontations

Senghennydd Railway Station.

with the management over the price of cutting coal in the different faces. As each new coalface was developed, pay levels had to be set against the basic standard of the sliding scale, a source of continuous friction and of several short strikes intended to focus the minds of the management. The issue was on the agenda of the East Glamorgan Miners in September 1899 and reached the point of a strike in January 1901 when the union agreed on financial support for the colliers.[6]

The managers continued to resist pay rises on the grounds of the fragile profitablility of south Wales coal: their claims may have rung hollow to the men in the light of the announcement that Sir William Lewis was to be the executor of the will of his friend, John Nixon, proprietor of Nixon's Navigation Colliery Company. Apart from his land and personal property, John Nixon left £1,145,658. It was noted that Nixon made no charitable bequest even of a symbolic nature.[7]

At the end of 1899 the Universal employed 731 miners and was producing around 3,000 tons of coal a week, figures which would increase two or three fold in the following decade. Sir William Lewis also rose with this prosperity, receiving a baronetcy in 1896. Rumours of a peerage in 1897 had led the *Glamorgan Free Press* to describe him, hyperbolically, as 'the genial baronet of Mardy' and the paper went on to claim that 'no honour ever conferred will have been more popular throughout the land than when Sir W. T. Lewis will receive the title of lord'.[8] The peerage did not materialise at that stage, but in 1900 he was a made a Knight Commander of the Royal Victorian Order, a personal honour from the monarch which must have given pleasure to the old Tory. In 1900 he floated his Rhondda mines on the stock market, amalgamating them in Lewis Merthyr Consolidated Collieries Limited. The new company had a share capital of £450,000 and had coal reserves estimated at 70,000,000 tons. Certainly the strike did not appear seriously to damage his fortunes for in 1899, before the flotation of his company, Sir William had bought Hean Castle in Pembrokeshire, together with 1,000 acres of land.[9]

From a far distance there came the rumbling gunfire of the Boer War which brought a touch of excitement to the village without involving the inhabitants as a whole in any hardship. Thomas Thomas of Senghennydd wrote stirring letters from the front to John Nicholas, the station master, and their publication in the local paper caused much interest. During the battle for Eastcourt, Thomas wrote,

> The first place we went to was Movi River, where we had a hot time of it with the Boers. They shelled our camp for three days. I can say this much, they are good shots, but I thought that they were firing sawdust at us. Their shells are no good, as they go straight into the ground, and do no damage to anyone. When we were under their fire some were laughing at them and some were reading penny novels . . . but our artillery did good work and had effect on them—blowing them up and killing about four hundred Boers, so they saw we were the best.[10]

Thomas accurately expressed the jingoistic mood of the time in his parting note: 'I won't say any more at present. We are getting ready for another attack on the Boers. We want a few more Boers and sows for Christmas and we will have them'. After the Battle of Colenso he wrote:

> It was murder on both sides. The bullets and shells came upon us like hailstones, but we went on and took no notice of the Boers and killed two thousand or more I should think . . . After the battle the Boers filled their trenches up with dead Boers. It was [an] awful sight to see.[11]

As always he signed off with some piece of hearty soldier's bluster: 'I must go now because we have to go and give the Boers their breakfast —a few 'B' pills to remove their pain'.

There was also pride when Major (later Colonel) Lindsay, the local landowner and Caerphilly councillor, who had been involved in the civic rituals of Senghennydd from the start, departed for South Africa with the Monmouthshire Militia. The relief of Ladysmith and the capture of Pretoria were celebrated with all night festivities and Saturday holidays, outbursts of enjoyment calculated to weaken the impact of local Liberals who asked if the war could not have been avoided in the first place.[12] Even in the patriotic effusions after the Relief of Mafeking, the liberal *Glamorgan Free Press* managed to maintain some distance from the prevailing jingoism by publishing a letter from one of the defenders: 'The Siege of Mafeking is no doubt a thing of the past, but up to date it has been a one-sided affair. The commanding officer [Baden-Powell] has finished playing to the gallery and, as far as I can see, treated with contempt the men who put him in the exalted position he now occupies.'[13]

In general, however, the mood was one of popular enthusiasm and when a wounded local 'hero' returned to the Aber Valley from Ladysmith, he was 'carried shoulder high right through to Senghennydd and the khaki dressed soldier was unceremoniously jostled about amidst the cracking of gunpowder and the hoarse shouts and songs of hundreds of men, women and children. . . others, having lost control of their better feelings, shouted themselves hoarse. . .'.[14] The managers of the mine gave expression to the popular mood when they renamed the underground districts of the mine, Mafeking, Ladysmith, Pretoria and Kimberley.

Apart from these passing excitements, in Senghennydd things appeared much as usual in the spring of 1901. It was a growing, prosperous pit village with all the social stress and exploitation associated with such a place but also with much of the bustling, busy importance which made mining villages so alive for their inhabitants.

By May 1901 there were 450 men on the day shift and 240 on the night shift, all under the charge of the thirty year old Edward Shaw who had taken over as manager on the death of his father ten weeks earlier. 80 men, many of them on overtime, were on the repairing 'half-shift' in the early morning before the main day shift arrived for work. The overmen and firemen supervised the work of the men in preparing the mine for the main day shift, repairing falls, checking for gas, and carrying out other safety work required by law. The mine was worked on the longwall system by which the seam was cut and carried forward on a long front moving away from the pit bottom. Each faceworker had his own 'stall', about eleven yards in length, in which he was responsible for cutting the coal. He worked with a younger miner who did not yet have his own stall: this would commonly be his son, a relation or a lodger in his house.[15]

The Universal appeared to be a good pit in which to work since the seams were fairly regular, without the geological faults and shifts of many south Wales pits. Above all, with the exceptions of a few areas and despite the difficulties during the sinking operation, the mine was dry, ensuring that miners did not have to work all day in wet clothes, lying on their sides in pools of water for hours on end, as they undermined the seam.

The very dryness, however, produced its own problems since it caused high levels of coal dust which was the cause of the chest diseases which crippled and killed miners. Coal dust was also the main factor in the spread of devastation beyond the immediate area of an explosion of methane gas. Gas explosions, in themselves, were localised in their destruction. The cause of the high death tolls in many disasters was the secondary explosion carried through mines by the build up of coal dust, which produced a continuing combustion along the roadways and workings. Although the exact nature of these secondary and more lethal explosions was not entirely understood, the basic cause and effect was clear long before 1901. In order to prevent such explosions, a number of innovations were being carried out in mines. In particular the trucks which carried the coal from the face to the pit bottom were now being designed with closed tops, to prevent the spread of dust. Legislation had been drafted to ensure that all trucks leaving the face would be watered by sprinklers in the roof and that safety men and repairers should clear dust from the roofs and sides of the tunnels on a regular basis.

In the year when the Inspector of Mines for South Wales had noted that the only important new workings in the coalfield were at Senghennydd, he had also made a general point about the occurrence of explosions: 'the past year was remarkable for its freedom from explosions of firedamp and their frequent terrible results'. He was optimistic that this happy situation was not merely fortuitous:

when the vast output is considered, and the large number of persons employed underground in producing it, together with the fact that this output is worked almost entirely from mines more or less gaseous, this is a satisfactory result. It proves that, with skill and care, it is possible to work such mines safely in this respect.[16]

On Friday 24th May 1901, the Universal Colliery blew up with a force not before known in the south Wales Coalfield.[17]

The night shift had ascended the shaft at 4.30 a.m., and the day shift was not due to go down until 6.00 o'clock: only the repairing half shift was in the mine. Shortly after 5.00 o'clock there was a loud explosion from 1,500 feet below ground. This was followed by a long rumbling vibration, indistinguishable from an earthquake. These manifestations were felt three and a half miles away on Pontypridd Road. The force of the first explosion was so great that, gaining momentum as it travelled through the mine, it erupted up the shaft blowing away the equipment in the pit-shaft and on the surface which then crashed down on the mine buildings. One of those in the last cage to arrive at the surface was John Morgan, (John 'Whitecross'): as he walked from the pithead he was blown to the ground by the explosions and both his legs were broken as the pithead equipment collapsed around him.

Edward Shaw and everyone on the surface immediately threw themselves at the tangled debris around the pithead, struggling to clear it so that a cage could be lowered. The after-effect of a mine explosion is to produce lethal carbon monoxide gas which can kill all who survive the explosion: their only chance of survival is if they can escape or be reached by rescuers before they are overcome by the gas. The speed of the rescue is therefore the vital factor which determines how many people will survive.

Miners and officials from every accessible point in the coalfield hurried to the scene as soon as they heard the news. Within two hours several hundred volunteers had reached the Senghennydd mine: but there was little for them to do until a cage could be lowered. Apart from the men who worked to repair the winding machinery and restore the pit, the others could only reflect with desperation on the minutes which were lost as men died of gas poisoning below. The volunteers joined most of the inhabitants of the village who stood near the entrance to the colliery yard, away from the pithead itself.

Relatives tried to get the wives of the trapped men to wait for news at home, anticipating the worst and trying to ensure that when it came the most vulnerable should have some degree of privacy.

By 7.30 a.m. Shaw and his helpers had cleared the debris at the surface and he was able to descend the pit together with a fireman and one of the pit officials. The destruction in the shaft was so great that they could not be lowered to the bottom and it was another hour and a half before a team managed to reach the working level. Even then the cage jammed 18 feet from the bottom and they had to climb down the guide ropes in order to reach the level and clear the obstructions. There they faced a scene of almost total devastation, with trucks thrown across the roadways, props blown away and the roof in a state of collapse. In one major respect they were fortunate for Senghennydd was a new mine and the furthest workings were only about a mile from the pit bottom; however even this seemed an impossible distance in the condition of the mine. The effect of the collapses and the deadly afterdamp was that the rescue teams managed to move only a little way forward by midday.

At midday there was a surge of hope among the crowd when men were lifted up the shaft and some were brought out on stretchers. It seemed that the rescue was at least partially successful. In fact the news was disastrous, for the men on stretchers were members of the rescue team. Elijah Tanner, Arthur Essery and Joe Townsend had been overcome by carbon monoxide fumes and exhaustion in their attempts to climb over the falls and reach the trapped miners: the rest of the team were driven back by the appalling conditions in the mine. Among the urgent problems was the replacement of the cage itself which had been so badly mis-shapen in the explosion that each trip up and down the shaft increased concern for the safety of the occupants.

In the early afternoon the rescuers came across horse manure on top of the dust of the explosion, an indication that at least something had survived the explosion. Further on they discovered the body of William Harris, an ostler, lying by the corpse of a dead horse. At first Harris was assumed to be dead, but when he showed some signs of life doctors were brought down the pit; his condition was too critical for him to be manhandled into the damaged cage. Eventually he was taken to the surface and then to his home, still unconscious, since there was no hospital in Senghennydd and it was too dangerous to remove him to Pontypridd or Caerphilly.

William Harris, the survivor of the 1901 disaster.

By this time an array of experts had reached the colliery. The Inspector of Mines had arrived as had Robert Rees, agent for the mine and a director of the company, as well as being a nephew by marriage of Sir William. Officials of the Lewis Merthyr Company and of the Bute mines were also present: these included Mr Richards, the general manager of the Lewis Merthyr Company, and Edward Jones, manager of the Lady Windsor Colliery. Tudor Davies was there with colliers from the Navigation Colliery, a part of the vast Nixon's Group, along with men and managers from Llanbradach, Coedcae, Treharris, Mountain Ash, Ynysybwl, Abercynon, Quaker's Yard, Wattstown and Clydach Vale. However the experts could only agree with the conclusion of the working miners that there could be no immediate progress to the work faces since the force of the explosions had brought down the roof in falls of up to a hundred yards in length.

Observers were impressed by the quiet solemnity and by the dignity of the village throughout Friday. This changed on Saturday when large numbers of visitors arrived, giving to the village something of a carnival atmosphere. Pubs and hotels spilled their customers into the street and large crowds of onlookers gazed at the damaged buildings in the colliery yard, drawn to the great spectacle of death. The hills overlooking the pithead were black with spectators. Newspaper moralists deplored what they saw as a morbid fascination: the newspapers, however, indulged that fascination to the full. For some people it was necessary to be seen at the spectacle: thus William Brace and John Thomas of the miners' union telegraphed their condolences and apologies for their absence. Most absent of all was Sir William Lewis, who had the misfortune to be caught on the Cote d'Azur at the time of the explosion. Each report which mentioned his absence emphasized that he was on the Riviera for reasons of health, ordered there by his doctors.

Three corpses were brought out of the pit on Saturday afternoon; George Warren from Stanley Street who had nine children, six of them still living with their parents; John Jones who lived in Kingsley Place with his wife and four children, and Thomas Coombes who lived in the High Street.

It was to be expected that the rumours which flowed around the town would find their way into the newspapers. Various sources

The makeshift hospital at the pithead in 1901.

maintained that voices had been heard in the mine; but the reality was clear. Reporting the events of the Saturday, the day after the explosion, the *Western Mail* wrote that 'all hope of any men who were in the Universal Colliery at Senghennydd when the explosion occurred on Friday morning has been abandoned by the government inspectors and officials of the colliery'.[18] Edward Shaw added that if anyone was found alive it would be miraculous: the voices, he said, could only be heard in people's imaginations.

An opposite and probably more dangerous rumour, started by one of the directors of the colliery company, was also believed. He told the *South Wales Daily News* that 'the prospect of getting through on the Western Side is very remote. He was afraid the pit would prove the burial ground of most of the unfortunate men'. Once hope had been abandoned nothing could have been better calculated to cause trouble since funeral rituals were of great significance in mining communities. The more hopeless and exploited the lives of the dead, the more symbolic importance may be attached to treating them with respect when they are buried: an assertion that, despite appearances, their lives amounted to more than a cost of production.[19]

Throughout the weekend the grim task of clearing the mine continued, with no hope of the risks being rewarded by finding anyone alive. The behaviour of George Beynon, reported by one of his fellow miners, was typical of the courage shown by the rescuers:

> When he was down this morning he volunteered to go on fifteen yards in advance of his comrades in order to bring out the body of William Thomas. The afterdamp was choking, but he crawled forward on hands and knees until he had brought out the body. When he came back he was so dazed that he could not speak for a long time.[20]

By Sunday afternoon most of the bodies on the East side of the mine had been found. Of the thirty bodies twenty had been brought to the surface. Most of them were identified immediately and put into coffins. It was clear however that it would take longer to remove the corpses in some of the districts of the West side. Even when the bodies were found it was a difficult job to manoeuvre them over the falls which almost blocked the main tunnels.

Above ground, the carnival atmosphere was firmly established in the streets and on the hillsides around the colliery:

The quiet solemnity which had brooded over the little village throughout the day of the disaster had been transformed into a scene that was not far from the element of disorderliness. People were pouring in from all points of the compass. Those who lived in districts not served by special trains walked over the mountains or rode on bicycles, while there was a steady stream of vehicles of all descriptions. The two, and only two, public houses in the village were quite unequal to the brisk demand for refreshments. The bars and smoke rooms were crowded, and even on the roadway outside scores of thirsty men were standing or crouching, as colliers have the special knack of doing, with quarts, pints and glasses in their hands.[21]

As in a fifteenth century painting, the carnival of life continued; 'the dogs go on with their doggy life', as death became the incidental. Hundreds could glory in their escape, even as they felt sympathy for people who had lost relatives: John Lewis of Commercial Street was particularly pleased as, years before, he had escaped the explosion at the Pentyrch Drift Mine as well as the disaster at the Great Western Colliery in 1892. Many members of the night shift, which narrowly escaped death, were to drink on tales of their escape for years to come: some were to be less lucky in 1913. Amidst the human tragedy, there were nice signs that business was to continue as usual. In a delightfully tasteless piece of public relations, it was announced, at the top of the list of the dead, that Messrs Colley and Sons had 'forwarded to the scene of the disaster, a quantity of cooked food for the rescue party'.[22]

Around the pit head the atmosphere was truly sombre. There the police only allowed members of the families of the missing miners and colliery officials. For most of the watchers this became a symbolic vigil, keeping faith with the dead until the bodies were recovered. The *Western Mail* reported that 'there was a total lack of any excitement. The one feeling that dominated all others was that no hope could be entertained of a single survivor being brought to the surface'. The names of the missing men recur throughout the history of the village: Coombes, Muller, Lower, Skym, Evans, Pugh, Crook, Parry, Rowlands. Keeping vigil with the families were Sir William's son and brother, Herbert Lewis and Colonel D. R. Lewis, together with their cousin Robert Rees.[23]

The reports tried to capture the agony of the inhabitants through images which penetrated beyond the carnival of emotion and the formalised grief of families. Various images were used at the time to symbolise the suffering of people whose lives were torn apart by the deaths of people they loved and nurtured. The bodies of James Fullalove (or Fullerlove) and his seventeen year old son Joseph were found in Will Evans' Heading; the father and son were locked in each other's arms. The oldest man to be killed in the explosion was the 72 year old George Tiler, a waller, who left a widow and six children. The 18 year old Philip Lower, whose family was to suffer in Senghennydd in the following years, was killed. That weekend the body of his brother, George Lower, was brought to the surface. The case of Mrs Anslow was particularly moving. She and her husband had seven children and were looking after the three children of William Anslow's sister, Mrs Lewis, who was in Cardiff Royal infirmary dying of cancer. On Saturday Mrs Anslow was informed that her sister-in-law had died during Friday night. Both William Anslow and William Lewis were killed in the explosion, leaving Mrs Anslow to bring up 10 children on her own. The Reverend David Roberts also reported the case of William Jenkins, three of whose brothers had already died, one of them in the explosion at the Albion Colliery in 1894, in which 290 men had been killed. David James, whose family was also to play a a major part in the village, left a widow and six children.

Dr James, who had walked over the mountain from Pontypridd to attend the colliers and villagers since the first days of the pit, presided at the mortuary where a strange air of calm was noted by several observers. The mortuary was the epicentre of human misery, and James shielded it from the direct gaze of the press and the curious. Many of the bodies had been terribly mutilated, adding to the distress of their relations; the distress was increased by the public airing of the details in the newspapers which simultaneously condemned the public's morbid curiosity. It was reported that the features of the dead were 'burnt into shapeless forms' and that many of the bodies were 'badly mangled, making the task of identification extremely haphazard'.[24]

The very horror, however, amplified the casualness and indignity of death. The father of W. D. Jones, from Pembrokeshire, identified the body of his son; he was then led to a second body, which he now identified as the real body of his son by the initials WDJ, which Jones had cut into a leather strap with a pen knife two weeks earlier.

Dr Philip James, Colliery Sergeant James and the mortuary team at the
Universal.

In individual and human terms it is unclear if there was much to be
learnt from the tragedy, though it may have brought some people to
a sense of human interdependence. Andrew Diegan was a single
roman catholic Irishman who had lived on his own in lodgings: a
sense of solidarity ensured that two hundred of his countrymen and
fellow miners accompanied his coffin to the grave.

The churches were naturally in the forefront of the attempts to help
the community. A joint service was mooted but the idea had to be
abandoned in the face of inter-denominational difficulties: it would
take more than the deaths of 80 inhabitants to bring the different
Christian religions together in a memorial ceremony for their
members. It was noted how few people turned up for chapel that
Sunday: a curious phenomenon at a time when people might be
expected to turn to religion for consolation and meaning, though the
same thing had happened during other mining disasters.[25]

From the newspaper reports it seems that the Reverend David

Roberts of the Salem Welsh Baptist Church coped best with the situation, in a notably unostentatious way. Having abandoned the Sunday service, he gave a reading from the Bible. He then made a brief reference to the explosion and 'appealed to those who were not affected to lend all the sympathy and aid they could to the bereaved relatives'.[26]

Though some of the sermons contained a degree of apparent sentimentality and religiosity which jars on modern sensibilities, it is worth remembering that there were many in the mining community for whom it was natural to turn to the heightened language of a highly emotional religion in the midst of disaster. A message, written by one of the doomed miners, had been found after the Seaham Colliery disaster in 1880 in which 164 miners were killed:

> Dear Margaret there were 40 altogether at 7 am. Some of them were singing hymns, but my thoughts were on my little Michael that him and I would meet in heaven at the same time. Oh Dear Wife, God save you and the chidren and pray for me Dear Wife Farewell, my last thoughts are about you and the children, be shure and learn the children to pray for me. Oh what an awfull position we are in.[27]

The vicar of the anglican parish, the Reverend Henry Morgan, took a rather higher profile than his colleagues. After visiting the homes of the bereaved, he reported to the press that

> he had witnessed sad sights in almost every home. The relatives, particularly the widows, appeared to have lost complete control of themselves, and several women in their grief tore away the hair from their heads. They moaned, screamed and fainted and formed distressing sights such as he had never seen before, and reverently hopes he will never see again.

With the vicar offering such vivid descriptions of the homes of the victims, intrusive journalism was made redundant. The vicar's story was particularly useful to the newspapers as, in general, the inhabitants had maintained a notable reticence which had struck journalists: ' . . . in Senghennydd there is not to be found those outward manifestations of general mourning usually associated with colliery disasters in South Wales'.[28]

Though it would be difficult for the clergy to offer any very plausible explanation of such suffering or to do more than offer comfort, the press reports suggest that a few did the worst that could be expected of them. That night the Reverend Henry Morgan preached to a 'very small congregation', arguing that 'there were many lessons to be learnt from the accident'. Most notably, the accident 'warned them of the uncertainty of human life'. This message was certainly true but none of its truth would have diminished by being kept for a week before being delivered to the reeling inhabitants. The message at the Methodist Chapel at least offered some hope, though it may have taken some believing in the circumstances: the Reverend B. T. Salmon said that 'although the cloud which hung above the neighbourhood was very dark just now, there was a day in the future when they should see, like Naomi of old, that the hand of the Lord was with them and not against them'. In general the ministers seem to have concentrated on encouraging their congregations to offer practical and emotional support and avoided the task of explanation.[29]

A second attempt to give meaning to the lost lives used martial imagery to link the miners to the war going on in South Africa. Beside the columns about Senghennydd were stirring headlines about the onward march of imperialism: 'Armoured Train Scatters the Raiders', 'Boer Attack on a convoy Repulsed', 'General Blood in the Eastern District' and 'Boer advance in Cape Colony: Colonel Gorringe in Hot Pursuit'. Much of the newspaper reporting, which was to be echoed down the years, sought to shroud the dead of Senghennydd in some of the glory and sense of purposeful sacrifice attaching to those supposedly dying heroic deaths in the war, even if the reality had more to do with cornering Boer peasants on the veldt and death from dysentery. The authentic tones of Henty were caught in numerous reports from the recently named mining districts of Ladysmith, Mafeking, Kimberley and Pretoria, below the Welsh hills in the Universal Colliery.

> But for this little storm of nature's forces at Senghennydd the little village would not be known, even by name, to most people, and fewer still would be aware of the fact that there is such a thing as a colliery there at all. But Senghennydd besides having a colliery, can boast of having a thousand men whose hearts beat as true as those of the most valiant heroes that ever won their countries laurels on the bloodiest of battlefields. At the very moment that the explosion shook the hills of the Aber Valley with the force of an earthquake on Friday morning, there was a rush of men almost frantic with eagerness to go down to the unknown dangers of the pit,

where 70 of their comrades needed all the succour that their fellows could give them—and more. It was a wild scramble for the honour of going down a a shaft of nearly a thousand feet in depth, which, for aught they knew, would be their death trap.[30]

In the current atmosphere of xenophobia engendered by the war, such imagery may indeed have sustained some relations of the dead miners, clouding the harsh reality of death in a fog of jingoistic sentimentality, as it was to do for millions during the Great War.

The *Pontypridd Chronicle* managed to combine the tone of the *Boys Own Journal* with that of Welsh nineteenth century lyrical poetry:

> If there is anything which brings out the chivalrous character of the Welsh miner it is when duty calls him to help his fellow-men and the disaster at the Universal will add to the lustre of the tradition. No soldier will face the bullets of an enemy more fearlessly than a collier will face death in the deadly afterdamp when the sacrifice of his own life may be the means of saving others. The scene at the pit head was in striking contrast to the pastoral surroundings, and but for the activity displayed immediately around the colliery, there seemed nothing to disturb the peacefulness of the surrounding hills, where the birds were trilling their morning song, and the sun shone on the placid landscape, making it beautiful in its early summer grandeur.[31]

The genuine heroism of rescue workers in these conditions should not disguise the reality of the relationship of owner and wage labourer which continued to operate. The rescuers worked in appalling conditions, in a broken gas-filled mine, struggling to clear vast falls of rock and coal, with the carcasses of decomposing horses around them and the constant threat of further falls or explosions. In these circumstances the rescuers complained to the management of the work pattern which was being forced on them: 'the first gangs of explorers were kept at work for six hours. They felt that this was too long a period to remain in a polluted atmosphere, and on Saturday night they made a representation to the management. They considered that four hours was quite long enough to remain down'.[32] The management had already been approached but had not given way and, when the next group was due to go down at six o'clock on Saturday night, the men held a last minute meeting at the pit head, only going down after 'advice' from the union leaders: even then there were absentees when the roll was called, as there were in the later shifts. Even in the first shift on Saturday morning, it emerged that 'a number of the men whose names were registered as volunteers to work in the first day shift, had not put in an appearance, and some difficulty was experienced in filling up the vacancies caused thereby'.[33] Senior members of the miners' union went down the pit to see if unreasonable demands were being made of their members. Meanwhile their comrades, laid off as a result of the explosion, were without wages until more work became available at the colliery.

In contrast to the largely anonymous miners working as rescuers for wages, the newspapers published lists of the notables in the colliery world who offered their advice and condolences at the pit head. Arriving on Sunday with the despised day trippers, these notables were welcomed for their human sympathy as well as for their expertise.[34]

The funerals started on the Monday after the explosion and offered an opportunity for the expression of communal grief. On Tuesday afternoon the bodies of George Warren, Thomas Coombes, Edward Bennett, George Griffiths and Llewelyn Llewelyn were buried at the Eglwysilan Churchyard. George Warren alone had nine children, seven of whom were married, and the extended family networks of the valleys ensured that these were large funerals even without the columns of miners who attended the funerals as a gesture of solidarity. The road from Senghennydd to Abertridwr was lined by silent crowds and from there the coffins were carried on the shoulders of the workmen along the winding country lane which leads to Eglwysilan Churchyard, 'the cathedral of the mountains'.[35]

Meanwhile inquests and a public enquiry continued the attempt to determine the causes of the explosion. This got off to a dubious start on the Saturday immediately after the disaster when the Inspector for Mines, who would necessarily be the main expert witness in any legal enquiry, was asked by the newspapers for his opinion on the subject. In view of the fact that it had been impossible to penetrate far into the devastated mine the Inspector started well. 'It was impossible', he said 'to state where or how the explosion occurred. Neither he nor his assistant had the faintest idea on these points'.[36]

He then mentioned the claim that the explosion may have been started by shot firing. If this was the case, he asserted, then 'the company appear to have taken all possible precautions to avoid accident', an assertion which could not possibly be supported by the evidence at this stage and one which was to prove highly inaccurate at the subsequent official enquiry. The Inspector went on to claim that 'there is nothing to show that there has been the slightest laxity in carrying out the regulations applicable to such a mine'. But he then said that whatever the cause of the initial explosion, it could not have been carried through the mine, destroying it in the process, if it were not for the presence of coal dust throughout the mine. The two statements, while possibly technically true in law, in that the minimum legal requirements for suppressing dust may have been met, would clearly indicate that the owners had failed to keep the mine clear of coal dust which was known to be the cause of large scale explosions.

The inquest was formally opened on Saturday 26th of May. In the first exchanges the coroner's comments indicated something of the distance between the professional and middle classes on the one hand and the working class on whom they depended. Mr Nicholas, the solicitor representing the Miner's Federation, asked that 'if possible some colliers should be empanelled on the jury'. The Coroner recognised that people acquainted with colliery work should be on the jury but said that 'he had given directions that men of intelligence and respectability should be summoned'. Since the jury included no working colliers in a society overwhelmingly composed of miners, this suggests either that the coroner did not see colliers as intelligent and respectable or that the jury was being packed for other reasons. Even the jurymen themselves seem to have jibbed at this: one of the jurymen asked if they could have a new jury. 'They felt they were not in the right place. They looked at it from the standpoint of the Miner's Federation, who strongly objected to them'.[37] But already, the day after the explosion, the coroner insisted that 'it was impossible for a fresh jury to be got together'. Lest anyone should think that the coroner was in any way prejudiced or unsympathetic, it was announced that 'expressions of sympathy with the families of the unfortunate men were made by the coroner'.[38]

The Reverend David Roberts of Salem Welsh Baptist Church was then chosen as the foreman of the jury, which was adjourned to allow the official enquiry to report its findings.

The enquiry set up by the Home Secretary was chaired by Professor William Galloway a former inspector of mines. Professor Galloway was an old colleague of Sir William Lewis, had assisted him in the testing of the Senghennydd site in 1889 and now held the chair of mining at University College, Cardiff which had been founded by Sir

William. The enquiry became a battle ground between the management and owners on the one side and the inspectors and Miners' Federation on the other. Two main questions confronted the enquiry: what caused the intitial explosion and what carried that explosion through the mine. The first, and probably less important question, was never settled. The different parties held different views about what caused the explosion and even about the area of the mine in which it had originated.[39]

The clearest information to emerge concerned the extraordinarily casual arrangements made for access to explosives. David Griffiths was the mine official in charge of explosives, which were kept in an underground magazine forty yards from the office in which the detonators were stored. The keys to both rooms were held by Griffiths and by each of the many designated shot-firers. During questioning Griffiths admitted that

> he did not know how many shot firers there were, or how many had keys. . .; that he had no control over the persons who took the gelignite, nor over the quantity they took, save that he provided the quantity generally; and that no-one had told him who were the persons entitled to take the explosives or detonators from the room. He kept no register either of the quantity which he took out of the magasine, or of the quantity which he gave out, or which was taken out by others.[40]

The questioning over the explosives suggested a mine slack in safety procedures but it did not necessarily throw light on the immediate cause of the explosion.

The second question concerned the reason why the explosion had spread through the whole mine. In itself an explosion of methane gas will kill and injure people in the immediate area, as was to happen six miles away in the Bedwas Colliery: but it is impossible for methane to build up to such an extent that an explosion could devastate a working mine consisting of miles of tunnels and headings. It had been strongly suspected since the 1840s that coal dust, mixed with air, could explode. Thus a small explosion of methane gas could, in a dusty mine, raise clouds of coal dust which would continue the explosion thoughout the tunnels and workings of a mine until some barrier brought the cumulative explosion to an end: the barrier might be in the form of a wet area of the mine, or of an area full of stone dust, either of which would keep the coal dust down. These facts had been known since Professor Galloway had experimented with controlled explosions on coal dust in the 1880s.

Senghennydd was known to be a dry, hot and dusty mine. At the coal face dust was created by the mining operations. From there the coal was taken to the pit bottom in open trucks, from which dust was blown by the air being pumped into the mine. One end of the truck was open so that coal could be shovelled into it. Once filled, two bars were placed across the end, allowing coal piled high above the top of the trucks to fall to the ground or to slip between the bars at the end. This dropped coal was then crushed to dust by the tread of men and ponies. The dust could be controlled in a number of ways: by laying down stone dust, by clearing away the dust at frequent and regular intervals and by watering the trucks and roadways.

Robert Rees and Edward Shaw accepted that the extent of the devastation had been caused by an explosion of coal dust: but both maintained that the mine was not exceptionally dusty, that the arrangements for watering were sufficient and that the dust was swept and removed from the roadways every night. This left the question of how, in that case, a coal dust explosion of that extent could have occurred. The fact, accepted by virtually everyone, was that the mine contained a dangerous concentration of coal dust which, once ignited,

created an airwave which swept though the roadways in every direction, raising the coaldust and mixing it with the air as it passed. . . . The airwave sent off a shoot into each roadway as it passed, and if the shoot found a sufficient supply of coal dust to sustain the flame, it became self supporting but, otherwise, it quickly died out. In this way the whole of the workings that contained coal dust were rapidly traversed. . .[41]

Whatever the immediate cause of the explosion, the lesson about the critical need to keep down the coal dust was clear and unequivocal. The failure to alter procedures to take note of that lesson was to cause the death of hundreds of people and to blight the lives of many more in the coming years.

While the enquiry sat and reports were written, the people of Senghennydd had to get on with living. From the dependants most directly affected by the deaths, the experience and the pain rippled out, affecting extended families and whole streets. Those affected included people who would nurse emotional wounds for the rest of their lives as well as people who gained status from their connection with the dead; people who tried to comfort the suffering as well as those who boasted of their miraculous escapes only minutes before the explosion. No doubt the widows also included both women torn apart by their grief and women who had been wishing their spouses dead for many years, but who now wept for lost hopes and memories of a young man before he was corroded by poverty, fear and the effects of alcohol. Mr (Sam) Edwards, who claimed to have narrowly escaped the explosion, managed to turn the experience to good use by publicly endorsing Dr Williams' Pink Pills for Pale People, which supposedly cured influenza and restored lost appetites.[42]

In practical terms most of the families were better off than they would have been in the past. All were now covered by the Workmen's Compensation Act of 1896, and this was the first major disaster in which the families of the victims received compensation under the Act. As a result of the high wages of recent years most of the widows received full compensation of £300 and there were further sums from the disaster relief fund to which many individuals and organisations had contributed. Until the compensation was paid the Miners' Federation advanced money to the families and the newspapers were probably correct in saying that this was the first occasion in which the families of the victims of a disaster were not faced with destitution—simply with a life of hardship which was taken for granted among their class despite the intermittent periods of relative plenty. Nor does the Senghennydd disaster bear out the miners' reputation for feckless behaviour and inability to prepare for the future: among the insurance companies which sent representatives to Senghennydd to pay out on claims for funeral and insurance benefits were the Prudential Insurance Company, the London, Edinburgh and Glasgow Assurance Company, the Pearl Life Insurance Company and the Wesleyan and General Assurance Company. The Senghennydd miners' own sickness and funeral fund, started eighteen months earlier, was bankrupted by the explosion in which 62 of its members had died.[43]

Despite this evidence of sensible provision on the part of the miners, a writer in the *Western Mail* felt able to deplore the failure of the miners to insure themselves with the scheme run by Sir William Lewis. As will be seen, Sir William's scheme had been developed, in part, with the explicit aim of undermining union membership which explains why, after the passing of the Workmen's Compensation Act, its membership fell rapidly. The *Western Mail* unctuously commented that:

> Unfortunately for those who mourn today, their breadwinners, with only two or three exceptions, were not members of that excellent institution the South Wales Miners' Provident Fund, so that outside the compensation money due to their next of kin there will be no other source of maintenance.[44]

The newspaper simultaneously deplored the fact that the miners were inadequately provided for, due to their lack of foresight, and also that their dependents would be unable to handle their sudden wealth. Three days after the disaster, in a nicely ill-timed piece of bad taste made worse by coy innuendo, the newspaper published an article questioning the ability of Senghennydd women to handle their compensation money. The piece made the reasonable point that the money might be best paid in instalments. The reasoning, however, indicated the view still held about the qualities of miners' wives:

> What is pointed out by those who are familiar with the habits and domestic conditions of life in the homes of the Welsh miner is that there is a danger of the money, if given in a lump sum, not being applied to the best advantage. Not that it would be wilfully frittered away in senseless extravagance, but that from the lack of foresight and reasonable economy it would not be devoted to the best purpose. Three hundred pounds to many a housewife would seem inexhaustable wealth, and, without labouring the point, it will be patent to every intelligent person that there is a very real danger of such an impression proving disastrous.[45]

The writer in the *Western Mail* no doubt meant well for the families of the victims: nevertheless the class assumptions implicit in the writing echo the coroner's distinction between the intelligent section of society and the miner's community.

Sir William Lewis himself was able to take a fairly detached view of the risks of coalmining. In his presidential address to the Institute of Mining Engineers, delivered later that year, he paid particular attention to the issue of safety, commenting that 'it is pleasant to be able to congratulate all those connected with coal mining... respecting the reduced risk in the conduct of coal mining operations...'. He conceded that there were still risks, but judged that 'the occupation as a whole ranks as particularly healthy as compared with other trades'.[46]

As might be expected the disaster brought out some of the best qualities of the south Wales valleys; generous and caring, wrapping the lonely in a rich web of attention and gossip. What could not be retrieved was a sense of security. The explosion had shaken the foundation of the community and the ratchet of fear was turned another notch, increasing the unspoken, insidious, corrosive sensation which accompanied every descent into the 'dungeon of darkness'.

Outwardly the town quickly returned to normal. The mine was cleared and production was restarted in a matter of weeks, just as, in the case of individual deaths in the mine, managers would insist that work was restarted immediately. Miners might be frightened about returning to work but the alternative, for most of the men, was starvation or the workhouse: almost all returned to work. The reported cases of drunkenness, of minor crime and of neighbours' quarrels grew rapidly in the immediate aftermath of the explosion and continued to grow thereafter in the period during which the community reached maturity.

The families of the dead survived because they had been bred into a common-sense acceptance of the hardships which almost inevitably awaited them. The appalling disaster, when it came, was different only in scale from what was already known to be their fate.

CHAPTER 4
[1] PC 1/9/1899
[2] PC 12/1/1901
[3] Kelly's Directory, 1901
[4] PC 12/1/1901
[5] PC 23/9/1899
[6] PC 5/5/1901
[7] PC 4/8/1899
[8] GFP 26/6/1897
[9] WM 9/3/1900: John Davies, *Glamorgan and the Bute Estates 1776-1947,* (University of Wales Thesis; 1969), 566, n243
[10] GFP 27/1/1900
[11] *ibid*
[12] GFP 19/5/1900: GFP 5/5/1900: GFP 9/6/1900

[13] GFP 15/12/1900

[14] GFP 23/6/1900

[15] PP 1902 Cd. 947 xvii, 749ff

[16] PP 1894 C. 7339 xxiv, (6)

[17] The following account is taken from reports in the *Western Mail, Glamorgan Free Press, South Wales Daily News, Times, Daily Mail:* See also J. H. Brown, *The Valley of the Shadow: an account of Britain's Worst Mining Disaster,* (Port Talbot; 1981); PP 1902 Cd. 947. xvii

[18] WM 27/5/1901

[19] WM 27/5/1901; SWDN 17/5/1901

[20] WM 30/5/1901

[21] WM 27/5/1901

[22] SWDN 25/5/1901

[23] WM 27/5/1901

[24] WM 29/5/1901; SWDN 29/5/1901

[25] R. Meurig Evans, *One Saturday Afternoon: The Albion Colliery, Cilfynydd, Explosion of 1894,* (Cardiff; 1984), 31

[26] WM 27/5/1901

[27] J. Benson, *British Coal Miners in the Nineteenth Century,* (London; 1980), 38; H. Duckham *Great Pit Disasters,* (Newton Abbot; 1973), 29

[28] SWDN 27/5/1901

[29] WM 27/5/1901

[30] WM 27/5/1901

[31] PC 1/6/1901

[32] WM 27/5/1901

[33] SWDN 27/5/1901

[34] SWDN 27/5/1901

[35] WM 29/5/1901

[36] WM 27/5/1901

[37] WM 27/5/1901

[38] SWDN 27/5/1901

[39] J. H. Brown, *op cit,* 54

[40] PP 1902 Cd. 947 xvii, 775

[41] *ibid,* 757

[42] GFP 7/6/1902

[43] WM 1/6/1901: see also Dot Jones, 'Did Friendly Societies Matter? A Study of Friendly Societies in Glamorgan 1794-1910', *Welsh History Review,* vol 12 (1984-5)

[44] WM 27/5/1901

[45] *ibid*

[46] W. T. Lewis. *Presidential Address of Sir William T. Lewis, Bart., to the Institution of Mining Engineers at the Engineering Congress, Glasgow, 3rd September 1901,* (NLW, Lord Merthyr Archive; 389)

PART II
LIFE IN THE VILLAGE

Chapter Five
The Social Life of the Village

During its first years Senghennydd had been a remote work camp, set apart from local communities. In the years after the explosion the isolation of the village was greatly reduced by the sinking of the Windsor Pit a mile and a half away in Abertridwr on the road to Caerphilly. Work on the new mine had started in 1898 and by 1902, when production started, a second pit village was growing rapidly, almost matching the size of Senghennydd by the time of the 1911 census. Thereafter there was a constant flow between the two communities for work, housing, courtship and chapel going. The rivalry between the two was such that despite the obvious advantages to be gained from sharing some facilities, virtually every voluntary organisation, from the denominational divisions among the chapels to the ex-servicemen's organisation, were to be duplicated.

The health of Senghennydd was largely determined by the success of the colliery company, and in the years after the explosion the company was not wholly successful. While Sir William's main company, Lewis Merthyr Collieries, continued to expand production, the Universal Colliery Company was sometimes in difficulty, having to compete in a notoriously volatile market against larger concerns. From 1904 until 1905 the men were on short time working while the Windsor Colliery in Abertridwr was working full time. In April 1905 all the workers were given dismissal notices and rumours circulated wildly about what was to become of the colliery. In fact Sir William was simply using the opportunity to buy out the existing owners and to amalgamate the colliery with his main company. The news brought relief. The *New Tredegar, Bargoed and Caerphilly Journal* announced that

> it is surmised that the colliery having changed hands will tend to better the trade of the district. If, as stated, Sir William Thomas Lewis is at the head of affairs we have no doubt that in the near future a more prosperous time may be seen.[1]

It is unclear whether the problem had been the inability of the single colliery to match the worldwide sales organisation of larger concerns, or whether it had been a self induced decline in preparation for the takeover by Lewis Merthyr Collieries. In any event once the amalgamation was complete the situation miraculously improved and the men were working full time within weeks of the takeover.[2] Thereafter the Universal thrived. Its purchase had been funded by a debenture issue of £150,000, and the following year Lewis Merthyr Collieries issued further shares with a nominal value of £125,000 in addition to the existing share capital of £450,000. In 1912 there was another share flotation, raising the nominal value of the company to £700,000.[3] Ownership of shares in the company continued to be dominated by Sir William and his family, in particular his son and heir, Herbert Lewis of Hean Castle, and his younger son Trevor, a shy and unsuccessful barrister. His daughters and sons-in-law also held shares, including Colonel and Mrs Forrest of St Fagans, Mr and Mrs de Winton and the Venerable Charles Green, vicar of Aberdare and later to be archbishop of Wales, and his wife Kitty (Katherine). Several of the great names of south Wales industry, including the Corys and the Crawshays, invested in the company. However the list of 400 shareholders also contained scores of more ordinary members of the middle classes: there were accountants, merchants, engineers, cashiers, butchers, chemists, and publicans, many of them only owning ten or twenty shares.[4]

The Universal now grew rapidly and soon became the largest colliery in the Lewis Merthyr group, a position it maintained from then on. In 1908 it employed 1600 men compared to 988 at the Bertie Pit, the next largest of the Lewis Merthyr mines. By 1913 the Universal employed 2,120 men, one of only ten pits in Glamorgan to employ over 2,000 workers.[5] Profits in the group also grew over the period up to the Great War, although the group suffered from the severe fluctuations which were endemic in the international markets for steam coal. In 1909 and 1910 profits were around £50,000 with reserves of £160,000. The following year profits rose to £117,000 while reserves fell by £60,000. In 1912 profits fell back to £56,000 but rose to £172,000 and £121,000 in the years immediately before the Great War.[6] It is probably unwise to pay too much attention to these figures since the known wealth of major coalowners suggest that fortunes were being amassed at higher rates than declared profits and share flotations suggest. By the time of his death in 1914, Sir William Thomas Lewis, Lord Merthyr of Senghennydd, had dispersed large sums to his eight children and he left over half a million pounds apart from his landed wealth.[7]

As Sir William piled up his private fortune from the labour of thousands of colliers, the village of Senghennydd also grew and prospered. For those inhabitants who were still arriving from the countryside Senghennydd was a lively social centre, comparable in size and resources to the small market towns of mid Wales.

The centre of the village was now the 'Square' where the memorial would later be erected. On one side of the Square stood the impressive three storey Gwern-y-Milwr Hotel and opposite were Miss Bussell's Post Office and some of the main shops. Commercial Street, which ran through the square, was half a mile long; it formed the backbone of the village and continued in one direction towards the Universal Hotel and the colliery yard. Further on, past the colliery yard and nestling into the end of the valley, were four small streets, banked so tightly into the hillside that each of them had a terrace on only one side which looked down on the street below. Other streets radiated from the Square. Station Road led over the stream to the railway station and to the two long terraced streets which lined the far side of the valley; above them, carved into the hillside, was the recreation ground. In the other direction Commercial Street, flanked by Caerphilly Road, led from the Square down the valley towards Abertridwr, Penyrheol and then Caerphilly. The High Steet climbed up the hill from the Square and led to the school which was perched at the top of the village. From Coronation Terrace, beside the school, the inhabitants could look over the colliery to the soft beauty of the

The Square with the Gwern-y-Milwr on the right.

An overview of the village from the end nearest to Abertridwr, looking over Caerphilly Road towards Station Terrace in the background and the colliery in the distance on the right.

hillsides, made tragic by the waste tips and the destruction that had been done to them. Above the streets were the quarries and reservoirs which serviced the village, and beyond them the relatively unspoilt hills and moors which harboured the dreams of many country bred colliers. Down below, among the tightly packed, blackened, over-crowded houses were the pubs, chapels and halls in which the inhabitants played out their communal lives.

This was a small close community which, despite the railway, remained remarkably self-contained. The growth of Abertridwr lessened the isolation but it remained an enclosed community. A surprising number of workers lived in the area immediately around the mine, though some of them would have been lodgers sending money home to families in other areas. It seems that about 71 per cent of the miners lived in Senghennydd, 17 per cent in Abertridwr or the Aber Valley, 7 per cent in Caerphilly and only 5 per cent in other places such as Cilfynydd and Llanbradach: only a handful came by train from Cardiff. As far as Senghennydd is concerned it may be that the dependence of miners and employers on the railways for travelling to work can be exaggerated.[8]

The shops and shows, chapels and pubs, boxing booths and sacred concerts contributed to a community humming with life; there were cricket, rugby and soccer teams, societies to cater for varied interests, summer outings organised by the chapels, visiting speakers at the Conservative, Liberal or Constitutional Clubs, special events at the Universal, Gwern-y-Milwr, Parc and Leigh pubs, all of which finally gained licences, first aid lessons at the 'Ambulance Classes' and a seemingly endless variety of other activities, even if the village could not offer the range of music hall and low life available over the mountain in Pontypridd.

The schools were by now an established part of the community. Despite the many problems with which they had to cope, Her Majesty's Inspectors reported in 1901, that 'the lessons are of a stimulating and intelligent character and the order and organisation [are] highly satisfactory'. Apart from the practical problems of space, the main difficulty faced by Dan Lloyd was that of bad attendance which was taken very seriously, not least because the grant to the school was based on average attendance figures. A resident of Llanbradach remembered occasions when, to achieve the reward of a half-day holiday for high attendance, 'children were sent out to encourage absent ones to come in even if they were unwell—they were told they could sit by the classroom stove if they came in'. The school log books record a continuous stream of prosecutions: in December 1905 no less than thirteen parents were fined for the non-attendance of their children. Some families were particularly regular in their absence. The Snailhams were fined several times for the absence of William and Arthur, whom we will meet again in the local court. Charles Waddon was fined for the truancy of his son David and daughter Florrie.[9] In 1910 the logbook of the Boys' School noted, 'Mr Waddon brought his son David, a confirmed truant, to school this afternoon'. Dan Lloyd added, 'home influence not of the best'; a nice understatement in view of Charles Waddon's appearances in the local court. George Thomas even suffered the ultimate horror of being dragged away to the residential truant school at Quaker's Yard. There the boys were washed in carbolic soap and had their hair cropped before being subjected to a routine designed to instil discipline and regularity.[10]

The progress of the Infants' School in these years indicates the importance of the schools in creating a mature community in the future. The efforts of the staff were still crippled by an inadequate building: in 1905 it was reported that there were 'no fires at all at the school... no nature lesson [was] taken as children had drill and marching until 10.00a.m. to get warm'. Gross overcrowding meant that classes still had to be held in the vestries of Noddfa and Salem Chapels. Problems over staff continued and on occasion the head reported that she and one trainee had to supervise 130 children. All these difficulties were summed up by an inspector's report which stated that 'this department is excessively overcrowded and the instruction is carried out under great difficulties. The staff too is inadequate... All these matters require immediate attention'. As with many other aspects of the village, these criticisms were endlessly repeated down the years.[11]

Despite the problems, the school established a distinctive reputation after the appointment of Catherine James as head. Miss James was born in 1880 and had worked as a pupil teacher in the Mixed School until 1900 and then in the Senghennydd Girls' School. In 1899 she passed the student teachers' exam in the 1st class and won a scholarship to Swansea Teacher Training College, before returning to Senghennydd. In 1903, at the age of 23 she was appointed head of the Infants' School with a staff of six.[12]

From the start she took a bracing approach to her staff. She reported of Jane Lewis, in the month that she became head teacher, that 'her work is carelessly done and her answers are not very intelligent. She has been spoken to.' Edith Jones was told that 'her teaching is intelligent but she talks too much'. Though Catherine James's approach may have led to staff shortages in the short term, it had remarkable results over the years. Despite continued worries over the staff, by 1909 there was a staff of eight, five of whom were certificated and in 1909 one of them was taking special Froebel exams in Cardiff.[13]

Teaching methods became more flexible as soon as Miss James took over. In January 1904 the teachers took the first class 'for a ramble this afternoon, in order to make their nature lesson for the next week more interesting' and on another nature walk later in the year the 'children returned at 4 laden with twigs leaves etc'. There was a range of events celebrating festivals and special events: 'May Day was celebrated by giving lessons on May Day customs, stories of Robin Hood and his Merry men and games in the yard'. Something of the atmosphere of the school is caught in the annual report for 1905 which commented that 'the Mistress and her staff do their work in a cheerful spirit, and a very commendable feature is the hearty way in which they join in the children's games at recreation time'.[14]

The fundraising events also suggest the enthusiasm generated by the school: the concert at Salem Baptist Church in 1907 paid off the debt on the grand piano, and it was decided to use the surplus to buy £10 of toys for the children as well as a maypole. The continuous collections for work with the lepers, the Society for the Prevention of Cruelty to Children and the children's ward of the Cardiff Infirmary indicate the level of commitment in the school.[15]

An important innovation introduced by Catherine James was the school open day. On the first such day only 12 parents (including a sole father) turned up although they 'showed on the whole an intelligent interest in the work and the methods used'. The word soon got around, however, and the following day 54 parents and friends arrived to see the working of the school.[16]

Catherine James's most impressive achievement was the lively way she integrated Welsh into the teaching of the school. W. Edwards, the Inspector, reported that 'perhaps the most interesting feature of the school is the attempt which the Mistress is making to revive some old Welsh folk games. These are arranged by herself with Welsh words and tunes and are entered into by the children with great enjoyment'. It may even be that the infants' schools were almost too successful, producing an ugly contrast with some of the dismal and authoritarian boys schools of the valleys, remembered by the pupils later in life as 'dreary teachers, dreary schools and dreary atmosphere'.[17] Catherine James continued to play an important part in the life of the valley for the next thirty years, but it was a real loss to the village when she resigned as headmistress in 1910 in order to marry. Her husband was William John, a stone mason, who was to be a strong support to her in her political activities: they had been childhood friends and their families had come to Senghennydd together from Aberdare.

Even more important than the schools in the life of the community were the many chapels and churches. It is almost impossible to separate the contribution of the chapels to the religious life of the community from their contribution to its social life in general. Up to the Great War the chapels were well attended. They were not, in the main, the product of a wealthy mineowner or landowner, building himself a gaudy monument to his godliness, although two of the churches were rescued by wealthy patrons during the post war

Ebenezer Chapel.

depression. Sir William Lewis had a poor reputation among non-conformist congregations: the history of the Welsh Baptists cites him as an example of wealthy men who 'strayed from the paths of [their] fathers' and became anglicans. It is also reported that 'when in 1874, Tabernacl Independent Chapel, Treorchy, decided to build a large new chapel, a deputation sought building land from W. T. Lewis. . . The deputation was met with blank refusal and gross discourtesy'.[18]

The chapels were a response to a real demand in the village; they expanded their buildings to accomodate the needs of a growing community and raised most of the necessary funds from intense local fund raising campaigns. The main external sources of money were the central funds of various denominations put aside to encourage 'missionary' work among the growing, and potentially godless, urban industrial masses of south Wales. Thus the Baptist cause in Senghennydd was supported in the early days by preachers from the 'Home Mission' which sent J. W. Williams and D. Hussey to assist the cause.[19]

They were the forum for a large range of activities; musical, educational, intellectual and purely social. E. T. Davies, in his book on religion in industrial south Wales, has written that 'these chapels were not only centres of spiritual influence, but were real cultural centres as well. . . . The debt of the communities thrown up by the industrial revolution to the Welsh chapels is incalculable'.[20] They ran activities on almost every night of the week and on Saturday evenings there would always be a larger gathering for joint functions between the chapels. As well as singing there were a range of popular 'games' such as the *darn heb atalnodau,* in which the participants would attempt to read unprepared passages of unpunctuated prose: often with catastrophic results. As well as various events throughout the year, they marked the passing of time with regular great celebrations at Easter, Christmas and other festivals.

The eisteddfodau, which brought together the people of the village and the school children, were the largest regular events. Once a year the village put on an eisteddfod open to anyone. The budget of the annual Eisteddfod ran to about £300. In 1911 the tickets raised over £100 which more than covered the £77 13s needed for the prizes. The better off were dunned for donations ranging from Dr Philip James's £5, through to Miss Bussell's half guinea and five shillings from Mr Gay the bootmaker.[22]

Those active in the churches were also responsible for a range of other clubs and societies in the town and they were often also officials in the mine, a link noted by E. T. Davies.[22] Arthur Peglar, an overman in the mine, was also an officer of St Peter's Church. Robert Jones was an official at the Universal and a sunday school teacher at Tabernacl Calvinistic Methodist Chapel as well as being active in the Ambulance Brigade: David Davies, the colliery blacksmith was also active in Tabernacl.[23] John Morgan, an official who was among the first to enter the mine after both disasters, was a Deacon of Noddfa Chapel.[24] David Roger Thomas who had worked in the mine from the start and who escaped from both explosions was a Deacon at Salem Baptist Chapel, an overman in the mine and active in the Eisteddfod movement as his father had been before him.[25] There were also links between the chapels and the trades men and women of the village. David Williams, the newsagent of Pentyrch House, Commercial Street, was a deacon at Noddfa Welsh Congregational Chapel and Mary Tilley Bailey kept the greengrocers at 64 Commercial Street while her husband was an official in the Universal from the 1890s until 1928; both of them were active in St Peter's Church.[26] Thomas Nicholas, the station master, was typical of other village dignitaries: as well as being a deacon, he was at one time president of the Chamber of Commerce, secretary of the Liberal Association, and president of the Senghennydd and Abertridwr Debating Society. Occasionally there were spectacular falls from grace as when Arthur Llewellyn Crockett, the very young treasurer of St Peter's Sunday School, was sentenced at the Glamorgan Assizes in Swansea to three months hard labour for stealing £29 from the Sunday School Fund. The incident probably only confirmed the suspicions of the non-conformists about the behaviour to be expected of those in the established church.[27]

Despite their patriarchal attitudes the chapels, with their committees which decided on policy and which employed the ministers, played a significant part in nurturing democratic habits in the community. The way in which the leadership of the chapels overlapped with power in the structure of authority at work and of relative commercial wealth in the community was partly balanced by the extent to which the local leaders of the labour movement were also nurtured in the chapels. Hubert Jenkins, the County Councillor and most distinguished of the group, was an active member of Ebenezer English Baptist Church as, at a later date, was George Worman, another Labour Councillor and Chairman of Caerphilly Urban District Council.[28] Later in the history of the village John Davies, also a Labour Councillor, was Secretary of Tabernacl Methodist Chapel, while William Bull, active in the 'Fed', the Labour Party and the Aber Valley Trades Council was a leading member of the English Baptist Chapel.[29] Another 'legendary' figure was the Reverend David ('D.M.') Jones, minister of Ebenezer Chapel from 1910 to 1943, and a Labour councillor and parliamentary candidate. The chapels both reflected the structures of power and authority at work and offered an arena in which those patterns could be questioned and the skills needed to engage in politics could be developed. E. T. Davies has written that 'the religious bodies which virtually formed the ecclesiastical, social and political Establishment in these parts were almost completely indifferent to the social problems which affected thousands of their members and tens of thousands of their adherents... Nonconformity in its official pronouncements revealed little or no concern with local problems'. At the local level, however, the non-conformist chapels, for all their conformist tendencies, did offer an important platform for debate and activity.[30]

Although the regular work of the chapels was part of the fabric of the village, there were also high points which focused the religious zeal of the community. The religious revival of 1904-5, fuelled by the activities of the young revivalist Evan Roberts, marked the climax of religious fervour in Senghennydd. The excitement built up in the village during November and December 1904 as Roberts's evangelical mission swept on from the Rhondda to Caerphilly. On the 6th of December he spoke to packed audiences in the Caerphilly chapels. On the surface the response was not so great as in the Rhondda, but it was argued that the crowds in Caerphilly contained a higher proportion of non chapel-goers and therefore provided a truer test for the mission. Nevertheless in a chapel packed with about 650 people, 30 to 35 'converts' declared for Christ. The singing and exhortation continued with 'For you I am Praying' and 'Come to Jesus just now', and by the time Evan Roberts left that meeting the number of converts had risen to 59. The meeting continued with the Reverend T. Bush and the Reverend C. Tawelfryn Thomas and when it finished, after four o'clock in the morning, the number of converts had reached 99.[31]

The next day the atmosphere returned to the rather more heightened and excited atmosphere of the Rhondda gatherings. Evan Roberts warned one of the congregations that

> it pained him to think of how many people in the Principality lived careless lives: how many lived drunken and sinful lives, and, oh, how many so frequently cursed and swore and used the sacred names of God and Jesus Christ in vain! When he pondered over that terrible fact he dreaded the sight which the judgement day would present.[32]

Amidst singing and exhortation

> the 'moving of the spirit' among the congregation was extraordinary. Without a word of warning a cry came from one man, who fell into a 'faint' of some kind. Mr Roberts asked the people not to be disturbed, but to pray for the man. That was done, and in silent prayer and expectation the congregation awaited the recovery of the man. While this was going on it was rumoured that the man's brother had become a convert, and the man who had fainted, after moaning, murmured 'O, Mam, mam! bydd mam yn llawenhau!' (O, Mother, mother! mother will rejoice!').

> 'Diolch iddo' broke out, and had scarcely been concluded when a man who had been under deep emotion for some time, but who had refused to listen to the invitation of his companions to 'confess', rose to his feet and shouted 'Christ for me'.[33]

By the time Evan Roberts and his associates reached Senghennydd on Wednesday the 7th of December, the village was in a state of ferment, 'the arrival of Mr Evan Roberts at Senghennydd ... [being] hailed with joy by large numbers of people'. At the Welsh Calvinistic Methodist Chapel, where he was expected, the congregation was warmed up before his arrival by Welsh hymn singing and the witness of the audience.

One woman told how, on the train to Senghennydd, she had tried to make another passenger turn to the Lord:

> She prayed to the woman, but at first without avail. She prayed again, and the woman accepted Christ, and then promised to try to influence her husband. Then the young woman added, 'I hope my brother is in this congregation. Will you pray for him?' Several prayers were offered, and ten minutes or a quarter of an hour later a shout was raised from the far end of the gallery. Her brother was converted and there was a mighty shout of 'Diolch iddo' and 'Songs of praise I will ever give to thee'.[34]

It had occurred to the evangelists that many people might be coming for Evan Roberts's performance rather than to hear the word of God, and they decided to face this issue.

> An expectant hush falls on the congregation as one of the lady evangelists —Miss Rees, Gorseinon—walked in. She immediately walked to the pulpit and bluntly asked, 'Are you here to see Jesus Christ, or to see Evan Roberts?' She then went on to say that in all probability they would not see Mr Roberts at this meeting as he had just gone to the Welsh Baptist Chapel.[35]

It would have been tactless to leave at this point to go to the young revivalist's own meeting so the congregation remained although, as it happened, Evan Roberts could have done with some support at Salem. There Roberts, accompanied by the female evangelists, Miss Mary Davies (Gorseinon) and Miss Annie Davies (Maesteg), was having a very slow start:

> there was a somewhat smaller congregation and ... the meeting was, for a time, decidedly colder—so cold indeed as to affect the young revivalist with deep emotion. He prayed and asked for others to pray for a downpour of the Spirit ... and presently there was a warmer feeling, the responses to the invitation to 'confess' being numerous.[36]

Among the congregations that day were ministers from Radnorshire and Monmouthshire, Portsmouth and Norwich, and at least one Welsh Member of Parliament. Unfortunately however, it was apparent that much of the interest was of less than Christian sincerity. It was remarked that nowhere else had idle curiosity in the personality of Evan Roberts been so great as in Senghennydd, and this was all too apparent in the highly charged meetings that evening which, it was feared, might become as 'boisterous' as those at Caerphilly. Appeals were made for calm and to avoid 'the disturbance caused through the excitement and rush to see the missioner on the previous night'.

> Judging however by the conduct of some of those who stood in the lobby, and positively refused to move or attempt to move to enable strangers to leave to catch their trains, a little while later on, the appeal thus made had not been listened to as it ought to have been.[37]

In the following weeks the 'harvest of conversions' from the 'fire in Senghennydd' amounted to 426. Probably the best measure of the profound effect of all this on the community is the report that 'among these was the greater part of the Rugby team who forswore the game as wicked and sinful.'[38] Even Caerphilly had only lost five of their

Members of the Wesleyan Chapel in Stanley Street, around 1910.

team to the fervour of the revival, so this was a special source of pride or lamentation depending on one's viewpoint.

Many people commented on the effect of the revival among the miners. In the *Western Mail* a writer described a prayer meeting underground in which 'one of the workmen was reading the 6th chapter of Matthew to about eighty comrades. He stood erect amongst the group, reading in a dim fantastic light. . .'. A historian of the revival noted that 'some colliery managers claimed that the revival had made their workers "better colliers" and that others spoke of "greater regularity in attendance of the men at work"'. He commented that 'the beneficial effect of the revival on industrial relations can hardly be over-estimated, and has hitherto been unrecognized'. Since the management noticed the effect it is to be supposed that many workers also noted it and drew their conclusions about the effect of religious enthusiasm on the socialist cause.[39] On the other hand it has been suggested that some managers regarded the revival as a menace which impeded production with spontaneous prayer meetings and that '. . . the revival generated reforming zeal and thus contributed to the industrial and political aspirations of the years that followed'.[40]

The historian of the Welsh Baptist Church commented that W. R. James, a missionary,

> was certain that the revival had been caused by a visitation of the Holy Spirit. He might well have looked for more earthly reasons. Many remarked on the crowd element connected with the movement, the processions through towns and villages to sweep others in. Everyone noticed that at the heart of the rejoicing was the transcendent love of Christ—an expression of mass rejoicing in a society torn by social conflict, an emphasis on the love of Christ in a grimly competitive society where the market price was more important than the standard of the Sermon on the Mount.[41]

The fears and hopes were, however, relatively short lived. The Rugby Club survived: 'in 1907 the churches began to record losses and, with the exception of some who remained faithful until the end, the new recruits disappeared as quickly as they had come in'.[42] Before long the various chapels returned to their traditional if less exhilarating role. They gave protection and some meaning in the desolation of largely unrestrained industrial capitalism and the many voluntary posts in the chapels offered a status and a role otherwise denied to most colliers. In view of the latter function it was fortunate that there were so many denominational divisions offering endless posts as Sunday school teachers, deacons and chapel elders for the self-improving workmen. 'The value of the Sunday school and of the night classes in the chapel vestries should not be underestimated and it would be a mistake to ignore the value of the puritan discipline taught under the chapel roof. It made possible some vestiges of civilised life and self respect under the atrocious conditions of the industrial revolution'.[43]

The fate of the Welsh language had also became tied into that of the chapels. Welsh had survived and indeed flourished in the early stages of industrialisation in the south Wales valleys. Since the main source of new labour had been the neighbouring agricultural counties in which Welsh was strong, the newcomers had brought with them not only the culture of the chapels, but the language also. When the proportion of English immigrants rose, it was not the absolute number of Welsh speakers which was threatened. Even the percentage drop of Welsh speakers in the population from 49.9% to 43.5% between 1901 and 1911 was not in itself disastrous.[44] These figures are however deceptive since they disguise major changes in the functional use of Welsh regardless of the number of people who, technically, could speak it. English had become 'the key to commercial, social and academic success'.[45] More importantly, in the valleys, for the survival of the language was the fact that English was also increasingly the language of the trade unions, local politics, the schools and the mine. Since English was, in general, the *common* language of immigrants and the Welsh, it tended to become the language of everyday affairs. Welsh was increasingly limited to the chapel and became closely linked with the fortunes of the non-conformist denominations. In the 1880s voters had been assured that Alfred Thomas, later the M.P. for East Glamorgan, 'worships in a Welsh chapel, it is Welsh that he sings and it is a Welsh Sunday School that he attends every Sunday': but like many others he was obliged to carry on the rest of his life in English.[46]

The chapels themselves were uncertain in their loyalties. The concern to involve the new industrial class of south Wales in the life of the chapel forced the congregations to offer their services in English: thus even the great revival led by Evan Roberts frequently held meetings in English, something particularly remarked upon of the mission in Senghennydd. Moreover the ministers themselves were often ambivalent about Welsh: D. G. Evans writes that 'one ambiguous element in the relationship was the growing admiration of ministers for the English culture. . . . English was accepted as a prestige-giving and status-conferring language'.[47] The realisation that Welsh culture as distinct from Welsh nonconformity, would have to be fought for, does not seem to have been very strong in the village until the 1920s.

One result of all this was that Welsh became increasingly placed in a compartment separate from everyday life: 'while English was the language of science, business and commerce, philosophy and the arts, Welsh was the language of religion'.[39] As a result it was increasingly seen as a second language, even as a second class language, by many people. An indication of some of the underlying tensions was a brawl which took place in Senghennydd after a bazaar at the Welsh Baptist Church. Anne Jones was summonsed for attacking Evelyn Beard who was with her friend, Vera Price. Anne Jones said that her children were being sneered at for being Welsh. Anne, with her daughter Maggie, had then allegedly bashed Evelyn Beard against the wall of the Conservative Club. As noted above, the Infants' School under Catherine James had been highly successful in developing the teaching of Welsh, and it had been an important part of the curriculum in all the village schools. An entry in the log of the Girls' School records the point at which the decline of Welsh reached a crisis: in 1913 there was a big turnover of staff and of the nine assistants, eight started their in-service training in that year. The log reports that 'most of the new arrivals are unaquainted with Welsh, and the teaching of this language has been practically suspended'.[50]

A meeting of the East Glamorgan miners in Caerphilly demonstrates the way in which Welsh was being marginalised in everyday use. The meeting, which was fairly rowdy, was addressed by Councillor Vernon Hartshorn, Richard Bell and David Watts Morgan, all of them present or future M.P.s. After several speeches in English, Watts Morgan was about to speak in Welsh when there were shouts from the floor

> and several miners rose from the front seats and left the hall. This brought from Mr Morgan an indignant rebuke, 'if the men who are English, and

who have made Wales their home do not think it worthwhile to remain here while I address others in the language which others understand, then they are welcome to go.'

The topic, however, was the need for all miners to join the union and the immediate logic of the union's needs therefore drove Watts Morgan to 'relapse' into English. The union needed English miners to join the union and English was the only common language.[51]

Welsh publications would have found it difficult to compete with the romantic novels which were the most popular books in the mining villages, and which were serialised in the local newspapers. B. L. Coombes had not long arrived in his new lodging at 'Treclewyd' when he was shown the nook where the young people in the family hid the novels from their elders: in later years there was disappointment when it was discovered that for every work of non-fiction, fifteen novels were borrowed from the Senghennydd Library. The nearest to the reality of the mining communities that this fiction reached were stories in which attractive young women happened to be in the mine when a disaster struck and they were then rescued from under the nose of the mine owner's son by a young collier. More commonly, aristocratic young women fell in love with heroes back from imperial adventures or, to connect with the world of the miner, fell in love with young workers who, in the end, discovered their lost aristocratic inheritance. B. Price Davies, in his autobiographical stories of 'Gorlan', recalled one serial in which 'the joyful ending revealed the boy to be a foundling and the lost son of a duke, while the girl proved to be also a foundling and the daughter of an earl!'[52] Through such stories the child learnt important things about the world; among them that there were societies outside the valleys and that in such places people who did manual work were by definition inferior.

As in earlier periods of the mining communities, the pubs played an important role in the life of the village, quite apart from the supply of alcohol. In the club rooms of the public houses met the large array of organisations and friendly societies which spanned the divide, such as it was, between the chapel goers and the drinkers.[53] Nevertheless alcohol did play a major part in the quality of life in Senghennydd: often for the worse. Almost every week the local papers published lists of the individuals convicted of drunkenness and related offences, many of them involving established local families in fights and other incidents. The lists of the drunks would be printed under headlines such as 'Senghennydd Usuals' and 'The weekly Tribute to Folly'. On occasion the reports would list seven Senghennydd miners on charges directly related to alcohol. It was a matter for something like pride when Evan Rosser appeared in Caerphilly Police Court in September 1909: the local paper announced 'Senghennydd: 90th Appearance'.[54]

Fairly typical of the persistent offenders was Daniel Parcel who was thrown out of the Gwern-y-Milwr Hotel in February 1902. He then returned and threw a jug of water over the fire, extinguishing it. Not surprisingly a fracas ensued. The bench clearly saw dowsing the fire as a peculiarly foul deed and the chairman asked 'Why should you return a second time and act so blackguardly?' before fining him a total of one pound. This failed as a deterrent since Daniel Parcel and Henry Gough, a member of another family associated with much rough housing in Senghennydd, repeated the performance two months later. On being told to leave they again poured water over the fire. This time Daniel Parcel was fined thirty shillings and had also to pay the costs of the case.[55] He reappeared regularly on the lists over the years, sending his wife to appear and pay his fines, until the magistrates lost patience and issued a warrant for him to appear before them in person. The fines alone must have had a major effect on the family budget, further exacerbating the extent to which the whole family suffered as a consequence of the wage earner's drunkenness.[56]

Though there are no statistics on the illnesses resulting from drunkenness in the village, there were a number of deaths in which drink was the major contributory factor. Morris Sullivan, a frequent drinker, attempted to kill himself on the 7th of February 1909. It is possible that his drinking and his attempted suicide were both the result of some other prior cause since the Sullivans suffered more than their fair share of tragedies associated with the Universal Pit. What he failed to achieve himself was accomplished by the official agencies since, following his suicide attempt, he was refused admission by the Master of the Pontypridd Workhouse and finally died of pneumonia in the Cardiff Workhouse a few days later.[57] In June 1913 William Davies of Stanley Street died after being hit by a train and in the same week Owen Morris fell down the stairs at Stanley Street, while drunk, and broke his spine: the Coroner, his interest aroused, commented that 'it is a very funny coincidence'.[58]

The regular results of this drunkenness were fights in the pubs which contributed to the performance at the next session of the police court. When the friend of Thomas Rees was refused a drink at the Leigh Hotel, Rees threw his drink away, splashing Miss Lucy Williams, 'a good looking barmaid'. Obadiah Meredith, the landlord, together with the cellarman threw Rees out and the court heard the usual conflicting evidence when Rees sued the bar staff for assault. The Rees witnesses testified that blood was gushing from his head, while the landlord's supporters claimed that there was no blood to be seen. One of Rees's witnesses failed to produce the expected evidence, and Rees won laughter and applause when he announced to the court that 'one of his witnesses had proved faithful, and one a traitor... Dallimore [the traitor] was courting one of the "slaveys" at the pub'. Rees's eloquence seemed to have worked on the court since he achieved a rare victory in winning ten shillings damages from the publican.[59]

The fights which resulted from the drinking were not confined to the pubs, nor solely to the homes of the wretched families involved; they spilled into the streets, affecting the whole public atmosphere of the village. The year 1906, a relatively quiet time industrially and politically, was typical. On 5th January John Booth and John Jones were fined for a public fight in Commercial Street on New Year's Eve. In April, Harry Bowen and Richard Morgan were stripped to the waist and fighting in Stanley Street: they were surrounded by a large crowd when the police arrived.[60] In May J. Mead and J. Reed had a public bout in Commercial Street and were both fined. In July James Smith and William Osmont were fined for fighting in High Street. In September the notorious Henry Gough was fined for fighting with John Jones, in Commercial Street, as were Thomas Donoghue and William Jones.[61] The spate of fights in 1906 confirms that the effect of the religious revival of 1904-5 was fairly short lived: indeed the fights may have had an added zest as the converted rediscovered the excitement of their previous excesses, or as the young discovered them for the first time.

In strike periods these fights often developed into riots if the police tried to interfere, but in normal times drunken attacks against the police were treated fairly casually. PC Pope became used to headlines such as 'Assault on a Pope', assaults for which the brawler would be fined ten shillings.[62]

While such fights were treated as normal in Senghennydd, and punished with fines of about ten shillings, the inhabitants of the village learnt that they were treated very differently if fights occurred in more respectable communities. Five Senghennydd men, including A. Weaver, a persistent drunk, were involved in a fight at a Caerphilly fish and chip shop in July 1903. Since the offer of cod instead of plaice could be taken as a sign that Senghennydd inhabitants were being looked down on and offered second best goods, it was not difficult for such fights to erupt. The situation was made worse, for all but the fish and chip shop owner, by the arrival of a police inspector in addition to the usual constables. The inspector took less kindly to being assaulted by Senghennydd miners than did his men and the offenders were given two months hard labour. There was public sympathy in the village when it was reported that, as the men's wives advanced to say goodbye to their husbands, the 'police hurried the prisoners through the court door leading to the cells'.[63]

Even in Senghennydd, however, the police had their methods of dishing out summary justice and were protected by the bench who were prepared to waive the normal constraints on the police in the light of the notoriety of the village. In April 1904, Isaac Jones was told by Constable Bevan to go home, to which he replied, 'I have as much right to this road as you have'. Isaac Jones, supported by various witnesses, claimed that he was then beaten and throttled by the police and again beaten in the police station. The bench supported the police, fining Jones and dismissing his claim against the police. But they made it clear that they accepted the essence of his claim by commenting that 'they had taken into consideration the difficulties of the police in carrying out their duty in such a district as Senghennydd... [but] they wished to caution the police against using undue rough usage to men in their custody'. They did not define precisely what would constitute 'due' rough usage.[64]

Drunkenness was overwhelmingly a male problem and was in general treated by the courts in a routine manner. Occasionally men might be told off by the bench, as when John White was reprimanded for leading his young son astray, but this was the exception. Certainly in this case the lecture had little effect since a month later White was sent to prison for 14 days for assaulting a policeman.[65]

Perhaps as a result of being lectured, women were more inclined to stand up to the court. Mary Evans was arrested in the street at 1.30

in the morning and Constable Fury claimed that she was drunk, to which she retorted that she was not drunk but angry, and that if she was drunk then it was on water.[66]

The archetypal drunken male, with just enough charm to rescue him from being totally vicious, was Benjamin Corfield who had gained a reputation in the village as a boxer in the competitive boxing stalls set up for popular amusement. He was also, by the end of 1903, the barman at the Parc Hotel. In January 1904 he had two experiences which were rare for him. The first was that of appearing in court as a witness against someone else, rather than as the accused in the dock. As an honest citizen he appeared against William Green, his fellow barman at the Parc Hotel, who was accused of a private line in selling the pub's beer. In the light of Corfield's subsequent career one cannot help feeling that there was more to the case than meets the eye: possibly Green was endangering Corfield's prior rights to the unofficial sale of the Hotel's beer.[67]

The second unusual experience for Corfield arose from the first, though it put him back in the dock where he may have felt more at home. He was on his way to appear as a witness against Green when he was stopped for travelling on the railway without a ticket. The suggestion that he was drunk was sufficient to convince the court that he had no intent to defraud the Rhymney Valley Railway, and Corfield had the interesting experience of being found not guilty.[68] The beer stealing case had its after effects, however, for in March Corfield was bound over to keep the peace in the sum of £5 after threatening the Manager of the Universal Hotel in connection with the case.

In April he got into his stride when Mrs Hinder refused to open the door of her house for him. He then smashed down the door and entered the house where he started to insult Mrs Hinder's daughter. The daughter fled upstairs and a neighbour extracted an invalid child from the scene, while Corfield started chopping up someone's clothes. He was gaoled for a month.[69]

Benjamin Corfield prospered over the years and by 1911 he owned at least two shops in Commercial Street. In March of that year he assaulted one of his employees and was fined £2 or a month in gaol. The insult offered by the bench in accepting the word of his employee rather than his own was too much for Corfield who harangued the bench, while almost incoherent with rage: 'This is justice is it, in

Caerphilly? Will you give me time to pay? This is justice is it? . . .
There is not a straight man in this court. . . .'.[70]

He also appears to have been one of the first people to own a car in
Senghennydd. In 1911 he was stopped by the police who rather
generously only prosecuted him for driving without lights. He had
been relieved when he recognised the constable who stopped him, and
greeted his acquaintance with the words, 'Oh it's you Harry—
Mum's the word'. The Chairman of the Bench asked, presumably
with heavy irony, 'Anything known?' about the defendant: at which
point Corfield sarcastically interjected, 'That's done it'. With great
tact and a careful choice of words, Police Superintendent Gill was able
to reply, 'He has not been on for this kind of offence before'.[71]

Corfield met his Waterloo when he engaged some hopelssly inept
accomplices to steal him 17 prize fowls from Cardiff. Their incompetence
betrayed him when he met them in his car at 4.30 in the morning to
collect the spoil. He continued to amuse the court, remarking that he
had 'first thought that the birds had been stolen as it was a funny time
to be with them'. On this occasion, however, his wit was not enough
and he was sentenced to eighteen months in prison. Whether one was
glad to see justice done and a brutal man put away, or rather missed
his brand of villainy, depended less on Benjamin Corfield than on the
individual's own point of view.[72]

The cliche that Welsh valley towns were divided between the
chapel goers and the drinkers, categories which were supposed to
coincide with the distinction between the respectable and the rough
working class families, was always an extreme simplification. Certainly
it suggests a clearer split in society than existed in Senghennydd.
Between these two institutions there were a range of other organisations
and activities in which the members of most families whose lives were
not entirely dominated by the behaviour of the male 'breadwinner'
would meet: the fact that there was no choice of school in the village
also made intermingling inevitable, though some children did go on
to the County School in Caerphilly or even to schools in Cardiff.
Certainly the lists of attenders at chapel and social events, of drunks,
child deaths and prosecutions in the Police Court suggests an intermingling of families rather than a clear division into camps however
much that would have been desired by some.

The first thing to strike a newcomer from the countryside was the
array of shops in the main street, with their large glass windows and

careful displays of goods flowing over the pavements. The effect was admittedly rather spoiled by the results of the street brawls. As one witness reported: 'The shop windows of Commercial Street, Senghennydd, are tastefully decorated. The attractive appearance, however, is destroyed by the large number of plate glass windows patched with wood'.[73] By 1914 about 100 people in Senghennydd were listed as running commercial businesses. These included prosperous and well stocked shops in Commercial Street which gave their owners considerable status in the town: the Brachi Brothers, ice cream makers; Abraham Shibko, the pawnbroker; Alfred Littlemore, the hairdresser; Francis Yendle, the bootmaker; Hazel, the newsagent; Starkey, the chemist; the Pitts, Rowlands, Kings and the important Marshalls. Theirs were lively shops, many of them owned by families whose names are listed in all the major events of the village: their members died in the mine or on the Western Front and contributed to the chapel as well as to the court performances.

There were also the small back street shops of the type found throughout the valleys and described by Frank Smith and others. The meaner shops were 'taken as evidence of poverty and a signal of distress. To open a shop is the last despairing effort to escape the reproach of pauperism. . . It is chronic invalids on meagre sick pay, or widows with large families who open shops. These shops are not glass fronted affairs dealing in a particular line of goods, but private houses turned with a minimum of alteration into a kind of general store', which dealt in odds and ends.[74]

The best description of shop life in a Welsh mining valley is given in the autobiography of the novelist Rhys Davies, who came from Clydach Vale:

There was a shop for locally slaughtered meat and one for ironmongery, flower-seed packets and punishment willow canes; also Ada Lloyd's shop for fruit and vegetables and, in her parlour behind hanging bunches of bananas, spiritualist seances; also a shop for sweets and ice cream kept by an Italian couple to whose daughter I suffered a token marriage; also Evans the Boot, selling what his nickname implied; and Eynon's for moleskin pit trousers, singlets, buttons, American oil cloth and 1s 11¾d per yard Welsh flannel out of which shirts and other distressing garments were made. . . .
The shop smelt of wholesome things. Golden sawdust thrown fresh every morning on the swept floor between the two long parallel

counters... an odorous coffee-grinding machine, mounds of yellow
Canadian and pallid Caerphilly cheese, rosy cuts of ham and bacon, wide
slabs of butter cut by wire for the scales, and bladders of lard. Behind the
counter over which my mother presided stretched wall fixtures stacked
with crimson packets of tea, blue satchels of sugar, vari-coloured bags of
rice, dried fruit and peas, weighed and packaged by hand out of chests
and canvas sacks on quiet Mondays. Soaps gave their own clean smell,
especially the flavoured kind which arrived in long bars and, cut into
segments, was used both for scrubbing houses and washing pit-dirt from
colliers' backs and fronts. Slabs of rich cake lay in a glass case on an
intersecting counter stacked with biscuit tins. Packets of Roger's tobacco,
black chewing shag, almonds and dried herbs occupied a row of drawers
under a counter, though not in the one always chosen by our cat for her
frequent *accouchements*. [75]

The largest stores in Senghennydd sold a range of brand names:
Brasso, Hudson's soap, Cadbury's and Fry's chocolate, Hartley's
jam, Colman's mustard, Carr's biscuits, Libby's tinned fruit and a
host of products now within the price range of miners in regular work.
This was a treasure trove of plenty for the half starved labourers
arriving from the farms of Herefordshire, Carmarthenshire and
Breconshire.

The years before the strike of 1912 and before the Great War
brought relative prosperity to the coalfield. In Merthyr Jack Jones's
two brothers,

> in order to remove the last tiny speck of coal dust from the difficult place
> under their eyes, applied sometimes best butter, sometimes cream. Fine
> linen they wore, and well-cut suits. Patent leather boots or shoes. They
> went not to the pub but to the dance, the stalls in the theatre, or for a game
> of billiards. [76]

The street life of the town was also alive with the hawkers who offered
their wares, often to the disgust of the shopkeepers. In 1909 Samuel
Llewelyn, a fruiterer from Abertridwr, had the effrontery to hawk his
strawberries in Senghennydd, and a prosecution was taken out
against him for noisy hawking which disturbed the peace. [77] The
police case was weakened by the fact that their chief witness was
Elizabeth Swaithes, a Senghennydd fruiterer who kept a shop at 120
Commercial Street: it was suggested by the defence that her strawberries
were selling at 9d and that she was being undercut by the accused who
was selling them at 6d. She angrily denied this to Lloyd, the well

known local solicitor, who sharply reprimanded her: 'Don't import any heat in this madam, I am dealing with you gently.'

The implied threat had little effect on her, however, for when he suggested that she should simply have spoken to Samuel Llewellyn about the noise, she haughtily replied,

'I could not speak to a man like him. I am not in the habit of speaking to men like him.'

On this occasion, however the alliance of Senghennydd shopocracy and the Senghennydd police was too brazen, for it then emerged that Louisa Rowlands, the second and apparently objective witness, was in fact yet another Senghennydd fruiterer, and the case collapsed ignominiously. Nevertheless it had been one of the star turns in the magistrates' court that month, and was greatly enjoyed by the regulars in the audience. The exuberance with which participants contributed to the court cases often upstaged their solicitors who sometimes had to use strong language in order to retain a role in the proceedings. One solicitor demanded of his client, 'Will you be quiet man, or I will sit down. Why do you pay me for spouting if you are going to spout yourself?'.[78]

There were also more professional street sellers, 'cheap jacks', such as Chekoh, the Wild West Herbalist, whose monkey was 'sent around the village during the day to attract attention to the great opportunities'. B. Price Davies, in his stories of 'Gorlan', remembered that on Chekoh's stall,

a man with a banjo, attired in clown costume and make up, would sing an occasional comic song. . . .

'Mary Jane, she never was the same
For when she left the village she was shy;
  But alas and alack!
  She came back
With a naughty little twinkle in her eye!'[79]

Senghennydd's local hawkers made up in volume what they lacked in subtlety. Gyngell (or Gingell) the Fish was fined a shilling after P.C. Williams testified that his voice could be heard 500 yards away. Gyngell managed to project his cry of 'Fresh Fish, Cockles Alive-O!' 'with a lit cigarette dangling from his lower lip supported only by the moisture on his lips, a vocal masterpiece'. In Caerphilly more exotic items could be bought in the street: Fred Ball, a photographer, was fined for selling vulgar postcards including 'life like pictures of my lady's bath'; he also had twelve copies of 'Aristotle's Works' in his coat pocket.[80]

On the streets also were the array of events described by Thomas Jones in the account of his childhood quoted below. Senghennydd boasted a continuous flow of showmen and amusements which set up on the patch of open ground by the stream, the Nant Cwm-parc. Swinging boats stayed for long periods as did the boxing booths in which the locals could try their skill against semi-professional boxers. Mrs Orton of the American Pavilion, erected beside the Leigh Hotel, took out a theatre license for two weeks at 2/6, renewable at 1/- a fortnight for the following three months. Scullett's Travelling Show was another popular attraction in these years.[81]

The Park Hall was the centre for bioscopes, dances and films. Though the films were silent the cinemas were far from quiet as the better educated children shouted out the captions for those who had not yet learned to read, above the noise of audience responses and the thundering of the piano. Walter Haydn Davies, in his description of childhood in Bedlinog, ten miles to the north, writes of how the pianist's

> 'Hearts and Flowers' rendering when there was a tragic or sad ending, such as someone dying, caused many a tear duct to flood and soft hearts to tick over in sympathetic unison with the music. When the film pictured sailors rollicking around the theme was 'Up with the Jolly Roger Boy'. The fast moving comics brought forth the 'William Tell Overture', the Red Indians stealthily following the trail, 'The Rosamunde Ballet Music' and the cowboys riding to the rescue, 'The Galloping Horsemen'.[82]

In the clubs and chapels, outside lecturers spoke on a range of topics from mineral formations to manure, and a fever of excitement might be reached when some famous visitor arrived to speak. Councillor Hubert Jenkins was in the chair when Sir Ernest Shackleton spoke about exploring in the South Pole, and at the end of the meeting Abertridwr Hall 'rang with cheers'.[83]

As well as these occasional lectures a number of voluntary groups, such as *Cymry Cymraeg* and the Allotments Society, ran series of meetings and talks. Events of great importance to the Nation were the basis for local celebrations, and committees would form to organise celebratory dinners. When the King visited Caerphilly in June 1912 to be welcomed by Sir William Lewis, now Lord Merthyr, a committee was formed and a 'capital' dinner was held, which was fully up to the standards demanded by the civic dignity of the village. Not all such patriotic gestures were a great success, however: the committee to celebrate the 1902 coronation had only managed to raise £13 from the Universal Colliery.[84]

The Conservative Club for which, at least in theory, only Conservatives and Unionists were eligible, saw membership rise from 137 in 1903 to a peak of 500 in 1908. The Senghennydd (or Aber Valley) Social Democratic Club was founded in 1904 with the stated purpose of nourishing 'mental and moral advancement and everything that would do away with the abuses of the drink traffic': the provision of a library was a key part of its programme. The Club was struck off in 1905 for abusing the licensing laws, keeping irregular membership lists and possessing only scraps of newspapers until the hurried purchase of 52 volumes of 'The History of Nations' immediately before it was raided. The Senghennydd Social Workmen's Club was also struck off for a similar list of offences. It was noted by the Liberal press that when the clubs in Senghennydd were raided, the Conservative Club, which had the protection of John Littlejohn and Colonel Lindsay, seemed suspiciously to avoid the attentions of the police.[85]

The rural background of many of the inhabitants and the closeness of the countryside meant that farming remained of central interest in the village. Each year the Eglwysilan sports day was attended by large numbers of Senghennydd folk some of whom enlivened the proceedings by fornicating in the long grass. Even the highpoint of the day, the ploughing competition, was given extra spice by the problems created by drunks falling into the furrows. The importance of the event can be seen in the interest generated by the award of prizes. Thus the formality of his tone cannot disguise the anguish of A. E. Taylor of the Windsor Stores in Commercial Street when he wrote to the *Caerphilly Journal* that he and not Mr Jerman as reported, had got second prize: 'The prize went to me, with mare named Ben. Kindly give same the same publication, and oblige, Yours Truly, AE Taylor, Windsor Stores'.[86]

The interest in farming, combined with good household management, created a lively organisation of allotment holders though the high minded never ceased to bemoan the fecklessness of Senghennydd

The Price family of Parc Mawr Farm haymaking for the pit ponies.

folk which prevented more of them from becoming involved. Men like Richard Hamar, who had started work as a gardener's boy on the estate of the Earl of Powis in Shropshire, could significantly improve the standard of living of their households by their work on the allotments. The Aber Valley Allotments Association held regular meetings and had a weekly column in the local paper. The importance of these meetings is indicated by the presence of Councillor Thomas James in the chair at a meeting of the Valley's Allotment Society in the Gwern-y-Milwr when a lecture was given on the subject of Manures and Fertilisers.[87] It is doubtful, however, whether the allotment holders' gain in cabbages, onions and potatoes can ever have made up for the jaundiced view of human nature which comes with trying to protect nature's return for labour and skill from the marauding habits of the more drunken and thieving members of a small community. Onion stealing was endemic despite the magistrates' occasional outrage that the miscreants should steal off their fellow men.[88]

    The complaints were not focused only on those without allotments. There was an equally ferocious attack on the fact that the bad habits of the inhabitants as a whole had infected the allotment holders themselves. Apart from the fact that the allotments became dumping grounds for rubbish, it was complained that the owners showed 'great partiality for non-descript erections of wood and corrugated iron for sheltering pigeons, fowls, dogs and other animals'.[89]

There was undoubtedly a real pollution of the locality: the major polluter was the Lewis Merthyr Company whose policy of tipping, without regard to the countryside or the amount of dust it created, worsened the quality of life for all the inhabitants. In doing this they reflected the narrow view of profitability and social costs taken by most industrial interests. But many of the inhabitants also were indifferent to the spreading rubbish. The strange constructions on the allotments were, however, not the result of indifference to the environment. In this case there was a genuine pride in constructing one's own retreat, a precious inner sanctum of individuality and privacy, and in doing this by using every available material which could be scavenged from the environment or extracted from the mine under the noses of the overmen. The result may have been a form of aesthetic pollution of the hillsides, or of what beauty was left after the ravages of industrialisation, but it is impossible to measure the profound psychological satisfaction of the exploited worker and harassed male as he retreated to his cave: a retreat occasionally to be shared with a compatible and favoured son as he grew to maturity.

For most of the inhabitants a fully human existence was something to be glimpsed in the parentheses between lives of almost intolerable exploitation and drudgery, 'outings' from the harsh realities of work and exhaustion. Many of the autobiographies and documentary novels of life in the valleys describe days snatched from the endless labour to walk over the hills and revel in the scents of the wild flowers and the flight of birds remembered from childhood in Merionethshire and Cardiganshire. Memories of such days have a dreamlike quality hopelessly at odds with the reality of life in the valley. On the hillsides and marshes of the apparently barren Mynydd Eglwysilan and Mynydd Meio could be found the bog pimpernel and the lilac coloured cuckoo flower, and the moorland was touched with the colour of harebells and sneezewort; in the mortared walls of the hill farms was black spleenwort, and the reddish-purple betony grew in the hedgebanks. To Walter Haydn Davies the hills 'were a corner of heaven itself, for the moorland appears like a carpet designed by god himself, with its intricate weave of heather and grass'. The wood anemone, to the lyrical poets a symbol of innocence and sweetness, nestled in the few woods allowed to survive and in the meadows and fields lower down the valley were the delicate pink yarrow, until they were blackened and destroyed by pollution from the colliery yard. The contrast between the experience of the mine and its natural surroundings has been celebrated by many writers: '. . . everything was bathed in a golden haze, and on all sides life was springing up warm and vigorous. Its youthful ecstasy was made up of the rustling sounds of the earth, the song of birds and the murmur of streams and woods. It was good to be alive...'. In these hours colliers could dream of saving up enough money to buy a small farm in their home villages and achieving independence; dreams which were destroyed in the depressions and strikes which wiped out the savings of most miners' families.[90]

Older miners would point out to boys, who had not known the farms from which their families came, the kestrel and buzzard and occasionally the grey heron nesting in open water, along with moorhens and coots. In the woodland, which was rapidly being destroyed, the sharp eyed might see the green woodpecker, the chiff chaff, linnet and the nuthatch while tawny owls still hooted at night. Tits, jays and jackdaws nested in the quarries glowering down at the village and yellow hammers in the hedgerows, while occasionally warblers and curlews might be seen near the local bogs. The next day, struggling in the residue of the ages to hack coal in the blackness of the underworld, that parenthesis seemed less like an outing than a dream which could never be realised. Buried in the blackness of the earth the miner could not even say 'a day without a black cloud. Almost a happy day'.

The reality of the land over which the old miner wandered was the farmer working to make a living while holding at bay the influx of over confident young miners who had little regard for his property or walls. Many farmers might have been willing to do without the voracious market for their produce, which had been created by the mine, in return for immunity from the habits of the mass of new inhabitants in the valley. Sheep killing cases were common and even the respectable Towyn Jones, shopkeeper, choir-master and secretary of the Chamber of Commerce, had suffered the indignity of a conviction for allowing his dog to attack lambs. In most cases dogs were the culprits though there were some spectacular prosecutions for killing sheep when the economic depression took hold in the 1920s. Senghennydd folk engaged in a range of country pursuits and the local gamekeepers and bailiffs, some of them employed by colliery companies, were constantly bringing cases of poaching: rabbiting, in particular, was popular for its combination of sport and good food.[91] Some of the poaching cases seemed to induce a fairly benign attitude in the court, at least when they came up before the Pontypridd Stipendiary, Lleufer Thomas. Thomas asked Richard Davies, a collier who had allegedly been poaching at Cilfynydd, 'Is there any game there?' But Davies, keeping his wits about him, cautiously replied 'There's supposed to be, Sir', which raised an appreciative laugh from his audience. He was nevertheless fined ten shillings.[92]

Many aspects of Senghennydd life came together when George Rogers was prosecuted for trying to steal what the indictment described as a goose. The attempt took place on 21st December 1909 when Rogers had been drunk. He enlivened the court by pleading not guilty on the grounds that the bird had been a gander and not a goose as stated in the charge. As he had been in custody for a week over Christmas, he was only fined rather than being jailed. Whether this was a farce or a tragedy, (as it might have seemed to his family without his company during Christmas), is unclear.[93]

Gambling was another important pastime. It was strictly controlled by law and offered the police wide scope for interfering in the activities of the villagers. In the main gambling was a male activity though there were some women among those prosecuted. It affected most age groups and occurred on very different levels from a modest game of brag to a meeting of two hundred people. Three teenagers were fined 5/- each for gambling behind Caerphilly Road in 1911, an example of how tightly some pit villages were policed and the behaviour of the population kept in check. Folk memory has it that in Stanley Street, a centre of gambling as of much else, there were well established escape routes from the police through the attics of the houses. At the other end of the scale there was a spate of cases in 1913 in which people were convicted for working as bookies's runners. In April William Davies was convicted of taking bets in Parc Terrace for Herbert Beckett, a Newport bookie. 29 girls, boys, women and men had gone to him with betting slips. Davies was fined the large sum of £10 which indicates the determination of the justices to stamp out street betting.

A week later there were further cases and in May there were again fines of between £5 and £10.[94]

Sunday gambling was particularly popular and the justices treated it with commensurate dislike. In 1911 gaming sessions involving 200 people were held in the neighbourhood of Caerphilly. Such sessions were well organised with outlying sentries to warn of the approach of the police.[95] Even this pastime could, however, have tragic side effects when combined with drinking. In 1909 a child was killed when a boulder rolled down the hillside and killed her. John Snailham was prosecuted for manslaughter despite the insistence of his friend, Arthur Booth, that it was a complete accident. At the trial Arthur Booth explained that he had picked up a boulder, which was found to weigh 89 pounds, and told his friend to watch his toes. John Snailham, acting as the responsible friend, then told Booth not to be a fool, took the stone off him, and threw it into a hedge. The death was therefore the tragic result of John Snailham's responsible action. This was the view of Mr Justice Coleridge who instructed the jury that there was no case to answer.[96] The memories of an old inhabitant of Senghennydd, recorded by Elias Evans sixty years later, throw a different light on the incident.

> In the early 1900s when there was no entertainment in the valley it was work, beer and gambling. Card schools were dotted over the hillside; these schools were strictly illegal and Dai can well remember the panic and the scattering when a look out spotted a copper. Dai (Junior) remembers one tragic experience he had when he was walking up the mountain at the age of six with his sister who was five. Near one of the card schools was a boulder lying flat. It was the occasional practice of the miners after a card game to challenge each other to up-end the boulder and hold it in its perpendicular position for the longest period. Dai and his little sister were coming up the mountain when the boulder, unbalanced, came tearing down the mountain catching the two young children. Little Irene had a huge gash in her skull. Dai nursed her, waiting for help. She died three days later. It is hard to convey an emotion in print, but Dai's feeling after all these years were very moving.[97]

Boxing, particularly bare knuckle boxing, was also popular and men would bet half a week's wages on the outcome. Boxing booths were a regular feature in the village and the inhabitants could try their luck against the professional boxer for a purse of between one guinea and

£5: in this way a good boxer could supplement his income with a minimum of outlay.[98]

Even formal fighting, however, could quickly develop into a drunken brawl, or at worst a riot, particularly if the police intervened. Daniel Hurley and Martin Watkins were stripped to the waist and fighting when PC Pope arrived on the scene. He parted the contestants and asked Hurley to go home. According to witnesses Hurley and PC Pope then fought for fifteen minutes, much of the time on the ground. Deprived of his fight, Martin Watkins decided to join in with Hurley and started kicking the constable on the ground, while a 'large crowd' enjoyed the fight. Martin Watkins's indignation was reserved for one particular accusation: 'I wasn't the man who threw the bottle and knocked the policeman's helmet off'. The surprise is that the helmet was still on after ten minutes. Someone in the crowd, angered by the way its spectator sport had been interrupted, tried to organise a rescue for Hurley and shouted, 'Now boys, let's get him from the . . .'. A quart flagon and various other bottles were thrown at PC Pope. Hopefully constable Pope, together with constables Zeal and Fury, had taken on the job because they too enjoyed fighting.[99]

One week in February 1913 can be used to illustrate the quality of life in the village.[100]

At the police court William Tidsley gave evidence against Thomas Jones for being asleep in the Universal Colliery; James Gardiner, David Croaks and two others were fined for gambling in the street and A. Davies was found guilty of being drunk and disorderly.

In sport all three local teams played matches, the highlight being the rugby match between Senghennydd 1st team and Machen. The game was won by Senghennydd thanks largely to Pharmo, their full back. The teams were congratulated on 'a very plucky and creditable show'. This was balanced by the bad news that their fullback, McGee, had succumbed to the attractions of the Adamstown team and was deserting Senghennydd. The football team added to the bad news with their defeat by six goals to three at the hands of the Caerphilly team.

It was also an active week for more sedentary games. The Senghennydd and Aber Constitutional Club visited the Senghennydd Workmen's Club for a games tournament which drew a large number of spectators. For sportsmen the highlight of the week was the visit of Freddie Welsh, 'the Welsh Wizard' boxer, who gave a six round demonstration with sparring partners.

The miners' lodge at Senghennydd held an important meeting during the week. The lodge had a major discussion and a vote on proposals to reorganise the Miners' Federation into a unified coalfield structure and on whether to demand a five day week with an expected drop in earnings. The Senghennydd miners, as will be seen below, rejected both proposals.

One of the main social events of the week was the concert put on by children at St Peter's Church. Over 40 children took part, organised and conducted by Miss Mildred Cole from Senghennydd School. It was such a large event that the church had to borrow the lecture room of the Conservative Club. As in all such events the names of the children were a roll call of those who were to fight in the war, who had died in the mine and who appeared in the police courts; Skyms, Bishops, Uphills, Baileys. There were piano solos, tableaux, short plays, songs and a scarf drill by fifteen girls. The climax of the evening was a play, 'Fairy Play-Jo's Dream', which was performed by fifteen children. The Reverend Campbell Davies thanked the participants, the audience sang 'God Save the King' and hordes of doting parents and relations went away glowing with pride at their offspring.

A normal week for the people of Senghennydd might include a visit to a play, a concert or an amateur production of an operetta; but 'Irene', the operetta on offer this week, was a special event since it was written and conducted by a local resident. The eighteen year old David J. Evans came from a fairly typical Senghennydd family which lived in Coronation Terrace: the father was a collier who was to be killed in the mine later in the year. David Evans had acted as the accompanist at many local concerts and eisteddfodau and now had a place to study music at university. The performance was given in the Abertridwr Workmen's Hall and was attended by hundreds of people. The hall was full long before the curtain was raised, standing space was entirely used up and it is recorded that 'hundreds' had to be turned away.

The build up to the event had been tremendous and generated a certain amount of competitive behaviour among the villagers. Dan Lloyd, the schoolmaster, was quick to claim the credit as 'the discoverer of the young composer's genius'. Unfortunately malicious tongues had been at work, and Lloyd had to assure the audience that David Evans had indeed written the piece and that 'it was all his own work and not someone else's as it had been rumoured'.

The music more than satisfied the demanding audience and several of the main parts were taken by local people trained in the various choirs of the Aber and neighbouring valleys. It was said that 'the composition really is a masterpiece and contains moments of exquisite beauty and climaxes'.

The plot of the operetta was entirely typical of the novels and short stories which were serialised every week in the local papers, and which coloured the fantasies and perhaps even the perceptions of the inhabitants.

'Irene' the young daughter of Lord and Lady Randall is brought to the depths of degradation and poverty by her mother 'Lily', formerly the wife of Lord Randall, who through the hand of fate became wedded to 'Jack Ray' a drunkard and loafer, whose vile influence and habits have ruined the life of his wife and child. Lord Randall, the husband of 'Lily', the mother of Irene, goes abroad and on his return is astonished to find that his wife and child have disappeared. Thenceforth his life is spent in one long, weary search for his loved ones. During this time, 'Jack Ray', has been leading a most degrading life, taking part in continued drinking and eventually leading to burglary.

He also makes his child go out singing, but Irene refuses to go, and during the interview between father and child, the child loses a locket which was given to her years ago. The father takes the locket and wears it in his watch chain as a kind of good luck in his burglary expeditions. 'Jack Ray' has decided to burgle the house of Lord Randall, his wife's first husband, and in his attempt to do so is captured and brought before Lord Randall, who during his observations finds the long lost locket, attached to Jack Ray's watch chain. He demands of the burglar news of where to find his wife and child, and sets off at once, with the result that he finds them in a poor flat and suffering greatly from poverty, and the drunken habits of Jack Ray. After Lord Randall's departure the messenger of peace alights and tries to comfort the wife and child, but life is too miserable to live. Eventually Jack Ray is tried at the Police Court on various charges, including persistent cruelty and neglecting of his wife and child and asks for her forgiveness which is granted, then her husband falls dead at her feet. Through his death the only obstacle to their future happiness and many years of sorrows are removed, and they are united once again. There is much rejoicing in Lord Randall's house where a well attended banquet is held to celebrate the re-uniting of the [hosts] . . . .

Lord and Lady Randall and family are heartily toasted. The guests sing the final chorus of peace and her angels. . . .

The evening was an enormous success and rounded off a week which may stand for the social life of the community in the years before the Great War.[90] From a mere agglomeration of individuals torn from their previous existences Senghennydd was becoming a web of relationships, institutions and social interactions; a community, now characterised as much by its confidence in a worthwhile future as by the instability for which it had been notorious in the past.

CHAPTER 5

[1] NTBCJ 15/4/1905
[2] NTBCJ 13/5/1905
[3] PRO, BT 31/16355/65300
[4] *ibid*
[5] *South Wales Coal Annuals,* (Cardiff 1903-1914)
[6] PRO, BT 31/16355/65300
[7] L. J. Williams, 'The Coalowners', in Ed. D. Smith (1980) *op cit,* 101: W. D. Rubinstein, *op cit,* 76-8
[8] P. Jones, 'Workmen's Trains in the South Wales Coalfield 1870-1926', *Transport History,* vol 3, no 1, (1970), 27 & 30
[9] Boys School Log 27/9/1901: D. G. Sellwood, *op cit,* 93: Boys' School Log 13/12/1905: *ibid* 23/11/1904: *ibid* 4/6/1906: *ibid* 7/3/1908
[10] Boys School Log 7/2/1910: *ibid* 14/10/1910: Girls' School Log 1/3/1906: D. G. Sellwood, *op cit,* 52
[11] Infants' School Log 15/3/1905: *ibid* 20/1/1908: *ibid* 4/7/1906: *ibid* 16/6/1907: *ibid* 11/10/1907
[12] Girls' School Log, May 1900: Mixed School Log 10/2/1899: Infants' School Log 28/9/1903
[13] Infants' School Log 30/10/1903: *ibid* 2/11/1903: *ibid* 3/8/1909: *ibid* 6/7/1909
[14] Infants' School Log 22/1/1904: *ibid* 13/10/1904: *ibid* 1/5/1906: *ibid* 30/9/1905
[15] Infants' School Log 1/4/1907: *ibid* 18/6/1907
[16] Infants' School Log 15/5/1907 and 16/5/1907
[17] Infants' School Log 30/8/1910: W. J. Edwards, *op cit,* 16
[18] T. Bassett, *op cit,* 365: E. D. Lewis, *The Rhondda Valleys* (London; 1959), 218n
[19] T. Bassett, *op cit,* 351
[20] E. T. Davies, *Religion in the Industrial Revolution in South Wales,* (Cardiff; 1965), 70: cf I. G. Jones (1987), 128-9
[21] CJ 12/1/1911

[22] E. T. Davies, *op cit*, 149

[23] CJ 12/3/32: CJ 16/1/1932

[24] CJ 16/5/1936

[25] CJ 9/9/1933

[26] CJ 18/10/1930; CJ 5/3/1932

[27] GFP 24/11/1900: WM 16/7/1912

[28] J. Saville, DLB, Vol 1, 193-4 ; CJ 25/4/1936

[29] CJ 23/1/1932; CJ 24/8/1935

[30] E. T. Davies, *op cit*, 91 & 158

[31] WM 7/12/1904

[32] *ibid*

[33] *ibid*

[34] WM 8/12/1904

[35] *ibid*

[36] *ibid:* see also W. H. Davies, (1972), *op cit*, 85

[37] *ibid*

[38] J. B. Phillips, 'Senghenydd 1890-1919', *Caerphilly*, 3, (June 1971), 44

[39] W. H. Davies, (1972), *op cit*, 80: W. J. Edwards, *op cit*, 106: Eifion Evans, *The Welsh Revival of 1904*, (Bridgend, 1987), 126

[40] C. Gwyther, 'Sidelights on Religion and Politics in the Rhondda Valley, 1906-1926', *Llafur*, Vol 3 (1) (Spring 1980), 33

[41] T. Bassett, *op cit*, 378-9

[42] *ibid*

[43] *ibid, 313*

[44] K. O. Morgan, *Rebirth of a Nation: Wales 1880-1980*, (Oxford; 1981), 121

[45] I. G. Jones, 'Language and Community in Nineteenth Century Wales', in D. Smith, *op cit*, 58-62: D. G. Evans, *A History of Wales: 1815-1906*, (Cardiff; 1989), 299

[46] T. Bassett, *op cit*, 319

[47] D. G. Evans, *op cit*, 300

[48] I. G. Jones, *op cit*, 61

[49] GFP 16/9/1910

[50] Girls' School Log 6/6/1913

[51] NTBCJ 16/9/1905

[52] B. P. Davies, *op cit*, 142

[53] I. G. Jones (1987), 130: D. Jones, *op cit*, 343

[54] GFP 16/2/1904: GFP 5/3/1904: CJ 9/1/1904: GFP 9/2/1906: CJ 9/9/1909

[55] GFP 20/2/1904: GFP 23/4/1904

[56] GFP 6/7/1906: CJ 3/4/1913: CJ 25/11/1909

[57] GRO file U/Pp, (records of the Pontypridd Workhouse)

[58] CJ 12/6/1913

[59] GFP 18/11/1905

[60] GFP 5/1/1906: GFP 6/4/1906

[61] GFP 20/7/1906: GFP 21/9/1906

[62] CJ 7/10/1909

[63] GFP 11/7/1903

[64] GFP 2/4/1904

[65] GFP 10/5/1902: GFP 21/6/1902

[66] CJ 28/8/1913

[67] GFP 16/1/1904

[68] GFP 23/1/1904

[69] GFP 2/4/1904

[70] CJ 30/3/1911

[71] CJ 23/11/1911

[72] CJ 11/7/1912

[73] NTBCJ 16/9/1905

[74] F. Smith, *op cit,* 34

[75] R. Davies, *op cit,* (1969), 9-11: R. Davies, (1941), *op cit,* 1-2: S. M. Tibbott, *op cit,* 20-31

[76] J. Jones, (1937), *op cit,* 123

[77] CJ 8/7/1909

[78] CJ 25/8/1910

[79] B. P. Davies, *op cit,* 144: W. H. Davies, (1972), *op cit,* 138

[80] GFP 19/3/1904: Elias Evans, *The Aber Valley: The Story of a Mining Community,* (Cwmbran; 1987), 93: GFP 16/5/1903

[81] J. B. Phillips, (nd), *op cit,* 14 & 18

[82] W. H. Davies, (1972), *op cit,* 142-3: Interview with Mrs Bull

[83] CJ 2/12/1909; CJ 14/11/1912: GFP 13/5/1902

[84] CJ 3/3/1910; CJ 8/8/1912

[85] GRO Register of Clubs: NTBCJ 5/8/1905: NTBCJ 17/6/1905

[86] GFP 19/3/1904; CJ 25/5/1911

[87] CJ 2/4/1914

[88] CJ 5/8/1912

[89] GFP 9/9/1910

[90] Rhymney Urban District Council, *Flora and Fauna in the Rhymney Valley and surrounding District:* W. H. Davies, (1972), *op cit,* 69

[91] CJ 10/7/1914

[92] GFP 29/3/1902: GFP 23/9/1905

[93] CJ 30/12/1909

[94] CJ 17/4/1913; CJ 24/4/1913; CJ 8/5/1913

[95] CJ 18/5/1911: reported to me by Neil Evans

[96] CJ 27/7/1909; 7/7/1909

[97] Elias Evans, *The Aber Valley: The Story of a Mining Community,* (Cwmbran; 1987), 82-3

[98] Elias Evans, *ibid,* 82; R. Davies, (1932), *op cit,* 43ff

[99] CJ 23/12/1909

[100] CJ 6/2/1914

Chapter Six
Women, Marriage and Patriarchy

The public world of the chapels, clubs, trade unions and political parties was dominated by men. It is almost impossible to reconstruct the experience of women in this period by examining the records of these organisations and such oral history of the mining valleys as exists has largely failed to capture 'matters such as courtship; parental authority; family relationships; incidence, types and treatment of sickness; home medicines and hobbies; marriage; motherhood; shopping for food and clothing; Christmas; pay day; childbirth...'.[1] In this chapter I explore the experience of women in Senghennydd, an exploration vastly constrained by the nature of the material which is available.

In attempting to reconstruct the social life of the town, the lives of women and the experience of children I have used a great deal of evidence which relates directly to Senghennydd; in particular the reports in local newspapers, as well as oral evidence and official reports. This use of local newspapers creates obvious problems, since newspapers tend to focus on exciting copy, be it heroic, criminal or simply scandalous. In using stories of violence, or sexual 'impropriety' it is difficult to know if one is focussing on utterly untypical behaviour, which is in the newspaper for precisely that reason, or whether the behaviour was widespread and the newspaper could only publicise that small proportion which became the business of the local magistrates' court. For this reason, among others, I have balanced the account of Senghennydd with contemporary semi-autobiobraphical material from other similar south Wales mining communities. In particular I refer to Frank Smith's 'Aberffrwd', B. L. Coombes's 'Treclewyd', Wil Edwards's Ynysybwl, B. Price Davies's 'Gorlan', Lewis Jones's 'Cwmardy', Walter Haydn Davies's Bedlinog and Thomas Jones's Rhymney Valley as well as using the autobiographies and 'documentary' novels of Jack Jones, Rhys Davies and others. The use of these writers does not entirely resolve the problem, since novelists and autobiographers also select their material for its dramatic qualities. But the use of these writers reduces the chance that the material on Senghennydd is merely idiosyncratic while simultaneously enriching the picture of the social and domestic life of such communities.

Even in the comfortable and working class family home in Senghennydd, (if not, perhaps, the homes of the most 'respectable' families), the atmosphere had an earthiness apparently lacking in longer established working class communities.[2] Frank Smith's memoirs of 'Aberffrwd' give a vivid description of the scene as miners bathed in a crowded house:

> from the backroom, come the strains of a male-voice choir. When we put our heads round the door, we discern through the eddying steam a bathtub on the hearth, and three young men, stark naked, washing away the stains of a day in the pit. In a chair by the bath sits a young woman, possibly their sister, or possibly not, but in any case interested in the proceedings. It is fair to say that such scenes were not uncommon in Aberffrwd, for the miners had to have their baths, and where else could the women sit?[3]

Wil Edwards remembered his brother Twm washing, watched by Olwen, one of the neighbours: 'he was standing upright in the tub rubbing his legs with one hand while the other hand held and hid his penis. When, reluctantly, Olwen left, I heard Twm mutter to Dai, "She stayed a bloody long time. I expect she hoped to see something".' In his autobiography of a south Wales miner's life, B. L. Coombes also describes the women's ribaldry as male lodgers or members of the family stripped for their bath in shared accommodation in a pit village.[4] A middle class perspective on the same practice was given by a Senghennydd curate, who

> made a vehement attack on the demoralisation associated with the domestic arrangements of the collier's daily life. He spoke of one of the doctors of the vicinity who said that on paying a professional visit he absolutely blushed to witness the indecency of the manner in which the collier took his bath surrounded by the grown-up female members of his family.[5]

This down to earth attitude, combined with a certain prudishness, seems to have extended to sexual relations among many young people. There was nothing particularly unusual about this. Various working class traditions accepted, even if they did not approve, sex between unmarried young people and protected the woman with the assumption that marriage would follow if she became pregnant, although the pressures against pre-marital sex were very great in some places.[6]

Russell Davies has compared illegitimacy rates between different Welsh counties at the turn of the century, and claimed that these statistics 'provide us with a good indicator of the geographical location of immorality'. Since the illegitimacy rate for Glamorgan was considerably below that for Carmarthenshire and Cardiganshire, Davies concluded that the theory that people enjoyed greater sexual freedom as they moved into the industrial areas from the countryside is mistaken so far as south Wales is concerned.[7] I suspect, however, that other factors were operating which make it impossible to draw such conclusions from the statistical evidence, at least in new settlements such as Senghennydd.

In Senghennydd there was a dramatic disproportion between men and women. The new mining settlement sucked in males of working age, and in particular those who had not already sunk roots in existing communities. The number of young single males living as lodgers and with limited opportunities for forming sexual relationships was a factor in the level of drunkenness as well as in the relationships between the men and women. As late as the 1911 census, when the population of the village reached 5,898, there were still 57 males to every 43 females.[8] This meant, among other things, that women were in demand and were in a strong position to find husbands, to insist on marriage when they became pregnant or, when marriages failed as they often did, to meet men with whom they could live. Illegitimacy rates therefore do not tell us very much about the experience of sexuality (or 'immorality') in new mining communities such as Senghennydd.

Davies offers a way out of the limitations of the statistics. He comments that 'illegitimacy has been quantified, it has been organised into tables, it has been conceptualised, it has been made to conform to certain set patterns, but the actual people involved have been ignored'.[9] The history of Senghennydd before the First World War offers a range of cases in which we can observe something of the sexual behaviour of the inhabitants. (It is worth repeating, however, that many of these stories were printed in the local press, an indication that, for one reason or another, they were of special interest or out of the ordinary if only because in general the press did not have the excuse of a court case to print the highly personal details of people's lives.)

There is considerable anecdotal evidence that, so far as sex was concerned, the code of the chapels was widely ignored among young people, despite varying degrees of disapproval by the older generations. This is suggested by reports of married couples who later divorced and by the records of the cases where women had to claim payments for 'illegitimate' children. Most couples got married in this situation and many of the men who did not want to get married paid up without a public fuss. Moreover, as many Senghennydd women discovered, the courts would not make an order for the customary 3/- or 3/6 per week unless there was strong corroboratory evidence. We are therefore inevitably looking at symptomatic cases rather than at a statistically reliable cross section of all cases for children conceived before marriage: Elizabeth Roberts, in her book on women's lives in Lancashire, has noted that a figure cannot even be guessed for the incidence of pre-marital sex. Nevertheless the cases in which it was agreed that the couple made love in the countryside on the first or second occasion that they met, or 'walked out' together, in proximity to the friends of the same sex who they had been with, suggest a rather different attitude to sex to that portrayed by Roberts on the basis of oral evidence from Lancashire.[10]

At the beginning of the century, in March 1902, Hannah Prosser summonsed Frank Gray, a Senghennydd collier, for contributions to the upkeep of her child. A week after Hannah Prosser went into service at Abertridwr she had met Frank Gray, and on the second time that they walked out together they made love, as they did on other occasions. Gray was not Hannah Prosser's first lover, but the family expected him to marry her when she became pregnant.[11]

At the other end of the period up to the Great War another case gives a similar impression of fairly casual sexual relations among some teenagers in the Aber Valley, though most of these relationships lasted for several months at least. In this case Beatrice Elias summonsed William Webb for maintenance. Beatrice was introduced to William by her girl friends when they were going for a walk in November 1911: she was fifteen. On that first evening when they met near the old thatched cottage, the two of them went for a walk by Penyrheol Cemetery where they made love. Like a well brought up girl she was home with her parents by 9.30 p.m. The next time they met they just went for a walk, but the following Sunday they made love near the hospital. Her girlfriend and her girlfriend's sweetheart were with them on that occasion: as in most of these cases the girl's friends were needed to support her story and there is no suggestion that the young women were breaking a moral code and having to do so in hiding from their friends. In the following months in between quarrels and reconciliations the couple made love in their old spot 'near' (this to spare delicate sensibilities?) the cemetery, beside the old mill and in the plantation. One of the Bowdens was quoted to the effect that he had seen Beatrice in bed with one of her mother's lodgers, but the Bowdens might well have been doubted in the flesh, let alone at second remove. As with Hannah Prosser it is interesting to note that both women were members of the respectable working class, possibly connected to such dignitaries as the part-time bank manager and the policeman.[12]

The same applied to Edna Jenkins, a Caerphilly schoolteacher who made love to John Hale on the hillside: he went to Canada when she became pregnant. The case of Mary Thomas, a nineteen year old who sued Garfield Jenkins for paternity payments, was also interesting. Garfield Jenkins was a promising young official in the mine who was introduced to Mary Thomas at the local parish sports day. They went for a walk and made love in the field within a stone's throw of the Eglwysilan rectory and within earshot of the crowds. Goodfellow, the solicitor who defended Jenkins in the paternity case, argued the improbability of this, so close to the crowds: a good defence against a charge of rape, perhaps, but against the accusation of fornication only convincing to a solicitor who had not experienced the pleasures of sexual passion in the long grass on a hot Summer afternoon. Mary Thomas won her maintenance payments, though the hint of rape was ignored.[13]

That it was not uncommon for young people to make love the first time they met is also suggested by various other cases: thus Annie Harper was undeterred by any religious echoes on Good Friday in 1914, the day on which she first met Alexander Davies.[14] A pattern of supporting witnesses emerges in these cases: the young woman producing a friend who had seen them together, preferably making love, and the young man producing a witness who had also 'walked out' with the woman or who had seen her in bed with another friend:

Charlotte Harris and David Thomas fulfilled these functions in this case for Annie Harper and Alexander Davies respectively.

There is thus significant evidence from Senghennydd to indicate the exuberance with which at least some of these young people threw themselves into sexual relations despite the morality of the chapels which enveloped them. Certainly the material raises questions about the claims that working class women did not in general enjoy orgastic sex.[15]

Many, perhaps even the great majority, no doubt acted according the prescripts of the chapels which they attended, with the occasional human wobble. Though love making and pregnancy before marriage were certainly common enough not to exclude people from the community, it drew varying degrees of disapproval from other inhabitants particularly if the woman was left on her own with an 'illegitimate' child. When Annie Harper started going out with another man in 1919 Emily Rowland, his sister, first remonstrated with her and then assaulted Annie Harper: an unmarried mother, though tolerated, may not have been good enough for a respectable woman's brother.[16]

As far as the man was concerned the penalty of unwanted pregnancy was not normally great assuming that he married his lover. If he came from a respectable or chapel going family there might be a stigma, unless he lied his way out of the situation, as in the case of the son of Evan the Overman, in Lewis Jones's *Cwmardy*.[17] The bench could be firm in making maintenance orders and in jailing persistent defaulters, but this was often in their role as protectors of the ratepayers rather than as guardians of morality on behalf of society.

The pattern of youthful sexuality and the reasons for choosing marriage are confirmed by the evidence of Frank Smith from his experience in an 'Aberffrwd' colliery doctor's surgery between 1908 and 1915. Smith seems to be a reliable witness, though one needs to bear in mind that he writes from the perspective of an ironic and sometimes cantankerous Englishman of professional and Home Counties background.

> Marriages are said to be made in heaven, but in Gwynfa Terrace they were all too often made at the surgery, where the simple question was whether the girl was, or was not, in a family way. If the answer was 'Yes', it meant marriage, and if 'No', it meant stay single and thank your stars for a lucky escape... Once it was clear that the girl was pregnant, it was

the mother's duty to speak seriously to the lodger about a hasty marriage. If the young man accepted responsibility, well and good. So long as it was discovered in time, a natural event of this kind was no slur on anybody... A certain amount of scandal did, it is true, arise if the wedding took place at a late stage, or even after the baby was born. But this was soon lived down. What was all-important was that the mother should be married, and when she had been the attendant circumstances were forgiven, if not forgotten... It was only the unmarried mother who had to occupy the stool of repentance...[18]

Frank Smith's suggestion about the role of lodgers in these relationships is borne out by the Eglwysilan parish register which shows that in a remarkable number of cases the bride and groom shared an address in Senghennydd before their wedding.

Occasionally there is evidence of women rejecting this almost inevitable dependence and asserting their independence. Mary Roberts preferred to bring up her surviving twin by Davis Jenkins on her own, rather than living with him without marrying.[19] In Bargoed, Lily Davies, having survived the stigma of local gossip for bearing an illegitimate child, rejected the belated offer of marriage by the father, William Jenkins.[20] Such independence was however difficult to achieve in a village where there was very little formal paid employment for women of the sort that existed in the Lancashire cotton towns, and relatively little of even the casual work described by Carl Chinn in his book about the Birmingham urban poor. A few young women might work as servants in one of the larger shops until they were 'obliged' to marry or as slaveys in the homes of the better off. However, even women school teachers were generally expected to resign on marriage, and should they become pregnant outside marriage they again had to resign.[21]

There was a recurring theme in the press on the need to get women out of the job market in order to maximise the number of jobs for the male breadwinner: since women were not in the job market in the valleys this simmering campaign must have been symptomatic of deeper fears than the explicit concern with jobs. The pressure on young women who might have wished to look for independence outside the valley, was increased by newspaper stories, which were largely true, of the exploitation of Welsh shop assistants in London stores who slept three to a bed in the dormitories of the stores, worked fourteen hours a day, and had the cost of board deducted from their

wages of eight shillings a week. Others warned of the 'white slavery'
which awaited young women with ideas of independence.[22] Without
strong family support the only alternative to economic dependence on
a partner might be the poorhouse, and there are cases of women
asserting in court that they would rather commit suicide than obey an
order to enter the workhouse. Once in the hands of the workhouse it
was sometimes difficult to escape the clutches of authority. In
December 1907 the five month old Isaac Morton was 'adopted' by the
Pontypridd Board of Guardians and his mother was examined 'with
a view to her being permanently detained as an imbecile'. When, two
months later, her relatives asked for her to be released into their care,
as a position had been found for her, their request was refused by the
magistrates. Apart from anything else the magistrates had to think of
the cost to the ratepayers of having to keep any further children.[23]

Where marriage was not wanted or was impossible, it was necessary
to avoid pregnancy, and it is clear that birth control was almost
entirely the woman's problem. The weekly newspapers, full of
reports of chapel activities, also carried coyly worded advertisements
for abortificants. Typical were the advertisements offering 'Valuable
information on how all irregularities and obstructions may be entirely
avoided or removed by simple means'.[24] These advertisements
would not have increased and continued for decades unless there was
a regular market for the products.

Many of the quack remedies were dangerous and unreliable and
were sometimes followed by 'infanticide', or by death as a result of
'neglect'. The pain and humiliation in these cases can be felt even in
the sparse accounts which are available. Thus in February 1916 a
dead baby was found in a wardrobe of the Gwern-y-Milwr Hotel. It
was wrapped in the skirts of a kitchen maid, Mrs Davies, who had
been a widow for four years. Whatever broken hope lay behind this
humble domestic tragedy she kept private, presumably to protect the
father: but this was counterbalanced by how public was the humuli-
ation she then had to endure.[25]

There is little evidence concerning abortions: few cases came to
court, in part the result of the courts' unwillingness to convict, or even
to have to face the facts, in such cases. Indeed respectable people,
while they could handle the concept 'child', seemed unable even to
mention the word 'pregnant' because of its sexual undertones, and
had to retreat into euphemisms such as 'in a certain condition' and

'*enceinte*': even Frank Smith in his memoirs of a colliery doctor, refers to his patients being in a 'family way'.[26] In such cases as are recorded, the suggestion for an abortion might have come from the man, though other expedients also seem to have been tried. Garfield Jenkins, the clerk and checkweighman, offered nineteen year old Mary Thomas £5 to leave Senghennydd and not disgrace him or his parents: alternatively he apparently offered to lend her a revolver with which to shoot herself rather than face the disgrace, though it seems possible that he was worried about his social position rather than hers.[27]

In many places the most tragic and public result of the hypocrisy over unmarried sexual relationships were the suicides of young women who became pregnant and who could not marry. In Senghennydd during the tumultuous period of growth before the Great War there seems to have been 'only' one case of a young woman killing herself because she was unmarried and having a child: this compares with five suicides in the Aber valley during the months after October 1913. I suspect that this is further evidence of a fairly unbothered attitude to sexual relations among many young people in Senghennydd at the time: in that community it would have been difficult to see oneself as a moral outcast or as peculiarly degenerate compared to one's contemporaries, however painful it may have been to live with the malicious gossip of a small community. But if that particular suffering of being treated as a moral outcast was less than in more established communities, all the other forms of pain associated with the rejection or betrayal of hopes and ideals were still present.

Catherine Jones from Stanley Street killed herself in 1906. One can touch the emotional bleakness and loneliness which faced her at the moment when she was at a period of heightened awareness, in an exchange between the coroner and her father. The passage gives a faint echo of the arid emotional relationship she had with her father and her lover, although it doubtless also indicates a determination by the family to close ranks against the official enquiries of outsiders.

In answer to a question by the coroner her father replied that he 'didn't see anything wrong with her except she was *enceinte*.'

'Did she ever fret about it?'

'I could not say.'

'Did she ever quarrel with her sweetheart?'

'Not to my knowledge.'

On 6th May she went to do her housecleaning job in Cilfynydd, a six mile round trip over the hills. She was found drowned in the canal in three feet of water.[28]

The time when a young woman was finding lovers was one of the periods in her life when she met men in a position which had some of the characteristics of equality. Driven by some mixture of lust, love and more practical considerations, both partners needed something from the other and were generally free to give it or not as they decided. If they were lucky they might have been sucked into that passion in which there seems to be a perfect equilibrium between lovers, even touching that ecstasy in which infinity is prefigured. For many that state of heightened feeling, even if partly self-induced, may have lasted into the early years of marriage when a lifetime of unselfish bliss seemed possible. B. L. Coombes was probably accurate about his own time when he wrote that 'we were as young lovers always have been: we longed for a home of our very own. The trees alongside the woodland walk heard our whispers of the furniture we would buy, and the grey stones in the houses were surely amused at our whispers of quiet rooms and places where no one should intrude'.[29]

From the start of a marriage, however, the period of the young woman's independence was at an end although, as Coombes suggests, this probably seemed a delight to some in the sentimental and domestic joys of building a home. Moreover the strength of character bred in the villages ensured that the women, though financially dependent on their male partners, would rarely be mere servants in their own homes.

In a significant number of cases, the man and woman married when the woman became pregnant. Even if she was not pregnant, aspects of life in Senghennydd made marriage almost inevitable. There was virtually no work for women and in any event there were very real reasons why, in the environment of Senghennydd, a woman might need a a man to protect her. Nothing is more difficult to enter than other people's marriages: the materials are not available, and even if they were it is the novelist's synthesising imagination that is needed rather than the historian's painstakingly reconstructed description. There are many examples of solid marriages which lasted for decades until one of the couples died and this was of course the pattern of marriage prescribed by the churches. Such marriages are celebrated in the documentary novels of Jack Jones and there are

autobiographies written by Walter Haydn Davies, B. L. Coombes,
Jack Jones, Arthur Horner and several other men which speak of a
lifetime's partnership which brought happiness. Even the more
jaundiced Rhys Davies describes such marriages in, for example,
Tomorrow to Fresh Woods.[30]

However the work which had to be done, the size of families, the
environment of a mining village, the fear of death and injuries and the
constant financial worries all served to reduce the chance of domestic
fulfilment.

In most of Britain the number of children in families was falling
from the large nineteenth century families of seven children towards
the twentieth century norm of two or three. Mining communities
were among the last to follow this trend. In Senghennydd and the
Aber Valley many couples continued to have children every second
year: in such circumstances the abandon of lovemaking was inevitably
destroyed by the increasing and corrosive fear of endless pregnancies.
In the fourteen years after 1900 Hannah and Edward Jones had six
children who survived until 1914; Margaret and Evan Jones had
seven, Ann and William Jones had seven, Louisa and Thomas Jones
had six, Mary and James Jones had eight and Polly and Thomas
Jones had seven.[31] The rest of the community followed the Joneses in
this respect as in many others. (Indeed it should be said that the only
reason that the Joneses, Evanses, Williamses and Thomases appear
from this study to have made less impact on the village than might
have been expected, is the near impossibility of identifying family
networks among the holders of these 'proverbially meaningless'
surnames, and therefore a tendency on the part of the historian to
focus, whenever possible, on the Marshalls, Lowers, Snailhams and
Bussells). Families of this size remained quite common and not only
put a vast strain on the mothers but also gave heavy responsibilities to
the older children and put a relentless pressure on the father to
increase his output in the mine. It should not be assumed, however,
that large families were necessarily the result of an irresponsible
disregard for the future and an utter insensitivity to the health and
welfare of women by their menfolk. Writing of the 1870s, Ieuan
Gwynedd Jones has argued that 'families were large, probably
intentionally so, and acted as a kind of natural mechanism in a
family's confrontation with the harsh realities of economic survival. A

large family, given reasonable luck, was a better insurance against old age than anything a friendly society could provide'.[32]

The average number of people in each house was over seven. The Company, anxious to accommodate as many miners as possible, made it a condition of many rental agreements that rooms should be sublet. While better off families might afford to live without lodgers, and might even afford the greatest symbol of status, a proper front parlour kept for best, nevertheless the majority lived in grossly over crowded homes, usually shared by two families, or else consisting of one family and a number of lodgers. Frank Smith describes the living arrangements in one 'Aberffrwd' house, a description paralleled by various other writers of the valleys:

> The Scotts . . . were quite well off though there were too many of them to be conveniently housed under one roof. They had to convert one of the two downstairs rooms into a bedroom, which left them only the kitchen for meals and the amenities of family life. To be precise, twelve people lived in a house of five rooms, four of which were bedrooms. In the first slept Mr and Mrs Scott with their youngest child: in the second two girls and a small boy; and in the fourth, on the ground floor, a married daughter with her husband and baby.[33]

This family was relatively well off and its members were living like this partly because of the housing shortage, but partly to maximise the income and pleasures of the family at the point at which many of them could earn good wages. Certainly, from the point of view of parents, there was a lot to be said for encouraging sons to sleep with their girl friends, rather than marrying and reducing the income of the family. Equally the marriage of a teenage daughter meant the loss of a cheap domestic help.

In other cases even families on the brink of disaster might struggle to maintain accustomed standards. Mrs Huish was left with seven dependant children when her husband, an engine driver on the Rhymney Railway, died in 1915 as the long term result of a railway crash. Mrs Huish survived on parish relief and by taking in two lodgers. She and her daughters slept in one room, her sons in another and the lodgers in the third bedroom: but she managed to keep the front parlour for best, as well as her living room in the small terrace house.

Even if a couple wished to marry, however, the shortage of housing meant that they would almost certainly have to lodge with another family. The astonishment of Coombes when he and his wife finally got a house to themselves makes the point well as does his description of the house for which they were so grateful:

> Just after the end of the War we had a wonderful stroke of luck—so unexpected that we could scarcely believe it to be anything but a dream: we got a house to ourselves. We had preference over a large number because the renter was a close friend of my wife's parents. I suspect that a deal of coaxing had to be done, because people there were prepared to go to any extremes in bribing or paying extra rent to get a house that became vacant; but, unbelievable as it was, we got it.[34]

Single men would either live with their parents, contributing to the family budget, or, if they came from outside Senghennydd, find lodgings in the town. The cheapest way of doing this, allowing money to be sent home, was to stay in a boarding house in which large beds were shared and men on different shifts would even take over the bed from those on other shifts. Beatrice Morgan looked after eight lodgers at her house in Stanley Street in addition to her own family. Frank Smith describes such a house in 'Aberffrwd', in which the family slept in the front bedrooms:

> It is difficult to say just how many people sleep in Mrs Potts's house, but they obviously exceed the number of beds. The [three] young men we have seen are lodgers, and they share together the back bedroom: they share it with two or three others as well, for it is the dormitory of Mrs Potts's guest house. One double bed sleeps four lodgers, provided that the first pair are on a different shift from the second... If we go upstairs and inspect the back bedroom, we find it contains a double and a single bed, occupied by three night-shift workers...[35]

All descriptions of pit villages emphasise the near impossibility of keeping anything clean in the presence of the coal dust, swept around in the wind and coating everything in a soft black film. The dust was carried into the homes at the end of every shift, and the women had to fill the tin baths in the living room for the men to wash, covering that room in dirt and ensuring that it had to be dusted and cleaned after each bathing session. A Rhondda housewife of this period wrote that 'by the time we had done our daily clean it was looking alright, until Hubby came home. Then after he had bathed and his clothes put to dry, and turned from time to time, there is a nice film of coal dust all over the room, and it means you want the duster in your hand continually'.[36]

Coombes describes one of the older houses thrown up by speculative builders, which was the answer to his and his wife's dreams:

> Having no back entrance, the returning collier, and the load of coal when it came, had to be taken through the front room, of which my wife was so proud. The floor was below the level of the street, and water ran down against the level of the front door. At the back it was too low for any drains to act, so we had to carry all the rain-water . . . We came down on several mornings to find the water in the kitchen, and during one wet winter we had the water flowing in through the back, while we swept it out the front as fast as we could. . . . When I did not step into water in the mornings I stepped onto black beetles, for there were thousands there, and they remained there, although we tried everything to clear them. We could hear the papers rustling in the night while they moved over them, and the pockets of my working clothes, and often the boots, were favourite places with them.
>
> Despite its many drawbacks, it was a home to ourselves, where we could talk without being overheard and where the girl could play as she wished. We counted it almost as a palace . . .[37]

Frank Smith captures the near impossibility of keeping up with the work needed in a household full of working men, if they were on different shifts:

> Her alarm clock woke her before five in the morning, when she had to get up, light the fires and get breakfast for the day shift. Having sent them off to work, she had to heat an abundant supply of bathwater for the night shift shortly due home, and give them their breakfast, or, more correctly, their tea at seven. The two children who went to school had to have their breakfast at eight. At half past twelve it was time for the night shift's supper and for the dinner of all the non mining members of the family. Three o'clock was the hour when the day shift returned, and again bath water had to be heated and a high tea got ready. Soon after the children had to have their tea on return from school. Between nine and ten was served the only meal of the day which suited everybody, that is, as breakfast for the night shift and supper for the day shift, the women and the children.[38]

In all large households it obviously made sense to try and get all the men working on the same shift, so as to reduce the household work to something like manageable proportions. This meant that when explosions occurred all the males of a family might be wiped out, including fathers, sons, sons-in-law and nephews.

For women there were very few alternatives to this drudgery or possibilities of making some money for themselves. Taking in lodgers might give them money of their own, but at the cost of further increasing the load of work. The households of some tradespeople, mine officials and doctors kept servants but the drudgery of such work was only slightly less than in their own home, in which women at least had the satisfaction of standing up for themselves verbally and having some control over their environment.

Coombes described the attempt of women who wanted some degree of independence to start shops: but in the uncertain economy of the valleys these could easily end up subsidising the poor and distressed of the district, particularly during recessions and strikes.[39] In the larger shops women were generally servants rather than proprietors and only worked in them until they got married, though there were exceptions such as Elizabeth Bussell in the post office.

Most women therefore settled for a role as a wife, mother and housekeeper. It is certainly possible that a companionable and loving relationship might be maintained in the circumstances of the village, but we cannot tell how often the apparently solid marriage masked a home riven with loathing or even straightforward dislike between partners. Certainly the longevity of a marriage, by itself, gave little idea of its warmth or happiness since the mesh of emotional and practical ties which it created were sufficient to bind all but the most determined.

The case of Elizabeth and John Thomas, who were married in about 1890, illustrates the point. Six weeks after they were married he had threatened her for being too friendly with a male friend of hers. John Thomas drank and appears to have had a vile temper. He would stay away for days but would explode in anger if his food was not made when he got back. Lodgers reported that he hit her, and in 1905 he broke her arm.

For women such as Elizabeth Thomas religion offered comfort, meaning, and some long term hope, through education and individual improvement, of altering the sometimes appalling quality of human relations. Religion however was to be a catalyst for their separation after nineteen years of marriage. The dialogue during their last quarrel has a frozen, surrealist quality in the court report:

> When their lodger left, John Thomas commented, 'The Godly man is gone'.
>
> 'Johnny, being as the young man is gone, let him alone', she replied.
> He picked up the bread knife: 'I'll ram this down your throat.'
> Then she was knocked from her chair, hitting her head as she fell.
> 'Johnny, I've had too much, I won't take any more.'
> He then started hitting her again, shouting 'I'll take the gallows for you before the morning.'

That night she walked over the hills to friends in another village. Later she applied to the court for a separation order, making it clear that she was not asking for any maintenance. The Caerphilly Justices dismissed the case on the grounds that there was insufficient corroborative evidence.[40]

Mary and George Price had made the mistake of coming back together again on numerous occasions. He had left her seven times, in between Mary bearing six children. In 1917 she alleged that she read his love letters to someone else, a story which he, somewhat implausibly, denied. He alleged that she threw jam jars and stones at him and chased him away with the poker, a story which she, equally implausibly, denied.[41]

Compared to Elizabeth Thomas and Mary Price, Mary Elizabeth Davies was fortunate that her husband left her after only three years. She had married Edward Davies in March 1911 when he was twenty five. She was pregnant. He drank, left seven jobs in a matter of months, would refuse to get out of bed and would then go off without leaving money or food. The burial of their second child was paid for by friends and by the parish. Despite her complaints about the marriage, his articulate letter to her suggests that she may have hoped for a reconciliation with him: 'You don't want to write again, because I won't answer your letters. You don't want to come up here, there will be no welcome for you'.[42]

The attempt to maintain a marriage despite all its shortcomings may reflect financial dependence, though it has been suggested that it reflects rather the woman's commitment to the welfare of the family regardless of her personal needs: indeed, that in such situations the woman was almost unaware of having needs separable from those of her family, so deeply had she sublimated her existence in the greater good.[43] Certainly neither the length of a marriage, nor a woman's commitment to maintaining it, was necessarily much indication of its happiness. On the other hand one should not confuse the almost inevitable stress and inconvenience of having to put up with the needs and demands of a partner with the forms of raw oppression noted above.

Given the inclination of the court to tell married couples to make it up, the cases of domestic violence that got to court were usually there because some other issue, such as legal separation or even harm to the husband, was involved.[44] We owe a significant amount of this evidence to the overcrowding in Senghennydd and the presence of lodgers in most houses. These lodgers were important as financial supports for the families, as witnesses in court and (occasionally) as potential lovers.

In 1904 a Senghennydd landlady ran off not only with the lodger but with all the furniture as well and the outraged husband had the two of them prosecuted for theft. The lodger pleaded guilty but his landlady put up a fine defence and was acquitted whereupon her lover changed his plea and was also acquitted.[45]

In February 1904 two men, one of them a lodger in the house, attacked Thomas Edwards as a lesson to him over his treatment of his wife. Thomas Edwards said he was dozing peacefully in his chair when he was ruthlessly set upon, dragged from his house, assaulted, kicked around the field and left for dead. William Evans, the lodger in the Edwards's house, and John Bryant, his friend, said that they found Edwards drunk on the floor, having been insulting his wife. According to them a fair fist fight then followed in the field, after which Evans and Bryant returned to the house. Margaret Edwards, it was said, was not too anxious to look for her husband after the other two returned: she and the two men were asleep by the time Edwards recovered consciousness and got back to the house. Evans and Bryant were fined one pound eighteen shillings each, including costs.[46]

It might be that Thomas Edwards was warned by the attack on him but the real significance of the case was the way in which, in such a society, many women were forced into a position of physical dependence. Margaret Edwards needed protection against her husband but the moment the protection was removed it seems clear that she was in danger of much worse violence. To escape from dependence on a violent man or from an unhappy marriage virtually necessitated relying on another man: independence was rarely financially or physically possible, and these situations are evidence of the most raw form of oppression.[47]

Beatrice Morgan ran a lodging house for eight people after her husband left her: the house was vastly overcrowded as she also had her own children to accomodate. She lived 'as man and wife' with one of her lodgers, George Edwards; the different accounts put this as lasting for between two and four and a half years. On June 30th 1909 Edwards beat her up and the next day she went to Cardiff with another man getting back at 11.00 in the evening. That evening Edwards marched into the house and again beat her up: according to Beatrice Morgan he then started systematically to smash up the furniture. There were two witnesses to the attack, Adeline Meyrick, Beatrice's friend, and John Sehars, another lodger, who 'bravely looked on'. George Edwards was found guilty and fined £1 for the attack on Beatrice Morgan. The lesson again seemed to be that without a physical protector a woman could not be safe, but that a physical protector might well be the person she had most cause to fear.[48]

Even in the court's best tempered moments women were likely to be used as the butt of public humour when they appeared, as often as not to hear the case and pay the fines of husbands who did not appear in person.[49] In 1905 a woman was summonsed for not having a dog licence. In answer to a question she replied: 'It's my husband's and he's been away for five weeks'. There was laughter in court when the magistrate asked, 'The dog or the husband?'.[50] Similarly when a Senghennydd woman was summonsed for keeping her two youngest children, from a family of twenty four, from school there was much laughter in court. Even when she held her own and, on being fined 7/6, declared that she would not pay it, there was further laughter. The courts were often ruthlessly insensitive to the position of women: Elizabeth Lower, a widow, was unable to pay the 7/6 fine imposed by the court for not having a dog licence and was ordered to wait until all the cases were finished, an inconvenience that was probably intended as a punishment. After some time she tried to tell the court that she had to collect her children from school but was taken to the cells for interrupting the proceedings without being allowed to make her point.[51] At worst the laughter could have a cruel edge side by side with the element of farce. When Sarah Kingdon was accused of being drunk and disorderly and of 'using language more forcible than polite' she, 'with a shocked appearance, blurted out that she could not think of such a thing' and that 'what the Sergeant said was nothing but a falsehood'. The Chairman of the Bench then asked, 'Is she a married woman?' and Sarah Kingdon was met by an outburst of laughter when she interrupted with the reply, 'Yes, but I have not got a husband, he has gone away'. Like many others she managed to nonpluss the court when given the choice of a ten shilling fine or a week in prison. She replied, 'I'll take the week', whereupon the Chairman had to go back on his words and threaten to send in the bailiffs to remove her possessions.[52]

Perhaps more seriously the court constantly assumed that violence was acceptable in certain circumstances, thereby ensuring that women would only appeal to the court in desperation. When Mary Anne Thomas asked Bert Phillips for the return of a loan and was assaulted by him, the bench wanted to know if she had sent him love letters and whether he was the father of her child.[53] In the same year, 1912, Annie Morgan summonsed her husband for desertion. Two weeks after the birth of their child William Morgan had forced her out of the house at knifepoint, as even the defence witness admitted. He was a violent alcoholic and after two years of marriage she claimed that she lived in permanent terror. C. Harrison, the chairman of the bench, said that there should be a reconciliation: 'It seems a great pity that they will not try to live together. For the sake of the children they had better make it up. Take my advice and make it up'.[54]

Ada Lewis kept house for David Jones but, she claimed, did not 'live with him'. Charles Wadddon who, presumably, was jealous of this arrangement, threatened to 'rip her up'; but both the oppressor and his victim were bound over for £10 to keep the peace despite her outraged protest that she would rather go to jail.[55] The attitude to domestic violence was made most explicit in a case before the Ynyshir magistrates in which Ann Williams and her lover had been attacked by her extremely violent, former lover. She sued her former lover and asked the court to protect her. The magistrate, Dr Lewis, won laughter in court when he replied, 'get your new young man to protect you'.[56]

The reverse side of the image of woman as dependant on a male protector was the image of woman as the temptress leading men astray. When John Moggridge was arrested for the theft of £9 10s from his landlady he made a moving plea to the court: 'I am very sorry for what happened. I gave myself up to the police. I think that my wife ought to be made to suffer as well as me. She helped to commit the crime'.[57]

It should not be thought that women passively accepted the role of victims in these cases: on the contrary there was a large number of cases in which they held their own against the threat of violence and the attitudes of the bench. However the courts had the sanction of punishment against women who held their ground and the patriarchal assumptions were so deep rooted that even when women tried to create an independent life for themselves and their children, they were liable to be seen as uncaring, if not immoral. John Dixon left Annie Dixon and their five children in October 1913. He was a heavy drinker, got deeply into debt, and sent the bills to her in Senghennydd. When, eighteen months later, he sent her £5 and wanted to return, she replied 'please keep your £5, as I don't want it. I have finished with you. . . . I have only one ambition left in life. That is to get enough money to keep myself and the children respectable and not turn out a disgrace to them . . .'. Charles Goodfellow, the local solicitor, asked in reponse, 'you think more of your business than of living with your husband?'[58]

When the ratepayers were affected by men who did not meet their responsibilities, the courts tended to be more effective. Thus Mrs James and her husband parted in 1906 and she went into service in Senghennydd. Her daughter was brought up by her husband's parents, and Mrs James did not pursue him for the maintenance payments ordered by the courts. In the end, however, she lost her job in 1911, as a result of his behaviour when he entered the house where she worked. At this point she was obliged to sue him for the maintenance arrears of £175 5s, for which he was gaoled for three months.[59] So too the court was unsympathetic to Edward James when his wife sued him for non-payment of maintenance arrears. He claimed that Adeline James did not act as she should, and came home late after attending balls and dancing classes. He said that he would keep his child, but not his wife. His appeal to male solidarity was unsuccessful and he was gaoled for two months, as he had been on a previous occasion.[60]

The courts' attitude to attacks on women may well have contributed to disturbing cases of rape. In October 1909 Jennie Gardiner, a 'servant' at the draper's in Commercial Street, was sent to deliver a dress to Mrs Olsen in the Huts, near the colliery. According to her account, she was walking towards Graig Terrace, after delivering the dress, when she was attacked by four men. She later described the attack in the Caerphilly Police Court. She recognised Thomas Evans and Phillip Davies but was' less sure about the other two. She screamed and struggled but they held her mouth and dragged her into the plantation by the stream: there they raped her in turn while the others held her down.[61]

There were a number of significant aspects to the case, in particular that men should be confident enough to sexually assault a young woman who knew them, and that they should then follow her around the town up to the point at which she went into the police station. It is also interesting that at the first hearing, and prominently reported by the newspaper, the local doctor volunteered the information that Jennie Gardiner had possibly already had a child. In such a society there would have to be strong additional factors before a woman would dare to expose herself in court to face a rapist.

Earlier cases of group rape in neighbouring valleys, sometimes where a husband or even a policeman were held at bay while it occurred, confirm that for women this society at times teetered on the brink of bestial violence in which any structures which offered ordered values and respect would be welcomed.[62]

Such incidents exemplified an attitude to women as merely serving a function for men, an attitude made flesh in the availability of prostitutes. There is no firm evidence of organised prostitution in Senghennydd itself though it was often used as a pejorative term about women who, it was supposed, had more than one partner: for this reason the women who lived in the boarding houses were sometimes described as prostitutes. On the other hand there were various cases involving men from Senghennydd with prostitutes in Cardiff, including two in the same week of January 1904. Thomas Cambell was out for an evening in Cardiff when Janet Taylor disappeared with the five shillings he gave her to buy beer for both of them. The wretched woman, who had a long list of previous convictions, was sentenced to six months in prison. Patrick Donovan also went down to Cardiff for a 'good time'. He said that he was drinking in pubs in the red light district when Mary Anne Jones, a twenty year old 'unfortunate', ran in, snatched his watch and ran out. The defence claimed that Donovan had given Mary Jones the watch to pawn and the court accepted her version of events, or perhaps accepted the worldly approach of the defence lawyer who asked Donovan:

'You came to Cardiff to enjoy yourself?'

'Yes.'

'How did you enjoy yourself?'

'Very good sir.'[63]

The climate of violence in Senghennydd, fostered by overwork, bad housing, illness and alcohol, extended to the relations between neighbours. There were regular explosions, some temporary, others the result of feuds which ripened over the years.

There was, for example, a big audience when William Hazel was charged at the Magistrates' Court with unlawfully wounding Sarah Parry, a forty year old widow who lived two doors down from Hazel in Station Street. Hazel, it was alleged, had thrown a stone at Sarah Parry, witnessed by two other neighbours, Mrs Agland and Charles Edgar; Dr Kindon described the stitches that were needed. The Hazels claimed that the Parrys had stolen their ashtub first, and certainly Sarah Parry's daughter Blodwen could be assertive for after the stone was thrown at her mother, Blodwen said that she picked it up and promptly returned it through the front window of the Hazel's house. It may be, however, that she had fabricated this story to protect her mother, for two weeks later it was Sarah Parry and not Blodwen who was found guilty of breaking the window, valued at 5/9 for which she was fined 1/- and had to pay the costs. Sarah Parry was also fined 1/6 for stealing the ashtub from the Hazels. It was a bad week for Mrs Parry since on top of all this she was found guilty of being drunk and disorderly in a separate incident. The saga was still developing two months later when Sarah Parry was found guilty of attacking the Hazels and was bound over to keep the peace. She was also sentenced to two weeks in gaol for assaulting a policeman though Blodwen Parry asserted that the policeman had caught hold of her Mama.[64]

Some families were involved in more than their fair share of assaults, though for some this was simply an unavoidable result of living in Stanley Street. Adeline Meyrick seemed to have played a protective role in the fight between George Edwards and Beatrice

Morgan; Harriet Meyrick was summoned for assault by Hannah Samuels; and George Meyrick was summonsed for throwing an enamel bowl at John Drummy. It was probably the contents of the bowl which made the hurt sufficient to bring the case to court.[65] There were insults so maddening that a fight was almost bound to result, even if the instigator came out of it smelling of roses. Sarah Morgan, who was 59 and should have known better, told Mary Jones, who was staying with Morgan's daughter-in-law, not to 'cock her nose up when passing in the street as she was cocking her nose at her betters'. As was normal in such cases, the court enjoyed a patronising glimpse of working class life while the village revelled in the theatre of the court, before the case was dismissed. Perhaps most provocative of all was the habit of pulling someone's nose, a certain prelude to a fight.[66]

While the court undoubtedly patronised and abused women on some occasions, there were also many occasions when it offered a stage which was used to good effect by the inhabitants. Indeed the repartee from the bench was often a necessary stimulus to the performers. In November 1912 Edith O'Brien came home late and abused Mary Howells with whom she shared a house. Mary Howells said that she had been called a common prostitute and hit, despite the fact that she was carrying a baby. Both parties had squared their witnesses, though these were unevenly matched in terms of mental agility. Thus when Francis Cadman, Mary Howells's witness, was called, Edith O'Brien interrupted 'He can't speak. He was drunk'. Francis Cadman was unable to read the oath but announced, 'I am a witness that the woman did do what she did do'. When asked what she did do, Cadman replied 'Mrs Howells told you that'. (Similarly Jerry Mead, after being cornered by the clerk into reading the oath in a different case, announced: 'I swear by almighty God that my evidence is as true as his'.)

The O'Briens had the best of the repartee for, when Cornelius O'Brien was called to support his wife, he claimed that he had not intervened, 'the complainant's husband being too small and the other witness too drunk, so I did not hit one of them'. Since Edith O'Brien was bound over, rather than being fined, it may be that the O'Brien verbal fireworks had an effect.[67]

The most spectacular eruptions, the ripples of which created repeat performances in the following weeks, resulted from tangled relationships in the narrow streets, in which the thin walls ensured that privacy was impossible. When Ann Rees took in the husband of Catherine Anne Rees, the latter assaulted Ann Rees, for which she was fined five shillings. Elizabeth Ann Chappel then kicked open the door of Ann Rees's house and marched in. Ann Rees was not there but her husband David hurriedly got out of bed, whereupon he was hit by Elizabeth Anne Chappel until, in his own words, he saw stars. P.C. Prosser claimed that the whole lot were quarrelsome and the case was dismissed after the spectators had enjoyed a good performance.[68]

There is much evidence that in defence of their home women would fight with desperation, something that was likely to happen when bailiffs tried to enter a home. Angelina Burr arrived home ten minutes after the bailiff had entered the house when only her daughter had been present: she immediately threw him out. In the street he had tried to refuse to give her the execution warrant, arguing that it was for her husband, to which she had declared that 'what is my husband's is mine and what is mine is my own'. In court the bailiff claimed that she had been 'half drunk' to which she replied with a force shown by many Senghennydd women, 'I don't like to call you what you are'. Even more dramatically, Sarah Evans had attacked the bailiffs when they came for her husband, laying about them with a poker passed to her by the lodger while her husband cowered in the attics. She also managed to smash a bowl over the head of one of the bailiffs.[69]

In defence of their children the ferocious pent-up strength of women could be irresistible. When the thirteen year old Wil Jon Edwards, a collier's boy in Ynysybwl, was sent back on his own to the pit bottom by his 'master' along two miles of tunnels, he was haunted by ghosts in the blackness and almost killed by a journey of trams. That evening he broke down and wept with fear in front of his mother: 'she got up, rolled up her sleeves, and marched out of the house and down the street and into Jim Thomas's house without pausing to knock on the door. The sleeve rolling was symbolism; . . . the most violent punishment she could have inflicted would have been a flea-bite compared with what she could do with her tongue'.[70]

The immediate cause of the fights was often alcohol although the root causes of the personal quarrels went back to the emotional stresses and social conditions of Senghennydd: many of the women mentioned above had seen their children die in the recent past. Though women as a group did not drink on anything like the same scale as men, there were many cases of drunken women. In the case of men, the court would simply announce the fine and move on to the next business. The normal procedure was for the women to appear and to pay the fines of their men, who would normally be at work. By contrast, drunk women were likely to be lectured by the court on the dreadful example they were setting.

In 1903 Margaret Flicker, whose children were also to die in Senghennydd, went to the Universal Hotel for some beer and gin but got into a row with Bates the barman. She ended by cracking a jug over Bates's head. In the ensuing fracas both her husband and Bates were involved, and there were cross summonses for assault, though only Margaret Flicker was found guilty and fined, with the alternative of going to gaol. The bench also warned her that the next time she came to the court she would be jailed without the option of a fine. However she was not to be browbeaten by the Court, and defeated them by saying, 'Well, I will go to jail this time'. It seems possible that she would have a quieter time with less work in jail, than catering for a family: it also had the advantage of saving £1 in fines.[71]

It is impossible to understand the apparent, and often real, censoriousness of the nonconformist chapels and women's willingness to accept their subordinate role within them, without understanding also the sometimes crudely aggressive male world from which they offered some protection and some hope of building a community in which overt violence would be clearly condemned and alcohol would be controlled. In the one women were made subservient by physical violence, or by its potential use: in the other they were subordinated to sometimes overbearing and self-righteous male authority. Yet the chapels at least attempted to inculcate ordered rules by which people could live, developed organisations in which women had a meaningful role, encouraged debate on current issues and discussed ideals for the future.[72] It was these women who, in their role of reproducing that society, carried on the major part of the moral and physical struggle to improve the quality of life for individuals and the community.

People alive today, who were children in the early period, remember a close and warm family life, with parents who were companions and who spent much time playing and singing with their children, even if the mothers rarely went out except to events in the chapel. It may be that the majority of marriages were happy and fulfilling: certainly if to reach three score years and ten surrounded by grand-children and in the centre of a network of family, friends and community is happiness, then there must have been many fulfilled people in the village by the time it reached maturity in the 1920s. Those who can remember speak of their good fortune in being born into such a caring and happy community. Even when this was not the case it has to be remembered that the domestic sphere and marriage offered one of the very few contexts for human development away from the destructive forces generated in the workplace. The family offered a 'space' in the anvil of industrial society in which the individual might develop as a full human being: if that potential was unfulfilled, it does not alter the fact that there was nowhere else to hide. For the woman marriage was full of paradoxes and contradictions. The years of hope and apparent adolescent freedom which immediately preceded marriage were a bad preparation for the role into which she was to be moulded. The dawning awareness that partnership was often illusory and in reality only a form of dependence was one that came with that seemingly endless series of domestic battles by which authority was asserted within that patriarchal society and through which wives fought to reserve their limited area of authority within the home. Maud Reeves convincingly summarised the way in which poverty created a struggle for inadequate resources within the working class marriage and the process by which mutual support was eroded and destroyed in that struggle. Many men, after a day in the underworld, assumed the right to spend their hard earned money in the pub, while the woman, after a day of drudgery, was justifiably resentful if she did not have the money with which to create a presentable home.[73]

For all this, and despite the pressures, there is a sense in which marriage and child rearing were 'chosen' by women. The way in which motherhood was sentimentalised in order to make women accept the role, and then devalued and stripped of power has been analysed by Kate Millett, and can be observed in the popular fiction serialised in the local newspapers read by Senghennydd women. Nevertheless many women positively valued child rearing and did so both for biological and conditioned reasons but simultaneously because it really did play a more creative part in human development than the whole male world of work.

It might be true that men could work to change the world in an organisation such as the trade union or the local branch of a political party, but the trade union in general only reacted to circumstances and its long-term effect was unknowable. By contrast child rearing, apart from being an apparently unavoidable role thrust on a woman by her sex, was also an obviously important and fulfilling job which offered hope for a better future: on this feminists, socialists, imperialist eugenicists, and ordinary working women might agree. The fact that Senghennydd became, between 1900 and 1930, a happier and better place, despite the appalling deprivation at the end of this period, was largely the achievement of the women and of the values of uprightness and solidarity which were inculcated in the home.[74]

Within a few years of its foundation Senghennydd contained a large number of social, religious and political institutions. On some occasions women entered this arena to claim their rights directly. In 1902 the twenty two year old Catherine James, whose brother Thomas was also to be important in the political life of the valley, convinced the audience at a debate between various chapels that

Catherine James, ('Megfam'; Mrs John).

women should have the vote. As the suffragette movement gained momentum, she addressed other meetings including one at which she spoke after the local M.P., Sir Alfred Thomas.[75]

Even in the arena of social events, however, almost all positions of strength were held by men and in general it was their activities which were reported in the local papers. Nevertheless under the titular leadership of men much of this activity was powered by the efforts of women. The head teachers, ministers and chairpersons of the various societies and committees were generally men but in the schools, largely composed of women teachers under male heads, and in the churches, women played an essential organisational role. The history of Salem Welsh Baptist Chapel is typical. All the formal positions in the chapel were taken by men and the brief account of the history of the chapel makes virtually no mention of the role of women: yet in the early days when the survival of the chapel was in doubt, nine of the congregation of sixteen were women. Maggie May James, Catherine James's younger sister, had been an active disciple of Evan Roberts, and like the rest of her family was too lively a personality to be kept in a subordinate role: but in the case of nonconformist religion it was necessary for her to emigrate to America, where she and her husband, Clifford Joshua, both became famous evangelical ministers, in order to make full use of her abilities.[76]

While the men provided the income, it was the women who were the managers of the home and the family. They were the rock on which the family was built and their strength is celebrated in many of the autobiographies of valley life. Something of this is caught in Walter Haydn Davies's description of his mother who seems to have had a fulfilling marriage despite the tragic deaths of several of her children: she was

> ...a devoted wife and mother, no sacrifice being too great for her, no obstacle too difficult for her to surmount, no sorrow too great a tragedy to overcome, and no burden too heavy to bear. She was typical of the valley mam of those days, that noble generation of women who constantly bore stoically 'the heat and burden of the day'.[77]

Wil Jon Edwards summarised a general feeling when he wrote that 'my mother, unsophisticated and but simply educated, was my strongest civilising influence'.[78]

The necessary strength of these women could sometimes develop into tyrannical behaviour, the chief victims of which were their own daughters. Lillian Griffiths's grand-mother visited the home of her widowed daughter, who took in washing to earn a pittance with which to keep her children in the Rhondda. Her grandmother tipped a day's finished washing into the yard and ordered her to rewash the lot as it was less than perfect and a disgrace to the family.[79]

The success of women in creating a mature structure based on the family should not be allowed to disguise the price paid by working people for the sexual division of labour. It is true that, particularly in the post-war period, there is ample evidence of women's involvement in supporting the miners' trade union activities and of the involvement of men in the home during the long strikes and the unemployment of the 1920s. Nevertheless the overwhelming pattern of division remained that of a labour movement organised through the union and based on assumptions of the primary importance of production and therefore of men in the formal sphere of political action; and a community of women committed to creating and reproducing the values of a mature community through the home.

The way in which men excluded women from the formal world of politics, even when it affected the women's half of the division of labour, was clearly illustrated by the issue of pithead baths. The greatest source of dirt in the home was from the blackened miners returning from the pits. But when the union branch at the Senghennydd Colliery received a circular from the Women's Conference on Pithead Baths asking them to arrange for women delegates to attend a conference in Cardiff, it was reported that 'the matter was allowed to lie on the table'.[80]

In his resounding claim about the authority of women among the urban poor, Carl Chinn argues that

> devotion to her children was the catalyst which ensured the centrality of mothers of the urban poor and which enabled them to exercise authority. This power could only be wielded in tightly-knit, highly parochial and spatially limited communities... Their lack of participation—or even interest—in such activities [political and trade union action] can lead to the feasible conclusion that they were weak and powerless. This would be erroneous. The poorest women did not have the time to consider the merits of organised co-operation, to debate a different social and political system, to demand a more comprehensive medical system or to seek an improved education for their children.[81]

In the context of Senghennydd in the first twenty years of its existence women undoubtedly had a central role in shaping the community. And Chinn is right in arguing that in the home and in the street they more than held their own. In the chapel and the school they also had an essential if subordinate role. Even in their immediate environment, however, they had to contend with a threat of violence which was endemic in that society. That constant threat reflected the fact that women were virtually powerless in shaping their lives in any context or through any medium away from their immediate surroundings.

CHAPTER 6

[1] South Wales Miners' Library, Oral History Project, *Final Report,* 180-1
[2] E. Roberts, *A Woman's Place,* (London; 1984), 73
[3] F. Smith, *The Surgery at Aberffrwd,* (Hythe; 1981), 44-5
[4] W. J. Edwards, *op cit,* 11: B. L. Coombes (1939), *op cit,* 39-49
[5] CJ 21/4/1910
[6] E. Roberts, *op cit,* 80
[7] Russell Davies, 'In a Broken Dream, *Llafur,* III, 4 (1983), 24-6
[8] PP 1912-1913, CXI, 441
[9] Russell Davies, *op cit,* 25
[10] E. Roberts, *op cit,* 73
[11] GFP 29/3/1902
[12] CJ 4/9/1913: GFP 16/1/1904: GFP 9/9/1910
[13] CJ 29/9/1910: CJ 24/3/1910
[14] CJ 3/9/1914
[15] C. Chinn, *They Worked all their Lives,* (Manchester; 1988), 141-2
[16] CJ 26/9/1918
[17] L. Jones, *Cwmardy,* 47-9
[18] F. Smith, *op cit,* 47-8
[19] CJ 27/1/1910
[20] CJ 2/2/1911
[21] CJ 29/9/1910
[22] CJ 27/10/1910: CJ 27/10/1910: CJ 19/5/1910: CJ 7/7/1910
[23] CJ 2/11/1910: Pontypridd Guardians, Reports of Committees, 27/12/1907 and 7/2/1908, (GRO. U/Pp)
[24] GFP 9/1/1904: GFP16/1/1904
[25] CJ 17/2/1916: CJ 15/4/1909

[26] CJ 27/8/1914: GFP 8/6/1906: CJ 27/8/1914: F. Smith, *op cit,* 47

[27] CJ 24/3/1910: CJ 3/9/1914

[28] GFP 8/6/1906

[29] B. L. Coombes, (1939), *op cit,* 61

[30] J. Jones, *Me and Mine,* (London; 1946): R. Davies, *Tommorrow to Fresh Woods,* (London; 1941)

[31] Lewis Merthyr Consolidated Collieries Ltd; Senghennydd Colliery Explosion Dependents Awards, GRO D/D NCB 171 (1)

[32] I. G. Jones, (1987), 144

[33] F. Smith, *op cit,* 80

[34] B. L. Coombes, (1939), *op cit,* 130

[35] F. Smith, *op cit,* 45

[36] Mrs Smith in M. Davies (Ed), *Life as we Have Known it,* (London; 1977), 67

[37] B. L. Coombes, (1939), *op cit,* 130

[38] F. Smith, *op cit,* 47

[39] B. L. Coombes, (1939), *op cit,* 142: R. Morgan, *op cit,* 17

[40] CJ 16/9/1909

[41] CJ 15/11/1917

[42] WM 1/10/1913

[43] E. Roberts, *op cit,* 203

[44] GFP 10/6/1910

[45] GFP 19/3/1904

[46] GFP 20/2/1904

[47] GFP 2/4/1904

[48] CJ 15/7/1909

[49] GFP 11/4/1903: CJ 17/7/1913

[50] CJ 23/9/1905

[51] GFP 4/4/1903

[52] PC 25/5/1901

[53] CJ 19/2/1912

[54] CJ 10/10/1912

[55] CJ 19/8/1905

[56] GFP 24/7/1897

[57] GFP 15/4/1910

[58] CJ 23/4/1913

[59] CJ 15/6/1911

[60] CJ 21/11/1912

[61] CJ 21/10/1909

[62] PC 30/10/1896: GFP13/8/1898

[63] GFP 16/1/1904

[64] GFP 12/4/1902: GFP 26/4/1902: GFP 21/6/1902

[65] CJ 25/7/1909: GFP 25/11/1910: GFP 31/8/1906

[66] GFP 31/8/1906: GFP 21/9/1906

[67] CJ 14/11/1912

[68] CJ 23/11/1911

[69] CJ 28/5/1914: PC 28/10/1905

70 W. J. Edwards, *op cit,* 54
71 GFP 4/4/1904
72 R. Davies, *Count her Blessings,* (London; 1932)
73 M. P. Reeves, *Round about a Pound a Week,* (London; 1979), 151-8
74 E. Roberts, *op cit,* 203: C. Chinn, *op cit,* 166
75 CJ 13/1/1910: CJ 4/11/1909
76 CJ 3/12/1921: CJ 24/3/1910: Interview with Dilys John
77 W. H. Davies, (1972), *op cit,* 36
78 Interview with Mrs Bull
79 CJ 4/6/1914
80 C. Chinn, *op cit,* 22

Chapter Seven
Children and the Home

It was in the years of relative prosperity from 1900 to 1914 that the established Senghennydd of the future was being created in the upbringing of the next generation. That generation which came to maturity in the 1920s and 1930s lived in a community with less of the domestic violence and drunkenness which had scarred the lives of many in the early period of its growth. It is likely that the discipline of the union and the political parties, the influence of the schools and above all the sense of commitment, order and respect inculcated in the home all played a part in reproducing the community in a form more mature and able to decide its own fate: it was a tragic irony, though an entirely predictable one, that by the time the community was reaching maturity, the material basis on which it existed, that is the profitable production of coal, was disappearing.

It is, however, precisely these processes of the reproduction and development of a community which are most shadowy to subsequent generations. As I noted above, the male world of the union and the political parties can to some extent be reconstructed as can, to a lesser extent, the worlds of the chapel and the school, in which women played important parts. But the environment of the home and the networks of which it was the matrix, which together formed the heart of that process of social reproduction, are almost opaque. It can be explored only through memoirs which tend to be by men, by oral history, which largely applies to the post-war period, and by communal memories in which the central role of the women is passed down in sentimentalised form as the Welsh 'mam', or as a memory of a matriarchy, although one which could not seriously challenge male control of the public affairs of the community.

While marriage all too often became a process of the withering of dreams and of ideals, children offered the hope that those ideals could yet be realised in the future. Those hopes, however, had to be realised in a dangerous environment in which the mere survival of the child was a matter for relief, if not of surprise.

The atmosphere of the miner's home is nowhere better described than by Coombes in a picture that is echoed in the folklore of the valleys. Describing the first time that he entered a home in a pit village, Coombes wrote of

> the shining passage, the bright stair carpet, the brass rod on each step. The kitchen was a'dazzle with brass. There was a row of brass candle sticks on the mantle and a strip of brass along the edge, as well as a thick brass rod beneath and another wide strip covering the upper part of the chimney opening. That fire did not peep from under the second bar, it filled the grate as high as was safe, and its white heat showed in the reflection of the fender.
>
> The warmth and comfort was something to which I had not been used. ...I was astonished at the clean comfort of this new abode.
>
> I have found most Welsh mining-houses as clean—or nearly so—as this one. The women work very hard—too hard—trying to cheat the greyness that is outside by a clean and cheerful show within.[1]

Not all witnesses draw such a glowing picture of the ordinary miner's home. Frank Smith commented only that 'the housewives of Gwynfa Terrace generally keep their homes tolerably clean and tidy against the prevailing odds'. We need to bear in mind Frank Smith's background in suburban London as well as Coombes's delight at the abundance of the miner's home in a period of prosperity after the poverty of rural Herefordshire. The better-off colliers, the shopkeepers and the colliery officials had the luxury, and the symbol of their status, of a front room kept for special occasions. The front parlour was incomplete without a piano, photos of the occupants taken for their wedding, portraits of Gladstone and the Queen, and some religious texts, depending on the political and religious affiliations of the owners. B. Price Davies remembered in particular one print which symbolised the stability and continuity of Britain: 'the group consisted of four royal generations, which promised that three kings should follow the queen in their proper succession. The Queen was shown with the baby Edward on her lap, while behind her stood her son Edward, Prince of Wales, and his son, Prince George, Duke of York'.[2]

The picture of the gleaming and secure home contrasts starkly with the polluted environment outside the house, and indeed the cheer of the home was consciously created in order to counter the sub-human lives experienced by many of the inhabitants.

From the start the village had been plagued by inadequate fresh water supplies and sewage disposal, and there were frequent references to the dangerous situation in the village. In 1911 it was alleged that horse manure, excrement, and the carcasses of a fowl and two dogs were found in or beside the reservoir, though the water company claimed that these could not enter the supply of drinking water.[3] Sewage and putrefying matter lay uncollected in parts of the village. As noted above, housing was dangerously overcrowded: most of the small terraced houses contained more than one family and many of them housed over twelve people, while in the boarding houses people slept up to six in a room. In 1913 when Mr and Mrs Thomas were prosecuted for living in a condemned cellar their defence was simply that there was nowhere else to live.[4]

Stanley Street, in which several families lived in cellars, was particularly subject to epidemics of whooping cough, diptheria, typhoid and smallpox which then spread to other parts of the village. Already in 1898, when the houses were newly built, cases of typhoid were reported in Stanley Street; in 1900 twenty cases of diptheria were reported in two editions of the local paper; in 1902 smallpox swept through the corrugated iron huts originally built for the families of the men who had sunk the pit; and by 1912 houses were being condemned as unfit for human habitation. In 1904 a smallpox epidemic started in 29 Stanley Street, where four cases were reported, before spreading to twelve centres in the village: a tent with eight beds had to be erected to cope with the overflow from the isolation hospital. It was curious, though fortunate, that in this outbreak the youngest victim was 22, considerably lessening the danger of deaths. Dr T. W. Thomas, the medical officer of health for Caerphilly, commented with a mixture of surprise and gratitude that he was 'devoutly thankful to a merciful providence that we were able to get rid of it in so short a space of time'.[5] A measles epidemic in the neighbouring Rhymney Valley killed 25 children in 1909 and the Senghennydd school was closed for three weeks.[6] It is also likely that the over-crowding and the sharing of accommodation with strangers was a contributory factor in those, admittedly rare, cases of the sexual abuse of children which came to court.[7]

Senghennydd had a reputation for a disgusting environment which, like much else, was blamed on the character of the inhabitants. In 1905, the Medical Officer of Health reported of Station Road, Station Terrace and Parc Terrace that their condition was 'disgraceful and a positive danger to the public health . . . In wet weather they are almost impassable, some 8 to 10 inches of liquid filth to wade through'. When an outbreak of diptheria in Senghennydd was discussed by Caerphilly Council, the Chairman, with a fine insensitivity, could raise a laugh by hoping that 'some lessons in the matter of cleanliness had been inculcated into the minds of some of the tenants'. A similar jibe was made when the scavenger for the Aber Valley was threatened with a £1 fine by the magistrates for not collecting all the rubbish and for leaving waste in the streets. He claimed that the inhabitants were incapable of putting out their refuse before 10.30 a.m., when they got up, and, when asked what was the best time to start, he raised a laugh and some agreement by suggesting that 'about 5.30 pm would be early enough for the people of Aber'.[8]

The willingness of some to allow rubbish to pile up in the back streets caused a serious problem over refuse but most villagers were conscientious in trying to create clean homes and a good environment. Whatever the failings of individuals, the main problem was environmental and social, the concentrated pollution of the whole community to the point at which it is surprising that people's morale remained high enough to retain even the standards which did exist.

After the 1901 explosion, journalists, priests, politicians and union leaders had sympathised with the suffering of the people and the miseries of women deprived of the emotional and financial support of their loved ones. Even when the dead were indeed loved and loving, however, the death of 80 miners was vastly outnumbered by the death over the years of hundreds of children to whom women had committed their lives: this was another constant fear which hung over every parent. The infant mortality rate in Caerphilly in 1905 was 166 deaths for every 1000 births and by 1911 it was still 140 per 1000: as indicated above, the situation in Senghennydd was considerably worse than that in Caerphilly as a whole.[9] The burial records for the parish of Eglwysilan give only one part of the picture of child deaths in the years from 1900-1914 since many people from Senghennydd would not have chosen to bury their children in the graveyard of the anglican church: even so the register records the burial of over two hundred infants and children from this one village in those years. The anguish hidden in the bare facts recorded in the parish register is difficult to imagine.

Hannah Llewelyn was buried in January 1905, her twin sister was buried seven months later, both of them less than two years old; three year old Sylvia Llewelyn died on the same day as Hannah. Two years later their parents had a son; he died in March 1907 aged one month. Reginald Morris aged 6 months died in November 1913; his sister Maria, aged five, died two months later; their two year old sister Catherine died three weeks after that; their mother Catherine Morris died three weeks later. In such circumstances the apparently glib statements on the tombstones, 'Released from Suffering', were very probably true.[10]

The spread of epidemics in houses crowded with more than one family is also clear in the records. John Donaghue aged 20 months and Kathleen Drummy aged 3 years both died in April 1910; both lived in 34 Stanley Street. James Mead aged twenty one months died a few weeks after the five month old Henry Marsh; both lived at 27 Grove Terrace. The smallpox epidemic in September 1902 killed Ada and Elizabeth Essery, (both aged under two), Mary Neal and William Herring; all these children had lived in the Huts. In March 1910 the parish register records the death of eight children.[11]

In the houses of neighbours the deaths of children could be every bit as tragic and concentrated as in the colliery explosions. Between 1907 and 1911 eleven children were recorded as dying in the ten houses in the row from number 32 to number 50 Stanley Street. 27 children died in Grove Terrace compared to the 17 men killed in the colliery explosion and 10 children died in the Huts compared to the violent deaths of six men.[12]

The register records the deaths of mothers who died in child birth leaving babies on whom the affection and hopes of families would be concentrated. Margaret Sterry died in August 1911 and her daughter was named after her, only to die four weeks after her mother.[13]

Very many families whose names figure in the history of Senghennydd have children buried at Eglwysilan: Chidsey, Herring, Coombes, Flicker, Hyatt, Humphries, Jacques, Alderman, Meyrick, Hill, Kestell, James, Wigley, Baverstock, Marshall, Harper, Surridge, Agland, Pope, Tasker, Gough.

As well as the outbreaks of smallpox, measles, typhoid and other fatal diseases there was a continuous series of deaths caused by the dangers of bringing up children in cramped conditions, with coal fires and tin baths full of scalding water. In 1913 the two year old Sarah Thomas who was suffering from scarlet fever, died from burns. Mrs Thomas found her daughter with her hair and clothes on fire after her small son had run to her with burning strings in his hand screaming 'I did not do it'.[14] In July 1910 May Davies died: forty of her fellow schoolchildren attended the funeral. For her parents the tragedy was all the greater as another daughter had already died of burns.

In a few days in April of the following year Mr and Mrs Davies buried their only son and Mr and Mrs Andrews of Coronation Terrace buried a son two weeks after their other son had died. The thirteen year old Edward Cole died and the sixteen year old Leslie Lewis was hit by a tram in the Windsor Colliery. He managed to walk back to his home in Caerphilly Road but he died the next day.[15] Some advertisers used parents' continuous fears for their children to boost their products. Jones and Sons, the makers of a tonic, announced: '*Mothers,* there's many a little one lost who would be here today if their mothers had not neglected them'.[16]

On occasion all the pressures of the social system combined to destroy an individual, producing results which were terrible even by the standards of Senghennydd. In July 1904 Mary Evans returned to her house where her mother-in-law was looking after Mary's nine month old baby, Mabel. She found her mother-in-law, Margaret Evans, holding the infant over the fire. To the police she explained, 'I took the baby from the cradle and it slipped on the fire. I kept it on a little bit and then took it off the fire and put it back in the cradle. I again took it out of the cradle and put it on the fire a second time. I am sorry for doing such a thing'. Constable Bevan, who had seen men disembowelled during the South African War, commented that he had 'never seen anything which distressed [him] so much as that presented by this little baby'.[17]

The unspeakable pain suffered by the parents of these children is recorded by many witnesses, making a nonsense of the claim that people were hardened and therefore insensitive to the deaths of children. Walter Haydn Davies, from Bedlinog, remembered how,

> as the years went by, and as the anniversaries of the dead children came and went, my mother would say sadly, 'David William would be so and so today' and, 'little Philip lying far away in Alabama would be so many years old. I wonder what they would have been like had they lived? David William was such a chatterbox and loved by all'.[18]

Of Philip, who had died in the U.S.A., he wrote that 'the loss of this child almost broke my mother's heart . . .'.[19] Frank Smith described the death of a young collier:

A Doctor has to harden himself to the sight of human anguish or he would lose his nerve altogether, but here it was not easy to steel oneself, for the bright young lad I had been called to see had only lately followed the family tradition and become a miner. And now he had been crushed beneath a fall of rock, and before I could reach him he was dead. As he lay there his mother sat beside him, her eyes empty of tears but clouded by the agonies of grief as she continued to moan distractedly. The neighbours, kindly folk, tried to console her by speaking of the joys of heaven into which her son had been received, but she did not seem to hear. All she understood was that the form of her son beside her was lifeless.[20]

The central role of the woman in creating a rich family and communal life is clear when one compares the descriptions of valley life handed down in folk memory with the evidence from the apparently rare cases in which women were unable to cope with these responsibilities. The point is dramatically made by the different effect on families of having a drunken father or a drunken mother. Countless households in Senghennydd were subject to drunken men. Their families suffered economically and emotionally. In some cases the men became virtually unable to work: but the women survived, managing on casual work, shop work or relief. That the majority of children in such homes grew up as normal if scarred human beings was the result of the women who held the homes together in the absence of the man. On the other hand the effect when the woman was alcoholic could be utterly devastating, reducing the family to an unimaginable hell which, in the eyes of the world, explained and justified the collapse of the husband.

If the newspaper reports are to be trusted, and there are no doubt class assumptions in the writing, then Mary Tasker was an alcoholic like those scores of men who had made the town notorious. Like many of the 'rough' section of the working class, she lived in Stanley Street, together with her husband and five children. John, the eldest, was sixteen in 1904 and earned three shillings a day. The younger children were sent to pick coal from the waste tip: they were also sent out petty thieving. They were often without clothes and none of them had a pair of shoes, which may explain the continuous absence from school of Lizzie Tasker for which her parents were fined. The walls of the house were damp, the atmosphere was dangerous to health and the smell was described as 'unbearable'. In a previous case Mary Tasker and her husband had been sentenced to six months for child neglect after one of their children had died. The children's clothes were 'extremely filthy and verminous'. The body of Edward, the seven year old, was a mass of vermin marks. Of Mary, who was four and the youngest of the family, it was said that 'her body was thick with dirt, and one mass of vermin marks, and her head full of nits and vermin . . . she was a thin miserable child, and seemed to have no life in her at all, and in appearance resembles a careworn old woman'. The father was described as heartless and gaoled for six months, but it was Mary Tasker who was blamed for the situation and she was sent to the assizes for a longer sentence. The newspapers, simultaneously accurate and myopic, concluded that the case showed 'the untold misery and suffering of little children as the result of having a drunken mother'.[21]

While this case was clearly unusual, it was by no means unique. There was a similar case in Stanley Street in 1906, and in 1910 the five chidren of Elizabeth George, who lived in Caerphilly Road, were sent to the workhouse while their mother was sent to Glamorgan Assizes for sentence for child cruelty. The children, aged between one and thirteen, were allegedly caked in dirt, the beds were verminous and the meat in the house was putrid although the children were said to be well fed. Again the immediate cause seems to have been alcohol since neighbours testified that she was a good mother when she had not been drinking. She had previously been gaoled for cruelty to children in 1907 although, as a widowed alcoholic with five children, it is not clear that gaol would do much to help the situation.[22]

These admittedly extreme cases highlight the central importance of women in creating and reproducing an ordered community and the collapse of the family if the woman gave way to alcohol.

In general, however, the material which is available draws a picture of an exciting and fulfilling childhood enjoyed by the generations raised in these families. Memories from the 1880s through to the 1920s and 1930s draw a remarkably similar and unchanging picture: even the advent of the car and lorry seem to have made little difference until after the Second World War since almost all traffic arrived in Senghennydd by rail, and local deliveries were almost all made by pony and cart. The changes are not between the earlier and later period, but between the periods of plenty and those of extreme hardship within each decade.

Children played in the streets and in the blackened brook which ran through Senghennydd. They climbed the hills and they played among the mountain streams, the wooded plantations and the remains of the prehistoric stones and circles which were being broken down by the influx into the valley. On the hillsides the reservoirs offered an alternative playground, while cattle and wild ponies grazed on Senghennydd Common on top of the hills.

In the village the chapels and the school organised a continuous series of events for the children: anniversaries, *gymanfa ganu,* eisteddfodau, concerts and street processions were part of the life of the village's children, bringing together the parents as well as the boys and girls for whom the festivals were organised. Travelling fairs and circuses visited for short periods, while swinging boats would remain for much of the summer.

Though he was writing of an earlier decade, one of the most evocative descriptions of childhood in a south Wales mining community remains that of Thomas Jones who was brought up in the neighbouring Rhymney Valley: as he writes, the 'games that children play are similar in all ages. . . I do not suppose that Rhymney has changed in this respect in fifty years' . . . .

. . . we played games, some in the High Street and some at the back of our house between it and the coalyard where a stream thickened with coal dust ran near some pig styes. We dammed its muddy waters into a pond and then suddenly opened the sluices and flooded the land, dooming our paper boats to instant destruction. We did this a thousand times and went home wild with joy, wet, dirty, excited, and as proud as the builders of the dams on the Nile.

We bowled iron hoops on the pavement, spun tops, stalked on stilts, stuck leather suckers on window panes, blew soap-bubbles out of saucers by means of a clay pipe, played marbles, leap frog, I spy. At the back of the house we played rounders and cricket and a game akin to them called 'bat and catty'. We flew kites and banged bladders about, which we got from the slaughter house of the company shop. Girls skipped and hopped on the pavement and played duckstones. . .

We played a bouncing rubber ball against the pine-end of a house, or we placed our caps on the ground in a row against the wall and pitched a ball into them from a distance of seven or eight feet. The boy in whose hat the ball rested had to pick it up and hit one of the others with it while they scampered away.

We played pranks, threading door knockers with black cotton and hiding in dark passages until scared away by the police or an irate housekeeper. There were tunnels to give spice to adventures, one under the surgery and Lawn, and one between the cemetery and Barracks Road. Or we went further afield near the isolated powder house, to a disused and forsaken pit-shaft into which we dropped stones and listened spell-bound to the resounding thuds as the stones struck the sides, fell into the booming waters, and sunk into eternity.

We watched the grown ups... and followed them with ferrets in their pockets and dogs at their heels when they went ratting around the pig styes. There were frequent cricket matches...

We had pancakes on Ash Wednesday and ducked for apples in the wooden wash-tub at Halloween. On wet days we dabbled with paint boxes and crayons which were more satisfying than freehand drawing, or we put gaily coloured pictures and transfers into scrap books, or played with photographs and a stereoscope...

For us children there were also annual excitements in the shape of Sanger's Circus, Wombwell's Menagerie, Poole's Myriorama, and Studt's Coach and Horses... The sight around the circus at night time was thrilling, the side shows lit with yellow naptha flares, the shouting showmen, the noisy merry-go-rounds, the shooting galleries, the boxing saloons (with a flaming tin man called Bill Samuel offering to fight with anybody for five pounds a side), the billy-fair play which provided a little mild gambling and rewarded the winner with a clock or a china dog for the penny risked. And of course there were quacks with infallible remedies.[23]

Memories like these are part of the story of most of the children of the Valleys in the times before the great depression of the 1920s, although girls may have been prevented from joining some of these activities, being expected to play a greater part in the home. The acts would change and the bigger circuses would have to be visited in Caerphilly or Pontypridd, but the experiences are part of the memories of all the older inhabitants and are recreated in the books of Morgan, Coombes, Lewis, Rhys Davies and others. The only part missing from Tom Jones's memoir is the annual outing to the beach at Barry Island or Weston-Super-Mare, the occasion of much exhilaration and strife and the subject of numerous descriptions in autobiographies and documentary novels.

In *Count Your Blessings,* Rhys Davies described the departure for the seaside:

Early in the morning the local station seethed with excited, shiny faces, bulging bags and baskets, which contained joints of meat, loaves of

A group of village children photographed in 1913.

Benton

bread, Caerphilly cheeses, fruit, and bottles of a smoky coloured liquid, cold tea. Slowly, with a subdued and frightened air, the train pulled in amid the screeching voices of the multitude and, pulling up with a quake, was immediately overflowing with a bawling mass of blue, white and red draperies, perspiring and frantic faces, tense legs and yellow straw hats. The prolonged wails of babies clawed protectively to hot breasts mingled with the abusive complaints of angry older women who could find no seats and the loud sexual cries of girls tickled advantageously in the crowd.[24]

Lewis Jones, in *Cwmardy,* describes the scene as the train arrived at the sea:

Never before had he seen ships, and his only sight of the sea had been the glimpses he occasionally had from the mountain-top of its glistening ribbon like winding around the coast. Its close proximity now gripped him like a dream. When the train arrived at the seaside station the sweat-soaked people poured out on the platform as if released from a steaming oven. Little children howled in the misery of damp clothes as their already wearied parents hurried them through the irritating sands to the beach. Here everyone sat down. The glare of the sun, flung back by the sea, blinded pit-darkened eyes for a while and forced tears where none were meant.

A nearby steam organ began to play. It filled the hot air with raucous noise, but the people soon caught its vague refrain and accompanied it with lusty singing. This stimulated their flagging spirits, and in a short time the receding tide was followed by bare-footed adults and children.[25]

And most chroniclers of valley life report that, while the adults and children amused each other, the adolescents, their senses heightened by the sensuous experience of heat and light, disappeared among the dunes.

The winter nights in the mining towns and pit villages could also be as exciting for the children as for their parents. Jack Jones described how, as an eleven year old in Merthyr,

when my eyes looked away from the theatre's frontage down the street the theatre of life was opened unto me. The gas-lit shops and public houses, the people moving along the pavements. The clip-clop of horses' hoofs on the metalled road; light laughter floating up to me. Stars thick as anything in the sky above. The night so full with promise, rich promise that almost made me cry—sometimes did make me cry for I knew not what.[26]

As the children grew up the pressures of adulthood enveloped them. The job of the mother in a large family would have been almost impossible without the assistance of older children, in particular the daughters. When necessary, children of only six or seven might be made to help in minding their younger brothers and sisters and were kept from school in order to do so. As girls grew into adolescence their role in keeping house for the rest of the family became increasingly formalised. After leaving school some girls might help in the shops and small businesses of the village and others worked as slaveys in the better off homes. The vast majority, however, filled their adolescence by working in their own homes, learning the skills of cooking, housekeeping and child rearing against the day when love, pregnancy, or the desire to escape from home, induced them to marry.

The adolescent boy was treated with tolerance and even the courts would relax their sternness faced by boys having a lively time. When a group of four teenagers were summonsed for wilful damage to fencing at the Windsor Colliery, the magistrates accepted that they were merely trying to reach the private colliery land on the other side and only made them pay a shilling each to repair the damage. More seriously two schoolboys, Willie Griffiths and David Thomas, smashed the insulation china on 23 telegraph poles on the Aber Valley railway line; even they got off fairly lightly, being fined five shillings each.[27]

There were instances of children organising quite sophisticated arrangements for disposing of the spoils of their carefully planned robberies. John Prosser and James Daniel Davies, both aged ten, managed to steal 11 pigeons from Edmund Evans, the licensee of the Universal Hotel, after breaking the lock of the pigeon house and removing the door. The boys intelligently waited until after the pigeons had been fed and settled for the night: in their soporific state the birds were more manageable. They had their buyers lined up and immediately sold two of them to Arthur Tilk, their schoolfellow, who paid one shilling and twopence for each bird. Unfortunately one of their friends squealed on them and the pair were caught. Their fate was sealed when Tilk, the receiver, turned King's evidence; the suspicion must be that he struck a deal with the police, since he was not prosecuted for receiving stolen goods. In view of the behaviour of the publicans of Senghennydd, it was perhaps shabby of the licensee of the Universal to testify against the boys, though he at least had the excuse of being the injured party and of being distraught over the fate of his pigeons.[28]

The transition from this world of exciting villainy to the underworld of the pit would have been intolerable if it had not been seen as a fulfilment by most boys. For most of them the initiation into adulthood was more abrupt and more frightening than the long drawn out involvement in housework, but it was an exhilarating fulfilment. The day when, at the age of fourteen, a boy went down the pit with his father was one of excitement. Almost all the recorded memories of miners agree on this, just as they agree that most parents wanted something else for their sons. Wil Jon Edwards contrasted the dullness of a dreary boys school with 'the friendly, helpful, comradely environment of underground life, a paradox if you like because it was only when I began to work in the darkness of the pit that the true light of learning shone'.[29]

The memories of miners' sons are full of hero worship for their fathers and of longing for the day when they would enter the man's world, helping and protecting their fathers from the endless small injuries with which they had returned from the pit over the years, and helping to feed the family. There was pride as they gave their first week's wages to their mother, being given two shillings pocket money in return. The emotions of many boys as they finished their first day in the pit is summed up in the memoirs of Joseph Keating, a south Wales collier who later became a journalist:

> My pride in being the associate of men could not be put into words. To be seen returning home at evening time with all the big miners and their boys, stained by dust and toil, was a thing that had, for years, filled my imagination as the most exalted achievement of a lifetime. Its heroic side did not concern me. . . . I wanted to be seen going home with the men from the pit, black, vivid black, so black as to be nearly invisible. . . .
>
> My wish was granted. I was seen by most of my friends in my black clothes, with my face black, my hands black, and my pit lamp and 'box-and-jack' black as I came home. My mother smiled at my comical appearance as I went into the house. But there was a sigh in her smile.
>
> 'God help us!' she said laughing, as she looked at me. 'He's as proud as a dog with two tails'.[30]

Though newcomers could be subjected to frightening initiation rites and humiliating practical jokes, miners often remember the care and gentleness with which older miners, and their own fathers, eased them into the life of the pit. The theme of the care with which older miners passed on their wisdom to the younger men is one which runs through all the literature.

Such care must have been all the greater relief in a world where the vicious habits of adolescent males could flourish in the miles of black tunnels and caverns. The world of adolescent initiation rites is not easily penetrated and there is no direct evidence that such rites occurred in the Universal; there is however evidence from other mines and it is a commonplace of young miners' story telling. Thus a Yorkshire miner reported:

> when we went down the pit we all had to go through our initiation ceremony, during which they used to pull our trousers down and examine our little sparrow. The size of that was very important. If we were well endowed, we were looked on with great respect; if we had a poor, weedy little thing, they used to cover it with fat and make fun of us for days, or else they used to paint it and hang a bit of a band on it and all sorts of things. . .[31]

There was also a more explicit sexuality, though one which has, inevitably, left few traces behind for the observer. In 1910 a newcomer to a Durham Colliery 'went to the place where putters and drivers assembled for their baits (lunches) and in so doing surprised two adolescents, RH and CC, who were on their backs masturbating in competition to find out which could produce an orgasm first'.[32] In the miners' pub, such stories will be told in the early hours once the beer has had its effect. In the close atmosphere no-one can miss the occasional physical relationship, sometimes between youngsters and the middle aged. But such things are taboo and are not to be spoken about: they leave no evidence behind.

Most parents would be appalled by the behaviour expected in adolescent sub-cultures: perhaps it is a mercy that parents are, in the main, able to hide from the details of this passing stage, however much the patterns and attitudes of adolescence may affect the relationships of the grown person.

In these children the hopes of their parents were reborn from the hardship and bitterness of the years. It was through the home, comfortable, ordered, traditional and disciplined that a new generation was raised through which those values would come to dominate the community even at a time when its prosperity and even the reason for its existence was waning: the values of the chapels and the union, brought together and inculcated in the home, would colour the labour movement and working class education throughout Britain as the emigration from the valleys gathered momentum in the 1920s and 1930s.

CHAPTER 7
   [1] B. L. Coombes, (1939), *op cit,* 21
   [2] B. P. Davies, *They made a People,* (Cardiff; 1947), 10
   [3] GFP 22/7/1910: CJ 17/8/1911
   [4] CJ 20/2/1913
   [5] GFP 9/7/1898: GFP 6/1/1900: CJ 31/10/1912: GRO Eglwysilan Parish Register:
GRO Medical Officer of Health for Caerphilly, *Annual Report,* (1904), 8-11.
   [6] CJ 9/12 1909
   [7] GFP 12/4/1902

[8] GRO Medical Officer of Health for Caerphilly, *Annual Report,* (1905), 13: GFP 15/8/1903; CJ 26/1/1911; CJ 18/2/1909

[9] GRO Medical Officer of Health for Caerphilly, *Annual Report,* (1905), 3: PP 1913, Cd 6909, XXXII, 7

[10] GRO; Eglwysilan Parish Register

[11] *ibid*

[12] *ibid*

[13] *ibid*

[14] CJ 9/1/1913

[15] CJ 20/4/1911; CJ 27/4/1911

[16] CJ 1/12/1910

[17] CJ 7/7/1904

[18] W. H. Davies, (1972), *op cit,* 59

[19] *ibid,* 51

[20] F. Smith, *op cit,* 113

[21] GFP 16/4/1904: Girls' School Log, 15/7/1903

[22] GFP 23/2/1906; CJ 20/10/1910; C. Chinn, *op cit,* 17

[23] Thomas Jones, *Rhymney Memories;* (1970), 53-7: W. H. Davies, *Ups and Downs,* (Swansea; 1975), 115-9

[24] R. Davies (1932), *op cit,* 10

[25] Lewis Jones (1978), *op cit,* 33-4

[26] Jack Jones, *Unfinished Journey,* (London; 1937), 61-2

[27] GFP 14/6/1905

[28] GFP 30/1/1904

[29] R. Morgan, (1981), 62: J. Keating, *My Struggle for Life,* (London; 1916), 53: W. H. Davies, (1975), *op cit,* 90-1: W. J. Edwards, *op cit,* 16

[30] J. Keating, *op cit,* 53

[31] J. Benson, (1980), *op cit,* 32

[32] *ibid,* 32

Chapter Eight
Politics

As the chapels were part of the general social life of the town so too politics was often a continuation of social activity by other means. A variety of political activities was promoted by the parties, clubs, chapels and schools. Debates were organised in the chapels on the right to strike, votes for women, disestablishment, land taxation and a range of other topics.[1] Politics was also a major topic in the pubs, on occasion providing yet another reason for ending up in court: in January 1904, Peter Stevens was prosecuted for using bad language in public. His explanation for his behaviour was that he had got over-excited in the course of a political debate. The chairman of the bench primly told Stevens that he had 'no objection to him speaking politics but that bad language must not be included', before fining him ten shillings.[2]

Senghennydd was founded and developed at the high point of the Liberal supremacy in Wales. This supremacy, closely associated with nonconformity, grew with the combined attack on the supposedly tyrannical power and entrenched rights of the rural landlords and of the established anglican Church. After the extensions of the franchise in 1867 and 1884 non-conformist liberals defeated apparently unbeatable Tory members of parliament in a series of famous elections. In several notorious incidents Liberal tenant farmers were then evicted by their Tory landlords, leading to an, ultimately successful, campaign for the secret ballot. In each case Tory support for the state church, imperialist foreign policy and the maintenance of the established order of society was confronted with nonconformist liberalism and Welsh cultural nationalism, battles which reached a peak in the Merthyr elections between 1868 and 1885. Sir William Lewis was directly involved in this confrontation since he stood as what was tactfully declared as the Independent, (a euphemism for Tory), candidate for Merthyr in the general election of 1880. The gap between him and his opponents, many of them members of the Temperance Movement, was indicated by the fact that the main plank in his election platform was opposition to the Sunday Closing Bill for Wales; a bill that was important not only as a step in the nonconformist attack on drunkenness but also as the first piece of legislation to acknowledge the political and cultural division between England and Wales. Lewis was defeated in an election which 'resulted in extreme violence and disorder. . . In Aberdare the Riot Act was read, and the crowds dispersed with police batons'.[3]

A significant factor in the Liberal hegemony in Wales was the growth first of Welsh cultural nationalism and then, by analogy with the movement for Irish home rule, of the demand for autonomous Welsh political institutions. The former was characterised by the campaign for a Welsh university and for the National Library. The movement towards political autonomy was expressed by the growth of a 'Welsh Party' in Parliament and of a growing campaign for a degree of autonomy, led by Thomas Ellis and David Lloyd George. In its day Welsh nonconformist liberalism was a brave movement, committed to extending the franchise and defending a supposedly classless Welsh culture. The essential nature of Welsh Liberalism at this time was, it has been claimed, 'a revolt against a static, hierarchical social order' and its radical democratic language had gained the allegiance of the working classes in the valleys by the time Senghennydd was founded in the 1890s.[4]

The member of parliament for East Glamorgan, the constituency of which Senghennydd formed a part, was Alfred Thomas who was in the mainstream of these forces in Wales. He was first elected for the constituency in 1885 and represented precisely that brand of Welsh nonconformity to which Sir William Lewis was so opposed, though both were industrialists and businessmen from similar backgrounds. Alfred Thomas was born in 1840 and was a lifelong Baptist. He 'entered the business of his father, a contractor and owner of a limeworks at Llandough, near Cardiff, assisted in the construction of the Rhondda Fach branch of the Taff Vale Railway, and carried on the lime works for a number of years; ultimately [he] devoted himself entirely to public and semi philanthropic work'. He was a Gladstonian Liberal, President of the Welsh Baptist Union in 1886, accepted a knighthood in 1902, and was created Lord Pontypridd in 1912, the year after Sir William Lewis became Lord Merthyr. In some ways the careers of the two of them were symmetrical.[5]

By the time that Senghennydd was beginning to take on the characteristics of a permanent settlement Alfred Thomas had already been the MP for the constituency for ten years. He attended various functions in the new village with its rapidly growing number of electors and he enjoyed encouraging the children and performing before the respectable chapel going adults; his personality expanded in the role of patron. His status in pit villages like Senghennydd was very different from that of MPs in a later period. In these villages his presence at special events was a matter of major significance of which the whole community would be aware. Other M.P.s might describe him as 'that worthy old pantaloon', and historians may dismiss him as 'patently a figurehead' or as 'quiescent and picturesque', but in Senghennydd he found a forum for his interest and his patronage. The extent of his power and concern is indicated by the well established report that it was his nomination which had secured the much sought after position of sub-postmistress for Miss Elizabeth Bussell.[6]

In 1902 Alfred Thomas spoke effectively at a packed meeting in the Senghennydd Welsh Baptist Chapel in support of the slate miners of the Penrhyn Quarries in north Wales who had been involved in a year long strike against the almost feudal position of Lord Penrhyn. From the point of view of the Senghennydd miners Alfred Thomas hit exactly the right note, attacking the autocratic power of this great Tory industrialist who was also a hereditary landowner. He was speaking after a serious dispute between Sir William Lewis and the miners at the Universal Colliery, and the people of Senghennydd almost certainly read into his words an attack on Sir William. Thomas assaulted the class legislation of the Government and then laid about the reactionary Lord Penrhyn. In his peroration, delivered to the applause of his audience, Thomas declared that 'Lord Penrhyn owned the land, the houses, the chapel—in fact everything in that district, except the manhood of the men, and they would not sell that to him'. Thomas's speech gave the impression that Welsh Liberalism was coming to terms with the industrial problems which were the basic issue confronting his constituents. This was largely an illusion, for the real target of Thomas, himself an industrialist, was not the depradations of industrialists but rather Lord Penrhyn, the feudal landowner, who happened also to be an industrialist.[7]

The gap was to become clear in Senghennydd. When, in 1913, a Liberal Club was opened, the opening speech by Clem Edwards M.P. did not focus on the rights of working people, but on the proposal to tax land values, an old policy based on the assumption that while landowners were simply exploitative, industrialists were the creators of wealth and prosperity. When, two months later, the Liberal Club held a public lecture, the subject was still 'The Land Question'.[8]

Alfred Thomas was a long standing member of the movement for a degree of Welsh autonomy and for the development of independent Welsh institutions, although he has suffered for his reputation as 'the worthy though unimaginative Baptist who represented East Glamorgan'.[9] He had 'fought unsuccessfully in the Commons for a measure of autonomy for Wales. In 1890 he pressed for the creation of a Secretaryship of State for Wales, and in 1892 his National Institutions (Wales) Bill sought in addition to establish in Wales a National Council, a separate Education Department, a Local Government Board and a National Museum'.[10]

Such views were kept, however, for meetings of Welsh speakers and like minded nonconformists. A large number of the Senghennydd electorate were not Welsh by birth or commitment, and were not religious. Without the support of the mining population of south Wales there was no chance that a modern Wales would achieve autonomy. There is little evidence that Thomas attempted to alter the views of these working class constituents to accept the need for a degree of Welsh political autonomy. The nationalism of the 1880s was rooted in the old nonconformity of the countryside: Thomas and his colleagues lacked the vision necessary to transform it into a policy which could unite the new Wales. Their vision of a Welsh nation therefore faded from the serious agenda of British politics, as their emphasis on the old heroic struggle against landlordism and the long saga of the campaign for the disestablishment of the state church waned into insignificance for most voters. The irony is that a Welsh dimension to the politics of the valleys may have been necessary if the needs of their inhabitants and the intelligent exploitation of mineral resources was to be considered against the drive for immediate profits which fuelled the thinking of most coalowners. It is no coincidence that D. A. Thomas, Lewis's cousin and rival, had been an early Liberal supporter of a degree of Welsh autonomy. His proposals for a cartel of coalowners to limit production was designed to raise prices, and therefore profits and wages, but also indicated a first modest way in which resources could be used for the good of the national community even within the existing structures of a capitalist market.

While Welsh Liberal nonconformity was failing to set a relevant programme for the valleys, (and without such a dimension it must also therefore have been an irrelevance for the Welsh nation as a whole for which the Liberals wished to speak), the growing labour movement largely ignored the Welsh national dimension. Instead the socialists confronted the ravages of British industrial capitalism with a progamme on a British scale, a scale in which the needs of the valleys could all too easily be forgotten.

In the past it was a cliche that this period in the history of the Welsh Valleys saw the decline of Liberalism, the growth of Labour, the irrelevance of Conservatism and the marginalisation of the suffragette movement in the overwhelmingly male dominated politics of the valleys. The reality is more complex. The Conservatives showed great energy and, while they were ineffective in terms of gaining parliamentary seats, they continued to have a considerable impact within the community. They did this despite the Liberal non-conformist traditions which equated toryism with ungodliness. In the 1880s, for example, the Monmouthshire Baptist Association pressed members 'to be loyal to their consciences and to the Saviour in the polling booth. . . and not to fail to record their votes in favour of the Liberal candidates'; Mathetes (John Jones) had asserted that 'the apostles were all anti-Tories' and a minister declared, of the Welsh Counties which leant towards conservatism, that 'their names stink and their memory will be accursed. I despise them as much as the beast with ten horns'.[11]

The Senghennydd Conservatives were subjected to a similar barrage of contempt from the two local papers, the *Glamorgan Free Press* and the *Caerphilly Journal.* In 1905 there was a scornful attack on the local Tories when 'the second annual farce entitled 'a Conservative Miners Demonstration' was given on the Common, Pontypridd'. The participants were, according to the *Caerphilly Journal,* brought in by train from outside the coalfield and in any event they were not miners. The *Glamorgan Free Press* said that it would be remembered in Pontypridd 'as the day on which the town was invaded by an army of men, of ignoble mien, of doubtful politics but undeniable thirst'. Equally there was an outcry when one of the local brass bands in the Aber Valley played for a Conservative candidate. Such behaviour on the part of the band was considered to be in extremely 'bad taste', and it was reported that 'considerable indignation exists among sections of the inhabitants'.[12]

Despite this, largely rhetorical, contempt the local Conservatives were full of life in Senghennydd. They had the advantage of a Conservative Club before the Liberals started one. The club, like many others in East Glamorgan and the Rhondda, was founded by John Littlejohn, the Conservative agent for the constituencies, 'a gentleman noted for his "polysyllabic verbosity"'. He made up for his wordiness by his ferocious energy in arguing the Conservative case in local politics and in the trade unions and won the grudging respect even of his Labour opponents. The club achieved a membership of 500 before the Great War although this entailed the embarrassment of occasional court appearances when the club was rent by a typical Senghennydd fracas.[13] The *Glamorgan Free Press* claimed that these clubs were 'formed to spread the doctrine of keeping workers down, but this obnoxious doctrine is covered by copious draughts of ale. The members get so fond of this ale that their vision becomes dimmed, they taste the ale but do not see the evil they are helping to keep up'. The Senghennydd Club's activities suggest, however, that it was more than a front organisation for bribing the electors with Tory beer, as their opponents claimed. Primrose Day was always celebrated by singing and a lecture, often on Disraeli and often given by John Littlejohn. The local papers satirised the diminutive size, frock coats and top hats of Littlejohn and his lieutenant; ('they were so disguised as gentlemen that one could hardly make them out'); but even the local press had grudgingly to admire the 'immense energy' of the Conservative agent.[14] In June 1912 the members of the Club organised an outing which involved walking to Caerphilly from where they took a train to Cardiff in order to hear the great F. E. Smith speaking. They no doubt enjoyed Smith's devastating contempt for attempts to dismember the British union: in a later debate over new Welsh national institutions he was to oppose change on the grounds that 'we [have] muddled along tolerably well for ten centuries'. There is no record of a drunken return so this may have been a *bona fide* political outing though it no doubt included a few well deserved pints after the walk to Caerphilly. The Conservatives were quite capable of holding their own in the local exchange of invective and of landing some well aimed insults on the Liberal Party.[15]

The man who, as much as anyone, stood for Conservative values in the area was Colonel Morgan Lindsay C.B. of Ystrad Fawr, Ystrad Mynach, and of Pencerrig House, Radnorshire. By birth and marriage he was part of the old-established local squirearchy, raised to astonishing wealth by the quirks of geology and genes. Landowner, soldier, horseman, justice of the peace and chairman of the Caerphilly Borough Council he carried considerable influence in the affairs of the district long after the agricultural society on which his position was based had ceased to exist. After the Marquis of Bute, Lindsay and his cousin, Clara Thomas, were among the main landowners of the district.[16] Colonel Lindsay and his kind would, however, have had much less influence had their traditionalism not been echoed by that of a large number of working class people, reflected by the likes of Dick Hamar, staunch supporter of the miners' union and of the Conservative Club. Wil Jon Edwards wrote of his sister,

> a stout conservative Liza, a Liza as grimly conservative in her own way and in her outlook as Lord Curzon, Liza the keeper of the tribal mysteries including Mam's thoughts and the chapel's thoughts. Liza who could say what she thought about agitations and drive a man half mad; and yet a Liza, being a woman, who could be sweet and pleasant when occasions demanded both, as, for instance, when Keir Hardie and Dennis Hird called to eat Welsh cakes, and to drink tea and sing.[17]

The pattern at local elections is difficult to analyse since at that period many candidates, and in particular Conservatives, stood as 'independents' although their political sympathies were well understood. At local elections these 'independents' made a significant impression. Edward Shaw, the manager of the mine, consistently won one of the three seats in the Senghennydd Ward of Caerphilly Urban District Council. In 1911 five candidates stood for the three Senghennydd seats; Edward Shaw, the Manager and by 1911 also the Agent for the mine; Towyn Jones the Liberal shopkeeper, pioneer of Senghennydd and veteran of the Chamber of Commerce; a Mr Parker who stood as a ratepayers' candidate against Council waste; Thomas James a former Lib-Lab candidate, now Labour, and the brother of Catherine James; and John Davies a miner, standing for Labour.[18] The results were:

Edward Shaw	619
Thomas James	400
John Davies	346
Towyn Jones	315
Parker	118

It may be that much of the vote for Shaw represented a personal vote for a man who, despite his unenviable position between Sir William Lewis and the miners, and despite the catastrophe of 1901, had won the sympathy of the voters by his immense commitment to the activities of the local community, his personal courage in 1901 and by his willingness to defend individual colliers when he felt it was right. Moreover as a committed Baptist and also the agent of Sir William Lewis he was able to draw on the loyalties of both nonconformists and Tories. Whatever the reason it was clearly an interesting result, as was the narrow defeat of Towyn Jones by the Labour candidate. In local elections this marked the point at which the new Labour Party began to take over from the Liberals. The combination of Thomas James as the local Labour councillor with Hubert Jenkins as the Labour county councillor, both of them previously Lib-Lab, was to become a stable and unbeatable combination. Even so the performance of the local mine manager was not simply an aberration or a final residue of nineteenth century patterns for when Shaw retired during the war his place both as manager and as a local councillor was taken by William Kestell who was to be equally involved in the life of the local community. Robert Rees, the agent of the mine until Edward Shaw took over, was also an active member of the Pontypridd Board of Guardians.

In making the break from the Lib-Lab alliance the local Labour politicians did not necessarily change their attitudes to their constituents. In 1909 Hubert Jenkins, speaking at Salem Welsh Baptist Chapel, summarised his record of the last three years, and managed to include some forthright comments about the dangerous and unhealthy state of the back lanes in the village and about the refuse which was dumped in them: '[I] might say in passing that if each householder would only take a little interest and pride in the portion of back lane directly behind their own premises the sanitary condition of the place would improve, and would possibly save expense'.[19]

The audience had immediate revenge for this *lese majeste* of the sovereign people by their servant and representative. Jenkins went on to develop the theme, in a somewhat martyred tone, that, as a result of the council's overspending for the good of the electorate, it was possible that councillors would be surcharged and bankrupted. Jenkins, evidently expecting a wave of sympathy for his self sacrifice,

Councillor Thomas James.

announced that in this event he 'would possibly have to pay some of the liability in Cardiff [prison]'. He was clearly taken aback when the audience showed their appreciation with hearty laughter and he responded with asperity that 'he believed he was truly representing the wishes of the electors in this respect'.

By 1912 when Sir Alfred Thomas was raised to the peerage as Lord Pontypridd, the Labour Party, independent of the old Lib-Lab arrangement, was gaining ground. In September 1909 the Party had held a lively demonstration in Caerphilly at which the main speaker was Keir Hardie and in 1910 the Independent Labour Party organised a Summer Campaign programme in the district.[20] Although Clement Edwards, who followed Sir Alfred Thomas as the Liberal candidate, successfully held the seat, it was already clear that the Liberals could no longer count on dominating the constituency in quite the same way.

Studies on the way the electorate voted in the East Glamorgan constituency confirm the complexity of party loyalties, a picture confused by the still restricted franchise. The total electorate was 23,979 of whom, it is estimated, 12,980 were miners; the miners thus composed 54% of the electorate.[21] In a predominantly working class constituency a significant proportion of the other voters would also have been trade unionists on the railways and in industries related to mining. Sir Alfred Thomas was re-elected without opposition in the general election of 1906. In the election of January 1910 he was challenged by a Tory, Major F. H. Gaskell; the Liberal vote was 14,721 and the Conservative vote was 5,727. In the December election of 1910 the voters were, for the first time, given three choices. Clement Edwards took over from Sir Alfred Thomas as the Liberal candidate; Major Gaskell again stood for the Conservatives, and C. B. Stanton, a populist left-wing miners' leader, stood for the Labour Party. The result of the election was;

Clement Edwards	9,088
F. H. Gaskell	5,603
C. B. Stanton	4,675

If only a quarter of Stanton's vote came from trade unionists other than miners and from other working class voters, then Stanton won only about 33% of the miners' vote for the Labour Party. The vote for Stanton in the first election in which Labour contested the seat was enough to confirm that the Labour Party would make a significant impact on the constituency; this came as no surprise to anyone. On the other hand the votes for Edwards and Gaskell show the depth of loyalty to other parties, since neither candidate could claim long standing personal loyalty from the electorate.

Although the cause of disestablishment was reaching a climax, Welsh political autonomy was not a major election issue in 1910 since the only proposals for autonomy related to a Wales which was receding into history. The distinctive Welsh movement had faded as first Thomas Ellis and then Lloyd George attained front bench positions within British politics.

'Clem' Edwards was never to achieve the close involvement with Senghennydd that Alfred Thomas had taken for granted: certainly there is no hint that he had sufficient prestige to be able to use his patronage on behalf of supplicants for important posts such as the sub-postmistressship of the village. It may be that just as Sir William Lewis felt that he had created Senghennydd through his industrial strategy, so Sir Alfred Thomas felt paternalistic about the village which, in its social existence, had been nurtured by the Liberalism and nonconformity of which he was the local patron.

Nevertheless, Clement Edwards appeared to be the ideal choice for the Liberals. He was born in 1869 into a Radnorshire farming family with small local business interests. This was a classic background for Welsh radical liberal politicians and, although his family was Anglican, religious doubts led Edwards to join the Congregationalists. He battled his way to become a journalist and, after moving to London, saw the hardship and suffering of the East End. He played a significant part in the development of the 'new unionism' in the 1890s as a journalist, organiser, lawyer and writer. His activities were in direct confrontation with the policies of Sir William Lewis since one of Edwards's 'campaigns on behalf of trade unionism was his vigorous exposure of the strike breaking organisations of the 1890s', in which Sir William was the leading figure, and Edwards was probably the author of *Free Labour Frauds: a study in dishonesty*. Edwards had given genuinely distinguished service to the trade unions and to the Liberal Party as the MP for Denbigh Boroughs from 1906 to 1910: it was unfortunate that, by the time he came to East Glamorgan, he should be confronted with a brand of trade unionism with which he was wholly out of sympathy.[22]

Finally, towering over the community without the need for the sound and fury of elections, was Sir Thomas Lewis himself who, in 1911, was raised to the peerage as Lord Merthyr of Senghennydd. In part his choice of title referred to his achievement in conjuring a community into existence where before there had only been bog, woodland, hill pasture and streams. But even more it referred back to the medieval Senghennydd which was the domain of his ancestors. The feudal fiefdom of Senghennydd had stretched from the sea at Cardiff to Dowlais on the outskirts of modern Merthyr, consisting of the commotes of Senghennydd Uwch-Caiach, Senghennydd Is-Caiach and Cibwr. In 1158 Ifor ap Meurig, known as Ifor Bach, to whom Sir Thomas Lewis traced his ancestry, captured Cardiff Castle from the Norman English and extracted concessions which gave semi-independence to the old *cantref* of Senghennydd. In the mind of the 'black baron', the scourge of the trade unions, was a romantic vision of the rule of the Welsh chiefs, iron but just, whose heritage he sought to symbolise in the hereditary title which he was shortly to pass down to his descendants. To the Welsh Nation has descended the collection of medieval titles and documents, uncovered by J. S. Corbett and others, with which Sir William Lewis sought to buttress his dreams.[23]

In the real world of the twentieth century changes were however occuring in Senghennydd over which Sir William had little control. As noted above the cause of votes for women had been nurtured in the area for many years. In 1902, in a debate with the residents of Abertridwr, Catherine James put the case for women's suffrage and the result was strongly in favour of votes for women. The newspaper congratulated her but was surprised by her ability as a speaker which, the report managed to imply, was rather unfair: 'Miss James obtained a decided advantage over her opponent, her remarkable oratorical powers being considerably to her advantage'.[24]

Over the years 'Miss James of Senghennydd' remained a powerful voice in the district. In 1909, for example, she was active in the cause addressing a large suffragette meeting in Caerphilly which was attended by various local councillors, including the ubiquitous Charles Goodfellow.[25]

Despite the work done in this period, the local paper could still report, of a large meeting in 1910, that 'many came out of curiosity to hear women speak'. By then the peaceful element of the movement had the support of many in local politics though some of the arguments were presented in the male language of politics at the time. Thus Alderman Evans announced that 'he had always been the friend of girls' education', and argued that 'no fabric could be built on a firm foundation without the men and women acting together. The women would also help the men to be men'. The last remark gained applause and laughter, though it is not clear that the aim of the movement was to encourage men to be men, rather than encouraging them to be people. The emphasis was on education, a theme set perhaps by the presence of Miss Winifred James, headmistress of Hengoed School. Alderman Evans claimed that the admission of women to London University had been 'the beginning of the end of the oppression of women, and the beginning of their emancipation'. Even if his analysis was over optimistic, it is interesting to hear the dignified alderman using the language of oppression.[26]

Winifred James's ideas were distinctly traditional apart from the claim about the rights of women. She articulated some of those ideas at her speech at prize day at Hengoed School, in the presence of Lord and Lady Aberdare. On that occasion she argued that girls should stay at school until they were nineteen so that they would have 'a definite idea of duty and with a purpose in life', and 'be able to give a good account of themselves'. 'The best form of socialism was the highest individualism', she claimed, and she praised organisations such as the League of Empire and the Young Helpers League as the sort of organisations to which her girls should belong.[27]

By 1910 the local papers had recovered from their shock over Catherine James's speaking ability, and reported, as though it was a matter of course, that the three speakers at a meeting at Beulah Chapel should be Sir Alfred Thomas, Professor Edwards and Miss James of Senghennydd. There was still however the unconsciously patronising rider, that James was there to speak 'from the woman's point of view'.[28] The road to equality was to be a long one in the valleys where the nature of employment gave dominance to the male worker and the miners' union.

CHAPTER 8
1. CJ 15/2/1912
2. GFP 10/1/1904
3. R. Grant, *The Parliamentary History of Glamorgan*, (Swansea; 1978), 57-8
4. D. G. Evans, *op cit,* 304
5. R. Grant, *op cit,* 255
6. K. O. Morgan, (1970), *op cit,* 167, 197, 241
7. CJ 11/7/1903
8. CJ 23/1/1913; 20/3/1913
9. K. O. Morgan, (1970), *op cit,* 109
10. R. Grant, *op cit,* 64
11. T. Bassett, *op cit,* 308, 299, 307
12. GFP 17/6/1905: CJ 20/1/1910
13. J. E. Morgan, *op cit,* 48-9: *Glamorgan County Times,* 21/1/1922: CJ 29/2/1912
14. GFP 17/6/1905: CJ 24/4/1913: GFP 17/6/1905
15. CJ 6/6/1912: K. Morgan, (1970), *op cit,* 292: CJ 8/2/1912
16. D. G. Sellwood, *op cit,* 9
17. W. J. Edwards, *op cit,* 232
18. CJ 23/2/1911
19. CJ 18/2/1909
20. CJ 2/9/1909: CJ 16/6/1910
21. R. Gregory, *The Miners and British Politics,* (Oxford; 1968), 141
22. B. Nield, DLB vol III, 69-77
23. W. Rees, 'Records of the Lordship of Senghenydd', *South Wales and Monmouthshire Record Society,* (1957 no 4) 33-5: M. R. D. Jones 'The Welsh Rulers of Senghenydd', *Caerphilly,* (1971; no 3), 16-18: NLR Lord Merthyr Archive, 359, 360 & 361
24. GFP 10/5/1902
25. CJ 4/11/1909
26. CJ 3/3/1910
27. CJ 14/4/1910
28. CJ 13/1/1910

Chapter Nine
The Union

The years after the strike of 1898 and the disaster of 1901 had brought important changes to the south Wales Coalfield as a whole and to the Senghennydd Colliery in particular. One historian has argued that the settlement of 1898 'was a personal victory for Sir William Thomas Lewis': but Sir William's very dominance was the catalyst for his final defeat for among both coalowners and miners there was a backlash against his rule.

The miners' defeat of 1898 achieved what years of argument had failed to bring about. The small unions and branches which were spread around the coalfield agreed to unite in a single union, the South Wales Miners' Federation or 'Fed', based on a lodge structure. Their common aim was to end the Sliding Scale Agreement and to affiliate to the Miners' Federation of Great Britain. From now on the survival of the 'Fed' was to be the first requirement of all action. The Union was the essential defence against increased exploitation and it was the organisational basis of all new claims for improved conditions and legislation. The attempt to build the union took place, however, in one of the most difficult periods for British trade unions.

Since the 1870s trade unions had appeared to enjoy a degree of immunity from civil claims for damages by employers whose profits were affected by strike action, even if the strike occurred while a contract existed between employers and workers. In 1900 the workers on the Taff Vale Railway Company, the largest of the railway companies in the coalfield, went on strike. The railway workers union organised picketing to counter the strike-breakers employed by the company, strike breakers provided by the National Free Labour Association of which Sir William Lewis was a driving force. The Taff Vale Railway company sued the union for damages and was awarded £23,000, a judgement which meant that, in practice, workers would be unable to strike while a contract was in existence with their employers. Senghennydd was one of the collieries where that inter-pretation of the law was to be challenged by the miners.[1]

It was inevitable that loyalty to the newly founded South Wales Miners' Federation should bring the Senghennydd miners into direct confrontation with Sir William Lewis. The confrontation extended from union membership, through membership of the different insurance and health schemes to which miners could belong, to safety issues. None of these issues was entirely separable from the others.

It is unlikely that the Senghennydd men would have maintained such a determined position in the struggle to establish and defend their union had it not been for the personality of their new check-weighman, Hubert Jenkins, who was to play a major part in the life of Senghennydd and the Aber Valley for the next forty years. Jenkins was born in rural Herefordshire in 1866. He worked as a miner from the age of thirteen and took part in his first long strike at the age of seventeen. He moved to Caerphilly in 1884 and worked in various local pits. Already in the mid 1880s, when he was still less than twenty, Jenkins was a delegate to the Caerphilly District Committee of the local miners' unions. Trade unionism was quiescent in south Wales at that time, as a result of the operation of the sliding scale, and an enthusiastic youngster was liable to find himself catapulted onto a number of semi-dormant committees.

Jenkins then went to America for three years, working in various mines in Ohio. He helped to found and became the acting secretary of a lodge of the United Mineworkers of America. When he returned from America in 1890, he again worked in the Caerphilly District becoming secretary of his lodge and he married in the same year. Photographs of him and his wife, even those taken in old age, show them as a handsome couple and as a pair they made a major contribution to the Aber Valley over the years. Like many other miners Hubert Jenkins had to move to different mines to escape from the petty victimisation of some employers against active trade unionists: the nature of coalmining made it very easy to allocate difficult and dangerous work, which would reduce wages, to specific men. It was against this possibility that the short strike at the Universal Colliery in 1897 had been directed.

During the 1898 coalfield strike the mine in which Jenkins worked was not affected since the company was not a member of the Monmouthshire and South Wales Mine Owners' Association. Jenkins played a major part in organising support for the striking miners from those still in work. It is evidence of his energy and personality that, although he had not been on strike, he was never-theless chosen as acting secretary to the East Glamorgan District of the new union. This was an unpaid role and he still had to find paid work to support his union activities.

Jenkins was elected as miners' checkweighman by the Senghennydd men in 1902 and their mood perceptibly changed in the following period. He was not the man to lead trade unionists into industrial action simply to make gestures, but nor was he a disciple of Mabon: 'he was always an advocate of settlement by conciliation and negotiation in preference to strikes, but he was not a "a peace at any price" trade unionist'.[2]

After 1901 the men made determined efforts to force all miners to join the union, a necessary part of the battle to ensure that safety and earnings together reached an optimum level: the two issues were inextricably linked since the method of piece work payments put pressure on everyone in the mines to take risks as far as safety was concerned. The Universal Colliery was one of several in which there was a sustained campaign to ensure that all colliers who enjoyed the benefits won by the union should contribute to the union both financially and by submitting themselves to the necessary, if sometimes unpleasant, disciplines which collective action entails.

On 16th June 1903 a delegation led by Hubert Jenkins met Edward Shaw and told him that the union members would refuse to enter the mine in the same cage as non-unionists, a practice tolerated by the management in some collieries.[3] The men wanted separate queues for non-unionists in order to expose them to moral pressure. Instead of giving the clear answer which he must have known would be the policy of Sir William, Shaw called in Robert Rees, the agent (or managing director) of the mine. Rees made it clear that he would not allow any such thing and that the owners would make no distinction between unionists and non-unionists. On the weekend of June 21st the management put up notices at the pithead announcing that they would take proceedings against anyone absenting themselves from work on Monday 22nd, a statement which may have worried those who habitually needed Monday off to recover from their weekend drinking.

On Monday Rees was present with Shaw when the morning shift arrived; it was a pleasant July morning as the sun rose above the hills which surrounded the stark machinery and corrugated iron buildings at the pit head. As the men gathered to descend the pit, the trade union members showed their cards. They formed up in ranks and some entered the cage at 6.30. At that point men without cards entered the cage; they were presumed to be non-unionists and the rest of the men refused to enter the cage with them. When it was full the cage descended. The names of miners who had refused to enter with non-unionists were taken down by the overman.

When the cage returned, the men who had refused to go down with the non-unionists said that they would now go down in the empty cage but Rees and Shaw refused to let them: 'No, we can't do that. You were told that unless you got into the cage in the ordinary course, you would not be allowed to go down now. The other men must come on in their turn'. Only two, however, were prepared to get into the cage beside the two or three non-unionists who had entered. Finally the cage descended with the five men instead of the normal twenty.

What was intended as a gesture to bring pressure to bear on fellow miners, was rapidly becoming a demonstration by Sir William's agents of the powers of management. If their own tactics had been thought out by the miners it was clear that Rees and Shaw were also following a carefully planned strategy.

Rees and Shaw now went along the ranks asking the rest of the men to get into the cage, but when it returned none would enter. It was now 6.40 and for twenty minutes the cage stood empty. 480 lamps had been given out but only thirty men had descended the pit leaving about 450 men waiting on the surface. Since no-one else followed, the trade unionists who were already down the mine now decided to return to the surface to join their colleagues. In all ten miners worked on that Monday. The demonstration was repeated at 6.00 on Tuesday morning. Later in the day a deputation called on Shaw and reiterated the point that no miners would work until all the men joined the union. Shaw repeated the position of Sir William Lewis. The men remained out throughout the week but returned to work the following Monday. The action had undoubtedly been effective in demonstrating the broad unity and discipline of the miners and in bringing pressure to bear on all the men to join the union. The success of such tactics was, however, partly in the hands of the courts, and both sides awaited the outcome of a case in which the company sued 402 colliers for £2 each in damages and lost profits for the week. The prosecution was brought under the 1875 Employers' and Workmen's Act.

The cases were heard on 14th July at Caerphilly Magistrates' Court. The company claimed lost profits for the day shift, based on a weekly profit for the whole mine of £1,219 made from the average weekly production of 6,563 tons of coal. The men's solicitor, W. Nicholas, admitted a breach of contract, but argued that the bench should give only token damages, since 'the non-unionists' conduct must be judged as manifestly unfair, seeing that they sought to obtain the benefits without sharing the burdens'. Nicholas was also sceptical of the figures put forward by the company; 'with regard to the output of coal, he knew there was a jealousy among colliery companies showing their books and therefore he must accept the figures regardless of the basis on which they had been worked out'. The Court decided in favour of the Company and awarded damages of over £800 against the miners.[4]

The liberal *Glamorgan Free Press* reported the case under the heading 'Non-Unionism at Senghenydd', while the Conservative *Western Mail* used the rather more catchy headline, 'Federation Tyranny'. In a rampant editorial the paper, founded by the Bute Estate, attacked the men in a welter of chauvinistic abuse; they were unmanly, un-British and tyrannical. The Senghennydd workers were held up as an object lesson of all the dangers inherent in an organised working class movement. 'If the members of the federation object to working with non-unionists, they have no right to put their employers to large financial loss in order to display a not very manly and British feeling towards men who have a perfect right to work unmolested.' The editorial argued that if the Federation condoned the action of the Senghennydd miners then 'it is difficult to see what particular value can be placed on any document which contains the seal and signatures of the Federation . . . to those of us who still value personal liberty and detest tyranny in any shape or form it appeals as an act of bad legality and worse morals'.[5]

The incident personally affected Sir William Lewis and drew from him a virulent attack on trade unionism. The occasion was the presentation of a small gift to Sir William to mark his work for the Miners' Permanent Provident Society, an event which will be described below. At the ceremony, two days before the court's judgement, Sir William took the opportunity to stress that there could be no distinction between unionists and non-unionists:

> . . . as you well know, the agents of the Federation and their members, by their persistent policy of coercion and terrorism, have forced large

numbers of our members out of the fund and to join the federation, and are continuing to do so by the most disgraceful conduct that has ever been witnessed in this district as evidenced at various collieries in the last few months.[6]

The question of the Provident Fund brought the differences between Sir William and the miners to a head on an issue which again raised fundamental principles of social policy and philosophy.

At the ceremony in 1903 Sir William was presented with a framed photograph of himself with the Board of the Fund, and in Dr Parry's warm speech of appreciation he was credited with initiating the South Wales Miners' Permanent Provident Society. The Provident Society had been founded in 1881 and partially filled a serious gap in welfare provision. It was reliable, solvent, and in the hands of a man with a rigid sense of conventional financial probity, characteristics lacking in several of the small funds started by the miners themselves. It also made a significant contribution to improved medical services for the men. Sir William was able to claim that the fund had alleviated 'the distress of many thousands of sufferers, directly and indirectly, . . . rendering them independent of spasmodic charity'. The fund was run on the rigorous self-help principles which governed the thinking of Sir William and was a symbol of his belief that the interests of the men were inseparable from those of their employers. He claimed, for example, that 'the working of our charity has been the means of creating and maintaining the best possible relations between the workmen and employers, greatly to the benefit, not only of these parties, but also of all interested in the South Wales Coalfield'.

In view of the fact that the fund was run for the benefit of the miners and assisted them when they were suffering from accidents and diseases resulting from their labour for the employers, there were some curiosities about its organisation. The miners, for example, contributed 75% of the costs of the fund, their contributions being stopped from their weekly wages. But while the fund was largely paid for by the men, they had little real control over how it was run: its workings followed the pattern of stony paternalism which the Senghennydd miners found so objectionable in their relationships with their employer. For the men, therefore, the Workers' Compensation Act of 1897, for all its flaws, was a significant improvement over the workings of the Provident Society, setting a national system for compensation which was not subject to control by their employers.

Since the diseases and injuries of miners resulted, in the main, from their labour in producing profits for their employers, the new Act also increased the employers' contribution from the 25% which had been the norm in the schemes run by the employers themselves.

The clash over the miners' control of the Provident Fund was directly mirrored in a battle over the Cardiff Infirmary of which Sir William was a leading patron. Working class organisations, including the Senghennydd branch of the 'Fed', paid over a thousand pounds a year to the Infirmary but received no representation on its management board while individual subscribers of £10 became governors with full voting rights. In 1901 the hospital board offered three seats to the working men's organisations and called a meeting to endorse its suggestion. In a speech which was constantly interrupted by applause, William Thomas, speaking on behalf of the Senghennydd miners, denounced the meeting as a farce and argued that 'it was high time that those subscribers in the Infirmary should have a full voice in the management of the institution. . . . The colliery that he belonged to would not be satisfied until the farce was ended and the workmen treated not merely as figureheads': and in seconding the motion, which rejected the offer of a mere three places, William Thomas clearly linked the state of affairs at the hospital to that of the Provident Fund.[7]

In south Wales the Provident Fund had explicitly been used by Sir William as a counter to the influence of the Union. In an appendix to a proposed biography of John Nixon, the great coalowner, Lewis wrote that

> by filling something more than the normal place of trade unionism in the way of sick and accident benefits it has no doubt weakened the fighting power of trade unionism in south Wales and the workmen have been less ready there than elsewhere to listen to the arguments and oratory of self seeking agitators.

In the light of Sir William's comments it is not surprising that the Union in turn tried to wean its men away from this voluntary fund into funds and medical services controlled by their organisation: the Workers' Compensation Act now incorporated the separate schemes and funds of the men into a national framework.

As already noted the clash between Sir William and the men of Senghennydd over union membership was the catalyst which drew from the coalowner his most explicit attack on the union over the Provident Fund. He also, perhaps unwisely, made it clear that for him the fund was intended as a means of preventing union membership, for if employees could get the benefits of improved wages and conditions without joining the union, and if they could get sickness and other personal benefits from the employers, then why should anyone want to take on the costs and constraints of union membership? Indeed Sir William counterposed the Provident Fund and the Union as a straight choice and also regretted that the Workers' Compensation Act, with its higher contributions from employers, had been the cause of employers leaving his anti-union scheme:

> . . .unfortunately, owing to the increased expense imposed on the employers by that Act, many of our best friends, in order to minimise the effect of the Compensation Act, seceded from our fund, and, by the estrangement consequent upon such proceedings, played into the hands of the enemies of our fund, who had for many years previously unsuccessfully attempted to sow discord between the employers and employed associated in the miner's fund.[8]

The effect of this was

> to add greatly to the mischievous power of our enemies, who, by constant misrepresentation and otherwise, have coerced a very large number of workmen out of the fund and to join the Federation, which, under the guise of conciliation, has created a greater number of disputes and litigation in the last three years than took place between the employers and the workmen in the district in the previous twenty years.

In fact Sir William was being disingenuous in suggesting that the defections from his organisations were entirely the result of external factors. If Sir William's autocratic dominance during the 1898 strike had been the catalyst for the men to build a strong union, it was also the catalyst for a revolt against him by some of his fellow owners who recognised that, in refusing to give any ground to the men, the owners had strengthened the hands of the more revolutionary elements in the union. In 1899 the Bwllfa and Dare Colliery Company, which had withdrawn its application for membership in 1898 and had profited from inflated prices for coal during the strike, renewed its application. Sir William was adamant that the company's application should be rejected and the issue was seized on by those owners who were tired of his methods. Sir William was outvoted by his fellow owners and resigned as chairman. When a delegation of owners asked to meet him to get him to reconsider, Sir William replied acidly that

> of course my fellow members in the association have a perfect right of selecting their own company, but I also claim the same privilege, and I do not feel justified either in giving my services on behalf of or co-operating with those who did their utmost less than twelve months ago to ruin every member of the association . . .[9]

In a rare public reflection on his own temperament, Sir William argued that 'I have often spoken strongly because I have felt strongly'. Before long the owners, surprised by their own temerity, were asking Sir William to resume his position: he firmly rejected their advances though he mellowed sufficiently to withdraw, for the time being, his threat to remove all the pits under his control from the Association.[10] Even so he never lost his reputation as a ferocious opponent. In 1903 the system which he had contructed over a period of twenty five years was partially dismantled: the old sliding scale was abandoned, wages were linked to other variables in addition to the selling price of coal and the owners gave in to the men's demand for an independent chairman of the conciliation committee. Sir William issued a fierce statement:

> I am bound . . . inasmuch as my name appears as one of the committee, to dissociate myself from all responsibilities in connection with its proceedings, and which I have no hesitation in saying cannot but be fraught with most disastrous consequences for the South Wales Coal Trade and the many important interests associated therewith.[11]

If, however, Sir William was no longer the main opponent of the Miners' Union as a whole, he remained the dominant figure in the battle over union membership at the Universal, a battle which continued until the Great War. The Senghennydd miners attempted to achieve 100% membership even when all but a handful of the miners at the pit belonged to the Fed. This was a relentless task due to the high level of mobility in the coalfield, particularly among young unmarried workers. To the men, union membership was not simply an organisational matter but one of profound principle in the face of what miners of all political persuasions were likely to see as harsh exploitation.

Although most of the older generation of liberal nonconformist preachers and ministers preferred not to be involved in these issues, the view that the colliers and their families were the subject of crude exploitation and that they had a moral duty to join the union was one propagated by at least some of the chapel ministers. Samuel Bowles, a Primitive Methodist preacher from Mountain Ash, told his congregation that the union was fighting for all workers and that it was selfish to take the benefits and not to join the union: 'If there were any present not members, then let them get into the Federation for very shame sake'.[12]

Inevitably the new Windsor Colliery in Abertridwr had some ground to make up in terms of union membership: in 1905 it was estimated that 200 out of the 850 men in the colliery were not in the union. The campaign against non-unionism therefore continued and in 1906 the trade unionists in the Universal and Windsor jointly gave legal notice that they would strike over the issue of non-union miners, when their contracts ran out.[13] In 1911, by which time Parliament had reversed the main effect of the Taff Vale Judgement, the Senghennydd men again voted to strike to bring pressure to bear on non-members. There were further actions in 1913. An indication of the general success of the campaigns is that in 1913 there were reported to be only 6 non-unionists in the Windsor Mine compared to the 200 in 1905. Such figures have to be treated with caution, however, for as an official of the Lady Windsor Lodge in Ynysybwl has admitted, 'the correct number of defaulters, when they were excessive, was rarely given, so that they might not know their ''strength'''.[14]

While there were indeed general principles involved, the issue of membership also had immediate practical implications. The colliers and their mates were paid according to the amount of coal they had cut, and the price of the coal was negotiated locally in each pit, differing between each seam. This involved a continuous process of negotiation, one in which the men would only be able to protect their interests if the union was seen to be in a position of strength so far as the membership of the men was concerned. The history of the Universal is littered with disputes over the price for working different seams; if the union was forced to accept a low price then each miner working the seam would be condemned to low wages thereafter, however hard he worked.[15] The Universal hauliers were also involved in a long standing dispute in 1906 and a major dispute over victimisation occurred in 1910.[16]

A great deal of publicity was made from these and similar strikes and from the damage they did in terms of lost production and lost profits. Much of this was only a part of the continuing campaign to encourage public suspicion of the miners' trade union and it veiled the reality of greater lost production for other reasons which were in the interests of the owners. The events of 1903 had shown that, until the effects of the Taff Vale judgement were reversed by parliament in 1906, the miners could be sued for breach of contract if they decided to strike while a contract existed between them and their employers. By contrast the employers could find a host of reasons for closing the mine if the market for coal was slack or if they wished to teach the men a lesson. In May 1905 the Company unilaterally decided to close the mine on Mondays and in June 1913 the mine was closed due to a shortage of trams, probably to make a point about the recent legislation which required the phased introduction of new types of tram.[17]

The nature of payments to workers in the mine necessitated continuous contact between the miners and the junior officials and was the source of much bad feeling. It was impossible to maintain in a mine the sort of discipline taken for granted in a factory. The Senghennydd Colliery consisted of over a hundred miles of tunnels and complex workings, shrouded in an impenetrable darkness only touched by the meagre light of the safety lamp. This was true despite the fact that the longwall system of extracting the coal reduced the level of the colliers' protection from officials compared to the pillar and stall method used in the North of England, one reason why the men resisted the introduction of the former method. The means of maintaining output was therefore the system of piece work, operated by the overmen and deputy managers. The price of coal and the level of profit was set on world markets: but it was the miner and overman at the coalface who argued on a fortnightly basis over the details of safety work which would determine how much money the miner would actually receive. The economic pressures, on officials to reduce the costs of production and on miners to maximise wages, created unavoidable conflicts and much loud denigration of each others' competence and personality. Some of this was noisy rhetoric, enjoyed by both parties and disguising a good deal of mutual respect. Thus J. E. Morgan of Ynysybwl, a longstanding officer of the Fed and a

Labour Party activist, while noting the biases and shortcomings of the colliery management, wrote of one manager:

> He had an obsession for safety precautions, and a critical operation to be done at any important point secured his personal attention until things were properly 'tightened up.' Scamped work he hated, and many a time labourers who had made a bad job of walling or pinning had to do it over again—in their own time.[18]

In the context of a serious fire in the Lady Windsor Colliery, Morgan wrote of 'the engineering ingenuity of the managerial staff' and argued that they were 'most vigilant in their supervision and care of the workers', though he went on to claim that the company was much less than generous in recognising the skill and bravery of the workmen. In a similar vein Cliff Prothero, another young miner active in the union and the Labour Party in Ynysybwl, wrote of his first manager that 'apart from being a good mining engineer [he] was very human and took an interest in the welfare of those who worked at the colliery'.[19]

There was however a sufficient number of colliery officials who abused their power to produce a very real loathing which reverberates down the years in the memories of colliers.[20] Events at the 1904 meeting of the South Wales Colliery Officials' Association, attended by two officials of the Lewis Merthyr Company, give some idea of the attitudes on their side. In a much applauded speech W. J. Heppell from Aberdare referred scathingly to 'the way men worked, or pretended to work', and claimed that '10 per cent more wages was being paid than ought to be'. He went on: '. . . if the workmen of South Wales gave an honest day's work for an honest day's wage they could afford to pay this extra ten per cent without the slightest difficulty. . . There was no class of workmen in the country he had a higher opinion of than the Welsh workmen, but they had one fault— they lacked moral courage'.[21] The cheering which greeted this outburst indicates the gulf between the men responsible at the coalface for maximising production and the miners themselves whose survival, both physical and psychological, depended on mitigating something of the destructive force of mining on human beings. If they used the blackness of the mine to take breaks, unseen by the officials, then it was because the nature of the work made it a virtual necessity, despite the fact that any break in individual production lowered that miner's wages.

Coombes, Lewis Jones, Morgan and other autobiographical and documentary writers more than reciprocated these feelings on behalf on the colliers. Something of this anger can be seen in the occasional fights between colliers and officials in the Universal. In June 1910 there were protests that men were being victimised in the mine and being underpaid in 'abnormal places' where a miner could not hope to achieve a normal quota of production. Later in the month James O'Connor attacked Harry Evans, an under-manager, hitting him in the face. James O'Connor claimed that Evans said that 'he had never seen an Irishman who was any good and threatened to kick him out'. The Under-manager produced a witness to the effect that he had spoken to O'Connor 'very nicely', and against the word of an under-manager and an employee, isolated in the darkness of the mine, it was impossible to disprove Evans's version of events. Nevertheless the relatively small fine of ten shillings, suggests that the bench accepted that there had been provocation. Even the newspaper headline, 'Injustice to Oireland', indicates the level of contempt that was regarded as publicly acceptable.[22] Later in the year Henry Gough was prosecuted for assaulting another official, Thomas Marriott. Henry Gough claimed that Marriott was looking aggressive and saying 'Hit, hit, hit'. Again the bench may have thought that there had been some provocation since they fined Gough, who was known for his brawling and hell raising, only ten shillings.[23]

Some of the prosecutions for offences in the mine related to thefts from other miners, offences which were likely to draw down on the culprit the contempt of his fellow miners; this contempt would be felt beyond the workplace in the small community in which most of the men lived. The colliers provided their own tools and were, in the main, paid for what they themselves produced. Such thefts were treated with great scorn and men who would not normally have appeared as prosecution witnesses were willing to do so in these cases. Thus Frederick Alderman, who was to die in the mine, and Hugh Pugh, one of a family more used to being in the dock, appeared against John Bowden, who was also used to being in the dock, and who on this occasion had stolen another man's axe.[24] The same distaste would not have occurred when the crime was stealing property from the Lewis Merthyr company, as in the case of John Wolf, who claimed that he could not afford to buy a lamp.[25]

More common were the cases of miners re-marking the trams so that their contents would be credited to them rather than to the colliers who had cut the coal. Brinley Hyatt appeared as a prosecution witness against Gilbert Jones who had re-marked a tram. The fine of £2 10s and costs of 4 shillings indicates the seriousness with which such offences were treated by the court: the fine was five times greater than that for assaulting a deputy-manager.[26]

One of the areas in which officials and miners inevitably clashed was over breaches of safety legislation, offences policed and prosecuted by Sergeant James, the colliery policeman from the early days until the 1920s. Though there might have been some injustices, those prosecuted were rarely defended by the union which supported the firm application of safety procedures in the interests of the entire workforce. Nevertheless it remains the case that the rules were applied with a partiality which was to decimate the village, bringing catastrophe on a scale rarely experienced in small communities. There was a constant trickle of cases brought for the possession of matches, cigarettes and pipes in the mine, for sleeping with a lighted safety lamp and for being drunk. Most of these cases were treated in a routine way, although the magistrates would sometimes try to enforce the moral of these incidents, as when they reminded Thomas Cody that by taking a match into the mine he endangered the lives of 1000 men.[27] On occasion, if the management believed that the presence of matches or tobacco was genuinely an oversight, they even appeared as witnesses for the defence. In July 1905 Edward Shaw appeared for James Collier, a haulier, 'giving him a good character' and arguing that he had no intention of breaking the law.[28]

Throughout the years before the Great War, men were killed and maimed in the mine. Almost every year produced fatal injuries. In 1905 the 17 year old Evan Morgan was killed by a tram and Guiseppe Marriotti was killed by a fall as repair men were putting up a wooden 'collar' to support the roof. In 1906 James Wyatt was killed by a fall. While it was true that the colliers, in particular the young hauliers, broke safety regulations it was also the case that more serious offences which could endanger the entire workforce were often allowed to pass, usually unnoticed and certainly unprosecuted. In 1906 the Inspector reported that he had made a general investigation of accidents which showed that

in many cases the rules are not observed and enforced as they should be.
It may be necessary, by legal proceedings, to remind the owners and
managers of some of these mines of the responsibilities imposed on them
by the Mines Acts.[29]

In general, however, this remained as only a threat: in practice the
colliers were prosecuted for actions which could *lead* to accidents,
while owners were only prosecuted, if at all, after accidents had
already occurred.

The following year the Inspector allowed himself an optimistic
note, commenting that 'I am very pleased to report that the year
passed without the loss of a single life from an explosion of fire
damp'.[30] Nevertheless, in 1908 five men died in the Universal. Two
deaths were the result of falls, two the result of accidents with ponies
and trams and one was an accident due to the system of mechanical
haulage which drew the trams to the pit bottom along the main
haulage roads, after the ponies had pulled them from the workings.
The Inspector commented that falls could be reduced at little cost, but
did not make the point that the system of payment created pressures
on both colliers and officials which were bound to lead to accidents.
Nor should one take the occasional deaths as the worst statistic: John
Benson has shown that for every death there were something like 100
accidents, some of them resulting in amputations and paralysis
following broken spines. In 1910 five more men were killed in the
Universal. It has been shown that in Llanbradach 88 men died in the
mine in the years up to the great war, none of them in accidents
involving more than ten deaths.[31]

The death of young boys in the mine was particularly tragic. Often
they had become miners against the wishes of their parents, and many
of the memoirs refer to the agony of parents when the boy's workmates
had to break the news. Coombes tells of taking the body of a dead boy
back to his parents:

Everyone along those miles that we travelled could see what was on that
stretcher. There was not one blanket to be had in the colliery, so we
covered him with brattice-cloth and our overcoats. We could not drive up
to the house, so we carried the burden the last hundred yards, and his
father ran down to meet us, calling the boy by name. He collapsed and
fainted right at my feet.[32]

An overview of the mine, with the railway trucks of the Lewis Merthyr
Collieries in the foreground.

Had the managers taken as much notice of their own responsibility for
safety measures as they did in prosecuting breaches in safety by their
employees the future of Senghennydd may have been different. One
reason for this was that while searching and prosecuting colliers for
occasional offences was a cheap and easily organised task, the
conscientious clearing of the coal dust which had devastated the mine
in 1901 needed constant and regular paid work away from the profit
making activity of cutting coal.

The level of trade union activity in the South Wales Coalfield
increased throughout the period from 1898 until the Great War,
culminating in a number of increasingly threatening disputes
between 1910 and 1914. There were a number of reasons for this
growth. In the first place even the most traditionally minded unionists
could feel an increased confidence in the union's ability to improve
their conditions: they were conscious of the growing strength of the
organisation built up over the years and of the support of a significant
group of Labour MPs in the House of Commons. Given a sense of
their increased strength it was inevitable that the miners would try to
use it to achieve the best combination of reduced hours, improved
conditions and increased pay. It was inherent in the nature of mining

that virtually all workers, regardless of their political or religious views, would see the miners as a group essential to the prosperity of the country, exploited for profit and deserving of better conditions. It is unlikely that men can be worked in a black pit, pushed to the limits of physical endurance by the threat of lowered wages, kept constantly at risk of maiming and death, (risks intensified by the demand for higher profits), faced by the virtual certainty of dreadful industrial diseases, and be housed in conditions which threaten the survival of their children and yet not develop a profound resentment of the economic order which does this to them. The coalfield, it has been said, is an area where 'grievances spread like wildfire for, when a miner could see his resentment mirrored in the face of almost every other man... it was not long before he thought a major issue of principle was at stake'.[33]

The second major force was the growth of a new generation of activists among whom 'syndicalist' ideas were increasingly accepted. At the heart of the syndicalist programme was the demand for increased power at the grass roots of the union to be directed at using union strength to wrest wealth and political control away from the owners, and to ensure that the profits of the industry went to those who produced the coal. It was a programme based explicitly on a theory of class war which was utterly alien to Mabon and his generation and at odds also with the moderate Labour leaders typified by William Brace and Hubert Jenkins. The changed mood of the coalfield from the conciliatory attitude of Mabon's years to the language of class war before the Great War reached a climax during the Cambrian dispute of 1910-1911 which lasted for almost a year.

The catalyst for industrial unrest was D. A. Thomas, Sir William Lewis's cousin and his opponent from the 1890s. Thomas had been defeated in the 1890s in his attempt to create a coal producers' cartel which would increase prices, profits and, it was hoped, wages. After his defeat at the hands of his kinsman, Thomas concentrated on his political career as the Liberal member of parliament for Merthyr Tydfil, which he represented from 1888 to 1910. Thomas's success in Merthyr would have given little pleasure to Sir William Lewis who, as noted above, had himself stood for the constituency. Though Thomas was a coal owner himself, he dominated the parliamentary politics of Merthyr Tydfil, the largest of the coal towns with an overwhelmingly working class electorate. His support played a large part in the election of Keir Hardie as the

Independent Labour and socialist member for the second Merthyr seat. In 1906, however, Thomas received a further major blow to his career when the Liberal Party returned to office after ten years in opposition. Campbell-Bannerman became Prime Minister and found no place for Thomas who, for the second time, had to look for a career which would absorb his enormous, if idiosyncratic and combative, qualities. He now poured his energies into turning the Cambrian Colliery Company into a dominant concern through which he could apply his ideas about controlling the supply of coal without the necessity of working through an alliance of 95% of the coal companies as his cousin had demanded in 1897. By 1910 the Cambrian employed 12,000 men and produced four million tons of coal a year.

D. A. Thomas was, in his own way, as autocratic as Sir William and in 1910 the Cambrian Colliery Company was involved in a dispute with its miners which rapidly escalated into a strike of national importance. Though the strike started on other issues it came to focus on the subject of a guaranteed minimum payment to miners who worked in 'abnormal places' in which geological conditions prevented them from earning adequate pay. Incidents became increasingly bitter and involved the use of troops in the Rhondda and the reading of the Riot Act. The strike continued until September 1911 when the defeated miners returned to work and it had a perceptible effect on the increased level of tension and strikes throughout the Valleys.

In Senghennydd there was a crescendo of violence and attacks on the police as the Cambrian dispute was ending. The Senghennydd violence coincided with a railway strike and then a general lockout of workers in the Rhymney Valley Railway, which prevented many miners from getting to work. Some valley communities found scapegoats in shopkeepers who allegedly raised prices when supplies were reduced as a result of the railway dispute.[34] Ugly anti-Jewish incidents occurred in several mining villages including riots against Jewish shopkeepers in Tredegar and Rhymney. In Senghennydd in the third week of August there were a number of disturbances in which what normally passed off as drunken brawling escalated into riots against the police.

One of the Prossers addressed a crowd on the subject of how he had beaten Constable Pope, after inciting the crowd with the words, 'Let us put the Bastard through it'. Sergeant Walters arrested Prosser but was then in turn attacked by Henry Gough who had incited the crowds in an inflammatory speech which referred to the Rhymney strike. When Sergeants Walters and James arrested Gough and tried to get him to the police station, David Thomas led a rescue attempt. That at least was the police version. On the other hand David Thomas supposedly said to the police, of Henry Gough, 'Let him get up and have fair play'. This might suggest that Thomas was expecting an unrealistically quixotic attitude to attacks on them by the police: it might on the other hand suggest that something nasty was happening to Henry Gough while he was lying on the ground in police custody. Whichever is the correct interpretation, the police alleged that the conduct of the defendants made the crowd 'very hot', which seems very likely, since on the face of it the police were close to finding themselves in the middle of a riot.[35]

A few days later Fine's furniture store in Senghennydd was burnt to the ground; the police and newspapers insisted that this was a pure coincidence and that that it had nothing to do with the disturbances in Senghennydd or with the anti-Jewish riots elsewhere in the Valleys.[36] It is conceivable that this was true, though it would be a quite remarkable coincidence. Certainly the escalation of public anger was causing the police and local newspapers to play down the violence for once, rather than making a sensation of it. It is unlikely, for example, that the inhabitants of Senghennydd, or even the policemen on the spot, were convinced by a newspaper's summary of the week's events: 'A squad of boy scouts armed with toothpicks could keep order in peace loving Aber and Senghennydd'.[37]

Despite the fact that, on occasion, the inhabitants of the valleys tested the tactics of 'free collective bargaining by riot', in the main it was the solidarity, discipline and confidence of the 'Fed' which dictated the level and form of union activity in these years. In 1912 the union organisation and the years spent building up a party of labour were tested in a great miners' strike throughout Britain to establish a minimum wage, a piece of legislation made more necessary following the Eight Hours Act of 1908 which reduced the hours of work of the south Wales miners, but often at the cost of lowered wages. The issue was particularly important in Wales where geological conditions were notoriously bad, causing miners who worked in 'abnormal places' to earn inadequate wages. The campaign for a minimum wage for those working in abnormal places went back more than a decade and the claim had been central to the Cambrian miners' strike. In the ballot, held throughout Britain, the miners voted by over three to one in favour of a strike for the minimum wage; in south Wales the figure was more than five to one in favour of the strike.[38]

The unions entered the dispute with high confidence and a greater than usual degree of political support. They had been negotiating for a minimum wage for over a year, during which time the employers used brazen delaying tactics. As the talks approached the deadline of March 1st the 36 miners' representatives met the 46 representatives of the owners. At this meeting the south Wales coal owners, led by D. A. Thomas, found an unconvincing excuse to walk out of the talks, leaving the rest of Britain's owners to conduct the negotiations. In their tactics and attitudes the south Wales delegation had proved themselves entirely worthy of the tradition established by Sir William Lewis. Indeed it was after 1907, in the years that D. A. Thomas was active as the managing director of the Cambrian Combine, that the cousins were reconciled: faced by a self confident working class demanding rights in the form of a minimum wage, they rapidly discovered that not all that much divided them after all.[39]

The position of Asquith's Government was a trifle sensitive as the national coal strike approached. On the one hand several coal-owners were government supporters in Parliament; but on the other hand many, if not most, of the miners were Liberal voters while various miners' MPs had been Lib-Lab Members of Parliament in the recent past and still saw themselves as government supporters, albeit from the perspective of their working class constituents.

Despite Asquith's links with Liberal coalowners such as Thomas, he therefore treated the union's position sympathetically even while he tried to extract concessions from the union leaders which would enable a compromise to be reached. The extent of the change from the position of previous Governments was made clear when Asquith said, of the die-hards like the south Wales owners,

> We do not intend that the resistance of what I hope is a dwindling minority of the employers of labour, should indefinitely delay the attainment of an object which we believe you have properly put before yourselves and which we have satisfied ourselves is consistent with justice and with the best interests of the community.[40]

Asquith was impressed by the selfless dimension of the miners' position: since the vast majority of miners were paid above the national minimum they were therefore striking to protect the worst off rather than in their immediate self-interest. The intransigence of the owners meant that despite a willingness to compromise among many of those involved, the strike nevertheless went ahead as planned on March 1st 1912.

As in 1898 there were reports of hardship in Senghennydd and the neighbouring districts:

> the workhouses are full and the relieving officers to the guardians have more than they can do to cope with the calls upon the poor rate . . .
>
> The collieries are still idle, men are lounging about, women are scolding, children hunger more often than not, and the tradesmen are handling but little money . . .
>
> In the poorer quarters of the valley scantily dressed children reveal the state of things at home . . .[41]

There certainly was hardship and it hurt all the more for the fact that the previous ten years had accustomed miners' families to increased security: but these comments came from the pen of a notably anti-trade union columnist, who revelled in what were clearly hyperbolic excesses intended to drive home a point rather than to be taken entirely at face value. He claimed for example that 'hundreds of fowl have been stolen in all parts of the [Aber] Valley but we do not think that they have been forwarded to the soup kitchens'.[42] In the main the picture was rather one of a calm and orderly strike in which the population felt secure from the disaster of 1898 and was rationing its resources. There is little of the sense that it was facing mass hunger as before: indeed there is even evidence that many people were enjoying the extended break after the relatively good times of recent years.

The papers reported the early days of the strike with headlines like 'Peace Everywhere'. Arrangements for soup kitchens and the setting up of hardship funds were well organised and the Union paid strike pay from the third week. The position of the Poor Law guardians had also become closer to the men since the strike of 1898: the trade unions and the Labour Party had been successful in having their members elected to the boards of guardians although the law had been tightened to limit the categories of people the guardians could assist during a strike.[43] The picture of ill-tempered and hungry mining families lounging unhappily on street corners is contradicted by other reports from Senghennydd and the Aber Valley:

The workmen amuse themselves by walking about the surrounding hills whilst others indulge in football and other outdoor games. Every morning this week a free concert is held at the Workmen's Hall, at which anyone can give a song and some excellent singing has been heard. On Tuesday morning the Aber Valley Silver Band gave several excellent selections.[44]

One historian of the cinema has even claimed that the strike 'failed to lead to the usual violence because the strikers spent their temporary freedom at the pictures'.[45] In the halls a range of local musicians and comedians took the opportunity to display their talents, and the hills around Senghennydd were positively alive with activity; walking, rabbiting, sports, children's adventuring and, it is safe to assume, a good deal of love making; all of which was a welcome change from the toil of cutting coal. Even the women's work was lessened by the absence of blackened miners washing and spreading coal dust all over the recently dusted homes, though there was a heavy price to pay for the pleasures of love making between people who were not worn out with work. J. E. Morgan, the union official from Ynysybwl, wrote that, while for the officials strikes were a time of extreme stress,

> most of the rank and file on the other hand, seemed to enjoy themselves in spite of short rations. The stoppages generally took place in Summer, and almost without exception were accompanied by extremely fine weather. Young lads went bathing, older men took to their allotments. In the later stoppages street carnivals were the order of the day.[46]

Although the hardship was real, the moment was nevertheless judged appropriate to announce a sacred benefit concert for Thomas Burrell, of Commercial Street, who had been injured years before and had been bedridden ever since.[47] The politically aware could take advantage of famous speakers holding meetings in the valleys. Keir Hardie in particular used the opportunity not merely to support the strike but to drive home the broader political lessons for the Labour Movement. At Bargoed he argued for women's rights and enjoyed tweaking the noses of his largely male audiences in the process. He expressed

> his pleasure at seeing so many females present. He was sure that they all admired the fighting attitude of a certain section of the females. (Hear, Hear). He believed that votes for women would become law before the next election. (Hear, Hear). All parties were agreed that women could exercise the enfranchisement. They must admire the magnificent

courage that the women were showing in their fight for their rights and he could only wish that the men would show as much fight for their rights.[48]

Already on the 19th of March the Government introduced a Bill which would force the recalcitrant owners to negotiate a minimum wages agreement. Although the south Wales coalowners were supported by some M.P.s, as well as by the conservative newspapers, they could count neither on the support of industrial interests, nor even on that of some fellow coalowners. Sir Alfred Mond, the industrialist and coalowner, answered the charge that the strike was the result of a revolutionary attempt to bring the country to its knees. He argued that the strike was simply

> an attempt by a certain section of the workforce to improve their industrial condition, a thing they have been trying to do for a long time, and a thing they have failed to do because the coalowners have refused to agree to their terms.
>
> When I hear of labour holding up the trade of the country I think it might justly be retorted that the coal owners are holding up the trade of the country... the country would be quite happy if the coalowners would accede to the men's terms, so that the men could go back to work on Monday. The country would certainly be pleased, though the coalowners might not.[49]

The extent to which the hardline position of the south Wales owners and their allies was becoming untenable is indicated by the speech of Sir Arthur Markham, himself a major coalowner:

> After all, the origin of this dispute may be traced to one fact and one fact alone. The miners labour in a most dangerous calling in which three men are killed daily and 500 are injured daily, and not one miner but thousands go home weekly with not more than 2s or 3s a day after a hard week's work. Are these men not entitled to strike for a decent living wage?[50]

The second reading of the Minimum Wages Bill was passed by 348 votes to 225, which indicates the extent of dissatisfaction with the owners' position.

The final Act, as passed by Parliament, did not meet the demands of the union. The Act forced a minimum wage agreement on the unwilling owners and laid down a procedure for determining that wage, but it did not meet the men's demand that an actual minimum should be set at five shillings a day for all adult underground workers and two shillings a day for boys of fourteen.

When the men were asked in a ballot whether they wished to return to work on the basis of the new Act, the results were interesting, particularly as far as south Wales was concerned. In Britain as a whole the miners voted by 244,011 to 201,013 against a return to work. In south Wales, which had voted 5:1 in favour of the strike, they now voted by 62,538 to 31,127 to accept the deal and return to work. It has been suggested that this was a collapse by the south Wales men due to their inferior organisation and lack of adequate strike funds.[51] An alternative argument is that in some of the coalfields the miners in reality wanted to use the act to raise the general level of wages and not merely to protect the worst off; in south Wales, where geological conditions meant that some miners really did earn very low wages, the Act to set a minimum was indeed the victory they had sought, despite its shortcomings. This seemed to be acknowledged in good humoured exchanges between the union leadership and Asquith when the dust had settled:

> The Premier: 'You have done very well in south Wales'.
> Mr Hartshorn: 'We have done fairly well'.
> The Premier: 'I see my old friend Mr Barker. He told us when we met before that ''We're out for cash''. You have got a good deal of cash out of this'.
> Mr Hartshorn: 'Yes, a good deal, but there are the matters referred to and 2d a ton would put them right.'[52]

Whether the strike was regarded as a victory or defeat, it appeared to the trade unionists as a model for the future. It was 'a ''new kind of strike which . . . led to a new kind of settlement'', the inference for trade unionists being that ''what could not be won through negotiation with the employers could be wrested from the government'' by massive and concerted strike action'.[53]

After the defeat of the Cambrian Combine strike and the limited victory of the national strike in 1912, the 'syndicalist' activists, co-ordinated by the Unofficial Reform Committee, had renewed their agitation for a new union structure in the South Wales Coalfield. They argued that the old structure, which gave power in each district to local union agents and which allowed the men who built up their reputation through this system to enter Parliament, was inherently flawed. The old leaders, exemplified by Mabon, were separated from miners by the very positions to which the miners elected them. They were given the status and incomes of the middle classes and the process of separation was supposedly completed when they entered Parliament. The result, it was argued, had been the ethos of conciliation which had tied the miners into the sliding scale agreement for twenty five years. Even the next generation of leaders who had forced Mabon to accept the abandonment of the sliding scale in 1903 had been sucked into this separation; William Brace and Vernon Hartshorn were themselves increasingly drawn into parliamentary activity and were involved in the process of minor adjustments to wages and conditions rather than the overturning of the whole exploitative relationship between owners and miners, the policy demanded by the Unofficial Reform Committee.

The British economy, it was argued, depended on coal. Without it there could be no production, no exports and no navy. What was needed therefore was a union willing to take advantage of this, rather than frittering away its strength and idealism in parliamentary activity which created leaders but inevitably separated those leaders from the people they were supposed to represent. The syndicalists therefore proposed a new structure which would create a union strong enough first to give power to the union members and then to use that power to wrest the industry away from the coalowners. The first step was to get rid of the district organisation, which gave control to the likes of Hubert Jenkins, and to create a single structure in south Wales. To achieve this there would be a single executive of twenty four elected members who would direct the union in response to grass roots demand.

There was of course, to put it mildly, an inherent paradox in the proposed new structure; for, in order to create this powerful new instrument of grass roots power, it was necessary to centralise power and weaken the districts and lodges; the paradox was not lost on either the proponents or opponents of the scheme. Among the latter, not surprisingly, were numbered the majority of the existing district agents.

In their campaign for a new structure, a campaign which lasted for several years, the Unofficial Reform Committee attacked the moderate Labour leadership with a corrosive contempt which was highly effective among people who already held the leadership in contempt. With other people it was liable to be counterproductive, being seen as divisive within the union, contemptuous of people who had served their members well and indicative of an immature understanding of the realities of power. At the end of the Cambrian strike the south Wales miners had voted for their representatives on the executive of the Miners' Federation of Great Britain. The three longstanding leaders, William Brace, Tom Richards and Alfred Onions were defeated by three 'socialists', George Barker, C. B. Stanton and Vernon Hartshorn.[54] Hartshorn came top of the poll in a victory which was widely seen as a triumph for the new militancy in the coalfield. But Hartshorn was then himself attacked in the *Rhondda Socialist* by W. F. Hay, one of the activists on the unofficial committee and a joint author of *The Miners Next Step,* the manifesto of the grass roots reformers. The disagreement over principles did not worry the mass of miners so much as the language used to describe a fellow trade unionist, miner and socialist:

> A bitter day of reckoning is coming for those who, like Hartshorn, Brace, Richards, Onions etc have seized upon, misled and betrayed the most important industrial movement of modern times. Chief among these traitors, occupying this despicable pre-eminence stands Vernon Hartshorn. Puffed into rapid and undeserved eminence, trading on the ideas and efforts of abler men, he stands today a leading figure in the coalfield...
> A politician by temperament, and a demagogue by training, he seeks the wider area of parliamentary life to gratify his personal ambition, and it is to secure this prize that he has assisted in the base intrigue that has caused our defeat.[55]

There was a series of conflicting moves at various conferences and meetings, first gaining general support for reorganisation and then moving towards a specific scheme to achieve 'abolition of districts and the centralisation of funds and administration'. The reformers had to face the vested interests of the existing district leaders and the innate conservatism of many miners, as well as widespread doubts about their own motives, abilities, realism and genuine commitment to local democracy.

The proposals were discussed at various lodge meetings in 1912 until the final ballot of the whole coalfield was held in February 1913. The result was a dramatic defeat for the Unofficial Reform Committee. It has been said of these and the following years that 'the victories of the militants within the federation proceeded apace but proved to be more paper than real ones in the sense that the militancy and power of the miners in south Wales, although at times overwhelming in appearance, were not reflected in an organisational framework': the reality behind this comment is that the reformers failed to carry the miners as a body with them.[56]

In the 1913 ballot the result was conclusive, with 43,508 voting against the reorganisation proposals and 24,016 voting for them. Even in the Rhondda, the heart of the reform movement, the vote was against change, although by only 5,775 to 4,928.[57] In the East Glamorgan District the vote reflected that in the coalfield as a whole with 1,590 voting against reorganisation and 934 voting for it. In Abertridwr the voting again matched that of the coalfield as a whole, with only a slightly greater proportion against reorganisation: the men of the Windsor lodge voted 244 against and 110 for the reorganisation.

Senghennydd was a contented village. The mine manager had received the largest vote in the local council elections; he was a major figure in their local community. Hubert Jenkins, previously the union checkweighman and now the secretary of their district and their Labour county councillor, was an equally popular figure. He had been effective in unionising virtually the entire workforce in the mine and in standing up for the interests of his members although he was one of the moderate Labour men vilified by the reform committee. There may also have been some resentment of the radicals from the Rhondda telling the Aber Valley how to organise, and perhaps a sense that when the men they had elected were treated with contempt they themselves were collectively insulted. Certainly it is true that Senghennydd was away from the main coal production of the Rhondda, Merthyr, Rhymney and Aberdare Valleys and was therefore subject to rather less of the reform agitation. It was also the case that it was a place wrapped in the positive social values and activities created by the chapels and voluntary organisations of the village, though it is not obvious that this was stronger in Senghennydd than elsewhere. And if the chapel or the relationships of the home could offer no refuge from the stresses of the mine then the pub could offer a warm fog of humanity; one which, even when the pleasant haze wore off, left a narrowly focused pain which diverted the mind until the end of the next shift again released the miner into the bursts of hilarity and good cheer at the bar of Universal by the pit gates.

Whatever the reasons, the Universal Colliery in Senghennydd seems to have produced one of the oddest, and possibly most suspect, results of the ballot: according to the local newspaper the miners voted by 542 to 16 against the reorganisation scheme, a majority of 526.[58] The miners of Senghennydd evidently did not resent the directness with which Hubert Jenkins reprimanded them for the dirty and anti-social habits; on the other hand nor did they take much notice of his admonitions and change their habits in response to him. They just went on with their accustomed lives.

They asked for little more than to enjoy their lives in the parentheses between the brutality to which they were condemned: they certainly did not blame Edward Shaw for the lives which they were obliged to lead. They got drunk, went to Chapel, obeyed the collective voice of the union, enjoyed and spent wages which were good compared to those of other manual workers and brought up a new generation with hopes and aspirations for a life which would be an improvement on that to which they themselves were apparently fated.

CHAPTER 9

[1] H. Pelling, *A History of British Trade Unionism,* (Harmondsworth; 1970), 123-5

[2] J. Bellamy, DLB Vol 1, 193-4

[3] GFP 27/6/1903

[4] WM 15/7/1903

[5] *ibid*

[6] WM 13/7/1903

[7] N. Evans, ' "The First Charity in Wales" ': Cardiff Infirmary and South Wales Society, 1837-1914', *Welsh History Review* Vol 9, (1978-9), 336-7: WM 12/6/1900 & 13/6/1900

[7] W. T. Lewis, 'Appendix on the Sliding Scale', (to unpublished biography of John Nixon), NLW, Lord Merthyr Archive, 388

[8] WM 13/7/1903

[9] L. J. Williams, (1957), *op cit,* 157

[10] *ibid,* 160: GFP 20/1/1900

[11] L. J. Williams, (1957), 170

[12] GFP 26/8/1905

[13] GFP 6/7/1906

[14] GFP 9/9/1905; GFP 6/7/1906; CJ 7/9/1911; CJ 11/9/1913: J. E. Morgan, *op cit,* 16

[15] GFP 7/11/1902; CJ 12/8/1909

[16] GFP 25/5/1905; CJ 16/6/1910
[17] CJ 5/6/1913
[18] J. E. Morgan, *op cit,* 4
[19] *ibid* 51
[20] *ibid,* 16,17,19: K. Howells, 'Victimisation, Accidents and Disease', in Ed. D. Smith, (1980), *op cit*
[21] GFP 16/1/1904
[22] CJ 16/6/1910; 30/6/1910
[23] CJ 13/10/1910
[24] CJ 1/9/1910
[25] CJ 22/2/1912
[26] CJ 10/2/1910
[27] CJ 20/6/1912
[28] GFP 22/7/1905
[29] PP 1907 Cd. 3449 xiii, 531
[30] PP 1908 Cd. 4045 xix, 481
[31] PP 1912-13 Cd. 6237 xli: J. Benson, *op cit,* 40-41: D. Sellwood, *op cit,* 57
[32] B. L. Coombes, (1939), *op cit,* 168
[33] E. Phelps Brown, *The Growth of British Industrial Relations,* (London; 1959), 156: M. W. Kirby, *The British Coalmining Industry, 1780-1946,* (London; 1977), 17-18
[34] CJ 24/8/1911
[35] CJ 14/8/1911
[36] CJ 31/8/1911
[37] CJ 31/8/1911
[38] R. Page Arnot (1967), *op cit,* 279
[39] Viscountess Rhondda, *op cit,* 120
[40] R. Page Arnot, (1967), *op cit,* 286
[41] CJ 21/3/1911
[42] *ibid*
[43] M. A. Crowther, *The Workhouse System 1834-1929,* (London; 1983), 79-80
[44] CJ 14/3/1912
[45] R. Low, *The History of the British Film 1906-1914,* quoted in B. Hogenkamp, 'Miners' Cinemas in South Wales in the 1920s and 1930s', *Llafur,* Vol IV (2), 65
[46] J. E. Morgan, *op cit,* 25
[47] CJ 14/3/1912
[48] CJ 7/3/1911
[49] R. Page Arnot, (1967), *op cit,* 303
[50] *ibid* 304
[51] R. Page Arnot, *The Miners: Years of Struggle,* (London; 1953), 109
[52] Arnot, (1967), *op cit,* 320
[53] M. Kirby, *op cit,* 21: E. Phelps Brown, *op cit,* 242-3
[54] R. Page Arnot, (1967), *op cit,* 268
[55] R. Gregory, *op cit,* 134
[56] H. Francis & D. Smith, *The FED, A History of the South Wales Miners in the Twentieth Century,* (London; 1980), 22
[57] R. Page Arnot, (1967), *op cit,* 325
[58] CJ 6/2/1914

PART III
DEATH

Chapter 10
The Disaster of 1913

On the morning of October 14th 1913, the usual routine continued at the Universal Colliery. During the night the repairing shift had been at work. One of their regular tasks was to clear the coal dust which accumulated on every inch of the mine's surface. These labourers shovelled up dust from the roadways, clearing different tunnels on different days: inevitably there would be a build up on some roadways. They did not clear the dust from the timbers, or walls or from the ledges and cavities of the roof, since the management had decided that this job could not be done effectively.

Two hours before the main day shift was to descend the pit, the firemen, overseers in charge of districts of the pit, descended to inspect their areas. They had a legal duty to inspect each working place in the mine in the two hours before the men started work. In the early days of the mine the meeting station for the firemen had been established four hundred yards from the pit bottom. Now the tentacles of the workfaces were over two miles away. As a result William Chidsey, the fireman for the Mafeking district, thought that he spent about forty minutes travelling to and from the workfaces before he could start his inspection. Even in ordinary conditions he could not fully inspect the forty four miners' stalls in his charge, and if any thing abnormal had occurred then his job became impossible. In practice his task was to move swiftly through each stall, noting any obviously critical problem but leaving little or no time to check on the safety of timbering or on potential falls. The miners were content to collude in this cursory inspection. In the main they shared the company's attitude to detailed legislation, considering that it often interfered with their aim of spending as much time as possible earning good piece rates cutting coal. The colliers were skilled and independent men who also had some contempt for most of the firemen. They preferred to trust to their own experience which had enabled them to survive thus far.

One of the fireman's jobs, on which the lives of everyone in the mine depended, was to check for accumulations of gas. The Universal was a gassy mine and moreover it was unusually subject to great rockfalls. The cavities which these falls produced were shored up with timber, but they left behind great caverns in which methane could accumulate. The firemen checked on the build up of gas by hanging their safety lamps on a five foot pole and then pushing it into the cavities: if the flame got longer then methane was present. The trouble was that at the angle thus created it was hard to discern the length of the flame which gave off one quarter of a candle's illumination. The company considered any other form of inspection to be too time consuming.

It was therefore in the nature of the job that William Chidsey and John Skym, his equivalent in the Ladysmith District, had to rush their inspections and that there was not time, when the dayshift arrived, to talk adequately to the colliers about conditions in their work places, as the act had intended.

Some of the safety checks which colliery officials were obliged to carry out did not need to be done at the Universal since the colliery had not yet complied with the relevant Act of Parliament. In particular, collieries were obliged to be able to reverse the current of air that was blown into the mine and which circulated through the miles of workings. If a fire occurred near the bottom of the shaft or in the passages through which air entered the mine, thus potentially causing the miners to be suffocated, the air flow could then be reversed, delivering fresh air to the workers through the second shaft and blowing the fumes away up the damaged one. The management of the Universal had twice asked for more time to carry out the necessary adaptations to the mine.

The day shift started work at six o'clock and soon trams heaped high with coal were beginning to be hauled back towards the pit bottom ready to be wound up to the surface. As noted above, the Universal was a dry mine so that the colliers did not have to endure working with their feet in water or lying on their sides in pools. Nevertheless the lack of water had side effects, since it greatly increased the amount of coal dust. The trams were filled with coal far above the height of their sides, and as they were hauled back to the pit bottom against the force of the air being pumped into the mine, coal dust was blown into the atmosphere. To counter the dangers which this created, there was a legal requirement that the coal in the 'journeys' should be doused in water in order to keep down the dust. Since a dust explosion had caused the death of their fathers, brothers and workmates in the 1901 explosion the threat was well understood among the Senghennydd miners. The water for the mine was brought in through a pair of two inch pipes and this was then distributed to the areas several miles apart in which over fifteen hundred men worked. The floors of the roadways were watered every night and in addition it was intended that three sets of sprinklers should water the trams which brought coal to the shaft from the workfaces, in order to minimise the dust. However the spinklers were a third of a mile from where the coal was actually cut and the whole system was therefore less than effective.

The vast majority of the day shift were colliers, as distinct from the much smaller night shift which was mainly composed of repairers, roofers, rippers and the like. By seven o'clock, in dark nooks and crannies spread around miles of tunnels and cuttings on the West side of the mine, nearly five hundred men were working at their full strength to cut the coal. The districts in which they worked, Mafeking, Ladysmith, Kimberley and Pretoria reflected the patriotism and the toryism of old Sir William Lewis, now ennobled as Lord Merthyr. By contrast the names of the headings and levels, where the men were cutting coal, reflected the miners's traditions, using the names and nicknames of local characters: Snailham's Dip, Beck's Heading, Beck Old Heading, Down's Dip, Drew's Deep Dodge.

In these workings were clustered the families of Senghennydd, in many cases fathers and their sons, or married men and their younger brothers, working together as teams. The fourteen year old Evan Twining was working with John, his elder brother, in the Pretoria District. Their two other brothers were working in the same district, together with another fourteen year old, Alfred Tudor who was the breadwinner for his family. Also in Pretoria were the three Edwards brothers who shared a house with their widowed mother: the eldest of the three lived in the house together with his wife and young child.

George Downes formed a team with his two sons Thomas and George Henry, while Rowland Lewis worked with two of his sons and their lodger, Griffith Roberts. The colliers formed seemingly endless chains of extended families some of whom, such as the Ross clan of Coronation Terrace, shared homes in the same street, while others had homes dotted around the small town.

In the neighbouring Mafeking District, more than two miles from the shafts, the Pritchard brothers, Henry and Frank, worked as part of a team: so did Benjamin Priest and his fourteen year old son, James, and his other son, Thomas; and Richard Kestell with his son, Thomas. Friends, neighbours and lodgers also chose to work together: thus the twenty five year old Henry Brooks was working with Frederick Alderman, in whose house he lodged. By contrast young door boys like the fourteen year old Glyndwr Williams, the son of a colliery overman, sat on their own in the long dark tunnels.

The men were not merely skilled in cutting coal: even more important for their survival was the experience which gave them a feel for the mine and its movement. The creaks and groans of the timbers spoke to them constantly of the shifting state of the mine, and it was their skill, experience and good luck which had combined to keep them alive this long. Working in family groups not only had economic benefits, but also ensured that experienced miners could look after the safety of the younger members of their family until they had the experience to fend for themselves.

That morning this wisdom, acquired over the years, was to prove valueless: instead the management's casualness in failing adequately to take a combination of apparently minor precautions led to the death of several hundred people.

At about eight o'clock there was an explosion in the mine followed by a second and much greater explosion minutes later. The force of the initial explosion was less than in 1901 but the existence of quantities of coal dust caused a rolling devastation which gained in momentum and power as it was fed by the accumulations of coal dust near the working faces. The accelerating eruption blasted its way through miles of tunnels, derailing trucks and forcing down timber props. In some places men were killed instantly by the force of the blast: many more were burnt, their clothes, hair and faces scorched by the flame of the explosion and their skin burnt into by thick layers of carbonated coal dust when they did not have sufficient warning to throw themselves to the ground. Many were knocked unconscious, regaining their senses in time to confront a worse fate than immediate death in an explosion. As the blast brought down timbering from walls and rooves, men were buried under falls, the roar of which added to the sounds of devastation which filled the mine. Some were killed instantly under the falls of rock, while others, pinned down by the falls, lingered on in the black, smoke-filled tunnels.[1]

Those who were not in the path of the explosion itself heard loud bangs and thuds followed by clouds of smoke. Then the air suddenly became still, the stillness broken in the workings by the sound of boys crying in fear.

In those first moments the lamps of most men were blown out leaving the whole of the West side of the mine in total darkness. The blast and flame were followed by thick clouds of dust which filled the narrow tunnels of the mine with a dense blanket which would in any case have made the dull light of the safety lamps useless. But already a more terrifying light was showing through the heavy fog, for the flame had caught hold, igniting the timbers and starting fires which lit the mine for survivors in some work places, threatening to suffocate them if they outlived the immediate dangers.

Well over three hundred men had survived the immediate effects of the explosions and were still conscious: all of them knew that the main danger was neither the fire itself, nor the smoke which it gave off, nor the falls of rock, nor the explosive and poisonous methane gas which would be released by the falls, but the non-explosive carbon monoxide, or 'after damp', given off by the explosions, which would kill the survivors if fresh air could not be got to them.

Throughout the West side of the mine groups of men and boys started to gather amid the destruction. They could not know the extent of the devastation but, since they were more than two miles from the pit bottom in a mine ripped by an explosion, all must have known that they were only just clinging on to life.

At the pithead the first sign of trouble came with the second explosion at about ten minutes past eight. This was a quiet moment after the rush of sending down the main shift and before the flow of coal to the surface gathered momentum. There were few people about and Edward Shaw was talking casually to Jim Morse in the lamp room. At this moment the surface of the mine gave little indication of the hundreds of people a quarter of a mile below the ground who depended on the resources of the battered sheds for survival.

By contrast the village was at its most lively with a thousand children preparing for school and beginning to fill the streets with noise and play.

In the middle of this scene the three ton iron cage was shot out of the Lancaster shaft straight into the winding gear, as a metal ball might be hurled from a massive cannon. The man in charge of the pit-bank, John Moggridge, had his head blown from his body and great clouds of dust engulfed the pit head as the accumulated power of the explosion which had ripped through miles of underground tunnels at last found an outlet for its force.

Within seconds of the eruption Shaw dashed across the yard to check that the ventilation fan was working, gave orders for repairing the damage at the pithead and then went down the apparently undamaged York shaft twenty yards away. His activities in the next two hours gained him a degree of respect from the local mining community which remained over the years; they probably also cost the lives of scores of miners.

As Shaw descended in the cage the colliery yard began to fill with the population of Senghennydd. From the second that the sound of an explosion echoed around the valley and the cloud of dust rose into the sky the nightmare of 1901 was alive in the minds of everyone in the community. In those first moments, a child cried to its mother, 'Daddy's gone'.

The manager's descent was painfully slow; hampered by the smoke and fumes, by having to disentangle damaged girders and by trying to make contact with the apparently undamaged East side of the mine. Half way down Shaw and a companion, the overman David Thomas, saw the legs of a man hanging from a tram in the ascending cage. They signalled to the surface to stop the descent and clambered over to the other cage where they found the corpse of a miner who had been blown into the tram by the force of the blast. They continued to the pit-bottom with the body.

Having worked their way to the base of the Lancaster shaft, Shaw and Thomas managed to put out the fires which were burning at the pit bottom. They tried first one and then other entrances to the working districts but all were on fire. Seven men were found. All were badly injured except Ernest Moses who was sheltering behind empty trams.

On two immediate actions depended the lives of nearly a thousand miners. The first was to evacuate the four hundred and fifty men on the East side which, on first sight, did not appear to be affected. The second was to put out the fire in the main Lancaster level. Along this main roadway was carried all the fresh air to the five districts on the West side in which more than 450 men were working. If that fire was not extinguished then hundreds of miners would be deprived of fresh air and would inevitably die of the carbon monoxide with which the explosion had filled the mine.

Shaw and one other man started to tackle the fires, sending Thomas and others to the East side of the mine. Everywhere timber was beginning to catch, and Shaw battled to put out the flames. All the timbering, row after row of supports disappearing into the blackness, was ablaze and soon the roof and sides would begin to collapse and the frames start to give way if the fire was not controlled.

The water pipes had been fractured and for over an hour Shaw used hand extinguishers on the flames. But without large quantities of water the fire could not be fought successfully and because of the smoke and fumes it was impossible to reconstruct a proper water supply without breathing apparatus. Although there were rescue teams at Senghennydd the nearest breathing apparatus was at Porth, in the Rhondda. With one companion Shaw struggled on until the collapses started and then he drew back and joined Thomas in putting out fires in one of the tunnels leading to the East side. Shaw attempted to enter another seam but was again prevented by the falls.

Finally admitting defeat in his immediate aim Shaw returned to the surface after 9.30 a.m. At 10.00 a.m., after his heroic efforts to reach his workers and nearly two hours after the explosion, the rescue services were at last properly alerted and the first arrived at Senghennydd within half an hour. The Porth rescue brigade arrived with their vital breathing equipment at about 11.00.a.m. It had taken three hours for the apparatus to arrive at the mine from the rescue station a few miles away.

On the surface the people whose lives would be most affected by the events underground had gathered and were watching silently. They were entirely dependent on others, a dependence from which there was no escape for most of them. All that was asked of them was stoicism.

While Shaw and his companions were struggling to enter the mine, those caught in the blast were fighting for their lives. Everywhere men struggled with smoke, fumes and flames, staggering through blackened tunnels lit in places by fires. In some areas flames flickered in the gloom, while in others raging furnaces consumed the timbers which collapsed, bringing down great rock falls the noise of which continued to reverberate through sections of the mine. Panic was immediate in some places as miners rushed in different directions to escape the smoke. Elsewhere individuals sat alone and still, waiting to see what would happen as the explosions were followed by strange physical occurences which they had never seen before: fires glowing at distances which could not be estimated in the dark and strange whizzing sounds as air found new channels of circulation driven into different paths by the burning furnaces, the falls and the destruction of the ventilation doors.

George Moore was working with his two sons when they heard the report and were then stifled by the polluted air. Like others throughout the mine they blundered down choking tunnels to be driven back by impenetrable clouds of dust and smoke. Others were stopped by the afterdamp, overcome by giddiness, until they collapsed in the roadways. Some, like Bert Williams, were unconscious for hours as a result of the explosion, only recovering during the night. All who were still alive were racked with coughing as they fought for breath in the poisoned atmosphere. As they recovered consciousness they saw around them in the black tunnels licked by flames the bodies of men killed by fallen rocks, by trams hurled around the cramped spaces and by the blast.

After arranging for messages to be sent and issuing a brief non-committal statement Shaw had again descended the mine to be joined at intervals by mining engineers, members of the inspectorate and the miners' agents of the union as they arrived on the scene. All were agreed that the first priority was to put out the fires; it was hoped that this would be completed by the next morning. Those who had survived the explosion would inevitably die unless fresh air could be got to them. Since the colliery had no means of reversing the air current, thus ventilating the mine and blowing the smoke from the fire out through the Lancaster shaft, the only way of getting fresh air to survivors was to put out the fire.

Throughout the late morning and the afternoon the men working in the East District were brought up the York shaft. Those in the more distant parts of the district had been unaware of what had happened four miles away until officials and work-mates arrived to tell them that the mine was being evacuated. Miners near the pit bottom were more conscious of the narrowness of their escape. Lamps were blown out after the explosion and then they too were engulfed in thick smoke. In the No 1 North tunnel leading to the East district men died of burns and suffocation. Among them was William Hyatt: his two sons,

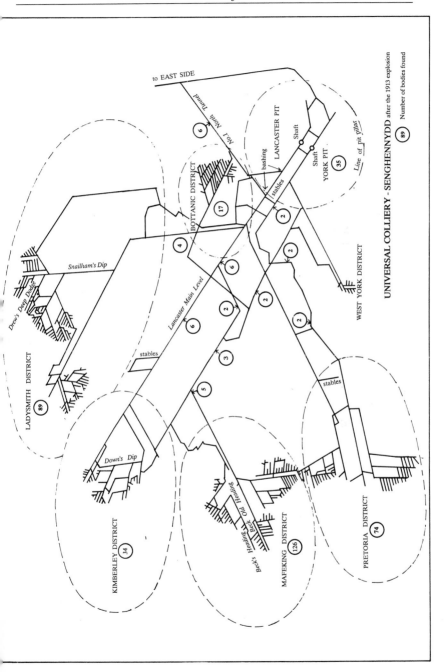

UNIVERSAL COLLIERY - SENGHENNYDD after the 1913 explosion

89 Number of bodies found

to EAST SIDE

No. 1 North Tunnel

6

BOTANIC DISTRICT

17

LANCASTER PIT

bashing

stables

Shaft

Shaft

YORK PIT

35

Line of pit pillar

WEST YORK DISTRICT

4

6

2

2

Snailham's Dip

Lancaster Main Level

2

2

Drew's Deep Dodge

6

2

2

LADYSMITH DISTRICT

89

stables

3

stables

5

Down's Dip

Beck's Heading Old Heading

PRETORIA DISTRICT

74

KIMBERLEY DISTRICT

34

MAFEKING DISTRICT

126

Charles and William escaped to the pit bottom after groping around for over an hour trying to find a way through the burning tunnels. Sidney Gregory helped a young boy who had started work that morning: 'he started to cry and asked me what was the matter. I told him that it would be all right. . . . As we were going I could hear the fire raging. It was awful; the timber cracking and falling and we could hardly stand the heat and foul air. The little boy was crying so I gave him some water and he got all right. At last we got to the bottom of the pit'.[2] The hundreds of men working in the East side of the mine had their clothes scorched as they struggled past the flames to be raised in batches of twenty eight throughout the afternoon. They were very fortunate to be alive.

The first to be brought up were the injured but there were few of those on the first afternoon. Of the seven men found at the pit bottom only Ernest Moses survived. John Herring, George Small and Charles Thomas all died after they had been rescued. Once the survivors had been brought to the surface the first eleven corpses were carried on stretchers to the improvised mortuary in the carpentry shed of colliery yard, to which relations were called to identify the dead. The community watched in silence as the bodies were carried past the stacks of coffins sent to Senghennydd from Cardiff. They had been brought by train together with detachments of police sent by the chief constable, Captain Lindsay, to keep order among the reverent community watching in frozen silence.

As the evacuation went on, the desperate struggle to put out the fires continued while exploring parties were formed to try and penetrate the working areas of the mine by alternative routes. After battling to clear falls and to put out fires the first rescue party to penetrate beyond the fire found twenty dead bodies. They brought out nine corpses and were forced to leave the other eleven. In their desperation the rescuers were reckless with their lives and the pattern for the whole rescue operation was established as more and more of the rescuers had to be carried to the surface gassed by the carbon monoxide or injured in falls. Shaw himself was brought up at five o'clock his eyes puffed up and blinded by the heat. Richard Williams, another rescuer, was knocked unconscious by falling rocks. As the day turned to night, volunteers from among those rescued from the East side of the mine were already re-entering the pit as members of the rescue parties.

Throughout the night the pithead wheels turned, bringing up tons of hot debris cleared from the falls which prevented further progress into the mine. The firefighting continued as groups of rescuers again tried to bypass the fires and penetrate further into the mine. Inevitably, however, these also became tied down in repair work once they lost touch with the main teams. One team took a long detour of over a mile and finally managed to reach the Bottanic district, having two vast raging fires between themselves and the direct way back to the shafts and safety. They came across five bodies. At last they found a boy, Evan Moore, and then further on William Jones, both of whom were breathing but unconscious. These were taken back to a point were there was fresh air and the back up teams gave them artificial respiration for two hours before they regained consciousness. Further on the rescuers, among them the flamboyant trade-union official David Watts Morgan, found sixteen more people alive all of whom, with one exception, needed oxygen before they regained consciousness. Among those rescued were two brothers, John and Evan Jones from Caerphilly Road, and James Hill the sixteen year old breadwinner for the family. Finally they found George Moore and his son George: together with Evan Moore, the first to be found, all the miners in that family had been saved. Those rescued were brought to the surface in the early morning of Wednesday. They emerged in ones and twos into a black night as a gentle rain fell. On the hillsides thousands had maintained their vigil throughout the night waiting for news of fathers, husbands, brothers, lovers and friends. There was a faint cheer as the first boy was brought to the surface but in general the rescued miners were carried or led through the yards in an aching silence. In the yard itself relations broke down as they were reunited. For each person who recognised a father or lover, there were hundreds whose vigil continued with increased hope. Some of the onlookers knelt and prayed while men took off their caps as a sign of respect to the rescuers. From the first some of the most experienced among the watchers had assumed that there was no hope for those in the mine but the rescue of eighteen men had altered the atmosphere despite the simultaneous discovery of a further thirty corpses.

Intermittently rumours whispered through the crowds, of further rescues, of knockings heard in the mine and then of another explosion. All were false.

On Wednesday the pattern remained the same. In the mine the rescuers struggled against heat and fumes trying to remove the burning rubble. The dangers for the rescuers were rapidly increasing as the fire damage spread: roof supports were weakened and roof falls released explosive methane gas.

That day the committee of seven mining experts met to decide whether the rescue operation could be continued in view of the risks. They decided to press on but, before going back into the pit, they wrote letters to their wives and three of them drew up wills which were witnessed on the spot. Several rescuers were injured that day and one of them, William John, was killed instantly by a roof fall as he was trying to clear the rocks from an existing fall.

The main decision of the committee had been to concentrate on putting out the fire rather than risking the lives of more rescuers on explorations into the mine. As long as the fires raged in the main air road into the mine, any survivors were being gassed by after damp and suffocated with smoke and fumes. Whether the decision was an attempt to increase the chances of survivors or whether it signalled pessimism about the likelihood of there being any more survivors, was much discussed in the newspapers and helped to maintain the dramatic intensity of the story.

In the mine the heat of the fires was so intense that the fire-fighters could only work for twenty minutes at a time. The greatest danger was of further explosions. The previous year there had been an explosion in the Cadeby Pit in Yorkshire in which 35 miners were killed: later in the day a second explosion killed 53 of the rescuers. That example was very much in the minds of those organising the rescue. The only way to prevent a dangerous concentration of methane gas was to force more air into the tunnels: but this in turn fed oxygen to the fire. Despite these problems each report spoke optimistically of bringing the fire under control. Colonel Pearson, the Chief Inspector of Mines, spoke for all the experts when he said to the press, 'expect surprises all the afternoon, for it is quite possible that living may be found among the dead'.[3] In the event, however, no one was found alive on that day.

During the day rescuers came across bodies which moved even men hardened to violent death: a boy cradled in his father's arms; comrades made unrecognisable by the explosion which had torn their bodies apart and burnt their faces away so that they appeared to be faceless; and others who had been gassed in such a way that they seemed untroubled in sleep and ready to wake at a touch.

As the bodies reached the world of the surface they were observed with a quiet undemonstrative dignity which impressed outsiders unused to the self-discipline of the valley people in the face of tragedy. To those on the surface the bodies were tokens from the other world less than half a mile beneath them, a world that might have been only a nightmare if it were not for the evidence of these blackened corpses.

In the temporary mortuary, away from the crowds, the horror of what had happened destroyed the steely dignity of the streets. Faced by the violation of the bodies and by the evidence of individual suffering, whether to a woman's lover or to a faceless and unknown stranger, the reserve broke down and anguished people had to be helped back to their homes to recover some equilibrium for what was to come. For many of them there were to be further horrors in the mortuary. Later some relatives were spared the visit: Edith Griffiths identified her husband by possessions brought to her home by Richard Hamar, whom she was to marry six years later.

The pattern continued into Thursday, but on that day the most pessimistic interpretations seemed to be confirmed when it was announced by William Brace M.P., a member of the executive of the South Wales Miners' Federation, that all work would concentrate on the fire and that no further parties of explorers would be sent out for the time being. In effect all the experts had given up hope of finding survivors. Against the experts, however, the newspapers suggested that men could survive by tapping into the compressed air pipes and many pointed out that in the Courrières disaster in France survivors had been found more than two weeks after the explosion. At each stage the experts hoped that they would be able finally to subdue the fire, but their hopes were not realised. As the rescuers slowly moved along the main roadway towards the coalfaces they were, in effect, driving the fire before them. The optimistic accounts of progress have to be measured against the actual advances: in twenty four hours the main group of rescuers advanced thirty yards down the roadway; they were still two miles from the coalfaces.

The bombast and celebration of heroism in some of the newspapers conveyed little of the nightmare unfolding in the rabbit warren of tunnels 1000 feet below the surface. Tom Purnell, a rescuer, later described the terror which overwhelmed some of the men in his team during Wednesday:

> ...we had gone in about 250 yards when one of the team lost his nerve. It was his first time down.[since the explosion]
>   He started to shout and run away as soon as he saw the bodies, so we had to hold him fast and bring him back. After that we had several accidents of a minor character but nothing serious until the twentieth body was being rescued by the Porth team.
>   I was holding my team in reserve until they returned. All at once three of them came rushing back asking for help. They had run away from their comrade when he fell and left one standing by him. This was the only cowardly action I ever saw at Senghennydd.

Purnell called for volunteers to attempt to rescue the man who had been overcome by fumes, and a small team then tried to reach him.

> We got the poor fellow out and he was very near gone as he lay 14 hours unconscious before he started to recover. After that, the inspectors wouldn't let me go in after the other [body] and it was a week before the body came out of that district.[4]

As hope faded the sheer scale of the tragedy and its effect on the town began to be understood. Thirty four men were missing in the High street, forty two from Commercial Sreet, fifteen from Graig Terrace, nineteen from Cenydd Terrace: each small terrace lost similar numbers.

Families were decimated. Elizabeth Twining's husband Thomas had died in September 1912: now she lost four sons, Evan, John, James and Ezra. Three brothers, Thomas, Morgan and George Edwards from 61 Caerphilly Road all died. Mrs Baker lost her husband Charles and her fourteen year old son, named after his father: the previous Saturday she had given birth to her twelfth child. George Downes was killed with his two sons as was Humphrey Jones and his sons, Thomas and Richard. John Maddocks died with his sixteen year old son. Benjamin Priest died with both his sons, James and Thomas, aged fourteen and sixteen respectively. The eight year old David James Jones lost his father, grandfather, two brothers, two brothers-in-law and two uncles.

The number of families left without breadwinners in a world which condemned such people to unremitting hardship was numbing. William Hyatt, killed with his eldest son, left a wife and seven children; Ben Hill, who died with his sixteen year old son, left a wife and five children; James Thomas of Brynhyfrydd Terrace left a wife and seven children; John Herring's wife had six children to support; Francis Clark left a wife and six children; Mrs Tudor, a widow, had relied on her eldest son to support the family: Ernest Tudor, the breadwinner, was fourteen when he died in the explosion; Mrs Ross in Coronation Terrace lost her husband, two sons, an adopted son and a brother-in-law: the household of ten people in the two bed-roomed house was reduced to the mother and her five daughters.

Many children were orphaned. Edwin Small, who lodged in Cenydd Terrace, died with with two of his sons, Arthur and Edward: his eighteen year old daughter Mary was left to bring up the six younger children. On the opposite side of Cenydd Terrace two brothers, Ernest and Arthur Vranch, both died: they were the breadwinners for Mrs Vranch, their widowed mother, together with her four younger sons and two daughters.

Just as tragic were the large number of elderly people, living with their children, who were faced simultaneously with the agony of the death of children and with the loss of any hope of comfort until they themselves died. In all, the dead miners had over nine hundred dependants.

The death of young people is always associated with the sadness of unfulfilled potential and of hopes suddenly become unrealisable. Fred Alderman's daughter, whose Christian name is not recorded, was to have married their lodger, Henry Brooks, on the Saturday after the explosion: her father and lover were both killed. James Lower, whose widowed mother had been sent to the cells by the magistrate in 1903 when she had tried to leave the court to collect her children from school, was killed. Two of the family had died in the previous explosion.

For many people the loss of children, unscathed by the humiliations of the years, brought even greater suffering than the loss of husbands: there were probably few parents who would not willingly have died in the place of their children. We know that many women lost husbands for whom, the day before, they would have said that only feelings of bitterness and dislike remained. The deaths not only forced on people the destruction of future potential in their children but also memories of youthful hopes burnt away by the acid of hardship and despair which were almost inseparable from the human condition in that

The scene outside the Huts as the inhabitants wait for news.

Benton

society. Many women must have mourned, not the husband whose personality had been tortured and warped, but rather the young man who had seemed her equal partner and with whom the possibility of happiness had seemed to be a realisable dream before it had withered with the bitterness of the years.

Scores of younger women were widowed in the first years of marriage, some of them treasuring, until their own deaths half a century later, an image of unsullied partnership. For some the hardship of surviving on their own was perhaps mitigated by the bitter joy of cheating death by recreating life. Gertrude Williams, who was married to the twenty one year old Llewellyn, bore a son the following year and Esther Morgan, whose husband Henry was killed, also produced a son the following May. Neither of the boys lived until they were twenty, both mothers experiencing the further suffering of their deaths in their teens.

For some the agony had a bitter twist, cruel even by the standards of the God who supposedly watched over Senghennydd. October 14th was the day that Mrs Hyatt commemorated the tenth anniversary of the death of her son George. Now her husband and their son Brynley

'A little mother waiting for news'.

Benton

were both killed on the same day: she had to wait for over a month before her son's body was found. On the 14th of October Thomas and Mary Cook remembered the second anniversary of the death of their seven year old daughter, Ada: the anniversary was now marked by the death of their son Thomas. 'The grave proves the child ephemeral': rarely more ruthlessly than in Senghennydd.

On Friday and Saturday the funerals started. Processions a mile long wound along the Aber Valley in the dull drizzle towards the municipal cemetery at Penyrheol. Among those buried were William Ewart Uphill, William Francis Davies, David Jones, the headpitman, and J. F. Carnell. At the Catholic Church they lost thirty two from their congregation, most of them Irish: in the previous explosion the sole Irishmman killed had been followed to the grave by his countrymen who had not known him: this time the Irish were a significant part of the community. Even more dramatic were the funeral processions which climbed the country lane to the old church four miles away at Eglwysilan accompanied by the Salvation Army band.

Against this background of suffering and pain, and the temporary solemnity which death lends to human existence, the continuing absurdities of life and the casualness of death stood out starkly even as the epic struggle continued a thousand feet below the hills. A furious correspondence erupted in the local newspaper about whether the cafes in Senghennydd should continue to serve food in the circumstances, and if so whether they should charge so much and if so then whether the food should at least be fresh. The position of the main correspondent seemed to be that when he or she went into a cafe to get some food, the un-Christian proprietor had the appalling bad taste to be open and serving food at a price. The debate involved much bandying of Christian principles.

When Evan Jones and his son Owen were returned to the lodgings they shared in Caerphilly Road, after their dramatic rescue from the Bottanic District, there was some difficulty about getting into the house where they had rooms. The houseowners had gone to bed and were sleeping soundly. Nor did the language of the survivors always match the official and dignified tone of the occasion: on being rescued, Evan Moore commented to reporters that 'once I got fresh air I was in the pink'.

Shortly afterwards the case came up in Caerphilly magistrates court in which Emma Williams summoned Elizabeth Pearce for breaking one of her windows in the weeks before the explosion. Later, Mrs Olsen of the Huts was considerably surprised when a wife turned up to claim the compensation for Charles Emery, her lodger: he had, as Mrs Olsen explained, 'passed' for a single man.

Even as the long drawn out tragedy continued, local sensibilities had to be sustained and local journalistic habits maintained: the music appreciation appropriate to the eisteddfod was echoed in the funeral reports. The *Caerphilly Journal* reported that in one funeral, 'the cortege was headed by the Aber Valley Silver Band, under the leadership of Mr S. Radcliffe, and the dead march was excellently rendered'.[5]

Throughout the week miners and relatives from the south Wales coalfield had arrived in Senghennydd to be with friends or to offer help: the watchers on the hills had been part of the awesome events. At the weekend, however, the atmosphere changed with vast crowds of sightseers arriving in the town as in 1901. It was estimated that well over a hundred thousand people visited Senghennydd.

Rescuers with a canary used during the rescue attempts.

Benton

. . . motor-cars, traps and brakes came from long distances, and curious men and women have descended on the stricken valley from every part of the South Wales Coalfield. Thousands walked over the mountains, and countless cyclists jeopardized their own and other people's lives in the congested roadway leading to the colliery. Senghennydd in its hour of sorrow, might well have been spared the intrusion of this multitude. The visitors were not callous, but they were merely curious sightseers. When they were thirsty they formed up in long lines outside the public houses, which, of course, are closed all day on Sunday in Wales except to travellers. When they were hungry they crowded into provision shops, which wisely opened their doors to them.[6]

Only within the colliery yard, around the pit head itself, were the inhabitants free of the casual visitors. The journalists were scathing about the vulgarity and intrusiveness of the inquisitive horde. In a sense, however, the masses were only trying to share in that heightened sense of awareness which great tragedy induces into a mundane existence and many, like the young Walter Davies and his school-friends from Bedlinog, went home altered by the experience. Moreover the smouldering taste for participation in tragedy was being fanned by the deliberately crafted words of the journalists themselves. While stimulating the desire to be present, one newspaper noted that 'most decent people would scrupulously avoid intruding upon the grief of the stranger and it may be hoped that some of these unwanted visitors went home less like picnic parties than they came'.[7]

Monday dawned with no hope left and it might be expected that the rescue teams would now progress in a safe and ordered way, not taking unnecessary risks which served no obvious purpose. The opposite was the case. Every day reports came in of parties being cut off and gassed as they struggled to reach the bodies of the dead. The fire in the main roadway continued to burn among falls which started near the pit shafts and which continued for over a hundred yards. To progress into the mine it was therefore still necessary to make long detours which cut parties off from direct escape routes.

Late on Tuesday night, one week after the explosion, a large party set out to try and bypass the falls in the main road and to reach the Kimberley District. It was composed of an advanced party, a reserve with whom they would maintain contact, and large gangs of workmen who would repair the roads on the main level between them and the massive fire. The small exploratory group went ahead and reached the nearest parts of the Kimberley District but in the meantime the workmen who were repairing the mine, closest to the fire, started to be overcome with fumes. The base group, between the workmen and the explorers, became concerned about those in front who were by now about a thousand yards ahead. They sent three messages to check that the party in Kimberley were alright. None of the messages got through. By now people whose purpose was to support the forward groups were themselves collapsing, able at the most to try and drag themselves back towards safety. At a late stage Dyer Lewis, a mines' inspector, decided to signal to the surface for help but by the time a rescue party arrived, wearing full breathing apparatus, several of the party were unconscious or suffering extreme effects from gassing. A further minor accident could well have cut off and killed twenty rescuers.

It is difficult to imagine the condition of the mine by this stage. Fires had now been raging for a week. Many south Wales mines were blisteringly hot, but the Universal was torrid with the mixture of fire and steam rising from all the water which had been poured into the mine. The mine was thick with the fumes and smoke of the fires and with poisoned gas. In the darkness the flames could be seen in lurid colours created by the gasses with which they were mixed. In the heat and smoke some hundreds of decomposing corpses rotted in the foetid atmosphere deep below the earth's surface while the tortured and broken bodies of horses lay in the roadways. After only three days the coroner had ordered that bodies be buried immediately after identification at the pithead because of the health hazards they posed. Rescuers described how they had to drag decaying corpses through areas littered with the disembowelled carcases of horses. Even the doctors faced with such corpses carried out the most perfunctory of autopsies; so much so that in scores of cases the blackness of decomposition seems to have been wrongly ascribed to burns. Underground, the rescuers, drenched in eucalyptus and with their noses pegged, worked in tightly enclosed spaces reeking of decomposition. Through all of this men struggled relentlessly in six hour shifts beneath mountains of unstable rock, risking their lives in reckless efforts to free the corpses of comrades they knew to be dead.

In the second week after the explosion small parties of men who penetrated over a mile from the shafts with the aim of reaching a particular district would clamber over falls, only to be stopped by concentrations of methane: they would than take an alternative route into the darkness in order to come out of the mine by another way to avoid the gas, to be stopped again, this time by massive falls. The most that could be achieved was to have located four dead bodies which could not in any case be brought out until the falls had been cleared. In terms of safety and of re-establishing the mine, a slow and steady effort was called for, and was decided on by those who were organising the operations. Within the mine, however, a desperation raged in the rescuers which is not explicable in simple terms. In part it was the result of wanting to put an end to the whole tragedy by knowing the worst. Many of the rescuers were the relations, often brothers, of the dead and this added to the sense of irrational urgency. In part the sense of desperation was due to strongly held feelings about the significance of a proper burial and of a horror, common in all coalfields, of leaving bodies in a mine. It was this which had added to the shock when new pipes were being laid, and the rumour had gone round that the whole mine was to be flooded and, later, that the mine was to be sealed off and abandoned. Above all was the futile and irrational sense that the mine was an evil presence, 'a monster gulping down his ration of human flesh', engulfing their comrades and friends, and that in recovering the bodies they were in some way snatching something back from the monster of death and defying it. This was an image that ran through much of the reporting.

Against the horror, meaninglessness and absurdity, this small victory in recovering the bodies and burying them according to their Christian and class rituals would somehow re-establish meaning and mastery. The funerals of the relatively few corpses which had been recovered became central to the pattern of the next weeks. A large proportion of the population walked in the columns which wound their way to Eglwysilan across the hills, the coffins carried on the shoulders of relays of miners. Brass bands accompanied the processions and journalists were impressed by the massed singing of Welsh hymns. The *Glamorgan Free Press* described the funerals of two members of the Salvation Army whose band played hymns on the three mile path to the graveyard: 'All the beautiful emotion and feeling that music can express was given forth by the bands composed of working men and boys... In the triumphant phrases of the changes of the melody the music seemed to defy the monster of industrialism which had robbed the mourners of their breadwinners'.[8]

Some of the funerals were held in the dark, the mourners holding lanterns in the graveyard of the old church nestling in the folds at the top of the hills between the Aber Valley and Pontypridd. No amount of healing ceremony could, however, dispel thoughts of the horror beneath them: 'even the impressive and sorrowful procession of death itself and the open grave were overshadowed by the despair of the women and children waiting for their dead which the mine still claimed and witheld from them'.

Within the mine the job of the rescuers was becoming, if that was possible, even harder. What was apparently the worst fire was near the shaft in the main tunnel which carried air into the mine. The rescuers realised that as they fought the end of the fire nearest the shaft they might well be pushing the fire further into the mine fuelled by the fresh air that was needed for the resue work. As the fire was quenched at one end, it simply extended at the other end, filling the entire mine with smoke and making the job of exploration impossible for days on end. It was therefore decided again to suspend exploration and instead to build a large barrier at the other end of the fire, thus preventing the smoke from being carried into the mine. However this entailed carrying several tons of sandbags through a long detour via the Bottanic District in order to get behind the fire. It also entailed laying over a mile of water pipes in order to be able to saturate the barrier with water. The fact that, once the decision to lay the water was taken, the whole job of pipe laying was finished in seventeen hours, indicates how rapidly improvements could be achieved when safety was seen as a priority. In the past the unwillingness to lay extra water pipes had meant that trams were not watered until they were up to half a mile from the coal face, causing the area of the faces to be encrusted with the dust which carried the explosion through the mine.

The job of laying the barrier was only just possible in a situation in which even ordinary tasks seemed like struggling in hell. The flames, smoke and fumes of a fire one hundred yards long were being swept down a tunnel into the mine: the rescuers had to go into the path of that holocaust in order to block it off from the mine. Men worked for between one and two minutes before having to give way to others. The special glass in the breathing helmets of the men laying the barriers was melted as they worked. The task of building the seven foot wide barrier, seventeen foot high into the fallen roof, took three days: even then it was insufficient, continuing at intervals to belch smoke and steam into the mine to such an extent that, a week later, repair and rescue work again had to be suspended while the barrier was strengthened.

In the heightened atmosphere of death and devastation in a village with deep Christian beliefs it was inevitable that the chapels would play a major part in the way the community experienced and came to terms with the tragedy. The work of the churches in ministering to the bereaved and the messages preached in the sermons were prominently printed in the local press. Many of the clergy confined themselves to comforting people but, since Christianity was so central to the life of the town, they also tried to explain the tragedy and the devastation of human hopes in the light of their beliefs.

Frank Williams, a local vicar, argued that '. . . the finest human qualities were only bred in adversity. . . ' and went on to say that 'many a comrade may have succoured his mate with some familiar memory of those happy hours when they walked in the House of God..'. Several claimed that the explosion was part of God's message to the world. The Reverend Arthur Sturdy, Curate of Saint Mathew's Church in Pontypridd, announced that '. . . God's voice, speaking at Senghennydd, had been heard throughout the length and breadth of the world'. He went on: 'these catastrophes were a mystery to many, but they might feel sure that through God's providence they were for man's improvement'. Sturdy's unshakeable certainty that all was for the best in the best of all possible worlds was to be unruffled even by the slaughter of the Great War. Even when it was not suggested that the explosion was a direct message from God, it was often claimed that there were lessons to be learnt. The *Birmingham Post* correspondent reported that the Salvation Army 'went in procession round the town holding meetings at street corners, seeking to enforce the spiritual lessons to be drawn from the disaster'.[9]

For some, to whom temperance, monogamous sex and respect for authority were the essence of Christian morality, the message was clearly a warning from God against Gomorrah: 'and Lo, the smoke of the country went up as the smoke of a furnace'. After the Wattstown explosion of 1905, in which 119 miners had been killed, the Welsh Independants had been explicit in the report of their Tredegar Conference:

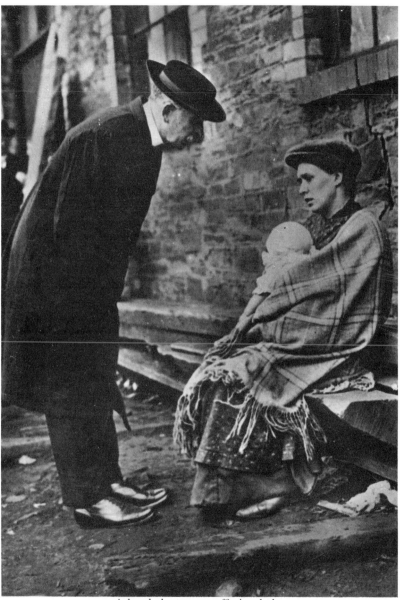

A local clergyman offering help.

Benton

... We can be certain now that the Lord has a loud voice directed towards us as a nation and especially towards the miners of our country, through this disturbing and sad event. If some of the miners of areas in the Rhondda and other places, have continued to be stubborn in the face of the powers of Evan Roberts' revival and 'not knowing the time of their visitation' have not known 'the things that belong to their eternal peace', we hope from the bottom of our hearts that they will listen to the serious words and warning of the Lord through this terrible explosion.[10]

But if God could deliver the lesson with ruthless savagery, it was more difficult for his ministers to say so openly. At any other time such a message might have been acceptable, but, at the very moment that it needed to be interpreted, the press and the public was so aglow with pity and compassion for the community that to say openly that it was being punished for its sins would have courted public outrage. The interpretations of God's message therefore had to be relayed in a coded form.

To less ferocious Christians, the plight of Senghennydd presented greater problems. If this was God's message then why, some asked, had he sent it in this way, and why pick on Senghennydd for sending no less than two such messages?

If it was indeed a message from God then it was delivered with a fine sense of the ironies of human existence. Those whose recent behaviour had seriously offended against the law were still safely in gaol, while those who had opposed the deepest moral assumptions of the community had long ago been forced to leave. John Snailham and his friend Arthur Booth, who had lied to get him off the manslaughter charge after the illegal gambling party, both escaped. It was the innocent who died in Snailham's Dip, trying vainly to escape the holocaust in the Ladysmith District. David John Jones, who had stolen from his aunt's house, was still safely in borstal: his namesake David John Jones, the father of three young children, died of burns and suffocation.

Those who had stolen from their mates in the mine had been driven from the town. John Bowden who had served fourteen days for stealing his workmate's tools had escaped as had Gilbert Jones, fined for stealing the wages of a fellow miner by remarking his tram of coal.

Of the four youths accused of rape in 1909 the only one killed in the explosion was John Davies who everyone, including Jennie Gardiner the victim of the attack, agreed was not guilty. Had he been found guilty he might have moved to a different town on being released.

Others who had abused or deserted their families, and who can be traced, were also spared. John Thomas who had terrorised his wife for nineteen years was living and working elsewhere having finally been separated from his wife, as was Joseph Dexeter who had persistently refused to pay maintenance. Edward Davies who left his wife and infant children penniless while he went off drinking, had now deserted them, so he too was safe.

Equally those who were fortunate enough to have been dismissed for damaging colliery property and those who had been victimised by the company were spared: George Truman, David Smith, Benjamin Williams and Joseph Morris all escaped as did J. Bennett, William Jenkins and Frank Bull, fined for having matches in the mine. Of all those convicted of offences, William Davies, fined for street betting, was almost unique in being killed by the explosion. Even the perpetual drunks seem on the whole to have escaped: perhaps some were saved by a bad hangover on the morning of the 14th.

The names of those who escaped contrast oddly with the effect of the disaster on the respectable churches and voluntary organisations within the town. The Salem Welsh Baptist Chapel lost twelve men including Benjamin Hill, one of its leading members; and the other nonconformist chapels lost similar numbers of their congregations. The attitude of the chapels had been nicely summed up by the Reverend W. Winks at the time of the exposion in 1901 when he said that 'it was always a comfort to them to learn when these things happened in Wales that a large proportion of those who had lost their lives were men who feared God', a statement to which both the chapel goers and the godless could answer 'amen'.

The stories of miners who were spared or caught in the explosion allow no more than an ironic recognition of the utterly absurd and meaningless path taken by individuals. However when the ministers argued that the tragedy was sent as a message from God it was surely permissable to suggest that, even by the standards of the late nineteenth century Christian God, it would be perverse to punish the moral and leave unpunished the vicious and cruel.

The Reverend W. Williams Millar, a Pontypridd curate, attacked the tendency of 'a certain class of person' to blame the disaster on God, an idea started by his fundamentalist colleagues. In a sensible and rationalist vein he argued that 'there was no mystery about the laws of explosions in mines. Any ordinary person knew that a certain portion of oxygen mixed with certain other gases would explode if a flame of any kind was brought near'. From this Millar drew the conclusion that blame should be attached not to God but to more prosecutable agencies: '. . . ignorance of any kind was culpable whether intentional or not when hundreds of lives were at risk'.[11]

This response might have been sufficient elsewhere, but the missionary work in Wales had flourished on the notion that God intervenes to reward and punish. In building chapels local notables sought, among other things, to confirm in stone that the righteous were rewarded with success. If the clergy were now to argue that the events of the world continued on their own paths without God's intervention then many people would direct their energies to changing the world rather than praying to God to change it.

The argument that God's ways were mysterious did not seem adequate in the face of the relentless and savage tragedy faced by Senghennydd, a tragedy which was soon to be amplified in the Great War. Senghennydd had tasted the experiences of the twentieth century which ultimately led to the closure of five out of its eight churches and chapels in the ensuing years, a pattern repeated throughout the country. Increasingly religion confined itself to the important work of offering comfort: but comfort, while essential, was a response to an intolerable existence, not an explanation for it and even less a way out of it.

The work of clearing the mine progressed at a painfully slow pace. At each stage the experts thought that a further twenty four hours would see the fires finally subdued and the mine opened up to inspection. In the event, even when the main fire was brought under control, a series of other fires were found in the main roadways to the different districts, and as the massive fall in the Lancaster main level was bypassed, further falls of up to a hundred yards in length were discovered. Blowers of methane gas forced work to be suspended even when the afterdamp had been driven from the mine.

At last during the third week after the explosion the Ladysmith district was entered and forty bodies were brought to the surface. Several of the bodies could not be identified: the coroner had to be satisfied with descriptions such as 'unknown: about 40' or 'identification impossible: 5ft 8ins long'. In some cases even these meagre descriptions were not possible and the victims were simply listed as unknown. One body was buried unidentified despite a tobacco tin with the inscription 'In memory of dear old Dad, 1912'.

Among those buried at last was fourteen year old Glyndwr Williams. Frederick Alderman was buried with Henry Brooks who was to have married his daughter. In the High Street Mrs Humphries and her five children could now bury King Humphries: Mrs Lewis and her three children buried Joseph Lewis and Mrs Prosser and her eight children buried William Prosser. Elsewhere David Evans and his son Evan were buried together. Elizabeth Lower buried her son Phillip after eighteen years of struggle.

After three weeks only one hundred of the victims had been recovered and buried. Finally, in the middle of November, the falls were cleared in the Mafeking, Kimberley and Pretoria districts, allowing a further three hundred bodies to be brought to the surface. None of the faces could be recognised: they were identified through the tobacco tins, boots and other personal possessions placed on top of the containers. One woman broke down when she could only identify her husband by the fact that one of his arms was longer than the other.

A funeral procession passes the shops at the bottom of the High Street.

Benton

It had taken over a month of extraordinary toil and courage to recover the entombed bodies in order to bury them according to the rituals of the inhabitants, rather than according to the whim of the industrial monster.

It was a relief that the waiting was over and that they could give them the 'decent' burial which was so important to a community for whom violent death was a commonplace. Though the community was used to sudden death and to the death of children, there is nothing to suggest that this lessened the pain: it merely gave to all existence a sense of the threatened quality of all ease or pleasure. Perhaps the most powerful means of bringing home the gravity of the tragedy were the photographs taken by 'Benton of Glasgow'. His powerful images, some of them posed, capture the pathos, the casualness and even the banality of the tragedy. They remain a remarkable example of photo-journalism of that period.

The disaster might have been used as an example of the essentially exploitative and destructive nature of largely unrestrained industrial capitalism. Instead the newspapers used the disaster to contribute to the strengthening of British national unity after the turmoil of the south Wales coalfield in recent years. The newspaper reports of the disaster at Senghennydd were cleverly, at times brilliantly, crafted to communicate the unfolding tragedy. They served to heighten the sense of loss among the public and generated a large amount of financial support for the families of the dead miners. The vivid and highly charged reports also created a mood receptive to national reconciliation. The complex, contradictory and often frightening world of the miner was reconstructed as a sociable, chapel-going community. The miners, usually presented as a threat to social stability, were now represented as heroic and self-sacrificing warriors: their wives, as the warriors' selfless and courageous supports. All were incorporated in an overarching image of a caring community which united all its members from the humblest labourer to the concerned monarch.[12]

Since it was over a month before most of the bodies were brought to the surface, a newspaper story that started as a dramatic episode developed into an epic. As it became clear that well over 400 miners had died the newspapers movingly reported the effect on the small community, using a variety of literary devices to communicate the awestruck atmosphere in the village. The contradictions between the newspaper accounts, though unimportant in themselves, demonstrate that the reports often owed as much to the dramatic requirements of the stories as to the actual events.

Many journalists used the scenery of the disaster, in romantic style, to create the atmosphere. The *Times* correspondent wrote that 'the bare mountain land of South Wales is. . . compelling in the intensity of its emotions; the setting of the tragedy is grand and wild'. But the *Western Mail* correspondent described the countryside in precisely opposite terms in order to highlight the tragedy underground: he wrote of 'the charming Aber Valley, bathed in the sunshine of a lovely October day, through fields of verdant green and trees clustered with foliage, showing few autumnal traces, nothing to suggest the grim tragedy which lay just beyond the bend'. The tragedy happened against 'a background of verdure-clad mountains, bathed in sunshine.'[13]

Some newspapers tried to maintain the drama of the story by keeping alive the possibility of there being more survivors long after the experts had given up hope. Thus on the day after the explosion the *Birmingham Post* headlined their report 'Hopes for more survivors abandoned' and by the second day the Chief Inspector of Mines confirmed this conclusion. However the *Western Mail*, while announcing the official verdict, maintained the excitement by discussing methods by which the trapped men might stay alive: a pebble in the mouth to produce moisture, a stocking dipped in tea to keep off the fumes and 'lying along the tram rails and breathing the air current which is always found there', were some of the suggestions made by their 'expert'.[14]

Individual cases were chosen to illustrate the effect of the disaster. The lists of the dead were awesome even without editorial comment, and the stories of personal tragedy were endless. Families were wiped out, terraces decimated, congregations and societies almost extinguished. In the heightened atmosphere of death the newspapers naturally gave prominence to the role of the local clergy, but they soon lost interest in discussions about the odd behaviour of God. Instead, their emphasis was on the role of the clergy in transcending barriers of class, language and nationality and creating a union of the whole community above such divisive elements.[15]

As the days passed into weeks without the fires being put out or the mine being cleared of more than a fraction of the corpses, the dilemma of the newspapers increased. Granted their assumptions

about newsworthiness, the national press could not indefinitely report
the dismal tale of a coalmining disaster.

The story had been looked at in detail and all the possible ironies of
the human condition had been explored. Readers were made to feel
the universality and unpredictability of death in such a way that they
could be brought to empathise with the plight of the otherwise alien
world of the mining community. The casualness, the arbitrariness
and the ironies of death were constantly reiterated.[16] Nevertheless
there was insufficient here for the likes of the *Daily Mail* which soon
dropped the story. While there had been undoubted courage shown,
there seemed ultimately to be something alien and distasteful about
this tale of blackened miners sweating below the surface to reach men
who, in the normal course of events, were only reported on because of
their criminal and anti-social behaviour.

By contrast, the fire on board the line liner 'Volturno', reported at
the same time, offered a more inspiring story. There was also death
on the 'Volturno', but in a situation which encouraged dreams of
British heroism. Instead of the decimation of a community, the
pattern was of a few deaths and many survivors, rescued by the
courage and determination of British officers. All this was reflected in
the headlines which announced 'Thrilling Stories of the Volturno
fire', 'Magnificent Bravery of British Officers' and 'A wonderful
drama of the Sea'.[17]

This story of the sea resonated with Nelsonian images compared to
which the 'drab looking colliery town, built on a monotonous and
uninspiring plan', described by *The Times,* did not seem to have much
to enthral the nation.[18] Several papers used the image of the theatre
to create a sense of a classical piece of drama unfolding. They referred
to the 'setting of the tragedy' and *The Times* accurately described the
valley as an 'amphitheatre' into which tens of thousands of people
poured.[19]

The newspapers tried to capture the imagination of their readers by
likening the rescuers to more traditionally heroic figures. As in 1901
the language and imagery of the rescue became one of war and the
heroism of the rescuers was made more explicable to readers by
comparing it to that of warriors.

Reporters and headline writers wrote of the 'forces of the Kimberley
District', 'the plan of campaign', the 'conquest of districts', 'relieving
forces', 'winning back lives from the corridors of death', 'getting the

better of the enemy', 'rapid advances through the fire' and 'gaining the upper hand of the enemy'. The *Western Mail* reported that 'the attack on the fire was productive of more than one thrill', creating from the disaster the tone of the *Boys Own Newspaper*.[20]

This image reached a crescendo in the reporting of a mining inspector's angry reply to the charge that more lives could have been saved if rescuers had forced their way into the Bottanic District sooner. The rescuers, Colonel Pearson said, had 'risked their lives in a burning mine, where the dangers are greater than anything reported from a battlefield, and to criticise them in their noble work by men who had neither the courage nor the manliness to take part themselves is cowardly, brutal and criminal'.[21]

The effect of the disaster on the town was also enhanced by military comparisons, *The Times* correspondent writing that 'we talk in awed terms of the decimation of a regiment in a bloody battle, but here a great community engaged in the pursuit of a peaceful vocation is threatened with the loss of at least a quarter of its able bodied manhood'. Later the same correspondent wrote 'and so the thrilling story has gone on from day to day in a burning mine where, to use the words of Colonel Pearson, the dangers are greater than anything ever reported from a battlefield'.[22] Insignificant military details were used to the full in the reports and even the names of the mine's districts, Mafeking, Ladysmith, and Kimberley, caused every report to echo with reminders of the supposed glories of British military imperialism. The imagery was expressed in more solid symbols when two members of the National Reserve were buried with full military honours at Eglwysilan Churchyard.

> Gun carriages were brought from Cardiff on which were conveyed the bodies. The coffins were covered with the Union Jack. . . There were 700 National Reservists present in charge of Sergt-Major Duffin (late of the King's Royal Rifles), also the Royal Field Garrison in command of Sergt Jenkins, Royal Field Artillery . . . The general arrangements were carried out under the supervision of Colonel Pearson, who was ably assisted by Colonel A. P. James, . . . The hundreds of people present at the Churchyard formed an imposing concourse and three volleys were fired over each grave by a company of National Reservists from the Rhondda including Porth. Trumpeter Broad of the 2nd R.F.A., Cardiff, sounded the 'Last Post' over the Graves.[23]

The imagery of war was particularly strong in the references to the men who were to form the 'forlorn hope', the small advance guard which gave up their lives in leading the assault on besieged towns: they

> prepared to lead the forlorn hope underground. But so desperate was the position that when they rose from the conference table these seven brave men walked to separate parts of the room and wrote farewell letters to those nearest and dearest to them. Three of them made their wills. It was a gamble with death on that first evening, but the seven won through, and a few hours later brought 18 men to the bank.[24]

All this was redolent of the novels of G. A. Henty about British military adventure and of Napier's highly charged romantic vision of the Peninsular War on which the middle classes had been reared. However when the courage displayed was described as a quality of workers, as distinct from honorary warriors, the oddness of the whole image became apparent. The *Caerphilly Journal,* for example, wrote of two rescuers, that 'both had the courage of facing death like brave British workmen never giving a moment's consideration for their own safety and considering the most advisable and expedient method to be adopted for rescuing their brethren who were entombed in the burning hell in the bowels of the earth.'[25] The tone is still authentically that of Henty, but the reference to courage as a quality specifically of British workers rings oddly against the backcloth of the years in which miners were seen as, at best, feckless and strike prone, and, at worst, as traitors.

The years to come were to bring savage reversals of this imagery. Within two years, during the brief strike of 1915, it was again to be argued in the press that the miners of the south Wales coalfield were comparable to an army and should be treated as such. On that occasion however they were seen as an enemy army:

> the enemy must be met literally by all the resources at the disposal of the State . . . attach all the trade union funds and prohibit strike pay. Food supplies could be held up, and the whole area treated as if it were an enemy's country. The men affected might be placed, by special enactment, in the position of soldiers, and placed under military discipline. Finally, to deal with any open violence or defiance of the law, the use of the military on a scale unexampled in normal times would be approved by the conscience of the community.

No sensible person will talk lightly of shooting down strikers and dragooning a whole population. . .[26]

The last sentence was not intended as a prelude to qualifying the maniacal tone of the proposals, but rather as a reassurance that when the eminently sensible writer put forward such suggestions, then the situation must have justified them.

If the newspapers honoured the miners by giving them the temporary status of soldiers, they gave to the women of Senghennydd the traditional role of warriors' wives: passive and brave, awaiting the return of the warrior or, if fate dictated it and King and Country required, then courageously facing the future alone. Women were portrayed as the passive victims of the tragedy, in need of comfort and support.

It would seem that the whole world of Senghennydd was powered by men and that the only role left for women was to mourn. In the small mining towns there was almost no paid work for women, and the whole economic and social structure of the town reinforced their apparent dependence. Yet in portraying the women as helpless victims and mere dependants the reports also served to reinforce an image which was far from the whole truth and which interestingly distorted the reality.

In the first place it is worth noting the extent to which the descriptions of the women's behaviour answers the dramatic needs of the story at different stages: their stoicism and strength are emphasised at one moment, their weakness and dependence at others. All built up the image of woman as strong in her dependence on her man and they paid moving tributes to the local community while reiterating the theme of the heroic British personality: 'they are not flinching; they are enduring their trial through this long and dreary night like British men and women'.[27] By contrast the *Western Mail* chose to highlight the emotional collapse of women returning from the mortuary:

'Oh dad, dad, he'll never come back again', continuously wailed a fine looking young woman of twenty while being led by sympathetic women from the mortuary to her home.

'Oh mam, mam', sobbed another in her agony, reverting to the mother love, while companions accompanied her along the sunlit road to the place whence had gone out husband and father to return no more.[28]

If the reports in the *The Times* and the *Daily Mail* were accurate then it may be that the women were in less danger of emotional collapse than was the *Western Mail* reporter.

Perhaps inevitably, all these reports profoundly mistook the nature of women's role. The misconception, starting as it did from the centrality of production, and therefore of man's essential importance, simultaneously reflected and misrepresented reality. If industrial production is seen as the sole focus of existence then the women were truly appendages, but if the reproduction of society is the greater whole, of which industrial production is only a major facet, then the role of the women is seen to be central though still excluded from formally structured power.

In the process of social reproduction the women took the major part through child birth, the rearing of children and the maintenance of the family and of the worker on which production depended. Placed in this context of suffering and hardship it is easier to understand that far from being the emotionally dependent, if stoical, appendages of men it was in fact the women who in many ways held this society together. They and their families were not going to collapse if the death of the wage earner once again forced them back into a life of hardship as against the comparative plenty of recent years.

Several of the women were the widows of miners who had been killed in the 1901 explosion.[29] They had brought up their children on their own only to see sons killed in their turn. The emotional distress may have been unspeakable but in practical terms the women would manage. It makes no sense to highlight the helplessness of archetypal Senghennydd women like Elizabeth Lower, who had faced up to the magistrates' court or Sarah Evans. It had been Sarah Evans who, when the bailiffs came for James Evans, saw them off with a poker and a bowl which she broke over their heads while her husband cowered in the attic and her lodger confined himself to passing her the poker.[30]

The women of Senghennydd were no doubt as much in need of emotional support as the rest of us but they were also tough, experienced, and the rock on which that society survived. From this dangerous cauldron the women produced generations of intelligent, hard working and committed people. To do this they fought to maintain the home as their territory in which their standards would apply. This has been distorted into the populist misconception that this was a matriarchal society: nothing could be further from the truth since in terms of structured power it was a virtually unquestioned patriarchy. Equally the role of women was sentimentalised into the image of the mother figure, the Welsh 'Mam'. An accurate picture would contain elements of all this, but in its gritty and unromantic quality it had nothing to offer the newspapers in their creation of an image of a unified British nation in which women played a purely supportive and sentimentalised role.

One would not expect journalists covering the disaster to engage with this complex reality: in circumstances like these death usually generates ritual orations rather than serious social investigation. Nevertheless the newspaper stories served to reinforce an image of women as helpless and passive sufferers. Now that their men were dead it was supposed that they needed someone else to be dependent on and it was here that the different themes of the newspapers came together in offering the warm community of the British nation, at whose head was a caring monarch, as the emotional, financial and psychological support for the bereaved.

The newspaper reports of the tragedy created a wave of public sympathy, and throughout the British Isles and abroad funds were started to help the victims. Newspapers, picture palaces, churches, societies, local authorities and trade unions all held collections.

As one would expect the largest donations came from the wealthy and from public companies. Every day the lists of the subscribers were published in the press and it is possible to get an accurate account of the wealthy people who donated to the fund since only a handful among the hundreds of subscribers chose to remain anonymous. Presumably it was pleasing to them to have their care and generosity made public. Occasionally wrong information was given and corrections had to be made, in case the generosity of these people was not properly recorded. Thus *The Times* wrongly ascribed a donation of £50 to Farrow's Bank (ltd) and had to publish a correction. *The Times* informed its readers that this was actually donated by Mr Thomas Farrow, the chairman of Farrow's Bank (ltd).[31]

Among the contributors were many south Wales businesses and some of the great families of south Wales. Lord Bute gave 1500 guineas, the Lewis Merthyr Company, owners of the mine, donated 1000 guineas and Lord Merthyr himself gave two sums of £100, (and possibly other larger amounts).[32] These were large sums. It is as well, however, to retain a sense of proportion. The Hon. Herbert Lewis of Hean Castle, Lord Merthyr's son and heir, had paid 500 guineas for a prize cow earlier in the month.[33] Lord Bute derived wealth beyond dreams from his mineral rights. He owned over 120,000 acres of land and nearly 50,000 acres of mineral rights. His income from mineral rights alone was soon to amount to more than £110,000 per annum apart from his income from the land, docks and railways which he owned. He owned the land on which the Senghennydd mine was situated, inherited from a sixteenth century ancestor, and was paid between 6d and 1s and 6d for every ton of the millions of tons of coal raised from the mine. It was from this wealth that he donated 1,500 guineas to the fund to relieve 900 dependants

John Bull grudgingly contributes to the relief fund.

Western Mail

of the dead and the hundreds of men, and their families, made unemployed as a result of the explosion.[34]

Public giving and shared sorrow became one of the major themes of the press and it reached its height in the reporting of the King's response. George V immediately sent £500 to the disaster fund and an admission charge to see the wedding gifts of Prince Arthur and the Duchess of Fife raised a further £1200. Headlines announced that Queen Mary had sent £200 and that Queen Alexandra, the widow of Edward VII had donated a further £100. The letters from the members of the royal family were printed in full. Only two years earlier troops had occupied the Welsh valleys, shots had been fired and the list of injured had run into hundreds. Now Senghennydd was used to draw the moral of a nation fundamentally sound and at one, in which all sections of the population were united. Columns on the generous response were headlined, 'From the Palace to the Cottage', 'From the throne to the humblest' and 'The Whole World Kin'.[35]

A report in the *Western Mail* quoted the Lord Mayor of Cardiff as saying that 'it was most inspiring and comforting to find that the nation was right at heart, that there was a flood of sympathy from his Majesty down to the meanest peasant'. A motion was passed which underlined the awe felt by his subjects, but also the kindliness and homeliness of the monarch's human response:

> in renewing to his most gracious Majesty the King the assurance of the devotion to his Majesty's person and throne, this council desires to express to his Majesty their most respectful thanks for his timely and handsome contribution of £500 . . . a kindly and thoughtful act which will be sincerely appreciated by his Majesty's loyal and devoted subjects in the Principality of Wales.

Sir John Curtis seconded the motion emphasising that 'the gifts showed that the King and Queen took a deep concern in the welfare of their subjects'.[36]

Lord Merthyr pointed out that expressions of sympathy had come from all classes, and particular emphasis was placed on 'the readiness of the employers to work hand in hand with the trade union officials . . . there has been absolutely no friction, and union officials and mine managers are working side by side in the mine, endeavouring with equal bravery and disinterestedness to bring succour to the unfortunate men who are missing'.[37]

The contrast was strong between the Senghennydd story and the treatment of another major story, about the Dublin dispute in which 18,000 workers were locked out or on strike. There was a clear implication that this harmony over Senghennydd underlay social relations as a whole and should survive once the immediate tragedy receded. Few papers seem to have reported the Welsh miners' support for the Irish strikers and their protest at the arrest of James Larkin. A single sentence lost in the dense columns of the four page *Caerphilly Journal* was not likely to dent the image, carefully created by the national and provincial daily press, of British national unity above the mere self interest of class.[38]

Several of these themes were illustrated in a much reported incident which was also used to suggest an older underlying sense of Welsh community which transcended class. David Watts Morgan, a miners' leader from the Rhondda,

> who has been one of the most capable and intrepid of the rescuers, met Lord Merthyr as he came from the cage after a long day underground. 'We are the masters at last', Mr Morgan said in Welsh, with a quiet strain of confidence. 'Thank god for that!' was Lord Merthyr's reply in the language which is used by nearly everybody in these valleys unless they are talking with strangers.[39]

Within a few years Morgan was to be metamorphosed by the First World War into Lieutenant-Colonel David Watts Morgan C.B.E., D.S.O., M.P., J.P. and immortalised in the valleys as Dai Alphabet.

As a result of the explosion eight hundred men were made unemployed at the Universal Colliery. For most of them their wages legally ended on the day of the explosion. In the ensuing weeks a plea was made by officials of the Miners' Federation that the unemployed should continue, at least, to get their concessionary coal but Edward Shaw was not empowered to answer the request. A deputation waited on Lord Merthyr whose main point was that the unemployed should be paid out of the public fund for the victims. When one of the funds agreed to pay £100 towards relief of the eight hundred unemployed miners and their families, 'his Lordship very generously intimated that he would make himself responsible for another £100. In consideration of the attitude of the Lord Mayor's Relief Committee his Lordship was prepared to co-operate with the local relief committee in the idea of relieving all necessitous cases, whether the families were bereaved or not'.[40]

Lord Merthyr's other main proposal was that 200 miners should transfer to his Rhondda pits where work was available. The delegation pointed out that most of the miners were tied to Senghennydd by the fact that their relations and immediate friends were still entombed. Lord Merthyr took the point 'but emphasised the fact that those who could obtain employment elsewhere should do so'. In the event the main source for helping the unemployed came from the miners themselves who carried out a monthly levy on all members throughout the south Wales coalfield and the owners generously assisted this fund by graciously agreeing to stop the levy directly from miners' wages. The Miners' Federation was able, in this way, to pay out 10/- per man and 1/- per child, to the unemployed at a cost of £350 per week.[41]

By the end of November when at last all the areas had been penetrated and while work was still going on to repair the devastated western districts, the men voted to restart work in the mine, in which eleven bodies were still entombed. It was a decision that no miners welcomed. After the explosion in 1901 the *Pontypridd Chronicle* wrote of the dead miners as men 'who had sacrificed their lives on the altar of duty'. It was not a sense of duty to a unified nation that drove them back to work in the lethal pit, but the harsh realities of unemployment and hunger for working class families in the context of the relentless drive to maintain profitable industrial production in a largely unregulated free market in coal.[42] This had been a bad time for the Lewis Merthyr Company and it was important to restart normal production as soon as possible.

At their best the newspaper reports had offered intelligent and moving accounts of the tragedy at Senghennydd: they were skilfully crafted presentations of reality. The differences between them reflect the sensibilities and insights of competing professionals. In his spare and effective reporting of the funerals for the *South Wales Daily News,* S. C. Fox wrote:

> In the presence of death, silence. Death itself is regarded as the shadow of the silence, and the whole district of Senghennydd was impressed with that spirit on Saturday... all excitement was hushed. The tension of feeling of the earlier days of the explosion has given way to stolid despair or submission to the awful facts of the mine.

By contrast, Wright of the *Western Mail,* in just one report, managed to collect enough cliches, mannered repetitions and alliterative excesses to fill a primer on purple prose. In that report he wrote of the 'horror of the blast', 'the roar of the blast', 'the theatre of the blast', and 'the resistless impact of the ascending blast': the 'reverberating roar', the 'thunderous explosion', 'the raging furnace', 'the deep descent' and the 'massive masonry': and of the rescue 'being watched with bated breath by kith and kin'. Effusions of sentiment in rolling alliterative prose trip over each other in a medley of overblown rhetoric. In a nicely ironic letter to his son, Fox wrote,

> I send you a cutting of the account of the funerals I did for the *Daily News*. It is not great, but it is a ¾ column written around the funerals which were *devoid of incident*. There was nothing to describe. The double column is a fine example of Mr Wright's style. It is a splendid specimen of 'how not to do it'. Examine it carefully *and smile*.[43]

Despite these differences of style and sentiment there was however a perceptible general thrust to the story that was being told. The newspapers sought to have their perceptions of reality accepted both nationally, through papers such as *The Times* and *Daily Mail*, and within the south Wales coalfield, through the *Western Mail*, the *Caerphilly Journal*, the *Glamorgan Free Press* and other local newspapers: and as there were differences between the perceptions of journalists so too different newspapers reflected conflicting views. However the reports were also expressions of an underlying ideology which incorporated images of man and woman, community and religion, into an encompassing vision of the British Nation.[44] Their success in getting that ideology accepted was demonstrated when, less than a year later, Welsh miners volunteered in their thousands to fight on the Western Front against German miners, encouraged by their own leaders.

The tragedy of Senghennydd throws into clear relief differing views of British society. As one might expect it was *The Times* which most clearly articulated the view that, beneath the differing degrees of hardship borne by different classes, there was an underlying human sympathy which bound all together in a British Nation. This view was expressed in an editorial at the time of the disaster:

> From all quarters messages of condolence and of sympathy are pouring in. None perhaps shows more truly the strength of the feeling which moves us all than that which the Royal bride and bridegroom of Wednesday bethought them of sending to the afflicted community 'in the

moment of their great happiness'. Grief such as the mourners' is indeed past cure, but it will find such mitigation as is possible in the knowledge that all sorts and conditions of men from the highest to the poorest, feel with them. Calamities so great as this are not appreciated all at once. It is only by degrees that the public mind can realise the immensity of the loss which the nation has suffered, and the extent of its consequences. As they come to ponder over the future of the women and children who have been suddenly plunged into mourning, and bethink them what enduring privation to those hundreds of sufferers the deaths of husbands and brothers and fathers may bring, they will resolve, we are sure, to do what in them lies to alleviate the hard lot of the widow and of the orphan.[45]

There were clear voices raised against this consensus. The *South Wales Worker* had commented in the week after the explosion:

bitter experience teaches us that in less than a few months the tragedy will be practically forgotten, and that the same persons who are now deploring the event and praising the heroism of the rescuers will, on the occasion of the next miners' strike, be equally ardent in denouncing the colliers who inconvenience the public for their own selfish consideration.

But such comments were drowned by the weight of reporting and editorialising which reflected the predominant ideology.[46]

Among the population of the valleys there remained, deeply internalised, the images perpetuated by press, churches, schools and by some of their own organisations: images of women which marginalised them within working class politics, of a Welsh Nation incorporated within British nationalism and of working class people in the bosom of an authority symbolised by a caring monarch.

Time was to show how much the loss was indeed felt to be a loss to the British Nation as a whole, and how far it could ultimately be ignored as the problem of what had become an industrial backwater.

The holocaust which enveloped the village showed the inhabitants to be capable of an iron discipline which gave outsiders little indication of their inner feelings. One measure of the emotional stress in the valley were the five suicides and attempted suicides which occurred during the following months, a figure in startling contrast to the small number in the previous fifteen years. Though not all were specifically caused by the explosion, they indicate something of the trauma felt in the community.

The seventeen year old Annie Gay cut her throat in her parents' kitchen in May 1914. She had been severely depressed since the explosion in which her sister's young man was killed. Dr James visited her parents' house earlier in May when he found that, while she was suffering mental torments, she 'was not insane'. Dr James reported that 'she was quite rational in her way and quite prim in her manner. She did not look strange but appeared to be depressed'. To Dr James she gave her explanation of what was troubling her: 'Oh dear, all those souls have gone home and I have suffered terribly'.

Two weeks later, on a Thursday night, she told her mother that she was writing to her young man and her mother asked if she was in any trouble. Annie Gay reassured her: 'Oh dear no, only now I am happy. I have told you'. It seems that having written the letter she experienced a sort of peace, having made her decision. Her wretched mother did not understand the significance of the letter until the next morning. Annie Gay got up before anyone else on the Friday morning and cut her throat in the kitchen where she was found by her mother.

For her mother and Henry Gay, the shoemaker of 22 Commercial Street, it added a further, almost unimaginable, quality to the suffering of the town. Possibly their membership of the Baptist Congregation gave them some comfort, though it had been insufficient for Annie Gay who was described as a faithful member of the Chapel.[47]

In October 1914 Robert Griffiths killed himself. He was from Penygroes in Caernarvonshire and his wife and child still lived there. He had been ill for nine weeks and had spent the time in North Wales with his family. He returned to Senghennydd on the Saturday in order to start work again in the mine the following Monday, but he could not face more of this existence and he too cut his throat. A verdict of 'suicide during temporarary insanity' was recorded: to an outsider his decision might seem rational.[48]

The following week the mother of one of the men who had died in the explosion killed herself in Abertridwr. Mary Saunders had been severely depressed ever since the explosion and drank carbolic acid. Her death was horribly drawn out, and while she was dying she claimed that she had drunk the poison by accident.[49]

There were also symmetrical cases of a young man and a young woman attempting suicide because of difficulties with their lovers. In April Elizabeth Ann Rees, aged 18, took an inadequate dose of poison. Elizabeth Ann's own explanation for her attempt was that she did it 'because she had been accused of causing her young man illness'. The crisis was probably brought to a head by her parents who threw her clothes out of the house 'because I had slept away two nights over the holidays'. She was lucky that Mrs Jackson of 24 Park Terrace was able to speak for her and that Mr Davies, the landlord of Park Terrace, was willing to take her into the house until she found a domestic situation.[50] This adolescent drama was matched by one in Abertridwr where a young miner attempted suicide because his girlfiend was unfaithful to him.[51]

Many people never recovered from the shock of the disaster. Ellen Owen, the mother of John Owen who was among the dead, had been active in the Congregational Church, had read her poetry at the *eisteddfodau* and had written essays for the Welsh press; after October 1913 she became a chronic invalid, dying a recluse twenty years later.[52] In another case, during the Great War, Ernest Wall's father was believed by the court when he argued that his son was 'more to be pitied than blamed. He is one of the survivors of the Senghennydd explosion and his senses have been affected ever since'. His father was urged to get medical advice for Ernest Wall.[54]

The effects of the explosion continued throughout 1914 as the grim experience of finding corpses continued in the Universal. On January 29th it was reported that the body of James Jones had been found in the mine. In May they found the body of William George King in the Kimberley District: on May 1st his wife Eliza had given birth to his daughter, Mabel, seven months after his death.

There was a sense of cheating death in the birth of children of the dead miners during the months after the explosion, though for some the burden of another mouth to feed must have outweighed the small victory. In all 39 children are known to have been born after the death of the fathers. The first, Robert William Evans, was born on October 21st, 1913 to Emma Evans, and was named after his father, as was Eva James after her father, Evan James. Margaret James already had six children, the oldest of whom was fourteen. Finally Teresa Moran gave birth to Margaret Moran just two days short of nine months after James Moran had been killed.

Altogether the dead miners left over 500 dependent children. The relentless hard work of having to survive and look after the children made indulgence in grief an impractical luxury. The relief fund provided ten shillings a week for widows and a further three shillings for each dependent child. Together with the compensation of up to

£300, owed by the company under the Workmen's Compensation Act, this ensured that the women had sufficient to survive: the wives of alcoholics were probably better off financially than before. Since wages had been high in recent years, most widows received the full compensation of £300. Annie Newell, the twenty three year old widow of Richard Newell, who had no children, received the full compensation, as did the two dependent children of Joseph Hopkins and other widowers. On the other hand the compensation was both meagre and petty minded in cases such as the two dependent 'illegitimate' children of Alfred Hadley. £47.10s was paid for the upkeep of Alfred and Edward, aged thirteen and eleven respectively. The two 'illegitimate' children of Charles Brown were treated in the same way: the four year old Griffith Davies and Gwendoline Llewellyn, who was not born until January 1914, received £40 between them, and the mothers were left dependent on relations or the Board of Guardians.[54]

The company fought a significant number of claims for compensation, and in many cases it managed to resist paying damages. In twenty nine cases no-one made a claim and the company recorded the fact that they did not admit any liability. In ten cases it was sufficient for the company to repudiate the claim for relations to desist from pursuing it. In a handful of cases, such as that of the sixteen year old William Attewell, relations pressed for compensation but the award was made in favour of the company and only the £10 burial fee was paid. Even when compensation was paid, it was fairly derisory in some cases. £8 6s 8d was paid by the company for the death of R. J. Evans, an eighteen year old collier boy. In a further 73 cases compensation was agreed for £50 or less, as in the cases of collier boys aged between fourteen and sixteen who had contributed to the family income. In most such cases, except those in which the child was the sole breadwinner, the company managed to resist paying damages.[55]

To the accountant handling these cases on behalf of the company the result seemed highly satisfactory, as he explained in his final letter to the Lewis Merthyr Co. Ltd: 'The average cost per case amounts to £172-15-9 and having regard to all the circumstances I think the settlements can be regarded as extremely favourable from our mutual point of view'.[56]

The village came to terms with the holocaust as the public ritual of inquests, public enquiry and legal prosecutions unfolded. The prosecutions for breaches of the Mines Act dragged on until July 1914. Even then, the decisions of the court were so lenient that the Mining Inspectorate appealed against the dismissal of various charges, and the legal processes against the Company and Edward Shaw were not finally settled until 1915.

The inquest on the dead added to the bitter, fatalistic expectations of the villagers when it delivered the verdict that the 439 miners had met accidental deaths. The verdicts at the inquest conflicted with the view, expressed later by Clement Edwards M.P., that 'there have been breaches in regard to ventilation; there have been breaches in regard to gas tests; there have been breaches in regard to the reporting of gas; there have been breaches in regard to electric sparking; there have been breaches in regard to the dusting of roads. . . most of the breaches appertain to one aspect or another of the provisions which have been instituted for dealing with and preventing explosions'.[57]

In many respects the pattern of the official inquiry was remarkably similar to that of 1901. Richard Redmayne, the chief inspector of mines, was appointed to chair the enquiry, 'assisted' by two assessors; Robert Smillie, president of the Miners' Federation of Great Britain and Evan Williams, the chairman of the Monmouthshire and South Wales Coalowners' Association. Again the inquiry was requested to find both the immediate cause of the explosion and the broader factors which caused the deaths throughout the west side of the mine. Since there was again disagreement about where the explosion originated, it was not possible for unanimity over why it erupted. It was argued that a fall of rock had released a large volume of gas and that this had been ignited either by a faulty lamp, or by sparks caused by electrical signalling equipment, or by a piece of falling rock creating sparks as it hit the stone below. Redmayne's view was that the electrical signalling equipment was the most likely cause. If this was the case then it argued a casual attitude to aspects of safety on the part of the management since this had been the cause of the explosion at the Bedwas Colliery only the year before, and the Inspectorate had circulated all colliery managers to warn them of the dangers of electrical signalling equipment.

Though much time was spent on the subject, both at the inquiry and in subsequent years, the exact cause of the initial explosion has never been conclusively identified. More broadly the inquiry pointed to a number of factors which led to the hundreds of deaths. It was suggested that the mine should have been watered more effectively, that the coal trucks should have had closed lids and that dust should have been swept and collected from the sides and roof, or blown from them with compressed air. The response of the management to these points varied. They pointed out that they were in the process of buying trucks with closed covers but that the rush to obtain them, in order to comply with the requirements of the 1911 Act, meant that there was as yet an insufficient supply. Shaw argued that he had tried to deal with the problem of dust on the side and rooves of the main tunnels by giving them brick arches but that the geological settlement in the mine was so great that these were destroyed by the weight of rock above. He argued that the use of compressed air simply blew the dust around the mine, causing even more to settle in the workings.

The one thing on which all could agree was that the management was so rigorous in ensuring that no miners took matches or tobacco into the mine, that the possiblility of the explosion being caused by a miner smoking a cigarette or pipe could be ruled out. This was good for the company in that it showed their efficiency in carrying out one aspect of safety work; on the other hand it made it impossible for them to argue that the whole thing had been caused by an irresponsible worker.

In several cases the manager and company were technically not guilty. As far as taking readings of gas levels, according to the requirements of the 1911 Act, was concerned the company was obliged to take monthly readings from 16th September 1913. The company therefore claimed that it had a further three days in which to carry out the requirement when the explosion occurred. Similarly, in the case of using closed coal trucks to keep down the level of dust, the company argued that they were not obliged to obey this clause of the Act until it came fully into effect in 1916. On the crucial issue of the ability to reverse the air current, the company was again able to claim that they had been given extra time by the Mine Inspectors to install a new system, and that in any event the current could have been reversed by some temporary expedients such as breaking through existing walls and installing new barriers. The precise legality of each point is, in retrospect, less significant than the general point, accepted by most observers, that the company failed to take a number of necessary precautions, known to everyone in the industry, regardless of whether, at that particular moment, the company was technically within or outside the law. The point was made by Richard Redmayne, who headed the inquiry, with regard to the supply of water:

> I am convinced that had there been available at that time an adequate water supply, and had brigades of rescuers attacked the three fires ... simultaneously, the fires might have been extinguished in a comparatively short time. I should have thought, in view of the fact that the colliery was such a gassy one, and as it had already been devastated by an explosion, that the management would have made arrangements for a supply of water adequate to meet an emergency of the kind that actually occurred.[58]

As it was, however, a pair of two inch pipes had been the total supply of water to a mine employing several hundred workers in coalfaces two miles apart.

Redmayne made the same point of principle when dealing with the company's argument that the spark produced by their type of electric signalling should not be sufficient to ignite a gas explosion:

> ... I can only regret that the safer plan of excluding sparks altogether was not adopted.
>
> It is all the more astonishing that the management should have faced the risk that the sparks produced might have ignited gas in view of the Bedwas Colliery explosion, which occurred on March 27, 1912, and which was proved beyond reasonable doubt to have been caused by the sparks of an electric bell.[59]

As far as the coal dust was concerned, the management was adamant that it was impractical to clear dust from the sides and rooves of the tunnels. Redmayne wrote that '... I have no doubt whatever that coal dust existed on the roof, sides and timber in dangerous quantity'.[60] He was 'not satisfied that serious efforts were, in fact, made towards removing the side and top dust, nor [did he] consider that its removal was impracticable' and concluded that 'the dust on the roof and sides was practically disregarded'.[61]

The point was repeatedly made that this this had been a comparatively small explosion. The vast majority of the men died of asphyxiation from afterdamp because they could not be reached as a result of the fires. Had water been available and rescue teams faster to arrive on the scene then more lives might have been saved. As it was there was a major delay in reconnecting the shattered water pipes because of the smoke which made the work impossible. The explosion had occurred just after eight o'clock. Redmayne commented:

> it was not until the arrival of breathing apparatus from the Porth Rescue Station—about eight miles distant—that a proper connection was made. As this was not until 11 o'clock—word not having been received at the rescue station until 10 o'clock—much valuable time was lost.[62]

Shaw may have speculated on how many lives would have been saved if he had alerted the rescue stations before descending the mine to carry out his heroic individual struggle against the flames. Redmayne seems to have liked Edward Shaw as a person. He wrote that 'Mr Shaw impressed me as an honest, industrious and in many respects, an active manager, and he gave his evidence in a clear and straitforward manner and assisted in the Inquiry to the utmost of his power'. There was also special praise for the courage of Shaw and the other men who entered the mine within minutes of the explosion. Nevertheless, Redmayne's conclusion was that 'some of these breaches [of the Mines Act] . . . may appear trivial, but taken in the aggregate they point to a disquieting laxity in the management of the mine'.[63]

In opposition to the general consensus Evan Williams, the owners' representative on the enquiry, maintained that the mine was well managed, that most of the alleged breaches of the law could not be proved due to technicalities and that such breaches of the act which existed were of a technical nature to do with the formality of registering specific information in books.

Broadly speaking the magistrates' court, which heard the case in July 1914, took the same view as Evan Williams. Of the seventeen charges against Edward Shaw, seven were dropped, and he was found not guilty on five of the remainder. Shaw was found guilty on three charges of failing to keep proper records, as demanded by the act, on the charge of being unable to reverse the air current and on the charge of failing adequately to clear the dust from the ground: he was fined a total of £24. The court decided that the company did not bear any responsibility and therefore found them not guilty on each charge. A local paper carried the headline 'Miners' Lives at 1¼ d each'.[64]

By then Sir William Lewis, Lord Merthyr of Senghennydd, had died. He left over half a million pounds apart from his land and personal possessions: the Hean Castle Estate and other properties had already been made over to his children during his lifetime. Among his

One of many souvenirs of the 1913 disaster.

peers he was remembered as a giant among industrialists and a stern philanthropist: 'in his inner heart he is ever solicitous for suffering humanity, and no one has ever done more really good service for the working man than Sir William Thomas Lewis'. In the mythology of the coalfield he was remembered as 'the hypocrite Sir William T. Lewis, the most vicious of all. He was a bugger, always prating about fair play this and fair play that, even while he was prepared to grind the miner into the ground to help him amass a fortune and gain a title'.[65]

In the wider world the orgy of sympathy which had enveloped the village soon faded away. In its place returned the customary indifference of the population as a whole to the problems of the alien world of the mining community, with its dismal terraces hidden from sight at the end of a polluted valley. The events in Senghennydd had already become insignificant beside the vast catastrophe that was enveloping Europe.

SENGHENNYDD

I roamed the dull streets in the valley blind
With mist and rain and the murk colliery smoke;
Churches I saw that to the passer spoke
Of many a soul that for God's peace had pined,
And refuge from man's multitudinous pain;
But darker far upon the valley lay
Than colliery smoke the shadow of the day
That saw that holocaust of strong men slain
On Wealth's soiled altars. In a room hard by
The men of law were met, with Mammon's crew,
Lords of the money bags, in long debate
Of whose the blame, and how it fell and why
Those hundreds went to flaming death,—and yet
Not one sat there but the whole secret knew!

T. Gwynn Jones
translated from the Welsh[66]

CHAPTER 10

[1] The account which follows is taken from the *Western Mail, Caerphilly Journal, Glamorgan Free Press, Times, Daily Mail, Birmingham Post:* the most comprehensive account is in J. H. Brown, *op cit.* See also N. Williams, 'The Senghenydd Colliery Disaster', in Ed. S. Williams, *Glamorgan Historian* vol. 6 (Cowbridge; 1969)

[2] J. H. Brown, *op cit,* 81 & 79

[3] DM 16/10/1913

[4] *South Wales Argus* 3 & 4 /11 1978

[5] CJ 23/10/1913

[6] *Times* 20/10/1913

[7] W. H. Davies, *Ups and Downs,* (Swansea; 1975), 185: *Times* 20/10/1913

[8] GFP 23/10/1913

[9] *ibid:* BP 20/10/1913

[10] Quoted in I. Jenkins, *Idris Davies of Rhymney,* (Llandysul; 1986), 25

[11] GFP 18/10/1913

[12] G. Williams, *op cit,* 195-6: the material which follows first appeared as an article, M. Lieven, 'Representations of the Working Class Community: the Senghenydd Mining Disaster, 1913', *Llafur: Journal of Welsh Labour History ,* Vol 5 (2), 17-29

[13] *Times* 15/10/1913: WM 16/10/1913

[14] BDP 15/10/1913; WM 17/10/1913: WM 18/10/1913

[15] WM 18/10/1913

[16] WM 16/10/1913: *Times* 19/10/1913

[17] WM 14/10/1913

[18] *Times* 15/10/1913, 16/10/1913

[19] *Times* 15/10/1913

[20] WM 18/10/1913

[21] BDP 20/10/1913

[22] *Times* 17/10/1913; *Times* 21/10/1913

[23] CJ 27/11/1913

[24] *Times* 21/10/1913

[25] CJ 23/10/1913

[26] R. Page Arnot, (1975), op cit, 74

[27] *Times* 15/10/1913: DM 16/10/1913

[28] WM 16/10/1913

[29] *Times* 15/10/1913

[30] GFP 4/4/1903: CJ 4/9/1913: PC 28/10/1905

[31] *Times* 20/10/1913

[32] WM 18/10 1913

[33] WM 9/10 1913

[34] PP 1919 Cmd. 359 xi 653

[35] WM 18/10/1913 & 16/10/1913

[36] WM 18/10/1913

[37] *Times* 17/10/1913: CJ 23/10/1913

[38] CJ 6/11/1913

[39] *Times* 18/10/1913

[40] CJ 6/11/1913

[41] *ibid*

[42] PC 1/5/1901: *Times* 25/11/1913: CJ 27/11/1913

[43] National Museum of Wales; Industrial and Maritime Museum, accession number 87.95 I/3. I am grateful to Dr Bill Jones of the Museum Staff for drawing my attention to this letter

[44] G. Williams, *op cit,* 195-6

[45] *Times* 17/10/1913

[46] R. Page Arnot, (1967), *op cit,* 366: *South Wales Worker* 25/10/1913

[47] CJ 19/3/1914

[48] CJ 29/10/1914

[49] CJ 5/11/1914

[50] CJ 23/4/1914

[51] CJ 20/8/1914

[52] CJ 14/1/1933

[53] CJ 8/7/1915

[54] Lewis Merthyr Consolidated Collieries, Senghennydd Colliery Explosion Compensation Payments; GRO D/D NCB 171 (1)

[55] *ibid*

[56] *ibid*

[57] quoted in R. Page Arnot, (1967), *op cit,* 353

[58] PP 1914 CD 7346 (p32) xxix

[59] *ibid*

[60] *ibid,* (p10)

[61] *ibid,* (pp 9 & 33)

[62] *ibid,* (p22)

[63] *ibid,* (p35)

[64] R. Page Arnot, (1967), *op cit,* 366

[65] E. Phillips, *op cit,* 202: W. H. Davies, (1975), *op cit,* 207

[66] T. G. Jones, 'Senghenydd', translated from the Welsh by H. I. Bell, *Welsh Outlook,* vol III, (Nov 1916). I am grateful to Neil Evans of Coleg Harlech for drawing my attention to the poem

Chapter Eleven
The Great War

On the 4th of August 1914 Britain declared war on Germany. Even more than in the rest of Britain, war enveloped Senghennydd while attention was on other things. At the start the village expressed little enthusiasm. Interest was focussed on the finding of the court that the Lewis Merthyr Company bore no share of responsibility for the deaths of 439 miners. For those who could think of anything else, the emphasis was on trying to rebuild families and the community and on organising the sports days and events for children which used to enliven their days.

In the first week of the war the Government received a clear warning that it could not take the response of the south Wales miners for granted. The miners' holiday was due and the Government, at the request of the Admiralty, asked them to work on Monday, Tuesday and Wednesday. With a few exceptions the Welsh miners refused, considering, (rightly as it turned out), that the position of coal stocks was not dangerously low, as had been claimed, and that they were therefore entitled to take an annual excursion from their underground world. The newspapers immediately drew disparaging conclusions about the loyalty of miners which they adversely compared to the apparently patriotic attitude of the owners:

> the Welsh miners, who were asked to curtail their holidays by working on Tuesday and Wednesday did not consent to help the government . . . and they went a step further and passed a drastic resolution condemning British interference in the war.[1]

The attitude of the miners was contrasted to that of the owners and of other workers:

> 'a hurried meeting of the representatives of the colliery owners was held, when a loyal response was given to the call of the government'.[2] Steps were taken 'so that the loading of the large fleet of collier transports . . . should go on continuously night and day, including Sunday, and also Bank Holiday and Tuesday, . . . Coal trimmers, railwaymen and others affected responded loyally to the call . . .'.

Few of the south Wales mines produced coal over the holiday, with the interesting exception of the pits at Llwynypia, the epicentre of the riots during the Cambrian dispute. It did not take long, however, for the jingoism of the times to affect the policies of the union leaders. An indication of the underlying strength of patriotic feeling occurred on August 6th when a meeting in Merthyr to demonstrate support for peace, to be addressed by Keir Hardie, was broken up by crowds mobilised by C. B. Stanton, the populist 'revolutionary' miners' agent who had been at the bottom of the poll in East Glamorgan in the election of 1910. By the end of August the miners' leaders had fallen into line with national sentiment and had committed their members to working an extra hour a day for the war effort: the Senghennydd miners stood out in their refusal to work the extra hour, one of the few signs that the horrors visited upon the town had produced any change in their political or social consciousness.[3]

Doubts about the justification for war were dissolved as inhabitants were overwhelmed by a flood of propaganda about the brutal Hun suppression of Belgium and Serbia, small nations overwhelmed by powerful neighbours: a connection was drawn between Wales and other small nations which apparently convinced Welshman of their moral obligation to fight for the British Empire, while avoiding questions about the relation of dominance between England and Wales. The highlight of the early recruitment and propaganda drive in Senghennydd had been a speech by John Littlejohn: his patriotic rhetoric was well suited to the genius of the valleys, full of *hwyl* and sophisticated historical references. An observer commented that 'it was one of the greatest speeches that he had ever heard and its memories would long be preserved by those who had heard it'.[4]

A fairly typical week in the early months of 1915 illustrates the social life of the town and the novel experiences created by the war for some of the inhabitants. In April a concert in the Senghennydd Conservative Club was chaired by Thomas Hitchings, a lifelong Liberal; Thomas James, the Labour councillor, was also on the platform. Hitchings opened the proceedings by commenting that 'during his eighteen years residence in Senghennydd, he had only once been in such an institution as this'; only patriotic enthusiasm could have broken down his aversion to the combination of conservatism and alcohol. Littlejohn then again delivered an oration which leant heavily on historical allusions; to the Athenian Parthenon, to Socrates and to Gibbon's *Decline and Fall of the Roman Empire*. His theme was the battle raging against Turkey in the Dardenelles and the attempt to retake Constantinople from the heathen.

> For nearly five centuries they [the Moslems] had guarded the faith of the false prophet until the Saint Sophia Cathedral had cried to the ages 'Oh! how long oh God before my profanation shall perish?' That question was being answered by the guns of the Queen Elizabeth, the echo of their discharges was being heard in the old Cathedral, the memories of her shame were turned to great drops of blood that fell down from her sapptured dome to the pages of time once more. Travellers had told them that when the Turks took the city in 1453, they covered the portrait of our Saviour with plaster. But the plaster was wearing away and the picture was being dimly seen again smiling in sorrow in its long sleep of the ages.[5]

In the same week a recruiting meeting was held in the Park Hall for the 3rd Battalion of the Welsh Regiment. The meeting was opened by Lieutenant Colonel Marwood-Elon who made a pedestrian speech which emphasised the heavy casualties and the consequent need for replacements: the speech finally became entangled in a discussion about the irrelevance of discussing horse racing in the present situation. 'It was not the future of horse racing that they were considering, but it was the future of the old country'. Something about the inconsequentiality of this issue suggests that the Colonel himself might have been happier discussing the Cheltenham results and that the lack of such discussions was rather preying on his mind.

The situation was rescued by Lieutenant Tudor Rees who declared that 'the whole heart of Wales was throbbing with enthusiasm and the mind of Wales was concentrated on France and Flanders as the flower of Wales was cut down there...'. After references to the Judas of Berlin, Tudor Rees was able to use the events of 1913 to engage the hearts of his audience: he 'made a touching reference to the Senghenydd disaster, where the men of Senghenydd and Abertridwr had done their duty with credit and he knew that the young men of the Aber Valley would again do their duty, and he hoped that they would discharge it immediately'. Further allusions were made to Welsh history and the national theme was underlined by a final speech in Welsh by a colliery under-manager.[6]

The following week there was a further lecture which nicely stands for the diet of half digested imperialist history and chauvinism which was now the weekly fare. In some respects Mr J. A. Lovat Frazer's tactics were not best adapted to maximising recruitment. He reassured the audience on the length of the war, which, he argued, would soon be over: 'whoever said that the war would last three years was speaking the language of ignorance . . .'. As a spur to recruitment, however, reassurance about a quick end to the war was unwise at this stage since it encouraged people to think that they could stay at home without weakening the war effort. He also revelled in party political points against the Liberals and against socialists in a way which went against the mood of consensus: in the valleys the Conservatives had more to gain by appearing to stand for national interests above party bickering. Frazer attacked Lloyd George for his pre-war attempts to reduce military spending and hoped that 'after this war they would not hear from the party that opposed them any talk of reducing the British armaments'. His enthusiasm was more successful on the theme of 'How Britain became Mistress of the Sea': the focus of his speech was the point that Napoleon had been finally beaten at the Battle of Trafalgar in 1805. 'He was really beaten at Trafalgar, but it almost took ten years to finally crush him'; Mr Podsnap in person could not have thought of a more splendid dismissal of Napoleon's defeats at the hands of the continental powers.[7]

In most ways Senghennydd was a very ordinary mining village, little different from scores of similar communities: the number of major recruiting events and speeches made in this one period of a few days is an indication of the relentless pressure brought to bear on the population to gain their support for the war effort. These recruiting meetings and lectures had their effect, and throughout the coalfield miners enlisted in large numbers. In Wales the problem for recruiters was not in the supposedly revolutionary coalfield but in the country areas where young men were disinclined to enrol.

While Welsh miners were willing to fight, they were less happy with the suspicion that their sacrifice and patriotism was not being matched on the part of the owners and that the sacrifices were being exploited for financial gain. The men worked longer hours on behalf of the war effort but watched the value of their wages decrease as war-time inflation began to undermine living standards. For the owners, however, the combination of increased demand and inflation was seen as leading to higher profits. Already by 1915, while exports fell, output per employee and profits had begun to rise.

The existing wages agreement was due to be renewed at the end of March 1915, having run since 1910, and the Miners' Federation of Great Britain gave the legally required notice that would terminate the existing agreements on that date. In all the coalfields except Wales the owners conceded most of the men's demands and new agreements were reached. The South Wales Miners' Federation then gave the three months notice required by wartime legislation to enable them to strike. The owners made no great effort to reach a new agreement since they could be reasonably certain that the miners would not force the issue to a strike in wartime conditions when the men could easily be represented as being lacking in patriotism if not actually traitorous. Quite apart from the damage to the miners in public opinion, it was clear that this was an image which the vast majority of the miners would themselves regard with disgust. As the weeks passed the government allowed the situation to drift until the real and immediate possibility of a coal strike emerged at the end of June.

In an atmosphere of crisis management the three Labour members of the Coalition Government induced the south Wales miners' leaders to agree to a further two weeks delay, until July 14th, while a new agreement was reached on the basis of proposals made by Sir Walter Runciman, the President of the Board of Trade. Runciman's interpretation of the miners' demands did not, however, satisfy the men. On July 15th, at the height of the most desperate war in which Britain had ever been involved, the south Wales miners, on whom the war effort depended, went on strike. The Senghennydd men worked on July 14th, refusing to come out on strike prematurely in order to force the hand of their leadership, as some colliery lodges did. But they voted along with the majority and struck on July 15th.[8]

Predictably, the strike brought down on the miners a storm of chauvinistic abuse and the widespread suggestion that they were being manipulated by agents of Germany. The *Daily Express* offered £5,000 for information leading to the conviction of anyone acting as agents of the central powers. At its worst the accusation was illustrated by a poem published in the *Daily Express,* entitled 'The Kaiser's Own Black Guards':

> They've captured England's coal supplies,
>   The life-blood of her fleet;
> They'll stop her factories and works:
>   Their triumph is complete.

> They're better friends to me than my own
>   Guards ever prove,
> For all my vast battalions could not make
>   so fine a move.
> As their occupation makes them black,
>   I'll show them my regards
> By giving them the title of 'The Kaiser's
>   Own Black Guards'.[9]

The south Wales miners were 'proclaimed' under the Munitions of War Act, thus making their action illegal and rendering them liable to a range of punishments. However it was clearly impossible to prosecute 200,000 miners, and the attempt would certainly have exacerbated the situation. Before long, however, the miners' case did start to be recognized in the press. Their record of recruitment showed that the charge of being unpatriotic was inaccurate and the complaint that owners were profiteering while the men made the sacrifices was widely aired. The *Daily Mail* and other papers used qualified support for the miners' case as an instrument with which to attack Asquith's allegedly ineffectual leadership. The *Manchester Guardian,* while condemning the strike, argued that

> in the first instance it is perfectly clear that the men had a strong case. Prices were going up fast, so also was [the] cost of living . . . Like most men when acting under strong feeling and in great masses, they will be found on impartial consideration to have been activated by a sense of right.[10]

The paper accepted that there was a very strong feeling among the men that the owners were profiteering and that the strike was not the result of extremists, enemy influences or desires other than the wish for adequate wages and fair treatment of a patriotic if resentful part of the community. Finally, when the strike was settled by Lloyd George over the head of Runciman, the *Manchester Guardian* drew the conclusion that the award meant that the 'justice of the men's claims [was] admitted'.[11]

In south Wales there seemed to be no reason why the tactics the miners had employed should not work again. Indeed their position was by now much stronger, for the belief that public pressure could stop them striking in war time had been blown away. Without Welsh steam coal the British navy could not sail, and the miners had shown that, if pushed to the limit, they were prepared to withhold that coal. The advantage was soon used by the men to settle one issue which had smouldered since the formation of the South Wales Miners' Federation; the struggle over union membership. In November 1915 the Senghennydd miners again held a show card day, with the threat that they would refuse to go down the mine with non-union men. The growing action throughout the coalfield against non-unionism was finally too much for the Government involving, as it did, lost production. In March 1916, under pressure from the government, the owners reluctantly accepted union membership as a condition of employment; but the qualification that this should be 'without prejudice to their position after the war' gave warning of trouble to come.[12] However, for the time being at least, the Senghennydd workers were revenged for their defeat in the courts in 1904; a satisfying victory.

But no amount of conciliatory remarks in the newspapers, after the miners had made their point, removed the underlying suspicion that the lodges were dominated by traitors leading a mass of honest men astray. Every time the miners stood up for one of their supposed rights, they were subjected to a renewed torrent of abuse, even from within south Wales. In the summer of 1916, for example, the two day holiday again became a major issue. The men wanted the holiday but the Admiralty asked them not to take it. The owners first refused and then granted an additional payment for working the holiday but a coalfield conference of 268 delegates, held on August 1st, decided, against the advice of their executive, to hold the holiday. After a flurry of activity by the executive a further emergency conference was held the following Saturday when the delegates did what the executive had intended them to do from the start and decided by 2,131 votes to 892 that the miners would work instead of taking their holiday.[13]

The next edition of the *Glamorgan Free Press,* in a major article, published a hysterical attack on the activists who had supposedly taken over the colliery lodges. The lodges had 'long since passed into the control of extreme Socialists and Syndicalists; men who are out to make mischief'.

In times of war they are that most despicable kind of traitor—men who have not the courage to openly declare their Pro-German sympathies, but who stoop to the most ignoble methods to stab their country in the back. . . Thus by thinly veiled suggestion, half-truths and falsehood they play upon the cupidity of the workers. They secretly hope that the country will be beaten—though they have not the courage to say so openly... What dirty little worms they are! They will tell you... that it really makes no difference to the workers who wins this war... If they really think so why don't they go to that paradise of the worker-Germany... They are eating into the vitals of the South Wales Federation like some vile cancer... Matters in numerous instances were left entirely in the hands of the lodges and consequently the pro-German element... But for a mere fluke which made a second conference possible, the name of the South Wales Miners would for ever stink in the nostrils of all right-minded people: and that in spite of the incontestable fact that the large majority of these miners are sane, patriotic and level headed citizens.[14]

It is not clear that the same could be said for the commentators in the newspapers.

While civic leaders enraptured audiences with references to Athens, Christian duty and the glories of empire, and regimental officers led miners to the slaughter at the Battle of the Somme, the grim reality of life in Senghennydd continued.

Contemporary figures for Wales as a whole suggested that recruitment was slightly higher there than in other parts of the British Isles, and recruitment in Senghennydd was higher than in neighbouring villages. It may be that young miners thought nothing could be worse than the underground holocausts which had decimated the village; or the heroic imagery of the previous year may have entranced some of the men. Whatever the reason for the high level of volunteers, Senghennydd was depopulated in the war years as a result of the deaths in 1913, the destruction of half of the mine which was not in full production until 1916, the recruitment of hundreds of the remaining miners and the deaths of many whose families then sometimes returned to the towns which they had left in order to find work in Senghennydd.

The increased wages won in the strike were no help to the families of men who had volunteered, and wartime inflation rapidly eroded the value of the compensation paid to the widows and dependants of the dead miners. For the wives of miners who enrolled, left behind in the devastated and depopulated village, the worst was yet to come. Wives of soldiers received 12/6 a week and a small allowance for children. These were starvation rates in the valleys where there was little work for women even in wartime conditions and where there were strong cultural assumptions that women should remain in the home. The allowance was paid in the aftermath of a period in which wages had been relatively high, accustoming families to a reasonable standard of living. The final twist was that as the families of enlisted soldiers were learning to survive, food and other commodities were in short supply and inflation was mounting at an unprecedented rate.

The payment of the allowance to the soldier's wives raised objections from some members of the community. They argued that it put money into the pockets of women who were unused to managing such sums and who frittered it away rather than putting the money into war bonds for when their husbands returned. Since the sums were in reality paltry, the complaints seem to have been triggered by the realisation that large numbers of women would have a kind of independence, albeit a poverty stricken independence: a deep seated fear was aroused by the idea of such 'freedom' away from the authority of a male.

The attack on wives living in the community, while their husbands were in France and at Gallipoli, extended beyond money to their morals and way of life. In Tredegar the Chairman of the Bench, Dr Jones, 'observed that it was full time to make an example of the some of the women whose husbands were at the front. He was speaking with an inside knowledge, which he could not make public. It was a scandalous thing how some of these women misconducted themselves, "both as regards drink and misbehaviour"'.[15] Patriarchal assumptions about the proper behaviour of women were internalised and sometimes expressed by the women themselves. Thus an Abertridwr woman commented on the extent to which the soldiers' wives had

> become public property. They are openly discussed in railway trains and public places of every description. One day I heard two ministers' wives discussing these women. Here at least I expected to hear them discussed with Christian charity, but no! You would have thought it was the qualities of a herd of cattle they were comparing in loud, coarse and strident terms. . .

'Why', this woman asked, 'do not some writers start their patronising of colliers' wives, or tradesmans', builders', doctors' and chemists' wives? Why is it that so many have an obsession for soldiers' wives?'[16]

In part, the answer is that the soldiers' wives were, for a period, not immediately subject to a man's authority and were therefore seen as in need of other forms of control. There was a male solidarity which, in the absence of husbands, allowed other males in authority to take over the supervision of the morals of their wives. In some cases the threat to male authority extended to the relatively few instances in the valleys where women took over men's work. At Ynyshir, for example, a man swore and refused to move when one of the newly appointed women bus conductors asked him to move from the platform of the bus.[17]

In reality the debate about the growing independence of women had the quality of a black joke, since a large number of families were going hungry and once again there were cases of children having to miss school because they did not have shoes.[18] Poverty on this scale had not been experienced in Senghennydd since the 1890s. The position of these families was made worse by the fact that on this occasion the hardship was not common to all the inhabitants, unlike the situation during previous periods of crisis. Those miners who had remained at home, and the newcomers who had moved into the village to take the places of miners who had joined up, were enjoying increased earnings as a result of the wages settlement in July 1915.

A. J. Baker, the Abertridwr woman quoted above, explained the financial problems of this group of women. 'An ordinary soldier's wife receives 12/6 including husband's allotment, from a grateful state to maintain herself, pay rent, insurance and the dozen other things pertaining to a household. For instance rent will cost (without the increase) 7s. She then has 5s 6d for coal, light, food, clothes, boots, insurance, parcels to husbands etc. True, here in Aber there is an allowance of 3s towards the rent, providing that she does not let apartments. Have you ever tried to keep a house on this sum?' She argued that 'most of their lives is one long torment, but they do not proclaim it to the world at large'.[19] Nor did the writers believe the insinuation that returning soldiers would criticise their wives for their spendthrift habits. Faced by a choice between their families having suffered or coming home to a pile of pawn tickets, the women seemed to think that their husbands would choose the pawn tickets. Indeed the tone of the letters from the women of soldiers' families suggests a confidence and strength in the relationships with their men. Mrs Baker wrote that she had known 'many soldiers in my time and have yet to meet one who will be grateful to the interfering busy bodies who try to run their homes for them during their absence' and she warned that the soldiers themselves would 'resent even more than do their wives the fact that because they are gone to fight for their country their wives have become public property'.[20]

The general attitude of stoicism, combined with a willingness to defend themselves, was summarised by Mrs Skym whose husband George had escaped the explosion of 1913, had been among the most active of the rescuers and who was now serving in France: 'I am not grumbling at my lot. I feel thankful for what we get and it might be worse, but let it be understood that it is to me and thousands of other soldiers' wives, what with the high cost of living, a sacrifice and a big sacrifice at that... Although we go on uncomplaining and try to do our part cheerfully we like to get a little appreciation'.[21]

The women and their husbands were all learning to cope with dominant ideologies directed to moulding the way they would perceive the nightmare, or alternatively the heroic struggle, through which they were living. The gap between, on the one hand, the official version of war and the attempt to maintain a public front and, on the other hand, the reality of private suffering emerges in a letter from William Fisher, who had been working in the Senghennydd mine before the war. In his letter he described the heroic spectacle of a plane being shot down but reflected on the devastation being visited on France:

> Great Britain is fortunate in being away from the mainland of Europe. It pains one to note the havoc being wrought in this country. This was an industrious place, and the work of ages lies wrecked around us— picturesque villages devastated, gardens with great shell holes, churches minus steeples, public institutions becoming just heaps of debris, railway stations becoming twisted iron and masonry... After the war this fair country will not be recognisable.[22]

William Fisher wrote of the value of Welsh miners in the engineering units of the army, with their knowledge of tunnelling and explosives, and he gave news of Willie Noon who, with himself, had escaped death in the explosion of 1913, but had now been killed by a shell. In the main Fisher gave a pleasing picture of the comradeship of war:

> The men enjoy the rest from the firing line, and stretch themselves out in the sun playing cards, or taking dips in the water. One also hears the strains of music. Our fellows are a jolly lot. The engineers billet anywhere... They were playing *The Merry Widow* this evening with a

'Four Aber Valley Lads' at le Havre before being moved up to the front in 1917.

couple of pals afooting it, and about it the guns boomed, shrapnel cracked and hissed, amd an aeroplane hummed, while within a stone's throw rude crosses marked a group of graves, the last resting-place of a few of the men who pay the price and give their lives for their country. . .

The concluding lines poignantly express the tragedy being experienced by ordinary people: 'I have a letter here saying that my little girl, five and a half years old, has developed tuberculosis as the result of a fall, and here am I, her father, out in Flanders'.

It was already noticed that, while the dead were glorified, those who had been horribly maimed were virtually ignored with something like embarrassment. One person wrote, in a letter designed to increase patriotic fervour, of a soldier who 'came home from the front terribly wounded. . . [and] discharged absolutely crippled for life. Aber never even pretended to be interested'.[23] This was the beginning of the attempt to make sure that after this war those who survived would not be thrown aside as had been the experience of men mutilated in earlier wars.

In Senghennydd moves were made to ensure that everyone returning from the war had some form of official welcome, though it took longer to establish such reception committees in Abertridwr. As so often it was Edward Shaw who took the lead. Local tradesmen were cajoled into decorating their premises when soldiers were expected home on leave, welcoming committees were organised to meet the soldiers at the station and accompany them back to their houses and funds were started to assist the wounded and recognise the sacrifices made by the veterans. A welcoming committee might also have prevented incidents like one in June 1916, when a soldier returning to the valleys found his wife in bed with another man and a woman: his young son's welcoming cries of 'here's Dada coming' had, not surprisingly, gone unnoticed.[24]

As the war continued without the expected quick victory, the need for more recruits increased and further pressure was put on men of military age. The *Caerphilly Journal* started to publish lists of all those who had already enrolled. From the Senghennydd Workingmen's Club there had been 117 volunteers and a further 89 from the Senghennydd and Abertridwr Conservative Club: more lists were promised. Most families in Senghennydd were represented in the lists: the Hyatts, active in the rescue in 1913, the Marshalls, who had three shops and the Meyricks, who farmed and kept a shop, were in the lists as they were in the parish register of dead children and in the lists of men killed in the mine. Mike and Martin Sullivan were both in Welsh regiments; John Sullivan had been killed in the mine in 1898 and Patsy had died in the 1913 explosion, while Morris Sullivan had died of pneumonia after he had been turned away by the Pontypridd Guardians following his attempted suicide in February 1909. Albert Hill, whose father and young brother had died in 1913, enrolled in 1914 and had been discharged with wounds. William Monaghan was also wounded; his fifteen year old brother had been killed in the mine in 1912. Among those serving abroad were the Bussells, Parrys, Rossers, Humphries, Coombes, Bowdens and Crooks.[25]

Families which had sent several men to the front were singled out for notice and their deaths were held up as an example and an encouragement to others. John Jones of 10 Grove Terrace had three brothers, a brother-in-law and four sons serving in the forces; by November 1915 only one was dead. The five sons of James Seagar were less fortunate. Richard Seagar, formerly of the Coldstream Guards, had been killed in the 1913 explosion, leaving his wife Catherine to bear a boy the following March; Sergeant John Seagar was killed in the Dardenelles in the Wiltshire Regiment and Percy and H. J. Seagar were both killed while serving in the 1st Wiltshires.[26]

The battle raging in the Dardanelles brought waves of death to the community. G. Turner of 3 Gelli Terrace and G. Dixon of 6 Gelli Terrace both died on August 10th 1915, as did Harry Lewis of Stanley Street. The slaughter in France took the lives of Hugh Jones, Trevor Shaw, C. Raymond and Charles Whitcombe in a few days in September 1915. The Pryce, Humphries, Roberts and Thomas families all lost their young men on the 10th and 12th of July 1916.[27]

Occasionally the public could see beyond the lists of heroes to a glimpse of the reality. The *Caerphilly Journal,* for some unknown reason, gave details of David Williams who was having to 'undergo another operation for the purpose of a further amputation of his leg'. He was wounded at the Battle of Loos and 'was struck on the foot by a piece of shrapnel but kept at it and on returning to the base he was medically attended to. When pulling his putty off, the lower part of the foot, where the shrapnel struck it, dropped off. He went under an operation and had it taken off but it has been found necessary to have it taken off again higher up'. As with all reports of the wounded, this one ended with breezy good wishes for a swift recovery.[28]

The wounded were not only used for propaganda purposes in print: in the flesh they could be even more effective. A wounded soldier was used at a recruiting rally in Merthyr in which he demonstrated his amputated fingers and the shrapnel in his head to storms of applause. In his peroration, a masterly performance in black humour which won a standing ovation, he exhorted the audience to join up; 'If some of you chaps came along, the fellows in the trenches would get a little more rest'.[29]

Many of the dead and maimed had volunteered in the first months of the war. Others had been enlisted in the waves of patriotism in 1915. But the numbers were still insufficient to satisfy the demands of the generals. The slaughter on the Western Front and at Gallipoli meant that even the million men who had volunteered since August 1914 were not enough. As 1915 wore on the debate on whether conscription should be introduced grew more intense. As a last attempt to maintain the voluntary system, in response to liberal opinion, a scheme was developed under Lord Derby, the new director of recruiting. Hitherto men in certain categories of necessary work, such as miners working in collieries which supplied the Admiralty, had been exempted from recruitment, though they had volunteered in such numbers that the supply of vital steam coal had been threatened. Lord Derby's scheme meant that all men of fighting age would be obliged to register with the Government: once the returns had been categorised, those who were eligible to fight were visited at home by citizens who would try to induce them to volunteer, while those who were in essential occupations were 'starred'. The aim was to avoid legal compulsion by exerting further pressure through public opinion, amounting to an extreme form of moral compulsion. In the parliamentary constituency of East Glamorgan it was found that there were 16,500 unstarred men, many of them drafted into the mines to take the places of men who had volunteered, and arrangements were made for them to be 'canvassed'. Clement Edwards, one of the presidents of the local recruitment committee, led the delegation to the Caerphilly District Council, formally to request its active support. He made the point that Lord Derby's scheme was designed to test the voluntary scheme to the limit: if that 'failed' then conscription would be brought in. Councillor Hubert Jenkins proposed the motion in favour of the Council lending its support to the scheme.[30]

As the war progressed and the threat of conscription came closer, the emotional pressure to enlist was increased. General Owen Thomas was responsible for raising a Welsh 'army', the hope being that recruitment could be increased by an appeal to Welsh national sentiment, while mollifying nonconformist opinion. Thomas, who was much quoted in the newspapers of the valleys, reassured a journalist that 'practically all the officers of the Welsh army are of Welsh parentage or descent... Two thirds of the officers are of Welsh nationality, the majority of them know and habitually use the Welsh language'. Most important in countering nonconformist impressions of army life was Thomas's assurance that 'we have in our ranks as non-commissioned and commissioned officers, nonconformist deacons, lay preachers, theological students and ordained pastors in addition to those who hold the distinctive rank of chaplain... This has tended to remove the last and the most serious objection of conscientious Welsh parents who feared to allow their sons to join the army'.[31] The appeal to Welsh sentiment reached an unmatchable pitch in General Thomas's rhetoric:

> Welshmen have never turned a deaf ear to their Country's Call. When Llewellyn, our last Prince, and the brave Glyndwr sent the war torch blazing through the land, the youth of Wales rallied to the Call. Their hearts aflame with their love of dear Wales, they rushed to arms from every commote in the land. Welsh hearts are no less brave today than in the days of of Llewelyn and Glyndwr...

Not wishing, however, to overestimate the finer feelings of his audience, General Thomas also appealed to their supposed atavistic instincts:

> It is by victories on the battlefields of Europe that our beloved country can be saved from oppression, our beloved homes saved from ruin, our wives and daughters saved from outrage, and our old people and children saved from massacre.[32]

The idealism which had inspired Welsh cultural nationalism, as well as aspects of late nineteenth century Liberal imperialism, was now all too often debased by the rhetoric of jingoism which might, in retrospect, sound funny, had it not been a solvent which destroyed even the residual ideal of an autonomous Wales: the war 'dealt the final blow to the radical idealism which had sustained the Welsh national movement in its long struggle for recognition'.[33] Welsh nationalism, rejected as a means for regenerating Wales, was now used as a populist slogan in the service of British military effort. Appeals to the miners of East Glamorgan and the Rhondda were made by various local political figures including John Littlejohn, Mabon and Alfred Onions of the Miners' Union, later to become the M.P. for the newly formed Caerphilly Constituency: all were part of the local structure of the Derby scheme. The churches in particular were targeted as useful agents for recruitment and special appeals were directed at the miners through them:

> We need not point out to you that this appeal is essentially a Christian duty. This war is a contest between our most holy faith and the brutal barbarisms of the modern school of German philosophy. ...We therefore ask the churches to assist us with canvassers who are not only fervent in church spirit, but who believe that there is a Providence that rules the world in equity. Persons ready to assist should call at the Council Offices, Morgan Street, Pontypridd, at once and oblige,
> Huw T. Richards
> John Littlejohn
> T. I. Mardy Jones[34]

Among those who answered the call to encourage others to fight was the Reverend Arthur Sturdy, whose comments had been unmatched for crassness at the time of the explosion. In a St David's Day sermon, after the Derby scheme had been superceded, he managed to link together praise for the glories of Welsh arms in France, a vitriolic attack on Caradoc Evans as a traitor (for his mocking descriptions of Welsh village life) and an outburst against the nonconformist campaign to disestablish the state church in Wales. It was, he said, 'very hard for them, as churchmen, to realise the significance of St David's Day to those who are doing their best to plunder and rob the church, of which the great St David was a pillar and an ornament'. The recruiters must have been relieved when he got to his main theme in which he did them proud, arguing that

> the best way we can prove our love of country is by our readiness to make sacrifices in its behalf and since Wales is the most ancient part of the British Empire, and we are not only citizens of Wales but citizens of the greatest empire the world has ever seen, loyalty calls upon us to make sacrifices to that Empire which, as the most optimistic concede, is to-day at death-grips with a merciless and unpitying foe.[35]

The London politicians, not satisfied with the chorus of patriotic enthusiasm from army officers, church dignitaries and leaders of the labour movement, also subjected the miners of the valleys to the patriotism of Mrs Pankhurst, as well as to her gushing enthusiasm for all things Welsh. Her colleagues, she said, had 'urged every man and woman to fit themselves to do their share in winning this war in defence of the civilization we loved'. To this end she too played on the wasted remains of Welsh cultural nationalism:

> You in Wales fought for centuries for your nationality and your language. You never gave up your national ideals, your language, your music, and all those things that make you a distinct nationality. For that the whole human race owe you a great debt of gratitude.

Even in regard to the position of women her rhetoric was indistinguishable from some of the jingoistic male speakers in their emphasis on the helplessness of women:

> We women who have given up our struggle felt that we have a right to say to you working men: 'Whatever your grievances, as you did not get them put right before the war, for God's sake postpone them till the end of the war. On your doing so depends our success. If our Navy fails for want of coal, may God help the women and children of this country.'[36]

Welsh newspapers can, however, have too much of enthusiasm and the *Glamorgan Free Press* referred to her demand for Welsh singing as 'naive'. And in any event no amount of jingoistic rhetoric, however brazen, perverted or morally diminished, could generate sufficient recruits for the slaughter on the Western Front.

The registration of potential soldiers had been useful to the Government, despite the failure of Lord Derby's scheme, since it could be used equally well for conscripting men into the army after holding the 'canvass'. Liberals, both in and out of the Government, could now argue that every means had been tried to recruit sufficient men on a voluntary basis and that, much against their will, they were forced to accept compulsion in the interests of national survival.[37] The Derby scheme had failed to produce all the recruits that were wanted: this was inevitable since the real aim was to enrol all the available men, and no scheme could achieve this since there were, necessarily, inefficiencies built into any system. Despite the endless threats, the politicians were obliged to do the thing openly if they wished to coerce men into the forces in the almost limitless numbers the army required. In January 1916 conscription was brought in.

As part of the system of conscription, tribunals were set up around the country to hear the cases of men who claimed total exemption from military service because of conscientious objections to fighting. The working of the tribunals is nicely illustrated by a case in Caerphilly. Councillor William James Jenkins appeared before a tribunal of magistrates largely composed of his fellow councillors, including Thomas James, Hubert Jenkins and Edward Shaw. The Chairman and the Clerk of the Court, William Spickett, confronted James Jenkins with a range of moral dilemmas including whether he would succour wounded soldiers; defend his mother and sister against being 'violated'; and destroy a German submarine just before it was about to sink the Lusitania: would Jenkins refuse to save the lives of hundreds of civilians or to protect his mother? Jenkins defended his position as well as is possible when faced with irresolvable moral choices, and he was effective when questioned about his attitude to those who were fighting:

> I have the greatest pleasure in according to these gallant men of having done what their conscience tells them, and I honour them to the greatest possible point. I honour them as heroes and as men. The only thing I regret on this occasion, I cannot go with them. I honour them for standing out for conscience, and I am standing out for the same also.[38]

Jenkins was interrogated for three quarters of an hour, after which the tribunal withdrew to consider its decision. It is a measure of the mixture of patriotism, solidarity, independence and tolerance in the local community that the tribunal granted James Jenkins total exemption and that the decision was cheered by the public in the court. Further evidence of that local temper emerged two months later when the decision was overturned by a military tribunal and Jenkins was taken under arrest to the barracks where he could face court martial for refusing to fight. He received support from articulate members of the community who themselves believed that eligible men should have volunteered to fight on the first day of the war. A correspondent wrote that 'I know that had you in August 1914 been able to see things as I see them you would have gone straight for the firing line'. The writer accepted that, in his way, Jenkins was defending precisely those values that the war was supposedly being fought to protect and prophesied, accurately, that the community would come to respect Jenkins's stand. The writer asked what was the point of the conscience clause if military tribunals made it impossible to use the clause: 'Jingoism has got into the blood and khakism into the brain'. The letter, prominently printed in the local paper, concluded: 'I wish I could persuade you to take up arms, but knowing the Provisions of the Act of Parliament I respect you for the stand you are making and deplore the fact that you have been treated as you have'.[39]

But even conscription could only temporarily satisfy the insatiable needs of the military to replace those slaughtered in France. In 1917 the pressure on men of military age to fight reached new heights of hysteria and venom after new regulations were introduced raising the age for conscription to forty one.

In May 1917 Clement Edwards M.P. spoke at a public meeting in Pontypridd. The thrust of his argument was that miners in his constituency had volunteered to fight in such large numbers that further recruitment had been suspended by the Admiralty, in order to protect their coal supplies. The Welsh miners had been replaced by immigrants to the valley who were immune to conscription. Clement Edwards's main point was that these 'immigrants' should be the first to be conscripted, thus attempting to divide the community which he represented. Edwards's campaign was backed by the *Glamorgan Free Press* in a front page editorial headlined, 'Clear Out the Funk Holes'. The article congratulated Edwards on rendering 'an important public service by exposing the scandal of the colliery funkholes. Since the outbreak of the war young men have flocked to the south Wales collieries, not in scores or hundreds but in tens of thousands.'[40]

The theme was taken up in further meetings later in the year. Mrs Drummond, another former suffragette, addressed meetings in the coalfield in the autumn and, playing on her previous role as a rebel, she attacked the 'shirkers in the Mines'.

> The best men in the trade union movement have gone to fight and what you are suffering from is those men who have migrated from North Wales and elsewhere into the mines since 1914 when your brave boys joined the forces. We find that these men are beginning to dominate constitutional trade unions in this country. These young men, for some reason or other—one of which is that they have no pluck to fight—come to the

mines to hide behind the backs of experienced miners and be exempted from service in the army.[41]

In another meeting, Owen Thomas Lloyd Crossley, Bishop of Auckland, delivered what was described as 'one of the most effective answers to the advocates of a premature peace that had been delivered in the district'. The Bishop was reported under the headlines, 'UP AGAINST THE PEACE CRANKS' and 'HOME TRUTHS FOR PRO-GERMANS'. The speech made the Reverend Arthur Sturdy seem a trifle reticent in his rhetoric. Crossley argued that, in the past, crusaders had risked

> everything in an effort to set free the sepulchre of our Lord from Turkish dominion. The Crusade of today was not to set free a tomb but to protect the cradle; not for Calvary but for Bethlehem. We were fighting for the child nations of the world—for Belgium, Serbia, Armenia. Nay, more, we were fighting for the child life of the world, the cradles of the whole world so that they might be free of the miasma of hate. We were fighting for our children. Were we worthy to bear the cross of this crusade, to be the champions of the cradles of the world? We were fighting for the Bethlehems of God. Were we worthy?[42]

The South Wales Miners' Federation stood out against the worst of these excesses and refused, at first, to aquiesce in co-operating with the 'comb-out' of miners who were eligible to fight. This refusal was backed by the threat of industrial action in support of their fellow miners who were threatened with compulsion. The actions brought down on the miners a storm of protest. William Brace, formerly the vice-president of the 'Fed' and now under-secretary of state at the Home Office, said that it was 'infamous that after three years of war such a decision should be come to, which has as its object the deprivation of reinforcements for the front and a shameful and ignominious peace'.[43]

Again the memory of the Senghennydd disaster was invoked, and the anti-war feeling was attributed to outsiders who did not share the manly attitudes of the miners: 'Can it really be that the South Wales Miner, whose courage in colliery explosions has been acknowledged, and whose boys have so heroically faced and outwitted Fritz, is really unpatriotic?' The writer of the article concluded that 'this contemplated treachery [by the Fed] at the behest of pacifist intriguers will have brought home to the Welsh Miner the evil in our midst, which should be shunned as a leper'.[44]

The suggestion that the south Wales miners were unpatriotic appalled Clement Edwards, among others, as is shown by the degree of his relief when the ballot demonstrated that the men were in favour of a further 'comb out' of working miners. In his relief at this demonstration of patriotism Clement Edwards wrote to Lord Stamfordham, George V's secretary, explaining to him that the ballot conclusively proved the miners' loyalty. The pre-war miners, he explained, were solidly in favour of the comb out.

> What is more, three fifths of those voting in favour of the comb-out are men and youths who are liable to service, so that in a secret ballot they had practically voted in favour of being called up themselves. It therefore means that the ballot has not merely inflicted a crushing defeat upon the syndicalists and pacifists, but has served as the most beautiful demonstration of patriotism that has yet come from any industrial population.[45]

Lord Stamfordham's reply brought forth a further effusion:

> I beg respectfully to thank you for your letter, and to assure you that His Majesty's gracious recognition of the overwhelming patriotism of the South Wales coalfield will be deeply appreciated by the vast body of the miners there. I am sincerely moved by the kind and flattering words of his Majesty as to my small success. . .[46]

In the midst of these excitements Senghennydd was settling into a pattern of war, however grim, and there were also older patterns which continued: war did not stop the flow of events, trivial to outsiders, which make up the lives of individuals and of the community. In May there was, as always, a fight in the mine and an assault on a policeman, P.C. Case. Evan Pugh, of the Universal Hotel, returned from service with the Welsh Guards to meet for the first time his twins who had been born the previous week. Clement Edwards, as always, was recruiting for the army: nearer home, patrols were mounted by the allotment holders to protect their potatoes from thieves. Dan Lloyd was filled with pride when his son, a second-lieutenant, was mentioned in dispatches and Thomas Thomas, the butcher from Woodland Terrace, was invalided out of the army after losing his right arm.

The general militarism was confronted by Mrs Ingram, a Caerphilly widow with five children, who sheltered a deserter on the grounds that he was too young to be sent to fight as a soldier. Jonathan Booth and Samuel Silcox, both teenagers, were sent for trial for breaking into a lodging house and stealing the large sum of £15-5s. Alice Roberts went on trial for murder at Pontypridd. She had stood up to a man who tried to rape her at gun point; he then tried a different tactic by giving her the revolver and asking her to give herself to him. If she refused then he asked her to shoot him: 'So I shot him'. In Senghennydd Elizabeth Jones was confronted by a man stark naked on the hillside: she could not, however, positively identify Hubert Hounsell who was therefore acquitted on the charge of assault. Beside all these continuities was the life of the land: in October the medieval Court Leet of Senghennydd Common met to determine the rights of freeholders in the coming year.[47]

Protests against war conditions were not confined to the mines, and from the early days of the war the inhabitants, often under the auspices of the local Labour Party, had organised themselves to oppose aspects of Government policy and to demand that the future should bring a more equitable society. In much of the protest, as in the colliery strikes, the driving force was the belief that individual owners were profiting from the sacrifices of the people. One form of alleged profiteering which united the community was the raising of rents, and much propaganda was made from the suggestion that soldiers would return from years at the front to face large rent arrears. The landlords, it was said, 'were reaping the fruits of the enormous sacrifices made by these men, and these men should return with a clean sheet with regard to rents'.[48] The key failure, Hubert Jenkins argued, was the failure of the Government to nationalise the mines early in the war and thus control the main element of profit; but the Government 'would not deal with employers of labour because unfortunately there were too many employers of labour representing the people in the House of Commons'.[49]

A major meeting to protest at the actions of 'the Landlords of the Aber Valley' was held in October 1915. Councillor Hubert Jenkins was in fine form, turning to the old radical theme of the oppression of the heroic Saxon by the ruthless Norman yoke: 'these landlords were only emulating the work of the barons of old'. On this occasion, however, Hubert Jenkins went further in his insults; 'the spirit which actuated these [landlords] because they were called upon to pay something, was the same spirit which was responsible for this great

European war . . . It was the same greed for power and all meant the same thing. Prussian militarism, which was dominating the Kaiser, was the same thing'. The spirit of the times moved Jenkins to use strong words, both raising the spectre of revolution and introducing a popular new phrase into the repertoire of the Valley: 'if these 'Huns of Britain' wanted to start a revolution in this country, let them start rising the rents'.[50]

The two main themes were patriotism and the need to offer manly protection to the women of the valley. Edwin Lewis said that 'these rag-a-muffins, dirty scoundrels as they were, went to the houses where the husbands were fighting in the trenches and sometimes buried somewhere, and told the poor wives that they would have to pay more or clear out. Rent rackers, as they were, were unpatriotic'. Dan Rees made the clearest statement about the need for men to offer support to the women: 'where there was a husband fighting in Flanders or in the Dardenelles, it was the place of the next door neighbour to look after his wife and family in regard to the rent question'.[51] Protest against capitalist landlords and coalowners was effectively wrapped in patriotic and chauvinistic rhetoric.

The main concern, however, was that the mistakes of the past should not be repeated after the war and that the slaughter should not have been entirely wasted. High on the list of demands was that those mutilated in the war should, this time, be treated with the respect they deserved. There was therefore an outcry when Government proposals seemed to suggest that a major part of the financial burden of supporting disabled soldiers would be left to charity. A large meeting was held in Pontypridd in June 1916 to protest at the Government's Naval and Military Pensions Act. Delegates represented 189 trade union lodges, 66 churches of various denominations, 15 trade councils, 3 Labour Party organisations and 6 friendly societies. The main thrust of the argument was that unless the people 'brought pressure to bear upon the Government they would again see one-armed and one-legged soldiers begging at the street corners'. Councillor John Davies, from Senghennydd, proposed practical action to undermine the working of the Act: 'why not ask the Urban District Councils throughout Wales to strike against administering the clauses? He had struck, and refused to sit on any committee appointed to work these clauses'.[52]

The brief strike of 1915 had taught the miners that they were almost invincible if they were prepared to back their demands with industrial action. The navy had to have coal and only the south Wales miners could provide it. After the strike the position of the men was considerably stronger. As Runciman had written to his wife in 1915, 'we are in the men's hands and humiliating as it is, I see no other end to it but Lloyd George surrendering to them'.[53] The Government's climb down in 1915 was followed by further collapses over wages in 1916 but these were insufficient to dispel the strong sense in the coalfield that, while the miners were simply keeping up with wartime inflation, coalowners and landlords were making windfall profits. As unrest over rent rises and profiteering in the Valleys grew, Lloyd George came to the conclusion that only Government control of the coalfield could ensure the stability of vital supplies. Government control was imposed on the coalfield in December 1916 and, despite their first suspicions, the miners soon realised that this was not merely a means of bringing them under military discipline. On the contrary, when Lloyd George took power from Asquith and control was extended to the whole industry, it soon emerged that there were real advantages to be gained by the miners in the new situation.

The structure imposed by Lloyd George between 1916 and 1918 was, for most members of the Government, an unpalatable action made necessary by wartime conditions. For the men it was a demonstration of their importance to the national effort and the baseline from which they would make demands after the war. Both sides knew the strength of the miners. A cabinet minute of July 1918 summarised the position of the Government: 'If an imminent strike appeared to be inevitable then the concessions asked for should be granted'.[54] The men had sensed their strength and intended to use it to create a different set of industrial relationships after the war.

The key element which underpinned the union's strength, the government's flexibility and the owner's new found willingness to settle was not, however, the war itself, but the fact that the owners were indeed making such enormous profits that wage increases seemed modest by comparison. In effect colliery company profits rose four-fold between 1914 and the end of 1918. The accounts of Lewis Merthyr Collieries clearly illustrate that growth. In the six years up to 1914, the company's profits averaged £98,000 while in the years 1915-1918 the figure apparently reached £200,000. The accounts underestimate the real situation, however, once profits took off in

1917. In that year declared profits stood at £177,588 but reserves increased by £220,000 to £340,900 and there was a further special reserve of £100,000. In the year ending in March 1918 profits rose again to £285,503 while reserves remained at £340,000. In the interim report of December 1918 profits of £418,807 were declared. Whatever the patriotic arguments, even in peacetime it would have been bad business to refuse pay increases and risk strike action at a time when windfall profits were available.[55]

As the war dragged on the hardship increased, though the families whose men were working in the mine were cushioned by high pay rises. Shortages of various items meant that many people, in particular the families of soldiers, were now going hungry, and rationing was introduced to counter the effect of spiraling prices. At some stages milk was unobtainable in the shops. In May 1918 Caerphilly Council decided that it could not supply shoes even though it was told that the wives of servicemen, who could not afford shoes for their children, were being fined for their children's non-attendance at school.[56] The agony was increased when, in the spring of 1918, military defeat was added to civilian suffering, and in May there was a further call up for previously exempted men in the age group from 18-32. However the pressure on men to enrol could all too easily undermine the war in other ways, since mining remained dangerous and physically demanding work which needed strong experienced colliers. In the midst of the holocaust, deaths in the mine were hardly noticed but they continued relentlessly: the 28 year old Tom Pearce of Stanley Street was trapped under a fall and fractured his spine in June. He died soon afterwards.[57]

None of this, however, prevented Senghennydd from revelling in a pageant organised to award medals for bravery to soldiers who happened to be on leave. The ceremony, which was organised by the local Reception Committee in February 1918, caught another facet of the atmosphere in the village and highlighted the experience of four fairly typical men in the army. Thomas James, now the Chairman of the Caerphilly District Council, presided and various notables including Thomas Hitchings, the local Liberal leader and guardian, were on the platform.

William Driscoll who lived at 13 Station Terrace had been wounded twice: his brother Patsy, also in the Rifle Brigade, had been wounded four times, but was still at the front. William Driscoll, by then a sergeant, had held his position when the Germans advanced and he later rescued a group of wounded men who had been left in the open for four days. He was awarded the Distinguished Conduct Medal for his bravery.

Sergeant Robert Clevely from the High Street had been a soldier for 12 years, serving through the Boer War, before returning to the mine in Senghennydd. In France he was mentioned in dispatches four times and was finally discharged after being wounded: when he was operated on the surgeon removed sixty pieces of shrapnel from his body. He was awarded the Meritorious Service Medal. Leonard Husk, of 146 Commercial Street, was also discharged after being wounded for the fourth time; he was awarded the Military Medal. Husk was luckier than Alfred Jones, from Caerphilly Road, who was killed in Mesopatamia. He too had been wounded before and had been mentioned in despatches, and he too was awarded the Conspicuous Gallantry Medal for rescuing wounded soldiers lying in the open while under fire. [58]

Colonel Morgan Lindsay C.B., R.E., J.P., who had been involved in the pageantry when miners were buried with military honours at the Eglwysilan Churchyard in 1913, presented the medals to the three 'heroes' and to John Jones, the father of Alfred Jones. The Colonel said that 'he was very proud to be present to present the gallant heroes with their distinctions. It was four years since he had been to Senghennydd and he was glad to see men of the old and new army receiving honours. They had all done well...'.

Thomas Hitchings then presented the men with gold medals. As a poor law guardian he made a point which was relevant to the honour of the country as well as to the pockets of his ratepayers. He expressed the hope that

> they would see that the heroes of this war would not be treated as the Crimean veterans had been, many of whom were to be found in their workhouses, whilst there were twenty-eight cases of soldiers who had to come and have such relief from this valley alone. [59]

The glowing report in the local paper was followed by a small item on the meeting of the explosion fund committee, which distributed funds to 134 widows, 408 children and 49 other dependants.

The martial event stirred a determination to stand up for individual rights against other forms of Prussian oppression which threatened

Colonel Morgan Lindsay C.B., landowner and colonel of the yeomanry.

the British way of life nearer at home. Under the guise of wartime efficiency and the need to maximise production, the temperance lobby were extending their ambitions for future legislation. At the end of March the beer drinkers of Senghennydd, led by the Aber Valley Licensed Victuallers Association, held a demonstration. The demonstrators marched from the Universal Hotel to the Park in Abertridwr where there were speeches praising the patriotism of beer drinkers. It was claimed that while there were no conscientious objectors among beer drinkers, many of them were to be found in the temperance movement. It was asserted that the principle at stake was at one with the great principles for which the war was being fought: 'while their boys were fighting for the liberties of the world, these people were taking advantage and trying to bring something before the country which they could not before the war'.[60]

Unfortunately, enthusiasm for pageantry and for the rights of beer drinkers was not matched by a willingness to work for the welfare of discharged soldiers. P. T. Pugh of the Leigh Hotel and Robert Hazel, the newsagent, held various meetings to encourage the inhabitants to support the Aber Valley Discharged Soldiers and Sailors Association, but they failed to generate great enthusiasm for the work involved, to their much aired patriotic disgust.[61]

At last, in the Summer of 1918, there was a breakthrough in the seemingly endless bloodletting, and allied troops advanced towards Germany. There was, however, no let up in the propaganda aimed at arousing anti-German hatred, which was to spill over into the peace arrangements. In August, as German resistance started to crumble, the *Caerphilly Journal* reprinted an article from *John Bull,* in which an American nurse was quoted as writing that

'Among the 1,800 (girls) for whom it is our duty to care, there are more than 900, all under 15 years of age, who are mothers, or who are on the eve of becoming mothers. And all—yes all—are infected with syphilis. About 600 girls, at the highest estimate 10 years old, have been violated by the Boche, and there is not one among them who has not been infected in this awful manner.' It is the tale of all the desolated districts of France and Belgium, as of every other country where the Hun soldiery has set its beastly hoof. . . . Is it not well that we should know what the Boche would do if he invaded England? Is it not well that we should know what sort of men are those German prisoners we allow to mix in practical freedom with our daughters at work on the land?[62]

The article was reprinted under the headline, 'DO THE PACIFISTS WANT TO "NEGOTIATE" WITH THESE MONSTERS?'

Ninety men from Senghennydd had died in the war and the village, like other communities in the valleys, had suffered terribly. Sensibilities, hardened by the sufferings of a mining community, had been deadened by the attitudes propagated in order to sustain a slaughter-house on a European scale. The ability of the community to remake itself after all the horrors is a measure of how far it had matured from the raw village of the 1890s.

CHAPTER 11

[1] CJ 13/8/1914
[2] *ibid*
[3] A. Mor-O'Brien, 'Patriotism in Trial: the Strike of the South Wales Miners, July 1915', *Welsh History Review*, Vol 12, (1984-5), 84-6: WM 20/8/1914: *Merthyr Express* 15/8/1914
[4] CJ 1/4/1915
[5] CJ 1/4/1915
[6] *ibid*
[7] *ibid*
[8] WM 16/7/1915: SWDN 15/7/1915
[9] R. Page Arnot, (1975), *op cit*, 75
[10] *Manchester Guardian* 17/7/1915
[11] R. Page Arnot, (1975), *op cit*, 74-7: *Manchester Guardian*, 21/7/1915
[12] CJ 25/11/1915: R. Page Arnot, (1975), *op cit*, 113-5
[13] R. Page Arnot, (1975) *op cit*, 121
[14] GFP 10/8/1916
[15] CJ 4/1/1915
[16] CJ 4/11/1915
[17] GFP 11/11/1915
[18] CJ 9/5/1918
[19] CJ 4/11/1915
[20] *ibid*
[21] *ibid*
[22] CJ 9/8/1915
[23] CJ 12/8/1915
[24] CJ 25/11/1915: GFP 11/5/1916: GFP 4/5/1916
[25] CJ 27/1/1916
[26] CJ 25/11/1915: CJ 7/10/1915
[27] Senghennydd War Memorial Committee list of dead, (Abertridwr Public Library)

[28] CJ 25/11/1915
[29] GFP 11/2/1915: J. Jones, *Unfinished Journey*, (London; 1937), 171
[30] CJ 28/10/1915
[31] CJ 12/12/1915
[32] CJ 25/11/1915
[33] K. O. Morgan, (1970), *op cit*, 274, 275-7: G. Jones, *Wales and the Quest for Peace,* (Cardiff; 1969), 93
[34] GFP 4//11/1915
[35] GFP 9/3/1916
[36] GFP 30/9/1915
[37] CJ 28/10/1915: GFP 4/11/1915
[38] CJ 16/3/1916
[39] CJ 18/5/1916
[40] GFP 24/5/1917
[41] GFP 18/10/1917
[42] *ibid*
[43] GFP 25/10/1917
[44] *ibid*
[45] GFP 29/11/1917
[46] *ibid*
[47] CJ 17/5/1917: CJ 31/5/1917: CJ 7/6/1917: CJ 16/8/1917: CJ 20/9/1917: CJ 18/10/1917
[48] CJ 23/3/1916
[49] *ibid*
[50] CJ 28/10/1915
[51] *ibid*
[52] GFP 8/6/1916
[53] M. W. Kirby, *op cit*, 28
[54] *ibid*, 35
[55] PRO BT 31/16355/65300
[56] A. Marwick, *The Deluge*, (Boston; 1965), 195: CJ 9/5/1918
[57] CJ 27/6/1918
[58] CJ 7/2/1918
[59] *ibid*
[60] CJ 11/4/1918
[61] CJ 23/5/1918: CJ 27/6/1918
[62] CJ 29/8/1918

Chapter Twelve
A Land Fit For Heroes

War had become a habit and the armistice demanded as great a readjustment as had the declaration of war, four years earlier. The sense of national unity, the hopes of a permanent peace based on a new international order and the post-war industrial boom all encouraged a mood of optimism for the future. The people of the Valley believed that there was to be a new beginning which would transcend the bitterness and conflict of the past. If, however, their demands were not met, then they thought that the wartime unity of the miners should be sufficient to force concessions from the owners. In the Caerphilly constituency an indication of the changes that had occurred was the victory of the Labour Party in the Khaki Election of 1918. Clement Edwards had moved to a more salubrious constituency and the sixty six year old Alfred Onions, at the end of a lifetime of service to the miners' unions and by now firmly on the right wing of the Party, at last won a seat in Parliament for which he had struggled for many years.

The will for change would however have to deal with the serious underlying problems of the coal industry. For over four years there had been an almost limitless demand for coal to fuel the industry of war. Old markets on the continent for south Wales coal had been closed but the Government, in particular the Admiralty, had absorbed all that could be produced. To safeguard its own supplies the government had taken ever greater powers over the industry which, by 1918, was largely under state control though ownership and guaranteed profits were still in private hands. Men from the mining communities of south Wales had given their lives in large numbers and had maintained the supply of the fuel without which war production would have been halted: the vital importance of the miners had been recognised by the speed with which the government had agreed to their demands. It now seemed logical and possible to push the government and British society one step further into nationalising the mines and getting rid of the private owners. Such a step would also help to resolve many of the half hidden structural problems of the industry. In guaranteeing prices, wages and profits the government had ensured that pits which would have been bankrupted, if subject to market forces, were able to go on producing coal. Despite the patriotism and lost holidays, output had fallen since 1915. Without the continuation of pooled profits to subsidise the weaker pits, there would be widespread closures: nationalisation offered one possible method of sharing profits and thereby easing the transition to an industry once again capable of surviving in a competitive international market.

These problems were however partially hidden by the continuation of wartime levels of profit into the first years of peace. The declared profits of the Lewis Merthyr Collieries rose from £418,000 in the last year of the war to £622,422 in 1919 and then almost doubled to £1,197,693 in 1920 compared to average profits of £98,000 in the six years before the war. In this situation the union felt confident in pressing its demands while the owners were equally confident in demanding that they should be set free from government controls and allowed to manage the industry for themselves.[1]

Early in 1919 the miners tested their strength when they demanded further wage rises to keep up with inflation. The Senghennydd miners voted by 701 to 390 to back their demands with the threat of a strike, a vote which reflected the feeling throughout the coalfield.[2] With the price of coal buoyant, Lloyd George's Government averted a strike by giving the miners an additional three to four shillings a day and setting up a Royal Commission to investigate the whole structure and future of the industry.

While the Sankey Commission deliberated, Senghennydd revelled in unprecedentedly high wages and the euphoria generated by the return of their men from war. The pride in a victory achieved through extraordinary determination and sacrifice, combined of course with a determination that no such barbarity could be allowed to happen again, were expressed by a ceremony in Senghennydd during the Summer of 1919. The occasion was again the presentation of medals for heroism, this time to eleven of the Senghennydd men who had been given awards. Thomas Polson, the chairman, described it as 'one of the greatest days in the history of Senghennydd', a remark repeated by Councillor Thomas James who had 'never felt prouder than that afternoon'. William Kestell, the owner's agent, was there with the colliery managers; D. Towyn Jones, as ever, conducted the Male Voice Choir and David Evans, the composer and

'Senghennydd Genius', and now a Licentiate of the Royal Academy of Music, led the United Choir.[3]

The procession was led by mounted men, followed by 'the heroes' driven in cars, sixty discharged soldiers in uniform and a further 200 in civilian clothes. Representatives of Public Bodies were driven in decorated cars and the ministers and doctors followed in more cars. The brass bands and choirs marched behind and the 2,500 inhabitants of the depopulated village watched them process in the decorated streets from the Square along Commercial Street to the Windsor Hotel, back down Caerphilly Road and then along Station Terrace to the recreation ground where there was an afternoon of speeches, music, and presentations. Again Colonel Lindsay presented most of the medals and there were many sentimental highlights which delighted the crowds. The modest minister of Salem Chapel, the Reverend David Roberts, one of whose sons had been killed, presented the Military Cross to another of his sons, John Roberts; and the little orphaned son of Corporal Williams wore his father's Military Medal to be photographed with 'the heroes'.

It was a day of reconciliation. Councillor Williams, representing Abertridwr, spoke in 'stentorian tones' as 'he grasped the hand of fellowship which had been tended to Abertridwr residents, although he remembered that nothing less than a European War could have swept away the little jealousy which existed between the adjoining townships of Aber and Senghennydd'. Hubert Jenkins, on behalf of the trade unions, hoped that 'the League of Nations would make it impossible for any great war to take place in the future'. The optimism was even greater for the future of industry: 'now we have to face the difficulties of peace, and he only hoped that as far as the industrial world was concerned, that the employers with the workmen's representatives, would reason matters out and be actuated by the spirit of President Wilson and Mr Lloyd George'. The mood was confirmed by the warm reception given to Percie Ward, the general manager of the Lewis Merthyr Collieries.

Ward had a link with the village, having displayed courage during the rescue operations of 1913, and he had a past which appealed to all but the committed socialists and liberal pacifists. He had played rugby for Merthyr, fought as a trooper in the Boer War and had worked as a colliery manager in south Wales before becoming colliery superintendent to the Assam Railway company in India, from where he had gone on an expedition to Tibet. Even his time as agent for the Cambrian Combine, during the troubles before the Great War, was forgiven in the euphoria of reconciliation.

An indication of the optimistic mood was the grandiose reception given by the civic dignitaries of Senghennydd to Percie Ward a few months later in the Autumn of 1919, to seal the spirit of reconciliation and mutual understanding. The dinner celebrated the work of the Senghennydd Reception Committee for Returning Soldiers and Sailors, and the event was intended to boost the efforts of the War Memorial Committee. Speakers referred to the £25 paid to the widows of the men killed in the fighting and the Christmas chocolate given to the children of men serving in the forces: they boasted of the record of the village men in gaining twenty one awards for bravery and above all they boasted with righteous pride of the achievements of the committee in raising money and dispensing over £1000 to the deserving. The evening had all that could be wished for in musical renderings and recitations, toasts and speeches; but underneath all the best of civic pomp and grandeur that could be created in the pit village was a recurring theme about the future rather than the past.[4]

The evening honoured Percie Ward and sought to tie him to the communal fortunes of the village. The main concerns of the Lewis Merthyr group were in the Rhondda and it was in the interests of Senghennydd that he should also feel a commitment to the isolated village. To this end Dr James and other speakers emphasised that 'he had identified himself with the interests of the inhabitants of Senghennydd'; as will be seen, it was not an evening for fussy attention to the accuracy of details. Ward came with colleagues from the Rhondda and brought more than £200 for the war memorial.

In keeping with the official theme of the evening Ward expressed his feeling that 'colliery owners and officials could not do too much for the men who had gone out and done their best'. He took the Senghennydd mine as an example for the future : 'he was proud to think and they would also be proud that they had not had a single stoppage at Senghennydd during the whole of the war'. This was a formula which ignored national industrial action and the stoppages caused by a shortage of trams and equipment. In the industrial relations difficulties that were to come 'he hoped that other localities would take Senghennydd as an example'; if they did the country would recover. The message of industrial peace referred not only to whole collieries, but to the individuals who worked in them. Ward used the example of a man promoted from modest origins as a haulier:

> One cannot get away from the fact . . . that although they often heard about class, that there are chances for men to come to the front and when they came to the front they were bound to respect them. A moment's reflection would show that in numerous instances the heads of industry today were men who had come to the front from the ranks through their own perseverance and energy and those were the men we lift our hats off to to-day.

Ward also took the opportunity to commend to them William Kestell who had succeeded Edward Shaw as Manager and Agent of the mine. Ward emphasised that in sending Kestell back to Senghennydd his local connections had been a major factor. Kestell was the archetypal manager who had worked his way up from collier's boy. He had worked in the mines since he was twelve, had attended night classes while working as a collier and had become first a fireman and then overman at the Albion Colliery in Cilfynydd. He started work as an official at the Universal at the same time that Hubert Jenkins became a miners' checkweighman and his family shared in the prosperity and tragedy of the town throughout the following years: two Kestells were among the dead in 1913 and their infants were buried at Eglwysilan. He was a major figure in raising money for the war memorial and for the Rugby Club.[5] In reply Kestell stressed that Ward took into account 'not only the interests of the officials, but also of the workmen and all concerned . . . They all wished for the success of the colliery, because by the success of the colliery it meant prosperity not only to the employers, but to the workmen and tradesmen and the community in general'.

On this hopeful note, which combined self interest, wishful thinking and a genuine commitment to the community by people on every side, the village prepared for the future. Already the government had rejected the recommendation of the majority on the Sankey Commission that the mines should be nationalised. However, the men had got a further two shillings per shift and a seven hours day as well as some continuing state controls over profits: the most vulnerable mines would continue to be supported by the levy on profits and, given the state of the industry, there seemed to be good reason for optimism even without nationalisation. Some people, perhaps, realised that a last opportunity to avoid catastrophe for the four million people and their communities who depended on the industry had been allowed to pass.

Senghennydd had other reasons for pride apart from the military achievements of its citizens during the war. In May, Councillor Thomas James of Senghennydd was presented with a photograph to commemorate his chairmanship of Caerphilly District Council in 1917-1918, a source of great pride to his sister, Catherine James, now Mrs John. In the same month Councillor John Davies, also of Senghennydd, took over as chairman. The activities of the Independent Labour Party in the Valley were another sign of the growing strength of Labour although this was never unchallenged in these years. The rise of James, Davies and the moderates of the Labour Party did not mean the eclipse of the old, or the stifling of new, political complexities. In December 1919 Thomas James retained his post as secretary of the Senghennydd miners; it was, however, quite a close election and one of his supporters unsuccessfully argued that 'to force him to a ballot to see whether members still have confidence in him is nothing short of an insult'. Thomas James had a great deal of support including that of Edward Shaw who had retired from the mine after nearly twenty five years service. It was reported that 'a glowing tribute to the valuable services rendered locally by Councillor James was paid him by Mr Edward Shaw M.E. (late agent at the local collieries) at the latter's presentatation, when he stated that if any person in the locality deserved the gratitude of the inhabitants, it was Councillor James who had rendered invaluable services of which he was personally aware'. The newspaper commented that 'such a tribute coming from a colliery agent speaks for itself': the miners seem to have agreed since they re-elected him by the narrow margin of 336 votes to the 291 given to S. Rogers, the Communist candidate; Thomas Polson won 98 votes.[6]

William Kestell, the new manager of the mine, carried on the pattern set by Edward Shaw and also won a seat on the Council, getting 768 votes to the 368 for Holder, the Labour Party candidate, and 290 for Thomas Jones, a self-styled 'Workingmen's Candidate'. Though Kestell stood as an independent, his affiliations were not in doubt, and later in the month he spoke at the Senghennydd Conservative Club on Primrose Day. He and his wife were to be found running the

church fetes, chairing the memorial fund and acting as president of
the Rugby Club. In Abertridwr also, the manager, E. S. Williams,
beat John Ellis, the Labour Party candidate, although only by two
votes.[7]

The mood of renewal led to efforts 'to raise the general tone of the
valley' and to spread the atmosphere of reconciliation even to the rival
choirs and rugby teams. Thus it was suggested that all the choirs in
the valley should unite behind David Evans in order to carry off the
prizes at the Mountain Ash eisteddfod. This was asking a great deal
of Towyn Jones, the doyen of choir masters in the valley, quite apart
from the problem posed by lesser people. The mood of national
reconciliation met an apparently insuperable obstacle in the musical
rivalries of the valley, and it had to be sadly admitted 'that there is too
much discontent in connection with musical matters in the valley
instead of unity and whilst such a state of affairs exists no good will
come of any movement [for unity]'.[8]

In other areas of cultural affairs there were fewer obstacles. The
local technical classes worked together to produce *The Merchant of
Venice* which was 'to be staged in the London style'. This was to be
only one of various offerings of which 'the object in view is to endeavour
to uplift and establish a higher literary taste in the valley'.[9]. In the
event both enterprises were highly successful. In the same week in
April, *The Merchant of Venice* was declared 'a very wonderful performance'
and David Evans and the choir won the first prize at the Mountain
Ash eisteddfod. Public lectures by writers were also part of the
attempt to raise the cultural tone of the valley; Silas Hocking, for
example, spoke at the Congregational Chapel on the theme of
'Misunderstood Men'.[10]

In most respects the community returned to the pleasures and
excesses of the pre-war years. The outings to Barry Island, Porthcawl
and Penarth were better attended than ever and the mountain sides
were again vibrant with love making; so much so that there were
complaints about dozens of married men spying on courting couples
around the church at Eglwysilan, 'dodging and hiding around the
walls and hedgerows and proving themselves a pest to young couples'.[11]
Reverberations of the social earthquakes set loose by the war were felt
when the Silver Bullets Monster Fete, Gala and Old Time Fair at
Caerphilly was opened by Princess Obolensky, a daughter of Tsar
Alexander II. Perhaps in her exile she was reassured to find a

A charabanc outing to the seaside during the good times.

continuing demand for the obligations and duties of nobility for which, alone, she had a training, while for the fair goers she added an exotic touch beyond that provided by dubious sherriffs from the Wild West.[12] The previous week A. J. Cook, the fiery miners' leader from the Rhondda, who had started his trade union career as a committee member for the Lewis Merthyr Collieries, had addressed an open air meeting in Senghennydd urging the miners to pay higher union dues; a difficult task when faced by men for whom the alternative temptations of the fairground were available.[13]

Extreme drunkenness was reduced as a result of wartime curbs on drinking, but Senghennydd still managed some notable excesses. The most dramatic was the exploit of Edwin Edwards and Theophilus Lewis who, on a day outing to Hereford, got drunk and stole a prayer book and surplus from Hereford Cathedral. Only supporting letters from ministers, the conductor of the local choir and the Chairman of the District Council and the Miner's Agent, all assuring the court that these were serious and God fearing men, led astray by their very inexperience with drink, saved them from gaol at the hands of the outraged Hereford bench. In a more modest way, better attuned to the traditions of the village, Richard Pritchard was fined a pound for stealing cabbages from the allotments; he too said that he had been drunk.[14]

Inevitably the public evidence of good cheer shrouded much private misery, even apart from families whose men had been killed during the war. In the prevailing hypocrisy over sexual morality, greater now than in the early, wilder, days of the village, there was much pain for women who had borne children whose dates of conception did not coincide with their husbands' periods of leave from the army or whose men had left them pregnant when they returned to the fighting. Emily Parsons, whose husband had died in the explosion of 1913, had borne two children to her husband's brother during the war. But he had gone off to fight and denied that the children were his: only her feelings for him which caused her to keep his letters, written when his emotional need for her had been strong, enabled her to nail the lie. The tragedies of childbearing also continued. Cecile Mathews, who had nine surviving children, died at the age of forty two. Her husband David was shocked when he learnt that she died as the result of an abortion.[15]

If there were private troubles there was also much happiness as families were re-united and fathers met children whom they barely knew. Perhaps the mood of hope encouraged Edith Griffiths finally to marry Richard Hamar who had brought her the evidence of her husband's death in 1913. He had courted her for the last six years, enlisting even the six year old fatherless Lillian Griffiths onto his side with carefully placed gifts of threepence for sweets. Edith Hamar died two years later in childbirth, together with their first child, but Richard Hamar demonstrated the loyal qualities of many Senghennydd men, bringing up the three children himself and becoming an idol to them.[16]

Private hopes and tragedies were overshadowed, however, by the uncertainties which were again hanging over the coal industry despite the euphoria of the post war boom, a boom caused in part by the temporary elimination of the French and German industries. The Government, while wishing to give miners some protection, if only because of the damage that they could do to British industry, were determined to relieve themselves of the responsibility for maintaining wartime controls over wages and profits. The miners and their leaders knew that the ending of those controls would return the industry to the uncertainties of the pre-war market place. In June 1920 the Government announced that it would end the levy on profits, and the wages which the levy underwrote, before August 1921; but as a result of the joint strike threat by miners, railwaymen and transport workers the Government of Lloyd George compromised again and agreed to guarantee an export price of seventy two shillings a ton of coal until the summer of 1921. In December 1920, however, the export price of south Wales coal slumped from 80 shillings to 40 shillings a ton. Up to November the high export price had paid for the government subsidy on wages for miners in less profitable pits; but by February 1921 each ton of coal in south Wales was being produced at an average loss of eighteen shillings and a penny halfpenny, as a result of which the Government brought forward the date of decontrol to March 1921. Again the situation of the Lewis Merthyr Collieries was typical of the coalfield as a whole with profits falling from £1,197,693 in 1920 to £150,027 in 1921. The maintenance of a minimum wage without a system of pooled profits would inevitably mean that many mines would be bankrupted and the miners gave notice that they would strike against the government action on April 1st. The government simply wanted to withdraw from the arena, while the owners wanted to ensure that, if there were to be major job losses, then they should be carried out by the Government before decontrol took place: in their view, it was the Government which was responsible for the impending crisis as result of its policy of subsidising loss making pits through the profits pool and guaranteed wages.[17]

As the coalfield drifted towards a major strike another event took place in Senghennydd which symbolised the reconciliation which, it was hoped, would emerge from the holocaust of war. For nearly two years the village had been planning a monument to the men who had lost their lives in the war. From the start there had been differences of opinion over what should be done: people variously argued for a hall, swimming baths, scholarships or a memorial. In the end 60 people had voted for a memorial, against the wishes of Edward Shaw and 27 others. Controversy had also surrounded the foundation of an ex-servicemen's club. Initially Senghennydd and Abertridwr had agreed on a joint club but, when the time came, local loyalties were too great and the Abertridwr men had 'seceded' to find their own premises.[18]

All this was forgotten on the great day that the Senghennydd War Memorial was unveiled. The unity of the community was symbolised by the position of Councillor Thomas James as president of the Memorial Committee with Councillor William Kestell as the vice-president and chairman of the appeal committee. Thomas Polson, unsuccessful against James in the union election, was chairman of the General Committee: Thomas Hitchings, the guardian, and William Marshall, the shopkeeper and rescuer of the rugby club, were also on the committee and David Evans, 'LRAM ARCM', was musical director.

On the great day the town again processed through the streets, led by bands and choirs. The Wesleyan Temperance Band headed the procession, followed by the ex-servicemen's association, the Red Cross and the Windsor Colliery Band all watched by thousands of local people. As always on such occasions Lieutenant-Colonel David Watts Morgan reminded the crowds of the heroism shown during the 1913 explosion and he was proud that more had gone from Wales than from other parts of the kingdom. Occasionally the listeners may have been rocked when a genuine emotion, unmistakably born out of experience, broke through the rhetoric as when Watts Morgan asked people to treat the ex-soldiers gently since people at home could not realise what they had been through in the trenches. The Reverend David Roberts of Salem addressed the crowd in Welsh and again referred movingly to his son who was buried in France.

Councillor J. J. Jones, chairman of the Lewis Merthyr Collieries, spoke to a theme which had immediate practical relevance; the need for trust and reliance between the men and their leaders:

> The men who fought at the front [were] united and felt that their officers would lead them well. The officers had that faith in their men that they would follow them so they worked together and achieved that triumph which they rejoiced over. By coming together in that manner and that esteem had resulted in developing a deep comradeship and he thought they should take their example in facing the difficulties they had to encounter. They should have respect for each other and work together and by their united efforts bring back to their country that peace and prosperity which they all wished for.

The highlight was reached when Percie Ward, general manager of the Lewis Merthyr Collieries, 'stepped forward in perfect silence and neatly withdrew the Union Jack which enwrapped the monument and thousands of eyes looked on the beautiful token of respect for those who had paid the supreme sacrifice'. The names echo those of the children in the churchyard at Eglwysilan and of those who died in the mine: Bussell, Coombes, Crook, Bowden, Jones, Milton, Pearce, Parry, Shaw, Whitcombe.

The Senghennydd War Memorial.

The whole event was a tribute to the civic feeling of the village and several speakers expressed the belief that the monument 'would last for years as a token that they would remember those whose names were inscribed thereon...'. It was a nice irony of the years that the names of the dead, carved in the stone, would be worn away by the weather and shrouded in moss, while the names of the dignitaries, engraved in metal, remained as legible as on the day they had gathered to raise a monument to the dead.[19]

Less than a month later the village was again in the grip of extreme hardship as the three month long strike of 1921 began.

The strike approached amidst the daily trivia of life in the village. In March Edward King, members of whose family had died in the mine, was fined for being drunk and disorderly; William Kestell, the manager, kicked off in the match against Cardiff to raise money for the memorial fund; and Eli Huish, Roy Earwicker and Willie Bennett, all teenagers, were fined 5/- each for playing football with a tin in the High Street. (The *Caerphilly Journal,* not appreciating its function as a newspaper of record, had a slapdash attitude to proper names and innacurately described the threesome as Eli Hurst, Roy Earicker and William Bennett, thus exposing the historian to a potentially infinite number of complaints from inhabitants deprived of their proper quota of convictions.) The intervention of Councillor the Reverend D. M. Jones, of the English Baptist Church, who assured the court that they were all respectable church going lads, helped to ensure that, as first offenders, convictions were not recorded against them.[20]

The Government did not back down in the face of the strike threat and for the union this was therefore the first major test of the strength and high confidence built up during the war and bolstered by the Triple Alliance of miners, railway workers and transport workers. The prosperity of recent years also meant that the miners started the strike with some cushion against hardship. Against this confidence was Lloyd George's assertion that 'Coal was no longer King' as it had been during the war, and that the miners would have to adapt to altered circumstances.

A mass meeting of the Senghennydd miners, chaired by Thomas Harpur, was held at the Park Hall Cinema, where the miners were reassured that if they stuck together the victories of recent years would be repeated. But that unity was cleverly broken by Lloyd George

whose offer of a temporary subsidy was sufficient excuse for James
Thomas of the railwaymen's union to urge a settlement and retreat
from bringing out his union in support of the miners. Among the
miners themselves there were major differences of opinion which
surfaced in public. Frank Hodges had urged a compromise only to be
disowned by his own executive. Hubert Jenkins defended Hodges in
April and again at the large May Day parade. The celebrations were
led by the Senghennydd Wesleyan Temperance Band and Thomas
Harpur and Thomas James supported Hubert Jenkins's renewed call
for a national profits pool as well as a National Wages Board.[21]

As always there were compensations for the inevitable sacrifices.
Time and the energy to enjoy it were luxuries for miners and now they
could indulge their enthusiasms. Coombes draws an idyllic picture of
life for some of the south Wales men throughout the long hot summer
as they played cricket matches against the neighbouring villages:

> we had matches every day and the village came to see them... The
> married men among us who had small babies used to bring the babies
> there while their wives did the housework. If these men were players, and
> it came to their turn to bat, another member of the team would try to
> pacify the baby while the father did his bit of slogging. Then, when we
> fielded, the spectators would mind the babies as part of the admission fee.
>
> We crossed over the mountain for one of the matches... More than a
> hundred and fifty of our supporters followed us the six miles there and the
> six miles back. They saw us win a grand game, watched by... every
> inhabitant, as well as the four policemen in that other village. We had a
> concert afterwards, and it was nearly midnight when they let us depart.[22]

Divisions were however showing at every level; between the miners
and the other unions, among the miners leaders and at the grass roots.
David A. Davies of the Rhondda, the secretary of the Lewis Merthyr
Collieries Benevolent Fund, was found guilty of embezzling £160
from the fund, offering a splendid opportunity for local newspapers to
publicise the activities of 'a prominent socialist and trade unionist'.
He was not to be the last who took this route to individual survival.[23]

Poverty gripped the town within weeks and the resentment exploded
when single men, who could not even claim the allowance made to the
families of married men, demonstrated in Caerphilly. On the last
Saturday of April, 300 men demonstrated against the Guardians,
demanding to see William Spickett, the Clerk to the Pontypridd Poor
Law Union, who was known to be in the area. That night trouble

A cartoon from the time of the 1920 industrial unrest.

Caerphilly Journal

erupted on a large scale. Doing his rounds of Caerphilly, as closing time approached, PC Hyndman saw a group of men standing around and he took the opportunity to approach them and tell them to move on. A few minutes later the constable returned and found the men still there, despite his instructions. Faced by this wilful disobedience, Hyndman then spoke to Ernest Hopkins, who evidently objected to be spoken to, for he then, allegedly, attacked the constable. Unfortunately for Hyndman, every time that he got the prisoner under control, someone in the crowd would interfere, for example by kicking him under the eye. In the end, Hyndman reported, he became quite dazed, and it was largely thanks to the presence of mind of Charles Goodfellow the solicitor, who arrived at an opportune moment, that nothing worse happened to the constable. Finally Inspector Griffiths and another constable managed to extricate Hyndman together with the prisoner, but before long they were themselves imprisoned in the police station by a crowd of between five and six hundred men some of whom stoned and mobbed the station demanding the release of Hopkins. The Inspector managed to keep the crowd talking while he despatched telegrams to Senghennydd, Llanbradach and Abertridwr calling for help. Their arrival was sufficient to restore order, but the Chief Constable took no chances and on Monday about fifty members of the Sussex and Essex constabulary, who were temporarily stationed in the coalfield, were sent to Caerphilly.[24]

The public troubles seem to have had some effect on increased levels of private violence. Phillip Lower was back in court for attacking a fellow lodger and Jeremiah Callaghan was in court for yet another drunken brawl. In January he and his brother John had been fined for fighting in Senghennydd Square.[25] Other items in the local court echoed the patterns which had evolved over the years. Redvers Harries, enthusiastically named after a Boer War general, had married his wife Doris when she was four months pregnant. He was extremely violent and after more than one separation she sued him for maintenance. Her husband offered to take her back and Doris Harries was under heavy pressure from the court and her husband's solicitor, Charles Goodfellow, fresh from displaying his own contempt for violent threats, to accept the offer. She stood up to Goodfellow and won her maintenance.[26] In another sad case Margaret Walters was fined £3 for stealing timber from the hillside. Her husband was found not guilty when she explained that he was a wounded ex-serviceman who did not fully understand what was happening to him.[27]

The strain of the strike told on the forces of law and order as well as on the striking miners and their families. Police Sergeant Walters of Senghennydd held an appreciative audience spellbound when he described to the magistrates' court the events on the night of July 4th when he had mislaid Constables James Richards and Ernest Williams. He had finally located them in the Conservative Club outside which he kept watch from 1.00 a.m. to 2.20 a.m. and within which he alleged that he had heard them singing ' ''Bonnie Mary of Argyll'' and other Welsh Hymns'; a confusion of categories which might, in itself, have cast doubt on the rest of the Sergeant's evidence. Finally Sergeant Walters entered the club in the early hours and found his constables with whiskies and a pint of beer in front of them. According to the Sergeant, P.C. Williams then said, 'I suppose Sergeant, that you have the necessary warrant, I presume to enter a registered club?' and when he, Sergeant Walters, asked them to leave, Williams replied, 'I am not leaving before I drink that pint'. The iniquity of the policemen's behaviour was made greater by the sergeant's evidence that corrupt offers had been made to him of bottles of brandy, laced with pleadings and threats from the club steward.

The court accepted the sergeant's story though the defendants told various tales of how the sergeant himself had used the club for late night drinking, how he had accepted the occasional bottle of brandy and of how he was driven by a personal grudge against the constables.[28]

For those whose memories stretched back ten years to the great strike of 1912, or twenty three years to the strike of 1898, events followed a familiar path of suffering: the soup kitchens, hunger and apathy on the streets. In Abertridwr the hardship was made worse by the actions of Francis Parry of Senghennydd, who was secretary of the Abertridwr Hardship Fund. At his trial it was alleged that many of the suppliers to the soup kitchens were paid by cheques for more than the amounts owed: there was no record of what happened to the change which Parry accepted in cash. He was also accused of receiving 3d in the pound from many of the tradesmen who supplied goods to the canteen.[29]

The men who returned to work in August, unlike the return in 1912, had a sense of wasted suffering as they went back on terms which were no better than those offered in April, three months earlier. Certainly the sense of invincibility which grew from the victories gained during the war had been destroyed. This was not a new beginning, but rather a return to all the problems and uncertainties of the pre-war period.

Some people feared that the 1921 strike was only a first stage in the annihilation of the British coal industry. They argued that state controls had been a massive exercise in subsidising the inefficient at the expense of the efficient. There were moreover other factors which operated against the industry, in particular the reparations clauses of the Treaty of Versailles according to which Germany was to repay France for the destruction of the Great War: the transfer of coal from Germany to France would have a terrible effect on British exports. Others noticed the shift to the use of electricity and oil in the place of coal. The natural conclusion of such an analysis was to expect the decimation of the British coal industry as it emerged from the cocoon of Government controls.

There were indeed job losses and dislocation in the aftermath of the strike, and the boom wages of 1919-1920 were soon a thing of the past.

One measure of the real drop in wages was the exceptionally large number of men in court for failing to pay affiliation and maintenance orders. The pattern was of relatively high amounts awarded to women during the brief period of high wages which, in the changed circumstances of 1921, miners found difficulty in paying, as wages dropped back to between £2 and £3. But while there was some unemployment, and much uncertainty about the future, the threatened catastrophe did not arrive. The optimists saw this as evidence that there was not a long and inevitable structural decline in the industry, but rather only the inevitable uncertainties of an industry which was subject to the fluctuations of international trade. In such an analysis, the sixteen week American coal strike of 1922 and the nine month long suspension of German coal production during the Ruhr crisis of 1923 were not fortuitous events which gave only a temporary reprieve to the British industry, but rather they provided useful extra time for the British industry to recover its long term stability after the recent dramatic fluctuations.

Among some of the experts there was quiet optimism, engendered in part by what was felt to be the healthy effect of the 1921 strike in reducing the expectations and confidence of the Union. The chairman of the Cambrian Collieries expressed the hope that the vastly inflated prices of 1920 were a thing of the past, since they produced a fever of expectations which were inevitably dashed as prices slumped. After the crisis of 1921 he thought that there was a good feeling in the coalfield and that they could hope for a period of stability and a lowering in the cost of living. Much the same sentiments were expressed at the Annual General Meeting of the David Davies Companies.[30] The position of the Lewis Merthyr Collieries reflected that of the coalfield as a whole. Profits fell to the level of the better pre-war years, apparently stabilising at about £150,000 compared to the figure of nearly £1,200,000 in 1920. Borrowings again increased, reaching £150,000 in 1921 and 1922 compared to pre-war levels of under £100,000, and money owed by creditors amounted to £317,588 in 1921 and £246,068 in 1922 compared to under £100,000 in the years before the war.[31] These figures, if they could be maintained, offered the hope of relative stability, but not the unaccustomed level of prosperity of the immediate past.

In Senghennydd the success of the Rugby teams in these years symbolised the renewed hopes and confidence about the future. The

1921-22 season saw the re-emergence of Senghennydd as a major team, with four of the side playing for Glamorgan against Monmouthshire; Will Crook, Jim Dallimore, Will Petherick and Bryn Edwards all came from families whose names echo in the history of the village. The first team played 28 games, winning 22 and drawing 3. It was a matter of vast pride to Senghennydd that Llew Jenkins, born and bred in the village and reared in their rugby club, should be chosen for Wales, and parties of Senghennydd men travelled to Paris in February 1923 to see Jenkins play for Wales against France. For Dan Lloyd, pride in the success of his former pupil brought reminders of his son Reggie who had played for Senghennydd and for Oxford University, and who had died of wounds after the war. In 1923 the first team won the Glamorgan League cup and, in delayed matches, also won the Lord Ninian Stuart Cup. The team was coached by Hippy Skym and it rang with the names of local dynasties; the Marshalls, Pughs, Prossers, Anzanis, Hoddinotts, Baverstocks, Evans and Beddoes, some of which were later to be nationally recognised names.[32]

Even the Rugby team had, however, been at the centre of a typical village struggle. When in 1920 a local journalist had suggested that the team did not put enough effort into training, Patsy Anzani, the treasurer, paid outsiders to play for the team, to the indignation of some of the locals who set up a rival team. The new team was supported by William Marshall, a rival to the Anzanis for the title of 'prominent local businessman' as well as being closely related to them by the marriage of his daughter to Patsy Anzani's son, Charlie.[33] However the success of the teams in 1923-1925 muted these clashes.

It was also a period of great activity for Welsh culture in the Valley. In January 1923 Saunders Lewis lectured at the Welsh Methodist Chapel on the poet Goronwy Owen under the auspices of the Aber Valley *Cymry Cymraeg* Society. In March 1923 Catherine James (Mrs William John) gave a talk in Welsh on the Seawalls and Dykes of Wales, (the thrust of her talk was on the need to extend them in order to hold back the tide of English language and culture), and in April there were performances of Welsh drama at the Tabernacl Welsh Baptist Chapel.[34] The realisation of the importance of the Welsh inheritance continued to grow: in one week in 1925 there were three major events in Welsh, including a lecture and the performance of a play, in addition to the regular chapel events. Several of those who were most active in the movement had moved to Senghennydd from the countryside; men like Evan Parry of Trawsfynydd who was an active member of *Cymry Cymraeg*, also contributed to the Welsh Press, was a Sunday School teacher and leader of the Band of Hope and, like many of those struggling to re-assert the importance of Welsh culture, was an active member of the Welsh Baptist congregation at Tabernacl Chapel.[35] James Harris was another important figure in the movement; as the librarian at the Senghennydd Miners' Institute and Library he had contributed poetry and essays to the Welsh Press under the name of 'Berian', won prizes at the *eisteddfodau* and was chairman of the Aber Valley *Cymry Cymraeg* for many years. Despite Harris's status in the cultural and intellectual life of the village, however, he remained firmly in touch with some of the broader cultural traits of Senghennydd. Later in the 1920s, when pestered by the Secretary of the women's section of the Senghennydd Labour Party (Mrs Watkins), the fifty year old Harris told Oswald Thomas, secretary of the Party, to step into a room where he would 'make a bloody pudding of him'. When Thomas asked him to moderate his language in the presence of ladies, Harris roared back, 'Do you call these bloody ladies?' He suffered the indignity of being bound over to keep the peace.[36]

The driving force behind the revival of Welsh was undoubtedly Catherine James. When she became chairwoman of the Caerphilly School Managers in 1921, in succession to her brother Councillor Thomas James, it was reported that 'as "Megfam" she is well known in Welsh circles as a speaker at Welsh conventions etc, a frequent writer to the Welsh Press and a successful dramatist. Five dramas for children by "Megfam" are now published by the Educational Publishing Co. The Welsh cantata *Plant y Pentre* written by her several years ago, is very popular and has been performed scores of times. She has also published volumes of games for infants. . . .'. She was active in a range of organisations connected with the women's movement, socialism and Welsh cultural nationalism: already by 1924 she had convinced the precursor of the B.B.C. of the need for children's programmes and for programmes in Welsh and she made many such programmes from then on.[37]

The village was proud of the academic achievements of its school leavers. In 1920 Willie Morris, Gladys Jones and Miss A. Davies all went on to teacher training colleges; and it was a particular source of pride when Miss I. Champion was appointed a lecturer in History at

Barry Teacher Training College, after taking her degree at the University College of Wales at Aberystwyth: (she was later to marry the pastor of one of the great Welsh chapels, the Reverend Merfyn Davies of Tabernacl Chapel in the Hayes, Cardiff).[38]

Optimism about the long term future remained high, and grand schemes were put in hand for the extension of facilities in the village. Thomas Harpur presided at a meeting at which it was proposed to raise £2,500 to enlarge the Miners' Institute and Library. By 1926, 17,564 books were borrowed in one year. For the high minded, however, the villagers' choice of reading matter was something of a disappointment since 16,399 novels were borrowed compared to a total of just over 1,000 books on Welsh, History, Religion, Science, Philosophy, Music, Poetry, Economics, Class, Biography, and reference combined.[39]

In the private sector also, local entrepreneurs were full of schemes. William Davies, formerly a boot maker of 106 Commercial Street, now carried on business as William Davies Boot Manufacturers and Co of Bristol House (106 Commercial Street). He also became a director of Davies Steel Specialists of Treforest and of the Principality Picture Palace Company: as a founder member of the Henry Pendrill Charles Masonic Lodge in Caerphilly he was in a good position to mix with the right class of person for picking up additional directorships.[40]

Other aspects of village life appeared to be almost timeless. Each year whole streets were left without water, forcing people to carry heavy pails up from the taps lower down in the village, while there were continued worries over the foul and polluted water which did arrive in other homes.[41] In this respect nothing much seemed to have changed since the 1890s, still condemning many of the women to unnecessary drudgery and insanitary conditions in which to bring up their families.

There were other echoes of the past. In October 1922 there was a religious revival in Senghennydd though it was not on the same scale as the great revival of 1904. Eleven people were baptised in one evening at the Welsh Baptist Chapel and the pastor, J. R. Evans, received 74 converts in all. His score was however topped by that of the Reverend D. M. Jones who baptised 132 people at the Ebenezer English Baptist Chapel, while a further 14 walked up after the baptisms were completed. The oldest convert was the 78 year old Ann Jones who was presented with a bible.[42] And Caerphilly District

The Reverend 'DM' Jones presiding at Harvest Festival.

Council was again the scene of protests about the abuse of allotments: it was again resolved to remove from Senghennydd the nuisance of pig styes, garages, fowl pens, and stables. [43]

Politically Senghennydd maintained some of the curious old compromises, despite the victory of Labour in the election of 1918. The Labour Party continued to grow in strength and in 1924 the Independent Labour Party re-opened a branch in Senghennydd; but the mine management retained much of their old influence. Percie Ward continued to be invited to open church fetes and events for ex-serviceman and William Kestell held his seat on the council despite the challenge from Labour, while Councillor E. S. Williams, the general manager of the Windsor Colliery in Abertridwr, was the Chairman of Caerphilly Council in 1923. By the mid 1920s, Williams had increased his majority over Labour from 2 to 443. In Senghennydd George Worman, one of the Labour candidates, was narrowly beaten by an 'independent' in 1925, but managed to reverse the vote when he stood against another opponent the following year. The old patterns are clear in the details of George Worman's campaign. In 1923, in the week that he stood as Labour candidate, he held a Party 'Social' which was attended by 300 people: the event was held at

Salem Chapel and the other main speaker was the Reverend D. M. Jones, minister of Ebenezer.[44]

Though drunkenness was less, the old names from the days before the war recurred in the magistrates courts. Daniel Parcel, who had dowsed the fires in the Universal Hotel in the early days and who was now 52 years old, was convicted in July 1923 of fighting in the street in Abertridwr, surrounded by a large audience. He was still on form, since he knocked out Evan Davies who was twenty years younger than himself and a seasoned street fighter in his own right. In court Parcel admitted to 36 previous convictions which seems suspiciously low; it perhaps reflected the fact that Parcel had mellowed and had not appeared so regularly in recent years. Similarly when Philip Davies was convicted of fighting in the street he admitted to 14 previous convictions, but the police spoke up for him on the grounds that 'there had been a distinct improvement in his conduct during the last few years'. The magistrate primly replied, 'I am glad you are improving. You will be fined twenty shillings'. In these years the worst fighters and drunks were the Callaghan brothers who were constantly in court for street fighting and drunkenness: Jeremiah Callaghan also had a history of brutality and was in court for beating up his wife.[45]

The grim tragedy of children's deaths in accidents was unchanged, many of them occurring as the result of adventuring in the dangerous environment. Hubert Gregory died after falling off a hayrick, John Williams was killed after falling from one of the rides of a travelling fair set up behind the Windsor Hotel, the four year old Haydn Edward died of pneumonia months after falling twenty feet from the window ledge of the Park Hall Cinema at a children's concert and Clarice Jones died from scalding while she was being looked after by her fourteen year old sister Phyllis. Only a month later, when the five year old William Husk was killed, the Coroner remarked that 'happily for the last two months I have not had so many cases of this kind': given the circumstances he must have been easily pleased. Occasionally there were cases of child neglect as when the three children of John and Annie Harford were found to be filthy and covered in vermin in a stinking house with food rotting in the kitchen.[46] There were also prosecutions for the sexual abuse of children, all of them unsuccessful.

Despite the uncertainties and tragedies, however, the feeling persisted that the coalfield and the village would ride them out, a mood enhanced by the greater maturity of the community as a whole. There were clear signs that the village had changed from the wild and sometimes even barbaric times in the early days of the community. The manic drunkenness of the days before the war when every week up to seven Senghennydd men would be in court had altered into the occasional court case, as had the cases of domestic violence. Those brought up in the village in the 1920s remember drunken outbursts but not the regular street brawls and fighting which had characterised some periods before the war. Their memories are confirmed by the evidence of the local press reports. Equally, older inhabitants still remember the shock of discovering when a contemporary became pregnant before marriage, an event which had been sufficiently common to arouse much less comment before the Great War. Philip Massey, writing about Blaina and Nantyglo, noticed the increasingly mellow atmosphere as the inter-war years passed and Arthur Gray Jones noted the same phenomenon in Ebbw Vale in the late 1920s.[47] The wartime legislation on drinking, which imposed various restrictions on opening hours and increased the price of beer, was one factor as were the depressed wages after 1921. A. G. Jones thought that the main factor was the civilising influence of the schools. It was also the case that in Senghennydd the balance between males and females evened out, resulting in many fewer single males without the ties, responsibilities and financial commitments of maintaining a home: moreover the single males who worked in the mine were now much more likely to be part of a family structure. Compared to the danger-ously violent atmosphere noted above, the home was increasingly subjected to the standards of the women: A. G. Jones wrote that 'the respect paid to the women is most noticeable . . . It is they who handle the money and in the home they are on terms of complete equality with the men'.[48]

The causes of these changing patterns can be glimpsed in the history of one extended family which played an important part in the growth of the village. In material terms the Marshall clan was untypical of Senghennydd, but the growth of the family and the web of relationships which it created mirrored that of most families and tells us a great deal about the changes that occurred between 1900 and 1930.[49] William Thomas Marshall arrived in Senghennydd at the end of the nineteenth century to work underground. By 1901 he was established as a grocer in Commercial Street and as the business

William Marshall, deacon and businessman.

Mr and Mrs Marshall surrounded by some of their dynasty on their golden wedding anniversary.

One of William Marshall's smart delivery vans with his son Cyril standing by the driver's door.

flourished he opened other shops over the years: a confectioner's, a cafe, a corn store and pet shop. He ran buses; built, in partnership with his brother Arthur, the short terrace of houses which makes up Clive Street; manufactured boiled sweets and ice cream at his warehouse behind his properties in Commercial Street; and was the tenant of fields at the top of the village, above Clive Street, where he grazed the horses which pulled his vans: the land is still known as 'Marshall's Ranch' by the village children. He and his wife Edith were a close couple who produced eleven children over the years, of whom six survived to adulthood. Marshall was a benevolent patriarch, too generous for his own good, who was almost bankrupted by the credit he gave to his fellow villagers and chapel goers during the times of crisis after 1926. An early member, and Deacon, of the English Congregational Church, he was also a founder of the Senghennydd Bowls Club and the major benefactor of the Senghennydd Rugby Team.

The greatest shock to this archetypal nonconformist entrepreneur was delivered by his beautiful eldest daughter, Ethel. In 1915 a sixteen year old Italian violinist, with strikingly romantic good looks,

Charlie Anzani and Ethel Marshall aged about sixteen shortly before their marriage.

arrived in Senghennydd as part of the three man band which played nightly at the Park Hall Cinema. Later in the same year Charlie Anzani, a conscientious roman catholic whose family originated in Milan, married Ethel Marshall who was just seventeen, the daughter of the leading nonconformist businessman. The marriage caused a major scandal in the village where almost the only roman catholics were Irish labourers. Marshall was too warm hearted not to accept and ultimately revel in his burgeoning family of grandchildren, the first of whom was born the next year. The Marshalls and Anzanis lived in adjacent houses in Commercial Street: an excellent arrangement for Ethel Anzani's four growing brothers who, after an evening drinking in the club, would creep back to their bedrooms through the attic fire door which linked the Anzani and Marshall houses, thus escaping the attentions of their teetotal father.

Though Marshall's affection for his daughter ensured that there was no split in the family, the Anzani children were to suffer for their catholicism at the hands of some teachers in the Senghennydd senior school. After leaving the infants' school the girls were therefore sent to Our Lady's Convent School in Cardiff, having to walk from the railway station every evening in their private school uniforms past children playing pitch and toss and 'dog and catty' in the streets. Anzani supported his growing family in their expensive needs with an entrepreneurial skill and an energy which matched that of his father-in-law. When he arrived in Senghennydd, as well as playing the violin at the cinema, he had worked underground as an engineman for the duration of the Great War: he was also responsible for the Marshall sheep in the 'ranch'. Later he took over the general stores as well as the corn stores and pet shop, for which his eldest son bred the exotic birds. Above all he led Anzani's seven man band, which played throughout the valleys and beyond. He too was successful, managing to afford a smart car in which the family had excursions to Penarth and Barry and employing maids from Senghennydd families, such as the Hyatts, whose plight would otherwise have been desperate after the deaths of 1913 and the Great War.

The Marshall children and grandchildren married into every section of the village: the Driscoll, O'Donovan, Grimes, Wilkins, Gardner, Evans, Jones and Thomas families all married into the Marshall clan, being set up in small businesses and shops. Members of the clan remember a rich family life with gatherings at the main festivals and anniversaries when more than twenty adults would squeeze into the front parlour and the furniture would be moved into the small garden from the back living room so that the young people could dance. Over the proccedings contentedly watched the ageing nonconformist deacon and his favourite son-in-law, the handsome violinist with the faintly melancholy air which added to his romantic aura.

Charlie Anzani's Band. Anzani is third from the left.

Charlie Anzani's open tourer in the 1920s. Anzani is at the wheel and Jack
Grimes, his brother-in-law and fellow bookmaker, is behind him.

It was these complex networks, now common to most Senghennydd
families, which altered the village from a cauldron, all too often
dominated by young males, to a community in which most inhabitants
were reared and socialised into a mesh of expectations, ideals and
assumptions, supported by the chapels, union and other institutions.
In this environment occasional excesses might be endured and even
tolerated, but they could not threaten the basic stability of the
community. The world had not been turned on its head but the
stability of the home, in the context of family networks built up by
intermarriage, imposed its standards to a greater extent than had
been possible in the raw atmosphere of new valley settlements.[50]

A sense of continuity began to develop as the older generation, who
had built up the village, handed over to their children's generation.
John Skym, the patriarch of a clan which had been at the forefront of
the rescue attempts in 1913, and which was one of the foundations of
the successful Rugby team, died in 1922, survived by a family which
was now embedded in the life of the village. The retirement of Dan
Lloyd as head teacher of the village school in 1925 symbolised the
continuities of village life, even among the middle class which might
have been expected to move away. Had things been different, he
might have been succeeded by his son Reggie who had died of wounds
after the war. Instead, to his great satisfaction, he was succeeded as

headmaster by John Roberts the son of the minister of Salem Welsh Baptist Church. The Reverend David Roberts had also lost a son in the war; William Roberts of the Air Flying Corps had been killed at the Battle of Cambrai. But the two older men were united in pleasure at the survival of J. H. ('Bertie') Roberts, who had been commissioned and won a Military Cross for bravery, and who had returned to Senghennydd as a school teacher at the end of the war, marrying Florrie Lloyd, the old headmaster's daughter.[51] Dr Philip James, who had walked over the hill from Pontypridd to attend to the sinkers in 1894, also retired. A collection in his honour raised the enormous sum of £430, a tribute to his courage in many mine rescues. William Watson, who had also won a Military Cross in France, now became the senior doctor in the village. His appalling experiences in France caused the villagers to tolerate his enthusiasm for the bottle, even when it led a teetotal and conscientious chapel going mine official to fall flat on his face, drunk, at the feet of his astonished wife, after a pre-Christmas afternoon in the company of the doctor.[52]

At the start of 1924 the mood was one of confidence for the future. The promise of 1919, with the hopes of a settled mining industry owned by the nation, had not been realised, but there nevertheless seemed to be good reason for hope. By the end of 1923 profits in the mining industry matched pre-war levels and in early 1924 the coalowners conceded a 12½ % increase to the miners. More importantly for the future, a Labour Government was in power for the first time; since Labour was not even the largest party in Parliament there was no excuse for illusions about major changes, but it was a portent of what might be achieved in the future.

In Senghennydd there was pride that Morgan Jones, their member of Parliament, who had been a school teacher and then a miner, after he lost his job for conscientiously objecting during the war, had been given a junior post in the Ministry of Education. The constituency expressed its pleasure through Caerphilly Council, which passed a motion congratulating Morgan Jones. The event was given typical local spice when the curmudgeonly chairman, Alderman Howells, commented that 'I am not against the motion but consider him a very lucky man. He was first a school teacher with £150 per annum, and then he was sent to parliament and had £400 per annum and now he is getting £1500'.[53] Even the Parliamentary Secretary to the Board of Education was, however, in no position to resolve day to day issues such as the shortage of water and the resultant problems of hygiene which had been plaguing Senghennydd families since 1896. Nor did political changes alter the long established pattern by which the colliery management took a major part in the voluntary activities of the town; thus it was Fred Wilcox, who had taken over from William Kestell as the Colliery agent, who presided over the scheme to improve the recreation ground for use as a cricket pitch and tennis courts.[54]

Hubert Jenkins was still the dominant leader of the Labour movement in the Aber Valley and he certainly earned his position through hard work. His diary shows that in one day he might attend meetings in Llanbradach, Bedwas, Ystrad Mynach and Senghennydd: he would dash from settling compensation claims, to a strike meeting, to the Glamorgan County Council and then be ready for branch meetings in the evening. He worked Saturdays, many Sundays and was often not home until after nine; sometimes it may have been too exhilarating for the important local leader now approaching sixty who recorded, after a meeting in Trethomas in the Rhondda, 'Home by Motor Cycle'. Since the diary appears to have doubled as a log book with which he could account for his movements to his masters, the workers, it may be that Jenkins was laying on some of the overwork with a trowel.[55]

Less noticeable than Fred Wilcox, the Manager and Agent, or Hubert Jenkins and Thomas James, the Labour leaders in the Valley, were a host of men and women whose qualities helped to transform the rows of terraces from mere batteries of human beings into a complex and fulfilling community. William Thomas was for twenty years the treasurer of the East Glamorgan District of Miners, a member of the Pontypridd Board of Guardians, Member of the Senghennydd and Aber Valley Co-operative Society Committee, Trustee of the Senghennydd Sick and Accident Fund, a member of the Library Committee and the Senghennydd representative on the Cardiff Royal Infirmary. Arthur Grimstead, who worked as an official of the Lewis Merthyr Collieries for sixteen years, was secretary of the education committee of the Senghennydd and Aber Valley Co-operative Society, a deacon of the English Congregational Church, a District Superintendent of the Independent Order of Rechabites, the temperance organisation, and the holder of various other posts over the years.[56] Elizabeth Whittaker was an active

Conservative, a sunday school teacher and a leading member of St Peter's Church, as well as bringing up a family.[57] Isaac (Ithel) Thomas was a miner who opened a grocer's shop in Commercial Street after escaping from the mine. He was a founder member of St Cenydd Welsh Church and was the warden for twenty years. He was a leading Liberal in the Aber Valley and, like many shopkeepers, went to the verge of bankruptcy in 1926 to give credit to his customers, as well as being active in the provision of.meals for schoolchildren. He was also the foreman of the inquest jury after the disaster in 1913, being both a respectable tradesman and an ex-miner.[58]

These cases were entirely typical of the hundreds of people who, on one level, held deeply opposed social and political views, but who worked together to sustain the activities and organisations of the Valley. One of the oddest comments of the Pontypridd Stipendiary, Lleufer Thomas, in his wartime report on industrial unrest in the Valleys, had been the judgement that 'the development of the civic spirit and the sense of social solidarity—what we may in short call the community sense—is seriously retarded'.[59] To the professional middle classes, the drunkenness and violence masked the equally strong countervailing forces of cohesion. No number of voluntary organisations will make a community, something based on shared experience and shared sympathy over time; but these voluntary associations articulated what would otherwise have remained private experiences, using them to bind families and individuals into the broader community.

The community was full of people willing to give up their time to support voluntary effort, whether through a sense of public service, private ideals, the desire for esteem and status or simply as a release from unpleasant home situations. It is fortunate that there were so many churches and chapels, with their divisions which seemed so esoteric to non-christians, all needing their own deacons and committee members, and so many voluntary bodies needing boards of governors; for how else could this large number of public spirited people have fulfilled their need to serve and to gain public esteem? It was these people who formed an 'elite' in the village. Ministers, trade union officials, shopkeepers, deacons, officers of voluntary organisations, educated miners, anyone with interests and commitments beyond earning a living, formed an intangible leadership within the community. It is true that, compared to the professional middle classes elsewhere,

Gwern Avenue, one of the 'better' terraces in the village.

they were relatively undifferentiated by the material symbols of class, living in the same terraced streets as the other villagers. Davies and Lloyd, the builders, Marshall the shopkeeper, Jenkins and James the union leaders, the ministers and teachers all lived in the village, rather than in detached houses on the hillside, set apart from the village streets. Even the mine manager and agent lived in a semi-detached house within the colliery. Behind the apparent homogeneity there were, of course, significant differences which were apparent to the villagers: the gardens of Caerphilly Road; the occasional stable and hayloft for a pony and trap; houses which, behind the similar facades, revealed spacious tiled hallways; Charlie Anzani's motorcar. Despite these differences it was indeed a community in which, to an unusual extent, all the inhabitants directly experienced the common good.

Both the union and the chapels, in their different ways, fostered a measure of democratic participation which became the norm in the community. It would, however, be a mistake to sentimentalise the reality. In March 1921 a delegate conference of miners had decided to make some changes in the levy of miners which supported union members who were on short time, and in the rules under which the payments to members were made. At a meeting of the Senghennydd miners, Hubert Jenkins then had to sell the new arrangements to his members. After a good deal of questioning the issue was put to the vote, and it emerged that Jenkins's rhetoric had been insufficient to convince the branch. This was an interesting test of the nature of the democracy; how would the local leaders respond to being 'defeated' by the membership of the voluntary organisation? In the event Hubert Jenkins lost his temper. He 'suggested that they should carry out their decision to its logical conclusion and decide to sever their connection with the Miners' Federation because it amounted to that whatever might be said to the contrary'. After being browbeaten by their Agent, something they were quite used to despite the fact that it 'created quite a consternation among the members', it was decided 'that a further meeting should be arranged on the first idle day to reconsider the matter'.[60] The servants of the people did not take easily to their advice not being followed.

An incident in the Aber Valley Trades and Labour Council, in February 1920, pointed to other structural weaknesses in the processes of democracy at the grass roots, when a single body such as the miners' union was so dominant in terms of numbers. In the previous local election John Ellis, a member of the Enginemen and Stokers' Association, had been an effective though unsuccessful candidate for Labour in Abertridwr Ward against E. S. Williams, the manager of the Windsor Colliery, who had won the seat by only two votes. The failure of Ellis to capture the seat may have been related to the fact, implied by the Secretary of the Abertridwr Lodge, that Ellis had received less than full support from the Abertridwr miners. Hugh Pugh, the Branch Secretary of the Stokers' Union, felt that Ellis should be allowed to stand again, in which case he should probably win. However the Abertridwr Lodge of the miners' union decided to nominate Edward Lewis, their own checkweighman. Thomas James, in his role as secretary of the Senghennydd Miners' Lodge, argued strongly that men from the non-miners union should be given a chance while Thomas Hitchings, the Senghennydd representative on the Pontypridd Board of Guardians, supported him. Although on a show of hands Ellis had won the nomination, nevertheless the combined numbers represented by delegates had meant that the Abertridwr miners' nominee had easily won the final vote. Hugh Pugh argued that 'by that system the miners could always fall back on their majority and they could carry out whatever they wanted, and he considered that it was not fair'. That however was the system in use and formally it had to be followed: nevertheless such use of their numerical strength hindered the miners when the time came for them

to ask for support of other trade unionists during the periods of crisis
which were to come.[61]

By the end of 1924 the situation was again changing. The pessimistic
view that the troubles of the coal industry might be pathological rather
than simply cyclical was again beginning to seem plausible. The
restarting of production in the Ruhr Valley reintroduced a major
supply of cheap coal to the export market and, as war reparations
were renewed, decimated Welsh exports to France as well as releasing
more French coal onto the world market. Electricity and oil were
increasingly being used for fuel and in 1925 the return to the gold
standard dramatically reduced the competitive position of British
industry in international markets. By the beginning of 1925 50%
of collieries were operating at a loss and 25% of miners were
unemployed.[62] Moreover the figure of 315,000 unemployed miners
disguised the even greater number who were employed for only two
or three days a week, reducing some families to penury. The weekly
production figures for the Universal in the mid 1920s indicate the
uncertain prospects of the miners. Even in the relatively stable period
of August and September 1925 the production of large coal fluctuated
between 5,500 tons and under 2,000 tons while total weekly production
varied between 10,700 tons and 3,300 tons.[63] In any other industry
many more companies would have closed at this point, but mining is
something of an exception: there are virtually no assets to sell unless
the business is a going concern, and a mine rapidly degenerates into
dereliction as workings sink and collapse, unless it is maintained.
Unlike a ship or a factory it cannot easily be mothballed. For owners,
therefore, there was a very strong incentive to keep the concern going,
sometimes at greatly reduced levels of production, rather than closing
down with the loss of vast capital outlay and little chance of capitalising
on the value of land, buildings, plant or unrealised resources at a later
date. Within a largely unrestrained market system, therefore, the
owners are locked into a suicidal battle for survival which, once
entered, has an inescapable logic to it.
    The accounts for the Lewis Merthyr Collieries clearly illustrate the
crisis. In 1924 profits slumped to £13,984 from the previous year's
figure of £165,826 and the post war peak of £1,197,693 while
borrowings reached a new high of £180,000. The figures for 1925,

when they were announced in December, were even worse. The notional profit of £4,064 was only achieved by transferring the entire reserves of £150,000 to the profit and loss account and the overdraft from Lloyd's Bank more than doubled to £400,000.[64]

In May 1925 there was a warning that the Senghennydd mine would close unless output was increased. Thomas Harpur, by then the chairman of the union lodge, presided over a mass meeting in the Park Hall Cinema, with Hubert Jenkins, still the miners' agent, and Thomas James, the lodge secretary.[65] The men agreed to work extra shifts, thus increasing the production of coal and contributing to a pattern which, repeated throughout the coalfield, was simply feeding the glut of coal for which there was a relatively inflexible demand. The following month the Windsor Colliery in Abertridwr was taken over by the fast expanding Powell Duffryn Company. All the men were laid off apart from 100 repairers who were kept on to help install the new cutting equipment and conveyors which would further increase production. Once the new equipment was fully installed some men would be re-employed, though it was known that there would be hundreds of job losses.[66]

By the spring of 1925 the position of British coalowners had hardened. They announced that after July 1925 the existing agreement would end; that in future the districts would revert to negotiating their own wage rates unfettered by national agreements; and that a first charge on earnings would be a 13% allocation to profits, regardless of the position of wages thus, in effect, ending the minimum wages won in the 1912 strike. There was also a demand for an extra hour on the working day. It was estimated that the package would result in a cut of up to 47% in wages in south Wales.[67]

The owners' terms were rejected by the men and the industry stumbled towards a major strike in which, it seemed to many of the men, they had little to lose, in view of the future that they were being offered. Faced by a strike which would cripple industry, Stanley Baldwin, the Conservative Prime Minister, gambled that the industry was simply experiencing yet another trade fluctuation and that a respite might be sufficient to carry the industry through to the next improvement in international prices for coal. The Government therefore gave a temporary subsidy to last until 1st May 1926, in order to support wages. (Opponents would claim rather that the Government was buying time in order to complete arrangements for the total defeat of the miners when the time was ripe and the inevitable strike would be allowed to occur.) Without the subsidy, 90% of the south Wales coal industry would have been running at a loss.

The crisis was underlined as each company delivered its annual report to shareholders and as local collieries closed down or worked short time.[68] In October 1925 William Kestell, who had left Senghennydd for the Albion Colliery a few miles away in Cilfynydd, had to announce that production would be reduced to a fraction of previous output, hoping to maintain the mine at minimum cost until the price of coal recovered on world markets.[69] The management at the Universal went for the opposite strategy, hoping by increased production and reduced costs to ride out the crisis: with this aim in view the mine actually took on more miners, absorbing many of those dismissed from the Windsor Colliery. Lewis Merthyr Collieries remained in business by reducing investment in machinery and modernisation with fatal effects in the longer term: in a report on the company in 1928 it was stated that resources were poor and that 'the collieries are not well equipped, though the coal is of fine quality and is extremely popular'.[70]

The pressure to increase production took its toll as safety standards slipped and miners struggled to maximise personal production. Evan Jones was killed in the mine: two of his brothers had died in the explosion of 1913. In October 1924 William Williams was killed when he was hit by a 'journey' of trams. James Griffiths, the father of seven children, was killed in July 1925.[71] In January of the same year, when 63 year old Benjamin Prosser died of a heart attack in the Windsor Colliery, the coroner used the case to praise the values of dedicated work for one's employer, saying that he 'was evidently an old workman who was going to work though not in a fit state to do so. There were, he was glad to say a good many like that about'.[72] The coroner did not elaborate on why it was admirable for workers to work when they were unfit.

It seems likely that the uncertainty of the times was partly responsible for the growing numbers of suicides as the crisis worsened. In May 1925 Jeremiah Callaghan, the unemployed father of a family of hell raisers, tried to commit suicide.[73] In August the stroke suffered by her mother proved too much for twenty five year old Ann Edwards who killed herself in the Senghennydd reservoir. Two months later 61 year old David Jones, who had a tailor's shop in Commercial Street, also drowned himself in the reservoir: Jones was part of the established families of the village and was married to one of the Bussells. At least the times produced a degree of compassion: by contrast when the seventy year old John Pember, who had been unemployed for nine months, had hanged himself from his bedstead in May 1923, the report had been headlined, 'Coward's Suicide'.[74]

Another effect of the continuing uncertainty was the growing number of people emigrating to Australia, Canada and New Zealand. The Hazels were an important family in the life of the village; now Jack Hazel, the son of the newsagent, left for New Zealand with his family, part of a growing stream which included some of the most active and able villagers.[75]

The miners, as well as the Government, had been preparing for the struggles which would inevitably come. In 1923 there had been continuous campaigns against non-unionism at the Universal, with a series of show card days and the handing in of strike notices to put pressure on both management and non-unionists. The result was a high level of unity demonstrated by the vote of 969 to 123 in favour of strike action in January 1924. The show card days continued up to May 1925, to ensure the highest possible level of union membership when the threatened national strike took place.[76]

At the end of November 1925, as the crisis unfolded, Percie Ward, the general manager of the Lewis Merthyr Collieries, died after an operation. His death shocked people in Senghennydd where he had been seen as an ally of the village.[77]

Altogether it was a threatening time and there were few of the diversions which had once enlivened the village. In the circumstances the villagers made the most of what amusements there were, notably the troubles of Edwin Pitt, now the chairman of the Senghennydd Colliery Lodge and miners' checkweighman.[78] Pitt, who was an active member of the Communist Party and lived in Caerphilly, was in trouble with Mr Williams, his landlord, who was also a miner. Williams, lived in the front downstairs room, the back kitchen and in one of the first floor bedrooms, while Pitt had the middle room downstairs and two bedrooms.

It was made clear, on Williams's behalf, that he was not too bothered about the non-payment of rent, but rather about the intolerable nuisance of being an unwilling host to a very active section of the South Wales Communist Party. Edwin Pitt, it was alleged, had turned the house into the headquarters of the party. About the politics of the party he had nothing to say. From early morning, afternoon and night and until midnight sometimes Communists from various parts of the South Wales coalfield met at the house to the extent of 10 to 12 persons at the same time. They used the rooms up and downstairs and also sat on the stairs. On Sundays some 20 to 30 persons met there. Leaders of the Communist Party stayed there as the guests of Pitt and there was literature all over the place. The result of all this was that Williams was unable to get any rest... sometimes people congregated at the house before breakfast and they discussed communism and attended the literature that was in the house.

In a pitiful litany, Williams explained that 'he had seen as many as seven and eight people in the kitchen at the same time discussing politics for hours'. It was not even as though Pitt was a single man: on the contrary. He was 'a married man with four children and he also had his niece staying with him, whilst her young man came there regularly and often stayed on the couch. He averaged that 50 people visited there during the week. Pitt kept papers in the pantry whilst he had some thirty communist collapsible chairs, some of which he kept under the bed and others in the pantry'. The audience were probably in as collapsed a state as the communist chairs at the end of this vintage courtroom saga. The story told by Williams may have dissuaded most people from playing host to local communist activists: on the other hand the description of lively debate, enthusiasm and political activity also explains why the Communist Party was attractive to people exposed to the unrelenting dehumanisation both of unemployment and of work in the pit, as against the apparent stolidity of the local Labour Party, typified by old stalwarts like Alderman Hubert Jenkins, Councillor Thomas James and Councillor John Davies.

By early 1926 it was clear that Baldwin's gamble had failed. The world market had not recovered, prices for coal were still disastrously low and the government was pouring money into the industry to subsidise wages. On 1st January a tea party was held at Beulah Chapel in Abertridwr for the 250 children of unemployed miners; the first time in the history of the valley that it had been necessary to organise such an event at Christmas time. The Conservative Club also organised a fund and distributed oranges and sweets to the children. In all there were 400 unemployed miners in Senghennydd and Abetridwr, largely the result of cuts made after the takeover by Powell Duffryn of the Windsor Colliery.[79]

A different Government might have reconsidered the option of nationalising the industry, in order to sort out its grave structural problems, as the Sankey Report had recommended in 1919. This government simply wanted to rid itself of any direct responsibility for the industry, with the least possible disruption. The owners wanted to get back to profitablility and saw lowered costs, in particular lower wages and longer hours, as the means to achieve this aim. The union was aware that the industry could not survive in the competitive world market in its present state. The leadership saw their main job as protecting the interests of their members, but if it came to a choice then Arthur Cook and the other union leaders would prefer to maintain existing wages and conditions, at the cost of some unemployment, rather than reducing all workers to grossly overworked and underpaid drudges. Better straight unemployment than intermittent days work and a weekly wage packet that could not keep a family.[80]

The position of the owners was made clear when Rufus Lewis, the new general manager of the Lewis Merthyr Collieries who had taken over from Percie Ward, was welcomed to Senghennydd as the guest of honour at a dinner for the colliery officials. Various speeches gloried in the risk taking and deserved profits of entrepreneurs, but the nub of the matter was put by Watkin Moss, the agent for Lewis Merthyr's Hafod mines. Moss argued that 'there was no doubt that Capital had suffered and there was no doubt that Labour had suffered. Labour was entitled to its just reward and capital was entitled to its just reward and unless the two got something worth living for the industry was bound to go down. As a practical man he was sure that if the Politicians would keep their hands off the industry and leave it to the men . . . they would be able to produce coal and compete with any country in the world . . .'. In short, and however sincere the respect expressed for the needs and rights of workers, the main thrust of the argument was that the owners needed to be set free from government regulations over prices and hours; and that the miners' wages would have to fall until they reached a level which was competitive in terms of the international costs of production.[81]

In these positions there was no obvious basis for compromise, and the government was already taking precautions to enable industry to withstand a widespread and long lasting strike. The men too were making final attempts to enforce union membership.[82]

As the months and weeks passed and the strike approached, men continued to be killed in the mine, arousing in retrospect the same feelings as when men were killed in the last weeks of the war. In January John Coles was killed by a colliery truck: such deaths were notorious among men made unfit by periods of unemployment. In April, Joseph Collier, of the High Street, was run over by a tram in the mine and was killed. His wife was already dead and he left eight orphaned children.[83]

Tension was mounting over the months but there were still moments of relief. In March, a large haybarn belonging to the Lewis Merthyr Company was set on fire on the mountainside and a big crowd turned out to enjoy the fun as three and a half tons of hay, intended for the pit ponies, blazed against the night sky. In April there was still enough money in the community for a party to visit Paris for the Wales versus France rugby match; but that must have been deliberate defiance in the face of the hardship which everyone knew was coming.[84]

For the miners it seemed that they had little choice. They could give in and accept longer hours for dramatically less pay, with higher chances of unemployment; or they could strike, with the support of the whole trade union movement, in the desperate hope that their action would force the Government to intervene as previous governments had done. Well informed miners knew, however, that whoever controlled the industry would be faced by the need to bring production and costs into line with the world markets. There would be hard times ahead whoever won although, in the long term, the best hope for the miners remained a nationalised industry which could make strategic plans rather than lurching from crisis to crisis in response to the fluctuations of a highly unstable international market.

On May 1st the long awaited strike, or lock out, finally started and three days later other major industries came out in support of the miners in accordance with T.U.C. policy. The misnamed 'general strike' was highly successful in gaining the support of workers on the railways and in transport, printing and other industries. However, when the Government failed to back down in the first few days, some of the leaders lost their nerve and sent their members back to work without gaining any concessions for the miners. Their reluctance unconditionally to commit their members to an indefinite strike on behalf of a union whose leaders seemed unable to work with other union leaders was understandable, but their inability to put their combined industrial strength to better use on behalf of the miners was condemned as pitiful. The other unions crept back to work on May 14th and the miners were left to continue their lone struggle which increasingly came to seem unwinnable. The intransigence of Arthur Cook, with his rallying cry of 'Not a penny off the pay, not a minute on the day', symbolised for many among the miners' natural allies the impossibility of negotiating or co-operating with the miners' leaders.

In the Aber Valley the community, as always, made the best use of a strike. All their talents for organisation and for stretching scarce resources to the maximum were put to use. Communal kitchens were organised and lessons were learnt from the embezzlements during the 1921 strike. At the Senghennydd Girls' School 140 children got three meals a day. Not surprisingly attendance was excellent at 97%, and the teachers kept the school open throughout the Whitsun holiday in order to provide meals. The infants school was serving 2,000 meals a week and a rota kept the kitchen open throughout the Summer holidays. Attendance remained at about 95% although it was noted

The Senghennydd school canteen committee during the strike of 1926.

that this would have been significantly lower had it not been for the provision of boots by the National Union of Teachers. Remembering those times, Kenneth Maher of Caerphilly wrote that 'we children of miners, between five and fourteen years, were better fed than normal'.

> The food was plain but good. For breakfast it was always porridge, bread and marge and jam, and cocoa. For dinner it was always potatoes, greens and rice pudding for afters. For teatime it would be, without fail, bread and jam and banana and two cups of tea. . . our parents were starving.[85]

In times like these the hardwork of the allotment holders was fully rewarded. Richard Hamar, who had married the widow of David Griffiths, one of those killed in 1913, kept three allotments and shared pigs with the local milkman. His produce helped to support the three children of his dead wife and his own children by his second marriage: his 'step-daughter' remembers the need for thrift but no real hardship in the family in the 1920s. Staunchly conservative, strongly anti-church and anti-chapel, and an active member of the 'Fed' through thick and thin, Hamar illustrates the complexity of the community as well as the qualities of self help and solidarity which kept the village together even in the midst of disaster. Some parents took advantage of a scheme run by supporters and their children were 'adopted' by families in London for the duration of the strike.[86]

There were other ways of solving the food problem and as always during strikes the hen coops on the mountainside allotments were very vulnerable. Even getting caught had its benefits. Emrys Griffiths, Idris Bull and Edwin Mathews claimed that they always went for a walk up the mountain at night, but the court accepted the version of an unnamed witness, who had been forty yards away in the dark, that the men had tried the latches of the coops. When the convicted men were given the alternative of a £5 fine or twenty eight days in jail, Emrys Griffiths remarked that 'It's free lodgings for a month anyway': it is unlikely that the labour involved would have seemed hard for a miner. Even rabbiting was illegal and received heavy fines.[87]

For the first few weeks the food kitchens and voluntary effort were enough to make the situation at least tolerable for most people, and the usual programmes of concerts and events helped to maintain morale. Particularly popular was a large horse parade organised by the canteen committee to collect funds for free meals. 140 ponies, released from the Universal Colliery by the strike, were enjoying an extended frolic on the company's farm and 100 of them were used for the event. After the parade there were competitions for grooming and presentation in which the hauliers entered with their favourite ponies. The high point of the event were the races and knock out competitions; all the more exciting since none of the horses had saddles. Only one rider was seriously hurt, and was carried off by the ambulance brigade which was proud to be able to display its skill. Here at least the terrible Callaghans were able to show their positive side and carried off two first prizes. The judges, in this event to raise money for the free kitchens without which the strike could not continue, were the management of the Lewis Merthyr Collieries who had lent the ponies for the day. Rufus Lewis, the general manager, was there, as was Fred Wilcox the agent and manager of the Universal. Tom Evans, the chief mechanical engineer, and Downing, the head of the Lewis Merthyr office staff, enjoyed the judging as did Councillor Evan Morgan, the Manager of Powell Duffryn's Windsor Colliery. There was as much jockeying for position off the race course as on but it is nevertheless an indication of the complexity of social relations in the valley that such an event could take place during one of the most bitter strikes in British history.[88]

In both cricketing and propaganda terms the Lewis Merthyr Collieries had the best of it when Rufus Lewis brought a cricket eleven to Senghennydd, later in the month, to play the village's team. Lewis himself only got two runs off Bryn Edwards, the Senghennydd butcher and noted rugby player, but Lewis's team won by 62 runs. Fred Wilcox, the manager and a long standing enthusiast for Senghennydd cricket, also scored only two runs; in his case for the home team.[89] The local papers were pleased to give such events considerable coverage compared to the scant coverage of the more routine events needed to maintain the strike.

These games were, however, only interludes in the unrolling crisis for the community. For some the strain had already been too much; in early June, Thomas Edwards, an injured miner from the Universal, cut his throat.[90] There was also an increasingly desperate element to the public demonstrations. While there appeared to be an understanding of the ground rules with the management, and perhaps something of the respect between adversaries engaged in the same business, outside propagandists were treated with scant regard.

When the Controller of the Women's Guild of Empire arrived to speak at Aberdare Hall in Senghennydd, the Hall was quickly surrounded by a crowd estimated at 600 people, booing and throwing old cans. Police reinforcements had to be rushed in from Caerphilly and Treharris to extricate the speakers and discourage the crowd from turning an enjoyable expression of community feeling into a full scale riot.[91]

An incident in June, which came to court in August, indicates the strength of feeling in the valley and also the tensions within the community.[92] A crowd of about three hundred was picketing the Universal Colliery as a small group of strike breakers loaded small coal in the colliery yard. A group of eight women set off from the Square in Abertridwr to inject some fire into the demonstration and the police alleged that the group was directed by two men whom the police described as members of the Communist Party. The group of ten included members of several of the long established families of the Aber Valley whose men had died in the 1913 explosion and in the Great War and whose children were buried at Eglwysilan; the Parishes, Parrys and Bishops. The police watched the group leave Abertridwr and phoned Senghennydd to warn the police there. In Senghennydd the women entered the colliery yard and Mrs Saunders confronted the man whom she took to be Fred Wilcox, though he was actually Police Sergeant Doolan. Mrs Saunders, who had died before the prosecution was brought, said to Doolan 'we have come to stop you filling the small coal', and Ethel Bishop accused him of 'starving us. You are well off'.

However the anger of this group was equally directed at the tamely legal tactics of their fellow workers and villagers who they tried to activate into greater confrontation with the colliery management. On the way to the mine, the group had tried to involve more people from Stanley Street and, in their disappointment at failure, had told them that 'You have got no guts in you.' Later, in the colliery yard, Mrs Saunders shouted at the crowd 'You have not the guts to stop them. Come and join us.' Although the village was solidly behind the strike, most inhabitants showed little inclination to support more aggressive action. The bench in its turn rejected the example of other areas in handing down severe sentences under the Emergency Powers Act and instead relied on the effective though less obviously repressive method of binding over all the defendants to keep the peace in the sum of £10 each. The Bench made no judgement on the issue but it seems likely that this demonstration was indeed an indication of the greater activism of the local Communist Party, regardless of exactly who were members of the Party. Fred Parish, for example, denied that he was a member of the Party, but by 1939, when as Secretary of the Senghennydd Miners' Lodge he stood for the local council, he insisted that he had left the Party three years earlier in 1936.[93]

As in all strikes the number of people charged with stealing coal for cooking and heating rose rapidly. In mid-July six men were fined ten shillings each for stealing coal from the Universal. In the same week three more Senghennydd men chose to go to prison rather than paying fines of £1 for taking coal from the tip behind the Windsor Colliery. Coal picking from the waste tips was well organised and took place while the police were occupied with pickets at the main gates. Since hundreds of people were engaged at one time or another the prosecutions represented only a slight deterrent. When the police did arrive there was sufficient warning for most people to get away, alerted by the likes of Bert Williams who was fined for obstructing the police, in the person of Sergeant Pinkard, after he shouted 'look out, here is that bastard Sergeant'.[94]

In the same month it was announced that the Senghennydd Rugby Club ground had been overhauled and new drains had been laid. Inevitably Rufus Lewis, the head of the Lewis Merthyr Collieries, was engaged to re-open the new ground. In the actions of the managers over the years, it is impossible to disentangle their motives which included a genuine commitment to the welfare of the village, as they saw it, as well as a relentless drive to win the confidence and votes of the community. J. E. Morgan describes a similar situation in the Lady Windsor Colliery at Ynysybwl, at which Edward Jones was the manager and agent for almost twenty years: 'Mr Jones had a fine sense of social duty. He was chairman of the Lady Windsor Institute for 29 years. He was regular in his attendance at the local Methodist Church, and his influence on the moral tone of the community was considerable'. And, despite the manager's antipathy to socialism and trade unionism, J. E. Morgan concludes that 'within his limitations, he was a valuable asset to the community, and to a greater degree, to the company'.[95]

In August, a fire at two o'clock in the morning at the Mens' Outfitters in the High Street offered an exciting diversion, as well as an opportunity to pick up some clothes. While the police and many inhabitants were helping to put out the fire, a fair proportion of the rescued stock disappeared. In the following week the local police carried out a series of raids throughout the village with the determination of Scotland Yard tracking down gold from a bank robbery. The police haul consisted of a few trousers and various socks from raids in Commercial Street, Brynhyffrydd Terrace, Caerphilly Road, and other addresses. The success with which they managed to track down odd pairs of socks, assuming that they had not sunk to planting socks on the defendants, argues that some respectable citizens were prepared to inform on their fellow inhabitants in the midst of a strike which was grinding the entire community into poverty. Samuel Milton was charged with the theft of one sock, which seems to have been overpriced at nine pence. He claimed that he had held it over his mouth while helping to put out the flames and had put it into his pocket as he helped with other tasks. Since he was busy as the caretaker of his chapel he had not returned the sock on Sunday. For his crime he was fined 15/-. The more heinous crime of removing a pair of trousers received, pro-rata, a fine of £3 or twenty eight days in gaol. John Moran who had managed to turn off the electricity in the burning shop, before helping to remove a flaming counter, and who had told the manager that he was taking some clothes and money to his house for safe keeping, also had to go through the indignity of a trial before being found not guilty. William Goodwin seems to have got off lightly with a 10/- fine for stealing three pairs of trousers, particularly as the police also found two revolvers during their search. Evidently the explanation that he had been in the regular army and had kept the weapons as souvenirs of his service in the Boer War had its usual positive effect on the bench.[96]

The miners and their communities held on throughout the Summer and Autumn as savings disappeared, heavily indebted shop keepers stopped giving credit, relief funds dried up and the community began to give up hope. Prosecutions for attempting to defraud the Guardians increased as the south Wales boards of guardians themselves sank into bankruptcy. Even the demonstrations against strikebreakers increasingly became a way of venting the anger of the community rather than serving an economic or tactical purpose in determining the final outcome of the strike. In November a crowd, estimated at 'several thousand', hooted and jeered at a single strike breaker escorted back by police to his home in Abertridwr from his work at the Universal. So great was the bitterness at the betrayal of the community that fifty years later such men would still be ignored and rejected as they drank in pubs, if they remained in the same community and refused to apologise for their actions. From the point of view of the owners also, what could be produced by such men was irrelevant compared to the symbolic statement that the union could be defied: and the state brought its weight to bear in attempting to protect such strikebreakers.[97]

In the end the underlying economic logic of the situation asserted itself. Coal was easily obtained on foreign markets and new developments suggested that it was slowly losing its strategic importance. Even a member of the Pontypridd School Board had proudly proclaimed that, thanks to electricity, 'we will soon be able to do without coal'; an astonishing boast from an elected public figure in the Welsh valleys.[98]

If the mines were to be run as capitalist enterprises, and there was no sign whatever of the Government wanting to take over the industry, then there would be lower wages, widespread closures and longer hours. However successful the union was in holding the line and preventing a slow, disorganised return to work, that economic reality of capitalist markets was unavoidable; and most people realised the fact once it became clear that the Government would not take responsibility. For many of the men the defeat in the strike was not the worst. The greater fear was that the defeat heralded the eclipse of the industry and the death of the communities which relied on it.

By the beginning of December men were beginning to crawl, despairingly, back to work. Among those too loyal, too afraid or too proud to return without union instructions other forms of escape might be possible. In Senghennydd the most dramatic was the announcement that Thomas Harpur, a major figure in the local Labour Party and Secretary of the Universal Miners' Lodge, was emigrating to Australia with his four sons. If there was despair at least there was not, as yet, 'the habit of despair'. The hopelessness, but also the miners' proud refusal to admit defeat, was clearly indicated when, in the ballot held at the beginning of December 1926 to give a mandate to the union negotiators to settle the dispute, only 261 miners voted at Senghennydd out of a workforce of over 2,000. The vote was 181 to 80 in favour of re-opening negotiations with the owners.[99]

The aftermath of the strike was grim. Hubert Jenkins reported that hundreds of East Glamorgan miners had not recovered their jobs by March 1927, and wages were forced down by the new piece rates. Work was intermittent and the Pontypridd Board of Guardians, with debts approaching £500,000, had cut their payments of relief. Even the physical environment was worse. Thomas James said that 'at Senghennydd they lived in dust, breathed dust and ate tons of dust. They could only dry clothes at night, while food could not be kept in pantries'. The management agreed to try to remedy the situation.[100]

Many followed the lead of Thomas Harpur, and emigrated. Bryn Edwards, formerly a local hero on the rugby field, who had played in the cricket match during the strike, gave up the family butcher's shop and went to Canada with his wife and children. Others settled back into the old routines. Mary Ann Davies applied for a separation order against her allegedly brutal husband who drank and beat her up leaving her broken and with black eyes during her pregnancy, only to be advised by the magistrates to make it up with her husband.[101] The endlessly stoical inhabitants of some of the terraces were again without water for drinking and washing and were told, as they had been for the past thirty years, that developments were on the way. Councillor Evan Morgan threatened that 'there is going to be a revolution in Senghennydd before long'; but it is difficult to see why the inhabitants should revolt at anything since they had almost certainly already put up with worse.[102]

Yet more inhabitants were fined for stealing coal, needed for cooking and for heat during the winter, while other batches of people were given last warnings that they would be gaoled if they did not pay off existing fines: meanwhile the company itself admitted that it could not carry out repairs to housing, due to its financial position.

When a council storeman's job in Caerphilly was advertised, there were 54 applications, an indication of the unemployment crisis. Many took jobs elsewhere, sending money home, and sometimes not returning. When Bert Hall left to work in Inverness he found a new partner by whom he had a child. He wrote to his wife saying,

> My advice is for you to go to court and make me pay and I will make arrangements for the children. If you don't take me to court I will send you money as I fancy . . . Please don't think of me as you knew me but as your husband that ran away with another woman and left you with five children.[103]

Young women who could not be supported by their families were also increasingly leaving for jobs as servants in London and the Home Counties where their accents and inexperience ensured that, although some revelled in new experiences and had sympathetic employers, many were treated with scant respect. The twenty year old Emma Chant, whose father had been killed in the 1913 explosion when she was six, worked as a servant for Dr and Mrs Atkinson in Streatham. She was pregnant when she returned to her mother's house in Grove Terrace. Emma Chant explained that the baby was that of her employer's father, sixty seven year old George Berridge; but her employers implied that she had been sleeping with a tramwayman, said that she had been sacked for being late for work and insisted that the money sent by George Berridge had been a mere kindness. The magistrates refused to grant Emma Chant a maintenance order against George Berridge on the ground that there was insufficient evidence to prove his paternity of the child.[104]

The economic depression was undermining virtually all voluntary institutions in the valley. Income at the Senghennydd Miners' Institute and Library had dropped from £30 to £9 a week. With an outstanding mortgage of £2000, it was clear that the Institute would soon be bankrupt unless a large number of people could be induced to renew their payments, a situation repeated throughout the valleys.[105] In Caerphilly the Red Cross Hospital was on the verge of closure as contributions dried up, the result of colliery bankruptcies and reduced subscriptions from union branches.[106]

Membership of the miners' union was decimated in the aftermath of the strike and a rival industrial union was making headway in Llanbradach: it was only a matter of time before the breakaway union attempted to recruit members at the Universal. In other mines, men like Albert Lower from Senghennydd, whose family had been killed in both explosions and had played a role in the court cases of the village, were active in restarting the Fed after the strike, in conditions of secrecy because of the threat of victimisation.[107]

While coal export prices remained in a trough and Powell Duffryn continued to buy up rival concerns to minimise costs and reduce the production of the coalfield as a whole, it became clear that the Lewis Merthyr Collieries were in serious financial difficulty. Work at the Universal had become increasingly uncertain as the management laid off men for days at a time to reduce costs. The balance sheet for 1926 made grim reading. With debts of over £400,000, property assets wildly overvalued at £1,193,870 in the context of a coal glut, and an operating loss of £193,872 the company had been heading for disaster for over a year.[108]

The end, when it came, was abrupt. An announcement was made on Friday, 30th March 1928 which merited only four sentences in the *Western Mail*:

> Workmen and officials numbering 2,500 at the Universal Collieries, Senghenydd, received one day's notice to terminate employment on Friday, which will come into operation today. (Saturday).
>
> The colliery is one of those owned by the Lewis Merthyr Consolidated Collieries (Limited) which are now under the supervision of a joint receiver and manager.
>
> It is stated that only nineteen officials are to be kept in charge of the collieries, which are to be closed indefinitely. All the workmen will descend the pit this morning to bring up their tools, while the horses will be raised on Monday.[109]

The Universal was bought as a disused colliery by the Powell Duffryn Company which was able to mine any remaining coal from their other pits in the area.

The colliery was never re-opened.

CHAPTER 12
[1] PRO BT 31
[2] CJ 27/2/1919
[3] CJ 30/8/1919
[4] CJ 1/11/1919
[5] CJ 22/12/1923
[6] CJ 21/2/1920: CJ 3/1/1920: CJ 6/12/1919
[7] CJ 3/4/1920: CJ 25/9/1920: CJ 11/4/1920
[8] CJ 9/1/1919: CJ 23/1/1919
[9] CJ 20/2/1919
[10] CJ 24/4/1919: CJ 8/11/1920
[11] CJ 12/6/1919
[12] CJ 3/7/1920
[13] CJ 26/6/1920
[14] CJ 25/9/1920: CJ 26/6/1920

[15] CJ 12/7/1919: CJ 28/8/1920: CJ 11/9/1920
[16] Interview; Mrs Bull
[17] M. Kirby, *op cit,* 55-6
[18] CJ 9/10/1920
[19] CJ 5/3/1921. The monument has now been fully restored and the names of the dead are once again legible
[20] CJ 2/4/1921; interview with Eli Huish
[21] CJ 23/4/1921
[22] B. L. Coombes, (1939), *op cit,* 146: J. E. Morgan, *op cit,* 25
[23] CJ 9/4/1921
[24] CJ 30/4/1921
[25] CJ 7/5/1921: CJ 14/5/1921: CJ 22/1/1921
[26] CJ 16/4/1921
[27] CJ 21/5/1921
[28] CJ 20/7/1921
[29] CJ 13/5/1922
[30] CJ 18/3/1922: CJ 8/4/1922
[31] PRO BT 31
[32] W. Boulton, *Senghenydd: The Village and the Rugby Club,* (Risca; 1982), 27
[33] *ibid,* 24: CJ 13/1/1923
[34] CJ 10/3/1923: CJ 28/4/1923
[35] CJ 28/2/1925: CJ 2/7/1932: CJ 25/3/1933
[36] CJ 9/8/1930: CJ 19/5/1928
[37] CJ 31/3/1923: CJ 28/5/1921: *Merthyr Express,* 7/6/1924
[38] CJ 25/9/1920: CJ 20/6/1925
[39] CJ 27/10/1923; CJ 13/2/1926
[40] CJ 27/1/1940
[41] CJ 24/3/1923
[42] CJ 7/10/1922
[43] CJ 13/9/1924
[44] CJ 21/7/1923: CJ 17/3/1923: 21/4/1923: CJ 11/4/1925: CJ 3/4/1926: CJ 9/4/1927
[45] CJ 30/6/1923: CJ 19/1/1924: CJ 26/5/1923: CJ 20/9/1924
[46] CJ 1/9/1923: CJ 31/5/1924: CJ 1/3/1924: CJ 11/4/1925: CJ 30/5/1925: CJ 18/8/1923
[47] Interview; Mrs Bull: P. Massey, *Portrait of a Mining Town,* (London; 1937), 34: A. Gray Jones, *op cit,* 187
[48] cf I. G. Jones, (1987), 140-2, 156
[49] Interviews with Doreen Jones and Pauline Thomas
[50] A. G. Jones, *op cit,* 188
[51] CJ 6/5/1922: CJ 31/1/1925: CJ 18/4/1925
[52] Elias Evans, *op cit,* 23
[53] CJ 16/2/1924
[54] CJ 19/4/1924
[55] Diary of Hubert Jenkins, (microfilm), Hull University Library
[56] CJ 3/10/1925: CJ 10/9/1921

[57] CJ 30/5/1931
[58] CJ 12/9/1931
[59] PP 1917-17 Cd. 8662 xv, 94
[60] CJ 12/3/1921
[61] CJ 14/2/1920
[62] M. Kirby, *op cit,* 68
[63] GRO DD NCB 17 3 (iii)
[64] PRO BT 31
[65] CJ 16/5/1925
[66] CJ 20/6/1925
[67] M. Kirby, *op cit,* 71
[68] CJ 30/8/1924
[69] CJ 3/10/1925
[70] Powell Duffryn Annual Report (27/3/1928)
[71] CJ 18/10/1924: CJ 25/7/1925
[72] CJ 12/12/1925
[73] CJ 9/5/1925
[74] CJ 15/8/1925: CJ 31/10/1925: CJ 5/5/1923
[75] CJ 7/11/1925: CJ 10/6/1922: CJ 30/9/1922: CJ 26/1/1924 (Australia): CJ 17/3/1923 (USA): CJ 30/9/1922 (Canada)
[76] CJ 5/5/1923: CJ 26/5/1923: CJ 1/12/1923CJ 19/1/1924: CJ 9/5/1925
[77] CJ 28/11/1925
[78] CJ 31/10/1925
[79] CJ 2/1/1926
[80] M. Kirby, *op cit,* 82 & 90
[81] CJ 13/2/1926
[82] CJ 13/3/1926
[83] CJ 30/1/1926: CJ 10/4/1926
[84] CJ 27/3/1926: CJ 10/4/1926
[85] K. Maher, 'Caerphilly', in N. Gray (ed.), *The Worst Times,* (Aldershot; 1985), 28
[86] Mrs Bull, interview
[87] CJ 22/5/1926: CJ 12/6/1926
[88] *ibid*
[89] CJ 19/6/1926
[90] CJ 5/6/1926
[91] CJ 3/7/1926
[92] CJ 14/8/1926
[93] CJ 18/3/1939
[94] CJ 24/7/1926: CJ 3/7/1926
[95] J. E. Morgan, *op cit,* 4
[96] CJ 28/8/1926
[97] CJ 20/11/1926
[98] CJ 11/7/1925
[99] CJ 4/12/1926
[100] CJ 8/1/1927
[101] CJ 15/1/1927: CJ 8/1/1927

[102] CJ 12/2/1927: CJ11/2/1928
[103] CJ 27/8/1927
[104] Interview, Mrs Bull: CJ 12/11/1927
[105] CJ 9/4/1927: P. Massey, (1937), *op cit*, 27
[106] CJ 3/12/1927
[107] South Wales Miners Library, Oral History Project, Interview with A. Lower
[108] PRO BT 31
[109] WM 1/3/1928

Chapter Thirteen
The Universal Colliery Closes

With the closure of the mine the original reason for the existence of Senghennydd disappeared. Even without the collapse of the industry the closure of individual collieries was entirely forseeable. Before the Great War, Sir William Lewis had warned of the need to limit coal consumption and wastage in order to protect coal reserves and extend the life of pits. The inhabitants too were aware of the very limited life of mines in a period of profligate fuel consumption. B.Price Davies recalled the refrain of an old village patriarch of 'Gorlan': 'Why are you building all these houses here, mun. The coal will be worked out in twenty years and these houses will be only houses for sheep'.[1]

A handful of men continued to work in the Universal after the closure, helping to dismantle anything of value, until the last repairer left in November 1928. The mine claimed a final victim in August 1928 when William Moulder, a member of one of the demolition teams, was killed under a fall. Even after its closure the mine continued to take its toll: George Taylor, who had been paralysed since his back had been broken by a fall of coal in October 1927, died in May 1929.[2] The deaths of Senghennydd men and boys now continued in other local pits, as miners cut corners on safety standards in order to increase production to maintain their wages. Two Senghennydd men were prosecuted in 1930 for working under a twenty three foot overhang of coal and rock weighing about eight tons which was wholly unsupported, an example of the recklessness and desperation to which some miners were driven. Evan Kirkham from Phillips Terrace was killed in the Llanbradach Colliery; his wife was left with memories of their three children buried in the cemetery at Eglwysilan including Evan, named after his father.[3] The problems were not reduced in the 1930s. In 1938, the fourteen year old John Thomas and sixteen year old Kenneth Clark were killed together as a result of a reckless disregard of safety.[4]

Relatively few found work. Those who did had to leave before five o'clock in the morning on the special miners' trains and return after dark: most had to work short time which meant that they were often almost as badly off as they would be on the dole. The vast majority of

A gang of coal pickers outside 1 Graig Terrace in 1929.

people who remained in the village and brought up families survived on that meagre dole. Many families obtained fuel from picking from the waste tips of collieries, though even this could be dangerous. The fifteen year old Arthur Morgan, who was unemployed, was killed when he was hit by a tram on the waste tip of the Windsor Colliery: there were six children of under fifteen in the family all surviving on the dole. One of the Bowden family broke his skull when he was hit by debris from an overhead conveyor on the same waste tip: he left a wife and six children to cope as best they could.[5] Faced by the desperation produced by destitution the police were rigid in their prosecutions for theft: Will Jones and his thirteen year old son were prosecuted for taking manure from the colliery yard of the Universal and putting it on their allotment and William Wynne and David Jones served fourteen days hard labour for the theft of 4/- of coal.[6]

In the circumstances, it was increasingly difficult to maintain general norms against theft, except where it affected other villagers. When a coke lorry belonging to the Great Western Railway broke down in the village, P.C. Harris arrived to find the inhabitants removing its load in buckets, boxes and anything else that came to hand.[7] Groups of young men organised themselves to retrieve what they could from the Universal. At night, with their faces blackened, they systematically raided the colliery and the locomotive yard. They removed the entire floor of the colliery engine house, and when one of them was caught he refused to name the remainder of the gang. Large quantities of fuel were involved: 23 hundredweight of timber blocks and 7 hundredweight of coal was found in the house and garden of one of the Hyatts whose family had been respected colliery officials, at the forefront of the colliery rescues and pillars of the sports teams and the chapel. When they had finished with the Universal, the gangs went over the mountain to other collieries. At the Albion Colliery in Cilfynydd, P.C. Smith complained that 'they came over from the other side in crowds and tried to terrorise the people. It was not safe for anyone to say a word to them'.[8] Apart from the need for the fuel, the work provided an excitement for the young men as well as offering a sense of having some control over their lives and a satisfaction in reclaiming their own product.

When James Dallimore, a key player in the successful rugby team of the early 1920s and a member of another old Senghennydd family, was prosecuted for assaulting the police in November 1929, Superintendent Griffiths said that

> during the last few months things had come to a certain state with a certain class at Senghenydd and things had become very troublesome. Several of his constables had been seriously assaulted and it was getting too bad. The conduct of the Senghenydd and Aber people on the whole, under the circumstances they lived, was all that could be desired, but there was a certain class that was causing a lot of trouble.

Faced by people who had too little to lose by a disregard for the law, the magistrates started to hand down exemplary sentences in order to create effective deterrents. They sentenced James Dallimore to six months in prison and warned him that he 'and other men must realise that the police must be protected in the execution of their duty, *especially in the industrial areas'*.[9]

Some exploits gave a heroic status to their perpetrators. The sheep skin found by Sergeant Doolan on Graig-yr-Hyvan Farm had, the Sergeant considered, been skinned by an expert. The evidence of expertise may have been enough to lead the Sergeant to Trevor Wilcox, but it is more likely that a neighbour betrayed him. In either event the Sergeant, supported by two constables, arrived at Wilcox's house in Cenydd Terrace to find him and William Ball 'seated at a table partaking of a meal of mutton chops', which was in itself suspicious behaviour in Senghennydd at the time. Meanwhile his mother was disposing of bits of sheep in the back garden. From there the police went to a house in Caerphilly Road where they retrieved two warmed shoulders of lamb from under the cushions of an armchair, the property of Ethel and Eva Wilcox. In court Trevor Wilcox gave a fine display of sensitivity and care for animals when he explained that he and Ball had found the sheep entangled in the barbed wire of the field and had only killed the suffering animal to put it out of pain.[10]

In these circumstances some of the recklessness of the Callaghans came to seem more acceptable. Jeremiah, the younger, was twice convicted of stealing coal from the Powell Duffryn Company in April 1930, and on the second occasion his nineteen year old brother James was prosecuted with him. The other brother John did more real harm: his marriage, in September 1929, meant that he was having difficulty keeping up the maintenance payments awarded only three months earlier to Gwenllian Rees for the baby she had just had by him.[11] The best qualities of the family were shown in April 1931, when a runaway horse and van bolted in the direction of a group of children near the Windsor pub: the 73 year old Jerry Callaghan, who had attempted suicide years before, was seriously injured when he threw himself at the horse and grabbed the reins.[12]

The closure of the mine removed some of their traditional work from the police and allowed them to keep an even tighter control over the behaviour of the villagers. The 57 year old Elizabeth Muller was British born, had lived in Senghennydd for thirty five years and had buried a member of the family after the 1901 explosion: she was prosecuted for failing to register her change of address, a necessary procedure as she had married a German forty years before.[13]

For a handful of men there was work with Davies and Lloyd, the Senghennydd builders responsible for much of the housebuilding in the early days. They now had the contract to build a new police station in Ystrad Mynach for £12,800. It was the only type of building for which there was much demand in the valleys at that time. Davies' and Lloyd's membership of the Henry Pendrill Charles Masonic Lodge would have given them matters of common interest to discuss with their clients in the Glamorgan Police Force.[14] In Senghennydd itself, however, the closure of the mine brought yet further closures in its wake. The worst was the shutting of the railway depot and the loss of over two hundred jobs. Most of the men were transferred elsewhere, leaving with 'sweet memories of the old Senghennydd sheds'. George Newell remembered the first trainload of coal to leave Senghennydd, which he had been chosen to drive. Others, like Alfred and George Crook, treasurer of the National Union of Railwaymen's branch and steward at the English Wesleyan Church respectively, left with memories of relations killed in the 1901 disaster and in the Great War. With their departure the English Congregational Chapel lost seventeen members: St Peter's Church lost nine, the Baptists eight, the Wesleyans seven and Noddfa Chapel lost six members of its congregation.[15]

There was virtually no work and no opportunities for anyone in the village: desperation forced them to leave the close community which had been created from nothing within thirty five years. In many cases it was those who were most active in the community who left, the men going ahead to find work, to be followed by their families: Daniel Rees, previously a miners' checkweighman and lodge secretary at the Windsor Colliery, was joined in Australia by his wife and three children: Thomas Pugh, a member of one of the strongest clans in Senghennydd and well established as the manager of the Leigh Hotel, also left for Australia. Others answered advertisements for emigration schemes like those run by the church army for boys and girls. The log of the Girls' School noted the fall in numbers and suggested that it was the 'best type of child' who was leaving.[16]

Advertisements appeared offering 'dowries' to young women who took up domestic work in London: the men left Senghennydd for the factories of the Midlands.[17] Someone may even have been sufficiently desperate to answer the advertisement in the *Caerphilly Journal* seeking 'Human Freaks of Nature for Exhibition Purposes'. 'Good wages [were] guaranteed to suitable curiosities' and 'anybody with anything peculiar about them' was asked to write to the proprietor of the freak show.[18] Others suggested even more drastic solutions to the problems of the valleys. Professor Ernest McBride, a zoologist of Imperial College London, argued that defectives who were only capable of unskilled manual work, notably the Irish and Welsh, were over-breeding. In the past this excess would have been killed off by disease and war but in the present circumstances 'there is only one remedy for the over-production of children that we can see. . . . This is compulsory sterilisation as a punishment for parents who have to resort to public assistance in order to support their children'. The professor seems to have been serious unlike Thomas Jones who suggested that the valleys should be evacuated and turned into industrial museums, target practices for the military and vast lakes for tourists. Thomas Jones's ironic suggestions are the closest to realisation.[19]

For the middle class there were jobs administering an Empire, which appeared to them to be as solid and timeless as ever. Of the sons of the Reverend D. Lloyd Rees, Captain Herbert Rees was in Ceylon, Stanley Rees was in the Indian Imperial Police, Frederick Rees was in the Nigerian Public Works Board, Thomas Rees was also out in India and Wilfred Rees worked for a company in Cuba.[20]

Over the years the population of the village slowly halved: it was a slow decline masked at first by the number of births. It was in holiday times, when all the young people returned to their birthplace from London and the Midlands, that it really struck home how many of the younger generation were leaving.[21] To an outsider the town had an air of death and infinite misery about it. One by one the chapels closed and many of the shops were boarded up. At one stage there was not even a resident doctor in the village since it was the colliery which had underpinned the medical service. The school logbooks contain a repetitive comment: 'attendance still poor. No boots'. In 1929 it was recorded that Dr Evans visited the school 'to examine children for malnutrition. As a result of the examination a number of children were recommended for extra nutrition'. Now it could be admitted that, even when there was no shortage of water, it was turned off simply in order to save money.[22] At times the situation reverted to the worst days of the 1890s before drainage was introduced; in November 1928 the council engineer reported that the water to Parc Terrace ran through a farmyard and a cesspool, and was unfit even for animals.[23] The situation was grim throughout the south Wales valleys and Senghennydd, lost from sight at the end of the Aber Valley, suffered exceptional hardship with hunger, insanitary conditions and disease as the inevitable consequences. The outbreaks of diseases, such as the ten cases of smallpox reported in April 1930, were largely the result of environmental factors.[24] Philip Massey in his survey of industrial south Wales, wrote that 'Senghenydd, having been based entirely upon employment at the one big colliery, and with the disadvantage of being a dead end town, is in a hopeless position today'. It was one of eight districts classified as 'derelict' in Lord Portal's survey.[25]

There was, of course, much political activity to confront the nation with the crisis of the valleys and the need for action. Alderman Hubert Jenkins, who had become the secretary of the Senghennydd Miners' Lodge back in 1902, was still active on behalf of the people of the Valley, as was Councillor Thomas James until his death in 1935. Their work was appreciated, and the inhabitants lined the streets all the way down the Valley when the funeral procession accompanied Thomas James's coffin to the cemetery at Penyrheol.[26] The Communist Party made the most stir, resting on the commitment of people like Albert Lower, Ted (Edwin) Pitt and Frederick Parish, who had been prosecuted under the Emergency Powers Act in 1926 and who, in 1929, was fined under continuing repressive legislation for collecting for the Party: his brother Albert had been killed in the 1913 disaster.[27] Despite anger at all the unnecessary suffering, the Communists had only a limited impact. In the general election of 1929, Morgan Jones, the Labour Candidate, was safely returned in Caerphilly with 21,148 votes: but the Conservative candidate still got a respectable 6,357 votes compared to the 829 votes for J. Wilson, the Communist candidate. Nevertheless individual commitment and sacrifice to the community gained victories for the Communist Party in some wards. In Abertridwr, Ted Pitt's friend and party colleague, Jack Roberts, carried on a relentless struggle against the coalowners and was arrested on several occasions, earning himself the nickname Jack 'Russia'. He was re-elected to Caerphilly Council while serving as a battalion commissar in the International Brigade in Spain, and held the seat for eighteen years ending up as the Chairman of Caerphilly Urban District Council, a worthy successor to Colonel Morgan Lindsay C.B. and Councillor Thomas James. The history of the Aber Valley seems to confirm the view of Peter Stead that 'the Welsh working-class for the most part has admired leaders who, whatever their labels, have displayed ability, industry and integrity in public affairs... Personality and style would seem to be more important than the purity of a man's theoretical position.'[28]

In local politics George Worman carried on the traditions set by Hubert Jenkins and Thomas James and held one of the three Senghennydd seats for Labour; he was active in the train drivers' union, a deacon at Ebenezer English Baptist Chapel and a member of a range of public bodies. In the local elections of 1929, the Labour Party tried to win the other two Senghennydd seats, while Samuel Rogers, whom Thomas James had narrowly defeated in the union lodge election, stood as a Communist. In the event it was the Independents, whose manifestos dismissed distinctions of class and party and who promised to protect the interests of ratepayers, who were victorious in a singularly dirty election. Mrs E. A. Williams had a fine record of voluntary activity in the Aber Valley; she had been headmistress of the Senghennydd Girls' School and was presently treasurer of the Senghennydd Chamber of Commerce. Her fellow independent was Griffith Lloyd the builder. He had been President of the East Glamorgan and Monmouthshire Valleys Master Builder's Association, and was presently deacon of Noddfa Welsh Congregational Chapel, secretary of the Senghennydd and Abertridwr United Welsh *Gymanfa Ganu* and treasurer of the Senghennydd Bowling Club and of the Senghennydd and Abertridwr Distress Fund. He was also active in the Henry Pendrill Charles Lodge of the South Wales Freemasons, along with Charles Goodfellow the solicitor and other local leaders. The voting figures were: E. A. Williams (Independent), 835; G. H. Lloyd (Independent), 772; E. Edwards (Labour), 695; A. R. Holder (Labour), 691; S. Rodgers (Socialist) 153. The exploitation and suffering which had been endured over the years had not reduced Senghennydd to a homogeneous community or destroyed the conservative and traditional attitudes inherent in the backgrounds of the inhabitants, including many Labour voters. Senghennydd and villages like it form a contrast to some of the more radicalised communities of the Rhondda.[29]

Senghennydd did not obviously conform to any one sociological model of the mining community. Although there was certainly class polarisation against the owners, the wide variety of political viewpoints which were expressed differentiated it from the, somewhat romantic, ideal of proletarian solidarity characteristic of Lewis Jones's novels and identified by David Smith and Hywel Francis in parts of the Rhondda. Nor did the village really conform to the theory of the 'isolated mass' put forward by Kerr and Siegel: the evidence I present suggests a community strongly integrated but never homogeneous and unitary in the way those authors suggest. If either of these theories was entirely satisfactory then Senghennydd, isolated and ruthlessly exploited, ought to confirm them. Both theories may help one to understand the experience of the village but are inadequate in themselves. Equally the shared experience of the workplace and the shared culture of the community was clearly significant: the fact that the community survived when its only industry collapsed is an indication of sinews apart from those of work. Nevertheless such theories of socio-cultural identity are empty unless set in wider social and economic contexts. Senghennydd does not conform to any one descriptive or explanatory theory of the mining community though it does share most of the characteristics, or conform to the 'ideal types', outlined by Martin Bulmer: it was physically isolated, dominated by one industry, inhabited by men who shared a dangerous occupation and by a population separated from other perspectives on society, characterised by very strong distinctions in the roles of men and women, humming with social activities and rent with conflict. These sociological and political models of the mining community perhaps offer fewer insights than the historical perspective developed by Ieuan Gwynedd Jones in his accounts of south Wales communities in the nineteenth century: certainly the continuities between the experience of Senghennydd and that of the earlier communities described by I. G. Jones are very great.[30]

In the extremes which it suffered Senghennydd, however, was exceptional: it was not so much *typical* of the mining community as a *symbol* of all such industrial communities. The experience of Senghennydd stood for all who had struggled to build humane communities in the storm of suffering and destruction created by industrial capitalism in an uncontrolled marketplace.

Nothing short of a change in the social and economic structure of the country, to ensure that industry served the needs of the community and of the nation as a whole, could have altered the condition of communities like Senghennydd. In lieu of such policies, the inhabitants had to make do with advice about the future and about their attitudes. An industrial expert assured the mining communities that 'the next upward period of good trade according to the cycle movements should be in full swing from 1931 to 1935 but it is due to begin some time in 1930'. To prepare for the upturn, the local paper quoted the advice of the *Daily Express*: 'every man and woman should think prosperity and plan means of achievement in their own sphere. When the tide turns and the whole nation is thinking of constructive prosperity—nothing can hold it back'.[31]

In his last Christmas message to his Rhondda constituents before, his death, Lieutenant-Colonel David Watts Morgan M.P., C.B.E., D.S.O., J.P., the old miners' leader for whom Senghennydd had often provided a stage, attacked the government for its lack of humane policies, and gave his good wishes for the future:

> let our wishes be animated with goodwill, service and sacrifice, teeming with sincerity and blessing, promoting and fostering our hope that in the time in front life will bring prosperity and joy back to the thousands of cottage homes and will allow sunshine smiles and happy contentment to beam once again on the dear faces of the men, women and children. . . .

The handsome old master of ceremonies, with his dashing moustache and a glint in his eye, seemed dizzied with his own words as the Vanity Fair, which had seemed so real, withered away before his eyes.[32]

The community never did die. On the contrary, in appalling circumstances it created a happy atmosphere remembered with great pride by the generation brought up in the 1930s. Looking back on his upbringing before the second World War, Trevor Evans, one of the most distinguished emigrants from the Valley who was to be knighted for his services to journalism, wrote that, 'whenever Abertridwr, Senghenydd, Caerphilly or Llanbradach are mentioned in my presence I am carried off on a magic carpet of growing up. Fate could not have chosen a more comforting location'. The most important events in most people's lives continued; birth, copulation and death. Eleven couples from the valley were married in one week of April 1930; Gough, Harrison, Howells and several Thomases and Evanses. Occasionally the inhabitants married someone who did not come from either Senghennydd or Abertridwr.[33] As young people moved away to find work it was noticeable that the births became fewer and the deaths of long established inhabitants increased. Those who were left ran clubs, collected money, and brought up their children to be serious and committed people: but without the mine or other local employment there was no real hope for the community. Instead there was an inevitably inadequate programme of relief works to mitigate aspects of the suffering; various educational and training projects, special treats for the children and fund raising. Salem and other chapels made each deacon responsible for an area of the village: the

The Salvation Army Singing Company during the depression of the 1930s.

Eglwysilan Churchyard.

minutes of the chapel record small grants to members of the congregation who could not afford coal or other necessities. The activists did not, however, become obsessed with their own local sufferings: George Worman had first drawn the attention of the inhabitants to the evils of fascism in 1923 and now Fred Parish organised a shop to support the Republican cause in Spain.[34]

It was a symptom of Britain's colonial history and its cultural patterns that Senghennydd, created to produce coal for the Navy of the British Empire, should despatch a 'Coon Band' and a 'Nigger Troupe' to raise money for worthwhile projects in the village. It was only one final irony that black labourers on West Indian sugar plantations should have sent £24-0-8, through their church, to buy boots for 81 destitute Senghennydd children.

A fitting end to an almost absurd story.[35]

CHAPTER 13
[1] W. T. Lewis, *Presidential Address to the Iron and Steel Institute, 1909*, 4-5, (NLW; Lord Merthyr Archive, 384): B. P. Davies, *op cit*, 165
[2] CJ 25/8/1928: CJ 18/5/1929
[3] CJ 18/1/1930: CJ 14/9/1929
[4] CJ 18/6/1938: CJ 24/9/1929: 25/8/1928
[5] CJ 7/7/1928: CJ 6/7/1929
[6] CJ 13/4/1929
[7] CJ 24/8/1928
[8] CJ 28/7/1928: CJ 6/10/1928: CJ 10/5/1930
[9] CJ 16/11/1929 (my italics)
[10] CJ 31/10/1931: Elias Evans, *op cit*, 24
[11] CJ 5/4/1930: CJ 19/4/1930: 15/6/1929: CJ 19/10/1929
[12] CJ 4/4/1931
[13] CJ 31/10/1931
[14] CJ 27/1/1934
[15] CJ 25/3/1931: CJ 22/7/1933
[16] CJ 16/3/1929: CJ 19/5/1928: CJ 4/5/1929
[17] CJ 31/5/1930: CJ 22/2/1930: CJ 29/3/1930
[18] CJ 18/7/1931

[19] G. Williams, 'Compulsory Sterilisation of Welsh Miners, 1936', *Llafur,* Vol 3 No 3: T. Jones, 'What's Wrong with South Wales ?', *Leeks and Daffodils,* (Newtown; 1942), 107-112.

[20] CJ 26/10/1929

[21] CJ 2/8/1930

[22] CJ 28/1/1932

[23] CJ 9/6/1928: 3/11/1928

[24] CJ 5/4/1930

[25] P. Massey, *Industrial South Wales: A Social and Political Survey,* (London; 1940), 38 & 61

[26] CJ 5/1/1935

[27] CJ 14/8/1926: CJ 30/3/1929

[28] CJ 8/6/1929: P.Stead, 'Working Class Leadership in South Wales, 1900-1920' *Welsh History Review,* Vol 6 (1972-3), 352

[29] CJ 30/3/1929

[30] H. Francis and D. Smith, *op cit,* 28-69: M. Bulmer, 'Sociological Models of the Mining Community', *Sociological Review,* Vol 23 (1), (1975), 61-92. For a recent and very detailed discussion of the concept of community in the context of mining villages see D. Gilbert, *Class, Community and Collective Action*, (Oxford; 1993)

[31] CJ 18/1/1930

[32] CJ 7/1/1933: CJ 4/3/1933

[33] CJ 26/4/1930

[34] CJ 28/1/1939

[35] CJ 27/12/1930

Afterword

> The gods had condemned Sisyphus ceaselessly to roll a rock to the top of a mountain, whence the stone would fall back of its own weight. They had thought with some reason that there is no more dreadful punishment than futile and hopeless labour.
>
> A. Camus, *The Myth of Sisyphus*

From the first days of its existence Senghennydd was doomed. Its survival depended on reserves of coal at a time when the profligate exploitation of those reserves was entirely in the hands of people seeking private profit, without any duty or responsibility to the village. However much colliers, trade unionists, women, or mine officials might, according to their own lights, seek the good of the community, they had no control over the aim served by the mine; the aim of maximising profits.

Nor was the mine subject to the needs of the wider Welsh national community, although it was subordinated to the demands of the British Empire during the Great War. The mine was created by the drive for profits, it destroyed people in that drive and it was closed when profit could no longer be obtained, leaving a community to wither. When a Labour Government came to power with a majority after the Second World War, the needs of places like Senghennydd were overshadowed by the massive scale of the problems facing the British multinational state.

The intense suffering experienced by the people of Senghennydd produced no great insights or single-minded commitments by the community. Other villages were more radical, more traditional, more religious or more violent. The horrors faced by the people produced nothing more exceptional than a desire for security and a sufficiency on which to exist. Even this was not refined by the experience of tragedy into something out of the ordinary: the commonplace peaceful existence for which people ached continued to be coloured by a taste for the raucous.

Coalmining has almost disappeared from the south Wales valleys. This does not mean that the lessons to be drawn from the history of Senghennydd have become irrelevant. The condition of workers employed by large companies throughout the world continues to demonstrate what happens to those communities and nations which are entirely subject to the whims of international markets, unconstrained by considerations of human need and the good society. In 1984, for example, three thousand people lived and died horribly in Bhopal because a corporation pursued profit with scant regard for the needs of a community and workforce.

Despite the desperate circumstances in which the inhabitants of Senghennydd found themselves they created a thriving village and, like other mining communities, they struggled to create a more just society. Even if that struggle was doomed it was nevertheless necessary.

Justice and the good society, like peace, may never be realised. But the inhabitants would have lived in a yet more nightmarish world if they had stopped struggling to realise those ideals, thus removing all restraints from the forces of raw exploitation. If the end of a just society was completely unattainable, then the need to struggle for it became even more vital.

Acknowledgements

This book has developed over several years during which time many people have helped me. Ray, Calvin, Sam Harris, Rolli and the other regulars of the Red Lion in Heolgerrig welcomed me to the mining community of south Wales. Ray and Mari Morris introduced me to other aspects of the valleys and Alun Evans has been a source of ideas and suggestions over a long period.

I am grateful to my colleagues at Fircroft College for their support and in particular to David Turner, Janice Wilcox, Hilary Hinds, Roger Kite, Louis Ross, Joan O'Hagan and Carl Chinn who have helped me in various ways. Aled Jones of University College, Aberystwyth encouraged me by publishing a part of my research in *Llafur,* the Journal of Welsh Labour History. Jane Monahan's maps have made the text much simpler to follow and she and Jim Monahan read an early typescript and gave me further encouragement.

The staff of the British Library, (at Colindale in particular), Birmingham University Library, Birmingham City Library, Hull University Library, the Miners' Library at Swansea University, Cardiff City Library, Fircroft College Library and Merthyr Tydfil Public Library have all helped me. No library, however, can hope to equal the pleasures of working at the National Library of Wales: I am immensely grateful for the intelligent and patient support of the staff at that incomparable institution.

My greatest debt is to Neil Evans of Coleg Harlech who has corrected errors, provided valuable references and made many interesting suggestions. He has been immensely generous with his time and knowledge to a total stranger. The book has been significantly improved as a result of his advice. Equally importantly he introduced me to his father, Viv Evans of Senghennydd. Viv Evans checked my factual statements about the geography of the village and introduced me to a range of people whose families had played a vital part in the history of Senghennydd. Viv and Glenys and Leslie Evans always made me welcome and showed interest in my endless questions even when they had more pressing problems of their own.

They introduced me to Gwen Edwards, formerly headmistress of the Infants School, who was full of knowledge about the village and of wisdom about the community. Ruth McCleod and Rene Morgan told me about their father Councillor Thomas James. Eli Huish and his sisters put me right about his own escapades. Dilys John was like an answer to a prayer just as I had given up hope of finding out more about her mother, Catherine James, ('Megfam'). Lillian Bull and her husband talked to me about her step-father, Dick Hamar and about the life of the village in the 1920s. Mrs Loram, a descendant of Lord Merthyr, offered to help, but unfortunately no private papers or memories seem to have survived beyond the meagre remnants in the National Library. I received a particularly warm welcome from Pauline and Ivor Thomas, and Doreen Jones, who talked to me about the Marshalls and Anzanis and allowed me to use their family photographs.

Viv Evans also introduced me to Bill Styles who has an exceptionally fine collection of postcards of Senghennydd and the Aber Valley. Bill Styles's helpfulness and generosity meant that I was able to use a large number of photographs with which to illustrate the book. The outstanding photo-journalism of 'Benton of Glasgow' deserves further research. Hopefully the whole of Bill Styles's collection will soon be available in book form.

The book has also been improved by the suggestions of Dr John Davies, who read the typescript for Gomer Press, and of Brian Davies and Chris Williams, who read it for the Welsh Arts Council. I am greatly in their debt for their advice, criticisms and encouragement. I am also very grateful to the Welsh Arts Council without whose support the book might not have been published.

I acknowledge the use of quotations from the following works, all of them published by Penguin Books: A. Camus, *The Plague* and *The Myth of Sisyphus*; A. Solzhenitsyn, *One Day in the Life of Ivan Denisovich*; W. Thackeray, *Vanity Fair*; W. H. Auden, *A Selection by the Author*; E. Zola, *Germinal.*

Beyond the people who have directly assisted me are the vast number of historians, amateur and professional, whose work I have used and which is so inadequately acknowledged in the footnotes and bibliography.

These and many other people have made a major contribution to the book. The flaws which remain are unmistakably my own product: as those who have tried to help me will know, some are the result of wilful wrong headedness.

Estimated Population Change in Senghennydd: 1890 - 1980

Appendix

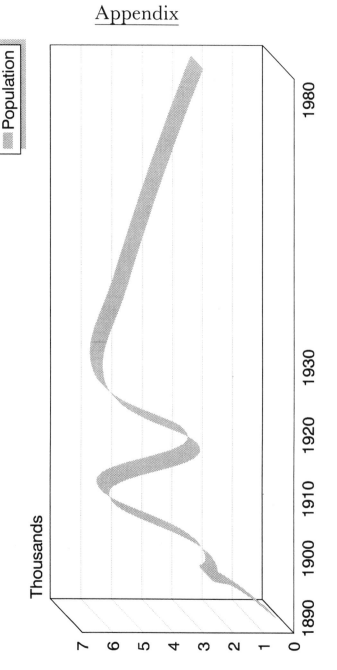

Thousands

Population

1890 1900 1910 1920 1930 1980

(Source: Census data, local reports and estimates based on newspaper items)

Bibliography

ARCHIVES AND DOCUMENTS
Glamorgan Record Office:
  Senghenydd Schools Logbooks, Records of the Pontypridd Workhouse, documents
  relating to the Universal Colliery, Eglwysilan Parish Register
Hull University Library:
  Diary of Hubert Jenkins
National Library of Wales:
  Lord Merthyr Archive
  Thomas Ellis Archive
  Records of the Monmouthshire and South Wales Coalowners' Association
Public Record Office:
  Records of the Lewis Merthyr Consolidated Collieries Ltd
  (BT 31/16355/65300)
South Wales Miners' Library:
  The South Wales Coalfield History Project Interviews

UNPUBLISHED THESES AND MANUSCRIPTS
Cartwright, J. A., *A Study in British Syndicalism: the Miners of South Wales 1906-1914,*
  (University of Wales Thesis; 1969)
Davies, James, *The Industrial History of the Rhymney Valley, with regard to the Iron Steel and*
  Tinplate Industries, Coal Mining, Lead mining, Smelting and Quarrying, (University of
  Wales Thesis, 1926)
John Davies, *Glamorgan and the Bute Estates 1776-1947,* (University of Wales Thesis;
  1969)
Evans, B., *A History of Trades Disputes and the Formation and Operation of the several Sliding*
  Scale Agreements in the South Wales Coal trade, 1870-1903, with special reference to the work
  of Sir William Thomas Lewis, first Baron Merthyr of Senghenydd, (University of Wales
  thesis; 1944)
Evans, Eric Wyn, *A History of Industrial Relations in the South Wales Coal Industry up to*
  1912, (University of Wales Thesis; 1955)
Lewis, W.T., *Presidential Address of Sir William T. Lewis to the Institution of Mining*
  Engineers at the Engineering Congress, Glasgow, 3rd September 1901. (NLW, Lord
  Merthyr Archive, 389)
Phillips, J.B., 'A History of Senghenydd up to 1918', (Typescript, n.d.: Abertridwr
  Public Library)
South Wales Coalfield History Project, *Final Report (SSRC; Department of History and*
  Economic History, University College, Swansea; 1974)
Williams, L.J., *The Monmouthshire and South Wales Coal Owners' Association, 1873-1914,*
  (University of Wales thesis; 1957)

OFFICIAL REPORTS

Annual Reports of the District Inspectors of Mines, 1890-1914

Report. . . on the circumstances attending an explosion at the Universal Colliery, Glamorgan, on 24th May 1901 (1901; Cd 947)

Report on the Causes and Circumstances attending an Explosion which occurred at the Senghenydd Colliery on Tuesday, 14th October, 1913. (1914; Cd.7346)

Report of the Commission appointed to enquire into Industrial Unrest, (1917; Cd 8662)

Report and Minutes of the Evidence of the Royal Commission on the Coal Industry, H.C. 1919, (Cmd 360).

Report on Investigation in the Coalfield of South Wales and Monmouth, (1928; Cmd 3272)

NEWSPAPERS

Birmingham Daily Post
Caerphilly Journal, (previously the 'New Tredegar, Bargoed and Caerphilly Journal')
Daily Express
Daily Mail
Glamorgan Free Press
Manchester Guardian
Merthyr Express
Pontypridd Chronicle
South Wales Daily News
Times

INTERVIEWS

Few of the people I was able to interview were adults at the time of the events which I record. Nevertheless the interviews were important in checking and altering general impressions, in suggesting new lines of enquiry and in correcting inaccuracies.

Gwen Evans. Headmistress of the Senghennydd School and daughter of an official in the Universal Mine.

Pauline and Ivor Thomas and Doreen Jones. Daughters and son-in-law of Charles and Ethel Anzani.

Ruth McCleod and Rene Morgan, Daughters of Councillor Thomas James, Chairman of Caerphilly U.D.C.

Eli Huish, Bessie Williams and Linda Griffiths whose father, a Senghennydd engine driver, died in 1915 after a railway accident.

Dilys John. Daughter of Catherine James. (Mrs John; 'Megfam')

Lillian Bull. Daughter of David Griffiths, killed in the explosion of 1913, and step-daughter of Richard Hamar.

Viv Evans whose family were shop keepers and businessmen in the valley from the early days of the mine.

BOOKS AND ARTICLES

Alderman, G., 'The Anti-Jewish Riots of August 1911 in South Wales', *Welsh History Review,* Vol 6 (1972-3)

Asteris, M., 'The Rise and Decline of South Wales Coal Exports, 1870-1930', *Welsh History Review,* Vol 13, (1986)

Barrie, D. S. M., *The Rhymney Railway,* (South Godstone; 1952)

Bassett, T. M., *The Welsh Baptists,* (Swansea; 1977)

Beddoe, D., 'Towards a Welsh Women's History', *Llafur, Vol 3, No 2 (Spring 1981)*

Beddoe, D., 'Images of Welsh Women', in T. Curtis (ed), *Wales: the Imagined Nation,* (Bridgend; 1986)

Beddoe, D., *Back to Home and Duty,* (London; 1989)

Bellamy, J. and Saville, J., *Dictionary of Labour Biography,* Vol 1-6, (London; 1972-1982)

Benson, J. *British Coalminers in the Nineteenth Century,* (London; 1980)

Benson, J. *et al., Bibliography of the British Coal Industry,* (Oxford; 1981)

Boulton, W. G., *Senghenydd: The Village and the Rugby Club,* (Risca; 1982)

Boyns, T., 'Work and Death in the South Wales Coalfield, 1874-1914', *Welsh History Review,* (1984-5)

Boyns, T., 'Technical Change and Colliery Explosions in the South Wales Coalfield, c.1870-1914', *Welsh History Review,* (1986-1987)

Brown, J. H., *The Valley of the Shadow: An Account of Britain's Worst Mining Disaster,* (Port Talbot; 1981)

Bulmer, M., 'Sociological Models of the Mining Community', *Sociological Review,* (1975) 23 (1)

Chinn, C., *They Worked all their Lives,* (Manchester; 1988)

Clegg, H. *et al., A History of British Trade Unions Since 1889, Vol I,* (Oxford; 1964)

Coombes, B. L., *These Poor Hands,* (London; 1939)

Crowther, M. A., *The Workhouse System 1834-1929,* (London; 1983)

Daunton, M. J., 'Aristocrats and Traders: The Bute Docks, 1839-1914', *Journal of Transport History,* (1975), Vol 3

Daunton, M., *Coal Metropolis: Cardiff 1870-1914,* (Leicester; 1977)

Daunton, M., 'Down the Pit: Work in the Great Northern and South Wales Coalfields 1870-1914', *Economic History Review,* 2nd Series, XXIV (No 4), Nov. 1981

Davies, B. P., *They Made a People,* (Cardiff; 1947)

Davies, E. T., *Religion in the Industrial Revolution in South Wales,* (Cardiff; 1965)

Davies, J., *Cardiff and the Marquesses of Bute,* (Cardiff; 1981)

Davies, M., (Ed.), *Life as we have known it,* (London; 1977)

Davies, Rhys, *Count her Blessings,* (London; 1932)

Davies, Rhys, *My Wales,* (London; 1937)

Davies, Rhys, *Tommorrow to Fresh Woods,* (London; 1941)

Davies, Rhys, *Print of a Hare's Foot,* (London; 1969)

Davies, Russell, ' "In a Broken Dream": some aspects of Sexual Behaviour and the Dilemmas of the Unmarried Mother in South West Wales, 1887-1914', *Llafur,* III, 4 (1983)

Davies, W. H., 'The Day of the Explosion', *Gelligaer,* VIII (1971)

Davies, W. H., *The Right Place, The Right Time. Memories of Boyhood Days in a Welsh Mining Community,* (Llandybie; 1972)

Davies, W. H., *Ups and Downs,* (Swansea; 1975)

Duckham, H., *Great Pit Disasters,* (Newton Abbot; 1973)

Earwicker, R., 'Miners' Medical Services before the First World War: the South Wales Coalfield', *Llafur,* Vol 3 (2) (Spring 1981)

Edwards, A. J., *Archbishop Green: His Life and Opinions,* (Llandysul; 1986)

Edwards, E. W., 'The Pontypridd Area', in M. Morris (ed.), *The General Strike,* (Harmondsworth; (1976)

Edwards, H. W. J., *The Good Patch,* (London; 1938)

Edwards, N., *The History of the South Wales Miners,* (London; 1924)

Edwards, N., *History of the South Wales Miners Federation,* (London; 1938)

Edwards, W. J., *From the Valley I Came,* (London; 1956)

Evans, D.G., *A History of Wales: 1815-1906,* (Cardiff; 1988)

Evans, Eifion. *The Welsh Revival of 1904,* (Bridgend; 1987)

Evans, Elias, *The Aber Valley: The Story of a Mining Community,* (Cwmbran; 1987)

Evans, Eric Wyn, *Mabon: A Study in Trade Union Leadership,* (Cardiff; 1959)

Evans, Eric Wyn, *The Miners of South Wales,* (Cardiff; 1961)

Evans, N., '"The First Charity in Wales": Cardiff Infirmary and South Wales Society, 1837-1914', *Welsh History Review,* Vol 9 (1978-9)

Evans, R.M., *One Saturday Afternoon: The Albion Colliery, Cilfynydd, Explosion of 1894,* (Cardiff; 1984)

Felstead, R., *No Other Way: Jack Russia and the Spanish Civil War,* (Port Talbot: 1981)

Fisher, T., *A Few Steps Away: Coal Mining in the Rhymney Valley 1816-1990,* (Ystrad Mynach: 1990)

Francis, H. and Smith, D., *The FED, A History of the South Wales Miners in the Twentieth Century,* (London; 1980)

Grant, R., *The Parliamentary History of Glamorgan,* (Swansea; 1978)

Gregory, R., *The Miners and British Politics,* (Oxford; 1968)

Griffin, A. F., *The Collier,* (Aylesbury; n.d.)

Gwyther, C. E., 'Sidelights on Religion and Politics in the Rhondda Valley, 1906-1926', *Llafur,* Vol 3 No 1

Haigh, H., 'The Miner', in (Ed.) B. B. Thomas, *Harlech Studies,* (Cardiff; 1938)

Hanley, J., *Grey Children: A Study in Humbug and Misery,* (London; 1937)

Hogenkamp, B., 'Miners' Cinemas in South Wales in the 1920s and 1930s', *Llafur,* vol IV (2), (1985)

Holmes, C., 'The Tredegar Riots of 1911: Anti-Jewish Disturbances in South Wales', *Welsh History Review,* Vol 11 (1982-3)

Horner, A., *Incorrigible Rebel,* (London; 1960)

Howells, K., 'Victimisation, Accidents and Disease', in Ed. D. Smith (1980) *op.cit.*

Hughes, G.T., 'The Mythology of the Mining Valleys', in Ed. S. Adams & G. R. Hughes *Triskel Two: Essays on Welsh and Anglo-Welsh Literature,* (Llandybie; 1973)

Jenkins, I., *Idrid Davies of Rhymney,* (Llandysul; 1986)

Jennings, H., *Brynmawr: A study of a Distressed Area,* (London; 1934)

John, A. V., 'A Miner Struggle? Women's Protests in Welsh Mining History', *Llafur,* Vol IV (1), (1984)

Jones, Dot, 'Did Friendly Societies Matter? A Study of Friendly Society Membership in Glamorgan, 1794-1910', *Welsh History Review*, Vol 12 (1984-5)

Jones, G. J., *Wales and the Quest for Peace,* (Cardiff; 1969)

Jones, H. C., *Old Caerphilly and District in Photographs,* (Barry: 1979)

Jones, I. G., 'Language and Community in Nineteenth Century Wales', in Ed. D. Smith (1980) op cit.

Jones, I. G., *Communities,* (Llandysul; 1987)

Jones, J., *Unfinished Journey,* (London; 1937)

Jones, J., *Me and Mine,* (London; 1946)

Jones, L., *Cwmardy,* (London; 1978)

Jones, L., *We Live,* (London; 1978)

Jones, M. R. D., 'The Welsh Rulers of Senghenydd', *Caerphilly,* 1971 No 3

Jones, P., *Colliery Settlement in the South Wales Coalfield, 1850-1926,* (Hull; 1969)

Jones, P, Workmen's Trains in the South Wales Coalfield 1870-1926, *Transport History,* 1970 3 (1)

Jones, P., 'Baptist Chapels as an Index of Cultural Transition in the South Wales Coalfield before 1914, *Journal of Historical Geography,* 1976 2 (4), 347-360

Jones, P., *Mines, Migrants and Residence in the South Wales Steamcoal Valleys: the Ogmore and Garw Valleys in 1881,* (Hull; 1987)

Jones, T., *Leeks and Daffodils,* (Newtown; 1942)

Jones, T. *Rhymney Memories,* (Llandysul; 1970)

Keating, J., *My Struggle for Life,* (London; 1916)

Kelly's Directory of South Wales and Monmouthshire, (London; 1901, 1906, 1910, 1914, 1920, 1926)

Kirby, M. W., *The British Coalmining Industry, 1780-1946,* (London; 1977),

Leng, P. J., *The Welsh Dockers,* (Ormskirk; 1981)

Lewis, E. D., *The Rhondda Valleys,* (London; 1959)

Lewis, J., (Ed), *Labour and Love,* (London; 1986)

[Lewis, W. T.], *Some Episodes in the Career of Sir William T. Lewis Bart., the Mardy, Aberdare,* (Merthyr Tydfil; 1908)

Lieven, M., 'Representations of the Working Class Community: the Senghenydd Mining Disaster, 1913', *Llafur,* Vol 5, No 2

Maher, K., 'Caerphilly', in (ed) N. Gray, *The Worst of Times: an Oral History of the Great Depression in Britain,* (Aldershot: 1985)

Mainwaring, M. J., *A History of St Peter's Church, Senghenydd: 1895-1945,* (Abertridwr; 1946)

Masonic Calendar, South Wales (Eastern Division) (Neath; 1926)

Massey, P. H., 'Portrait of a Mining Town', *Fact 1937,* (November) 8: 7-78

Massey, P. H., *Industrial South Wales: A Social and Political Survey,* (London; 1940)

Morgan, J. V., *Welsh Political and Educational Leaders in the Victorian Era,* (London; 1908)

Morgan, K. O., *Wales in British Politics, 1868-1922,* (Cardiff; 1970)

Morgan, K. O., 'The New Liberalism and the challenge of Labour: The Welsh Experience, 1885-1929', *Welsh History Review,* Vol 6 (1972-3)

Morgan, K. O. *Rebirth of a Nation, Wales 1880-1980,* (Oxford; 1981)

Morgan R., *My Lamp still Burns,* (Llandysul; 1981)

Mor-O'Brien, A., 'Patriotism on Trial: the Strike of the South Wales Miners, July 1915', *Welsh History Review,* Vol 12

Page Arnot, R., *The Miners: Years of Struggle,* (London; 1953)

Page Arnot, R., *South Wales Miners: 1898-1914,* (London; 1967)

Page Arnot, R., *South Wales Miners (1914-1926),* (Cardiff; 1975)

Paynter, W., *My Generation,* (London; 1972)

Pelling, H., *A History of British Trade Unionism,* (Harmondsworth; 1979)

Phelps Brown, E., *The Growth of British Industrial Relations* (London; 1959),

Phillips, E., *Pioneers of the Welsh Coalfield,* (Cardiff; 1925)

Phillips, J. B., 'Senghenydd 1890-1910', *Caerphilly 3,* (June 1971)

Phillips, J. B., *Abertridwr through the Ages,* (Newport; 1991)

Prothero, C., *Recount,* (Ormskirk; 1982)

Redmayne, R. A. S., *The British Coalmining Industry during the War,* (Oxford, 1923)

Rees, W., 'Records of the Lordship of Senghenydd', *South Wales and Monmouthshire Record Society,* 1957, No 4

Reeves, M. P, *Round About a Pound a Week,* (London; 1979)

Rhondda, Viscountess, *D. A. Thomas, Viscount Rhondda,* (London; 1921)

Roberts, E., *A Woman's Place,* (London; 1984)

Rubinstein, W. D., *Men of Property,* (London; 1981)

Saville, J., 'Arthur Jenkins', *Dictionary of Labour Biography,* (London; 1978), vol.1.

Sellwood, D. G., *Llanbradach: 1887-1914,* (Caerphilly; 1988)

Smith, D., (ed.), *A People and a Proletariat,* (London; 1980)

Smith, D., *Wales! Wales?,* (London; 1984)

Smith, F. M., *The Surgery at Aberffrwd,* (Hythe; 1981)

Spring Rice, M., *Working Class Wives,* (London: 1981)

Stead, P., 'Working Class Leadership in South Wales, 1900-1920, *Welsh History Review,* Vol 6 (1972-3)

Stearns, P., 'Working Class Women in Britain, 1890-1914', in ed. M. Vicinus, *Suffer and be Still,* (Bloomington; 1973)

Thomas, B., 'The Migration of Labour into the Glamorgan Coalfield 1861-1911' in Minchinton, W. E., *Industrial South Wales 1750-1914,* (London; 1969)

Tibbott, M. S. and Thomas, B., *The Gwalia: the Story of a Valleys Shop,* (Cardiff: 1991)

Walters, R. 'Capital formation in the South Wales Coal Industry 1840-1914, *The Welsh History Review,* 1980-1, Vol 10

Wilkins, C., *The History of the Iron, Steel Tinplate and other Trades of Wales,* (Merthyr Tydfil; 1888)

Williams, C., 'The South Wales Miners' Federation, *Llafur,* Vol V (3), (1990)

Williams, Gareth, 'Compulsory Sterilisation of Welsh Miners, 1936', *Llafur,* Vol 3, No 3

Williams, Glanmor, *Religion, Language and Nationality in Wales,* (Cardiff; 1979)

Williams, Gwyn, *The Welsh in their History,* (London, 1982)

Williams, L. J., 'The Coalowners' in Ed. D. Smith (1980) *op. cit.*

Williams N. 'The Senghenydd Colliery Disaster, in Ed. S. Williams, *Glamorgan Historian* Vol, 6 (Cowbridge; 1969)

Williams, R. and Jones, David, *The Cruel Inheritance: Life and Death in the Coalfields of Glamorgan,* (Pontypool: 1990)

Zimmern, A., *My Impressions of Wales,* (London; 1921)

Index

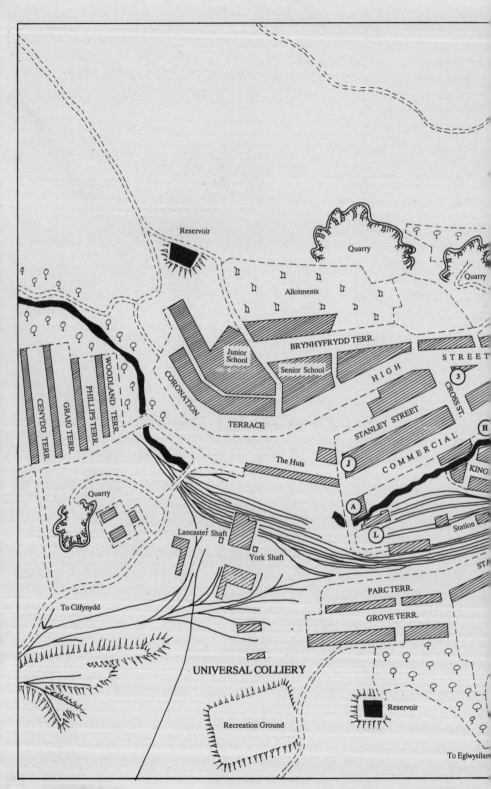